Introduction
to the
Peoples and Cultures
of Asia

COLIN E. TWEDDELL
and
LINDA AMY KIMBALL
Western Washington University

PRENTICE-HALL, INC., Englewood Cliffs, N.J. 07632

Library of Congress Cataloging in Publication Data

Tweddell, Colin E.
     Introduction to the peoples and cultures of Asia.

     Bibliography.
     Includes index.
     1. Asia—Civilization. 2. Ethnology—Asia.
I. Kimball, Linda Amy. II. Title.
DS12.T88 1985   950   84-17763
ISBN 0-13-491572-0

Editorial/production supervision: Colleen Brosnan
Cover design: Lundgren Graphics, Ltd.
Cover illustrations: Courtesy Dover Press. Upper left:
     Pah-Kwa and the Great Monade—charm against evil
     forces (Chinese). Upper right: Shri-Yantra—cosmic
     design (Hindu-Vedic). Lower right: Seal and
     signature of artist Kinya Ritsuo, lacquer painter,
     1663–1747 (Japanese). Bottom right: Mohammedan
     Magic Circle (Indian).
Manufacturing buyer: Barbara Kelly Kittle

Cartography by Eugene Hoerauf
Illustrations by Megan McCormick

Printed in the United States of America

10 9 8 7 6 5 4 3 2 1

ISBN 0-13-491572-0   01

Prentice-Hall International, Inc., *London*
Prentice-Hall of Australia Pty. Limited, *Sydney*
Editora Prentice-Hall do Brasil, Ltda., *Rio de Janeiro*
Prentice-Hall Canada Inc., *Toronto*
Prentice-Hall Hispanoamericana, S.A., *Mexico*
Prentice-Hall of India Private Limited, *New Delhi*
Prentice-Hall of Japan, Inc., *Tokyo*
Prentice-Hall of Southeast Asia Pte. Ltd., *Singapore*
Whitehall Books Limited, *Wellington, New Zealand*

Contents

PART II

Lands of Fervor, Fuel, and Feuds: Southwest Asia 34

Preface

Asia is a panorama of nations, some rich with the written wisdom of 6,000 years, some so new the ink has barely dried on their certificates of membership in the Assembly of the United Nations. ASIA is a brotherhood of communities attuned to compassion for the exploited peoples, yet also is a seething cauldron where Asian fights Asian only too often. ASIA is the fountainhead of the world's great religions, of philosophies of rectitude, and of epic poetry. ASIA is a continent of men, women, and children—Abdul and Indrani, Mei-lin and Akira—each needing recognition, dignity and fulfilment, and ready to welcome all persons of goodwill. ASIA, then, is a living organism, pulsing with life, a living tapestry continually being woven by myriad hands upon the countless looms of time.

In these pages the peoples of Asia are verbally portrayed living on their coasts, grasslands, deserts, mountains, and teeming cities. Among them the past infiltrates the present, and the physical environment enshrines the community with its guided yet optional life-styles. The themes outlined in the Introduction will be referred to and illustrated together with the social and national problems and international pressures which affect the structures of their societies and their adaptive cultures. Chapter 1 will comment briefly on some broad overviews of the continent as a whole, and Chapter 2 discusses some facets of religion, identity, behavior, and daily speech among Asia's peoples. Then come the regions of Asia in orderly sequence.

TO THE INSTRUCTOR

This book is definitely multidisciplinary in both intention and content, although written from an anthropological point of view. Every region and nation in Asia is mentioned—with widely differing degrees of detail—and representative major and minor peoples are described. These facets of history, geography, government, and society provide multiple springboards from which these topics may be pursued and compared in depth. Every endeavor has been made to provide accurate information, whether in map, chart, or text. A formal style has been used to provide information, but a relaxed, descriptive style when surveying the environment or in visualizing past events and current scenes.

GENERAL PLAN AND ORGANIZATION

The book consists of seven major sections, each of approximately the same length: a general Introductory overview of Asia, then consecutive sections on Southwest Asia, South Asia, North Asia, East Asia, and Southeast Asia, followed by a Conclusion on the whence and whither of Asia. The primary intention is to show nations and peoples as products of their histories who have adapted to their environments and prevailing technologies.

Format

The general format adopted for the above purpose is utilized both for the five sections and many of the individual chapters: (a) the geographical environment, (b) the historical background, (c) some characteristic or distinctive social patternings of the region or people, and (d) vignettes of representative national (majority) and minority peoples.

Themes and Viewpoints

The conceptual basis is represented by a cosmic-type mandala and is actualized as interweaving themes developed in Part I. Briefly the themes are as follows:

1. Each individual is a member of a cultural community.
2. A community is the product of its past.
3. A community lives in an established environment and territory.
4. A community's total environment is a composite of many factors.
5. A community's way of life is distinctly patterned.
6. A community is concerned with social, national, and, often, international problems.
7. Social change results from alterations in the basic community pattern.

These themes find illustration and application throughout the book. They are not forced upon the content, but, like the topics mentioned later, arise naturally during the course of discussion or description.

TOPICAL COVERAGE

Within the small compass of a continent-wide survey book, topics usually can be discussed or illustrated only in one setting. It is left, therefore, to the initiative of the instructor to guide students into the development of the subject. One such topic is that of minorities which remain minorities in spite of constant contact with a majority population for hundreds of years. Majority-minority relations crop up many times, but are discussed in detail for the situation in Southwest China, where the Balk Line stalemate situation existed between the Han Chinese and the tribal peoples. The range of topics includes also geopolitics and colonialism, nomadism and altitudinal residence, the Islamic legal system, social layering and invaders, religion and *bushido,* population growth and internicine warfare, art, religion, and the dynamics of social values, as well as the effect of geographical environment upon residence and occupation, as modified by improvements in the level of technology applied to the situations.

ACKNOWLEDGMENTS

During the years the manuscript was being revised, a number of colleagues, principally at Western Washington University, have read parts or the whole of the manuscript, and have contributed many valuable suggestions. We tender thanks, therefore, to Professors Vinson H. Sutlive, Jr., of the College of William and Mary, Angelo Anastasio, Michael H. Fisher, Howard L. Harris, Leonard M. Helfgott, Edward H. Kaplan, Milton H. Krieger, Richard E. Salzer, Henry G. Schwarz, James W. Scott, and Herbert C. Taylor, Jr., and to Dale McGinnis of Fort Steilacoom Community College. We have profited from all of them and have incorporated most of their suggestions into the text to the best of our ability. Ray McGinnis, head of the Reference Department and Social Sciences Librarian at the Wilson Library at Western Washington University, provided valuable reference and bibliographic assistance throughout the period of the project. However, all errors of interpretation, omission, or commission are strictly the responsibility of the authors.

Thanks are also due to our cartographer, Eugene Hoerauf, for his painstaking work, and to graduate student Megan McCormick for her unusual illustrations. And, if it were not for the efforts of the editorial, production, and marketing staffs at Prentice-Hall, this book still would not see the light of day.

All of the embassies or consulates of the nations of Asia were requested to supply whatever information was available for a project such as this book. We wish to thank the following embassies and consulates for maps, magazines, and other promotional material: Brunei, the Peoples Republic of China, the Republic of China (Taiwan), Cyprus, India, Indonesia, Iraq, Israel, Japan, Jordan, South Korea, Kuwait, Malaysia, Oman, Pakistan, Philippines, Qatar, Saudi Arabia, Sri Lanka, Syria, United Arab Emirates, and the U.S.S.R. We trust that none of the names of our generous contributors has been omitted. Our only regret is that more of the information contained in this literature could not be utilized within the compass of this small book. We are grateful to all of them.

Colin E. Tweddell
Linda Amy Kimball

PART I
Asia: A Preliminary Overview

Introduction

A FLY-BY GLIMPSE OF ASIA

Fly with a satellite over Asia—preferably with a map in hand—and you will see a huge land mass, stretching from the Pacific Ocean westward beyond its Ural mountain boundary into the sea-girt lands of Europe. Note that its southwest corner joins the smoothly contoured mass called Africa. Somewhat off-center tower the icy Pamir mountains. Radiating from this "Pamir Knot" and the nearby Tibetan plateau, mountain systems and mighty rivers extend to every ocean that borders Asia. And this land is home to 2.6 to 3 billion people.

People! People who mount everything from camels to oil rigs, who farm everywhere from malarial swamps to barley fields high in the Himalayas. People whose weapons grade from bamboo arrows to nuclear warheads, and whose functional architecture ranges from a brush lean-to or a felt yurt to a marble Taj Mahal, cyclopean ironworks, and earthquake-resistant skyscrapers. Their societies and nations range from longhouse communities of farmer-hunters, pastoralists, and tribes united by kinship, language, and occupation, to agricultural and industrial nations with populations in the hundreds of millions. Out of this kaleidoscope of peoples speaking a thousand different languages, wearing perhaps an embroidered G-string, a silken scarf, or the latest Western fashions, come philosophic concepts or writings from 3000 B.C. to the present. Here lie the breeding grounds of massive migrations that have changed the flow of history, and have the dynamism to change it again.

BOX I-1 *A PRELIMINARY OVERVIEW OF MISCELLANEA ABOUT ASIA*

ASIA is the largest continent (16,988,000 sq. miles; 43,998,929 sq. km.), nearly one-third of the planet's land surface.

ASIA encompasses:

—Seven of the world's thirteen longest rivers: Yangtze, Amur, Yellow (Huang Ho), Mekong, Ob, and Yenesey.

—Four of the world's seven largest islands: New Guinea, Borneo, Sumatra, and Honshu.

—Over 100 peaks higher than the loftiest summits in other continents.

—The highest spot on earth, Mt. Everest, and the lowest, the Dead Sea.

—The largest lake, the Caspian Sea, and the deepest, Lake Baikal.

—The deepest river, in the Gorges the Yangtze is 500 feet (153 m.) deep.

—A lake seven times saltier than the oceans, and containing fabulous mineral wealth—the Dead Sea.

—The center of the world's population lies about 500 miles (800 km.) northeast of the Aral Sea.

—Chemical battlements hundreds of feet high deposited by hot mineral springs at Pamukkale in Turkey.

—A medieval empire and the world's most secretive land —icy Tibet—lies on a vast high plateau which, if leveled out, would average about 16,000 feet (4,880 m.) above sea level (higher than Pike's Peak in Colorado, and the Matterhorn in Switzerland).

—Astronomy and mathematics provide the key to the perfect architecture of Kampuchea's Angkor Wat, the largest temple in the world.

—Three of every five persons in the world are from Asia; seven out of ten Asians are either Chinese or Indian.

Asia is no longer the ends of the earth; it is the land where our neighbors dwell. Today, from satellite technology to a Philippine woman etching a love song on the bamboo box that holds her betel chew, this infinite diversity has produced what one sees in the dignified and expectant face of every Asian—history and life. This is the mandala of Asia.

HUMANITY'S PATTERNED UNIVERSE: A MANDALA

The *mandala,* a Sanskrit word meaning "circle," originally was a diagram displaying symbols for the forces of the cosmos or universe. The mandala diagram used here depicts something of the purposes embodied in this book.

Humanity is surrounded by questions to which all people endeavor to find answers. Turning inward from the outer circle of nebulous questions, the square

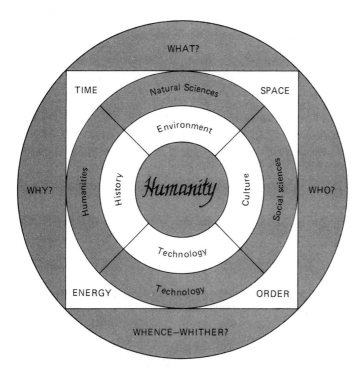

FIGURE I-1 Humanity's patterned universe: a mandala.

contains the names of the four elements which compose the universe: *time, space, energy,* and *order.* Academically the outworking of these elements in our world system has been systematized into four general categories. The *natural sciences* (biology, chemistry, geology, geography, physics), the *social sciences* (anthropology, economics, law, political science, sociology), and the *humanities* (history, philosophy, religion, and linguistics) must be augmented by *technology* (mathematics, medicine, engineering, computer science).

However, the personal universe of the human being is much simpler. The individual is directly concerned with the surrounding physical and geographic *environment.* He or she is born and raised within one or more *cultures* that considerably mold the person's way of life. Culture includes the expressive arts, language, and the whole realm of ideas, philosophy, and religion. The lights and shadows of past events and the decisions of long-dead persons have culminated in the world of today. This is the *history* of yesterday. Lastly, we are surrounded by the *technology* or mechanics of daily living, from G-strings to armor plate, from bow and arrow to intercontinental ballistic missiles, from fire sticks to microwave ovens, and from reading bumps on the head to CAT electron scanners.

The understanding of Humanity's Patterned Universe depends upon comprehension of both the separate units of the mandala and upon their patterned yet ever-changing and multiple interactions. Since many of these aspects and relationships are described for the peoples and societies of Asia, the mandala will come to life as they appear on the pages of this book.

Themes and Viewpoints

A number of intertwined themes show how history and geography and the flow of social and political change have combined to mold the peoples and nations of Asia.

1. *Each Individual Is a Member of a Cultural Community.* Each person both affects and is affected by his or her cultural community, by the customs and events which shape people's lives. At the core of the "thought tools" of patterns, grouping, and generalization, used here, lie the individual lives of countless people with all their meaningful strivings and personal worth.

2. *A Community Is the Product of Its Past.* History and environment comprise the twin guidelines between which societies and their members move, molded by their culture and aided by their technology. To be useful, guidelines must be explicit, yet within such guidelines the paths followed may vary. For instance, Iran and some other nations are trying to turn their cultural clocks back, endeavoring to restore to their present societies the standards and customs of Islam in the A.D. 600s and 700s. Other Muslims, as well as some Buddhist and Hindu sects, are actively mounting missionary programs, seeking converts in the West. Both movements are the making of history. History here is viewed as the dynamic and cumulative development of societies and the lifestyles of their members. Historical sections are included in this book to indicate aspects of the past which have added some characteristic the society still possesses. History, however, is only half the story. Someone remarked that "We can forget history, but we cannot forget geography," for the physical environment confronts us all day and awaits us next morning.

3. *A Community Lives in an Established Environment and Territory.* Sectional introductions show traditional cultures and technologies climatically adapted to life in the desert, the arable plains, river valleys, sea coasts, and the varying altitudes up the mountainsides. By adding new alternatives, modern technology has placed towns on the Siberian tundra, asphalt highways over Arabia's desert dunes, and gold mines in the mountains of the Philippines. Even in the jungles of Southeast Asia steel mat runways provide a base for airplanes.

4. *A Community's Total Environment Is a Composite of Many Factors.* These factors include, for instance, the physical terrain, the sociopolitical structures, the behavioral value systems, the spiritual beliefs, and intercommunity relations. Just as stranger meeting stranger asks polite questions to "place" the other person in terms of his or her geography and history, language and lineage, technology or occupation, so this book describes both major and minor communities and nations so that the reader may recognize and appreciate Asia and its infinitely varied peoples.

5. *A Community's Way of Life Is Distinctively Patterned.* The totality of each such pattern uniquely identifies regions and communities. Southwest Asia is described as a "mosaic civilization" and South Asia as a "multilayered civilization." The separate civilizations of the nations of East Asia are distinctively monolithic. Iran and Kampuchea exemplify the staggering effects of changes in the national patterns that were too radical and too fast—both nations floundered in chaos. Loss of patterning results in loss of predictability, and engenders social instability; repatterning is the only answer.

6. *A Community Is Concerned with Social and National Problems.* Energy sources, agriculture, population control, nutrition and health, illiteracy and educa-

tion, water conservation, industry and employment, and national security all affect the resources and endeavors of every government and society. Philosophies probe even deeper, for they underlie choices and actions. For good or ill, concepts such as individualism, humanism, relativism, authoritarianism, and a creeping permissiveness, all disturb the age-old balance between stability and change.

7. *Social Change Results from Alterations in the Basic Community Pattern.* The principal components of the basic community pattern are population size, community organization, the physical environment, level of technology, and the culture and value system of the society. Any significant alteration in one necessitates corresponding adjustments in the others until a new stable pattern is established. However, neither individual, nor community, nor nation stands alone, even in the matter of self-identity. So it is that self-determination for the community, self-government for the minority, nationalism for the nation, and ascending levels of regionalism which culminate in slogans such as "Asia for the Asians" are all difficult to reconcile with the concept of world-brotherhood.

Explanations: Whom and What the Book Is About

This book's unusual proposal is to cover briefly all the regions and every nation in Asia. The necessarily selective coverage means that, while the subject-matter is "a mile wide," the limitations of space result in the treatment being only "an inch deep." This presentation of Asia's peoples as seen through their histories, environments, and cultures includes representative national and minority communities—including some of the "little people" so often overlooked.

The inclusion of the introductory mandala serves to emphasize mutual understanding between the whole pattern of Asia and its parts, for each illuminates the other. Mountains of books discuss parts of Asia in depth, hardly one sketches the whole continent. A representative range of topics can only be highlighted in one or two places. Invaders, for instance, are discussed in Southwest Asia, and the interrelationships between nomads and villagers, and townsmen and city merchants are detailed for Arabia and Iran and partly in North Asia. Superimposed layerings of peoples and religions have been described for South Asia, and partly in Indonesia. Migrations are dealt with in North Asia, colonialism in Southeast Asia, altitudinal residence in China and in Southeast Asia, and the "balk line" as a way of understanding group identity and boundary behavior is brought to life in Southwest China, and obliquely for modern China. History is treated to show the past influencing the present, and the physical and other environments as setting limitations or challenges for societies. All these discussions compose so many springboards for further thought, research, and discussion as they are to be found elsewhere in Asia and in other regions of the world. Standard spellings have been used for place names; for instance, "Persia" has been used in historical contexts, and "Iran" elsewhere.

Chapter 1

The Many Faces of Asia I

Asia is a panorama of nations, some rich with the wisdom of six thousand years, some so new the ink has barely dried on their certificates of membership in the United Nations. Asia is a brotherhood of communities attuned to compassion for the exploited peoples, yet also is a seething cauldron where Asian fights Asian only too often. Asia is the fountainhead of the world's great religions, of philosophies of rectitude, and of epic poetry. Asia is a continent of men, women, and children— Abdul and Indrani, Mei-lin and Akira—each needing recognition, dignity, and fulfillment, and ready to welcome all persons of good will. Asia, then, is a living organism, pulsing with life, a living tapestry continually being woven by myriad hands upon the countless looms of time.

In these pages the peoples of Asia are portrayed living on their coasts, grasslands, and deserts, their mountains and teeming cities. Among them the past infiltrates the present, and the physical environment enshrines the community with its guided yet optional lifestyles. The mandala provides an overall scheme for the book, for its captions summarize the concerns of Asia. The themes outlined in the Introduction will be referred to and illustrated together with the social and national problems and international pressures which affect the structures of Asian societies and their adaptive cultures. This chapter will comment briefly on some broad overviews of the continent as a whole, while the next discusses some facets of religion, identity, behavior, and daily speech among Asia's peoples.

WHICH ASIA SHALL WE VISIT FIRST?

Shall we first visit tourist Asia? War-torn Asia? Religious Asia? The Chinese have a saying that *Hua bing bu chong ji,* "Picture cakes don't satisfy hunger." But we have only words with which to visit the land of oil rigs in the desert, a buried city of terra cotta soldiers in China, the island of Celebes with 60 peaks over 10,000 feet (3050 m.) high, and the fastest train in the world in Japan. If we merely see the spectacular sights and miss the people—some who believe the left hand is the side of honor, and some whose ancestors dressed in silks when Europe's folk dressed in bearskins—we will have misjudged Asia and misunderstood ourselves. One useful approach to understanding people is to know the environments in which they live.

THE MULTIPLE ENVIRONMENTS

People live enveloped in a number of environments. The survival of the human race, for instance, depends directly upon liveable relationships with its *physical* environment. The *social* environment is the cultural and behavioral world of the community. Beyond this lies the *national* environment of the structured arrangements operating within and between nations. These three environments are tangible, while the next two are intangible: first, the *mental* environment of the conceptual world within us, and second, the *spiritual* environment of the human spirit, the supernatural, and the Deity. The specific patterns of these environments differ at all levels from person to person and group to group.

Ecology and Harmony

Ecology concerns the human relationship to the physical environment, which can be considered *physically* as mountains and plains, *integrationally* as interrelated climatic zones and geopolitical regions, and *dynamically* as the homelands of living peoples. A stable existence requires the maintenance of harmonious relationships with all the environments. Asia's dual requirements for survival and stability—*ecology* and *harmony*—will be discussed under the following topics: geography, demography (study of populations), society, economy, religion, politics, and linguistics. For these discussions the maps should be consulted.

PHYSICAL ASIA: WHERE ASIANS LIVE

Terrain

No Asia, no Asians, is a simple truism. In the geological past two small chunks of land mass joined the shifting geologic plates that make up Eurasia. One we now call Arabia. The other, the Indian subcontinent, rammed so resolutely into the Asian land mass that it formed the bulging plateau of Tibet and its icy mountains. If leveled, Tibet and the nearby mountains, would average about 16,000 feet (4,880 m.) above sea level, higher than Pike's Peak or the Matterhorn. The southern

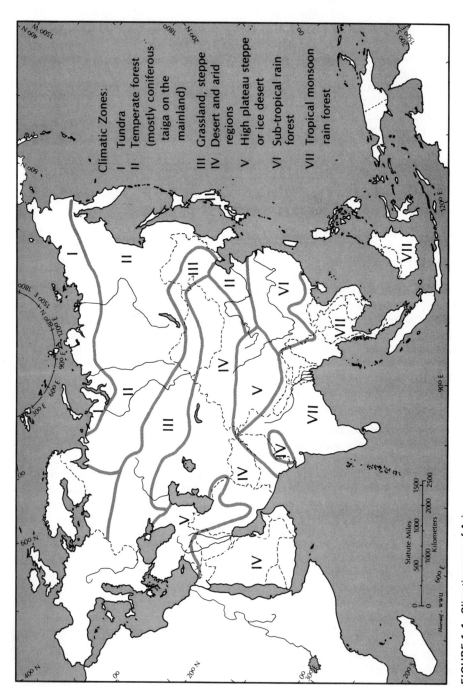

Climatic Zones:

I   Tundra
II   Temperate forest (mostly coniferous taiga on the mainland)
III Grassland, steppe
IV   Desert and arid regions
V   High plateau steppe or ice desert
VI   Sub-tropical rain forest
VII Tropical monsoon rain forest

Statute Miles

Kilometers

Hortval - WWII

FIGURE 1–1 Climatic zones of Asia.

BOX 1-1 *ASIA'S FOUR GEOGRAPHIC REGIONS*

ARCTIC ASIA. Two icy zones extend laterally across northern Asia: the treeless tundra along the Arctic coast, rich in oil and gas, and to the south the once trackless and endless taiga forest.

MOUNTAIN ASIA. The skeletal terrain system of great ranges radiating out from the "Pamir Knot" and Tibet: Himalayas to the southeast, Hindu Kush to the southwest, Kun Lun and Tian Shan to the Kamchatka mountains in the northeast, and the Caucasus, Elburz, and Taurus ranges in the west.

ARID ASIA. A broad band of desert and dry areas extending from Jordan and Arabia through much of Iraq, Iran, Afghanistan, Pakistan, and Central or High Asia to Mongolia. This covers about one third of Asia, between 6.5 and 9.8 million square miles (16.8 to 23.4 million sq. km.) of land unsuited to more than minimal human occupation, unless enhanced by modern technology.

SUBTROPICAL AND MONSOON ASIA. The generally fertile and heavily populated regions of South, East, and Southeast Asia.

edge of this massif, the Himalayan mountains, were picturesquely named by the Indian people "The Abode of Snow," while the crowning peak of Mt. Everest to the reverent Tibetans was Chomolungma, "Goddess Mother of the World."

Climate

Climatic belts extend across Asia from west to east as indicated in Figure 1-1. In all these zones the peoples and their occupations vary widely, each adapting to the conditions around them according to the level of their technology and the flexibility of their social systems. These Asian zones also affect outlying regions. For instance, the cold air mass above icy Tibet and the frozen tundra seasonally flows like an invisible torrent down Asia's eastern coasts and island chains to displace the warm air over the equator. The continent also fends off the successive typhoons (from the Chinese *tai* meaning "great" and *feng* meaning "wind," that is, a storm), which aggressively circle west and north from the Caroline Islands through the Philippines to Japan.

The Coasts of Asia

Although nearly ringed by oceans and seas, Asia's land boundary with Europe follows the line of the Ural Mountains and thence south to the Caspian Sea. The coastline is ruffled with gulfs and bays which provide ready access to the sea lanes for villages and trading seaports. The almost circular string of volcanoes around the Pacific Ocean, including Asia's outlying island chains, has been referred to both as the Ring of Fire and the Southeast Asian sector as the Earthquake Arc. Many oceanic archipelagoes have resulted from such volcanic activity, and fertile volcanic soils have provided abundant crops for the Javanese.

Features of terrain and climate in Asia, with resulting differences in fauna and flora, have combined to make the main mountain chains the border lines of

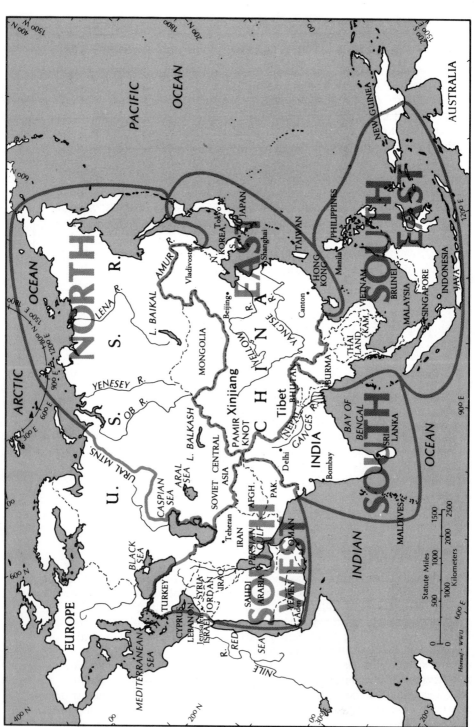

FIGURE 1-2 Asia's five regions.

major physical and political divisions. This book uses five such divisions: Southwest Asia (SWA), South Asia (SA), North Asia (NA), East Asia (EA), and Southeast Asia (SEA). These are shown in Figure 1-2. The major divisions of the book, and the general order of presentation of details, follow this same sequence.

DEMOGRAPHIC ASIA

Natural Population Sites

George B. Cressey, the well-known geographer of Asia, has remarked, "If a geographer were limited to a single map, it would be one of population distribution." Such a map points to the irregular distribution of people on the globe, and mutely asks why this unevenness exists. Areas of alluvial soils, with river or irrigation water or sufficient rain, plus warm sunshine, can support huge populations of plow agriculturalists. The densest farming populations live in the rich river deltas. Where the climate is cold, as along the big Siberian rivers, Russia was able to populate them only with concentration camps until the recent advent of modern amenities. Even here, however, the indigenous inhabitants had developed their own forms of comfort. Lopsided distributions are common. Of Southwest Asia's 2.417 million square miles (6.26 million sq. km.), one million are desert or arid, one million are mountainous, and only 125,000 square miles (324,000 sq. km.) are prime agricultural lands. People naturally cluster around these favored lands where water is available and industry might flourish (Cressey, 1963:3, 8).

Sites Enhanced by Technology

Technology can provide another foundation for high density, as in areas of irrigation, industry, and trade. Note the manufacturing and communication centers of Bombay and Tokyo, and the air transfer points at Singapore and Hong Kong, as well as administrative centers such as Delhi, Beijing, and Manila. Some places combine several of the above criteria: Istanbul sits at the crossroads of Europe and Asia, where emperors and sultans grew wealthy on trade. At the other end of Asia the tricity of Wu-han—composed of administrative Hankow, industrial Hanyang, and agricultural Wuchang—is the river and railroad hub of China. Waterways, railways, and airways all draw people to such centers.

The triangle of fertility in Russia's Central Asian steppelands is dwarfed by one million square miles (2.59 million sq. km.) of tundra, four million of taiga forest, and two million of barren desert and semidesert to the south. Nevertheless, with the extensive use of airplane and steamer transport and the importation of massive industrial plants, for which rivers have been dammed and electricity generated, over fifty million European Russians have been added to the expanding native populations. This industrialized belt coincides with the environs of the two Trans-Siberian railroads.

It has been said that if Asia were just somewhat more humid, great fresh water lakes would be formed, and Lake Balkash and the Aral Sea would flow into a double-sized Caspian Sea. From there the water would flow into the Black Sea with its outlet to the Mediterranean and the Atlantic Ocean. One could speculate what effect this would have upon the crop-raising potential of the vast steppelands, the food chain surpluses, and the redistribution of populations.

SOCIETAL ASIA

Civilization and Culture

The total ways of life of a community reveal two aspects: society as the organized aspect, and culture as the behavioral aspect. Civilization may be described as an advanced stage of social culture, characterized by a surplus production of food to support urban centers, and by systematized progress in writing, metallurgy, religion, and government. This development followed the introduction of agriculture soon after 10,000 B.C. in the Fertile Crescent, in Southeast Asia and on Taiwan, and flourished in Egypt, the valleys of the Indus and Yellow rivers, and in Southeast Asia. In contrast, isolated areas of snow, sand, and forest harbored communities which preserved their age-old cultures into the nineteenth and twentieth centuries. Such cultures could only transmit verbally what knowledge they possessed. Only a literate civilization could continually accumulate knowledge.

Control Systems

Out of Asia's traditional patchwork quilt of empires, kingdoms, sheikdoms, and chieftaincies, the last three types of social control still exist as national entities. The other nations are republics, as shown on the chart of the Independent Countries of Asia. Seven of these republics are or have been dictatorships of some sort, nine are Communist or Marxist states, and two are Islamic religious republics. The remainder, from Israel and Turkey to India and Singapore, operate on the foundation of representative government under free and open adult elections. These organized societies set overall guidelines within which their behavioral cultures may function, yet the guidelines are different.

Organization and Behavior

Society may be viewed as a wheel revolving around a hub. In these hub-oriented societies, organization merges with conduct. In Communist countries the administrative and control hub is the party committee, and the operational hub has been the commune. Commonly throughout Asia the countryside activities pulsate around a market town or city, a circle of markets, or the village which acts as the residential hub for its network of surrounding farms. On the other hand, the nomads' economic cycle of seasonal migration constitutes the extended hub around which their pastoral livelihood and village-nomad exchanges are organized.

In the village, and elsewhere in the commune or the city block, may be found the grassroots structures of society. Here people find spouses and family ties in the biological and cultural structure of the kin-and-family system. Family discipline, the neighbor's opinions, and the headman's advice or decision lay the early behavioral groundwork of the system of social control that becomes, finally, the government and judiciary system. Moreover, without the village products and purchases there would emerge no nationwide economic system. Similarly, without the village shrine, temple, or church, even peasant religious conservatism would find difficulty perpetuating the religious system. The educational system touches every member of society, by teaching the children their own customs and culture, using observation, imitation, and formal instruction in the village school.

The Interplay of History and Geography

History and geography are so inextricably interwoven in the experience of humankind that a Harvard geologist declared, "History is geography in motion." It also has been said of Christianity that "If Palestine is the cradle of our faith, then Mesopotamia and Egypt are the rockers (under) that cradle." Geography often will show the occupational options available to a people, and their history may record their efforts to capitalize on these alternatives, but neither history nor geography alone determine a people's culture, language, or values. Asian examples abound. The ancient Philistines had been one of the marauding Sea Peoples from the Aegean Sea, but once established on the agricultural plains of Palestine, they gave up seafaring entirely. Riverine peoples along the Euphrates, Ganges, and Yangtze river still exchange their goods, but as much by road and rail as on their traditional river craft. Kurdish and Pathan stalwarts, and girls from the mountains of Taiwan, emigrate from their farms and sheepfolds to seek jobs in the burgeoning cities.

Ethnocultural Diversity

Asians differ from each other in various ways: physically in build and facial appearance, culturally in language and religion, or in residential and behavioral patterns. The permanent differences are called ethnic traits, which are culturally developed on the basis of some biological continuity. Elmer S. Miller phrased it this way:

> Ethnic groups are biologically self-perpetuating, share and express common cultural values, demonstrate internal interaction, and are considered by themselves and others to be a distinct group. (1979:178)

Diversity may underlie apparent similarity of cultural patterning. Thus if the architects, stonemasons, and sculptors who built the fantastic pagodas of Burma could join with their counterparts in Thailand and the Cambodian builders of the monumental Angkor Wat, and all traveled to inspect the tremendous structure at Borobudur in Java, they would find only some Buddhist beliefs and stoneworking skills to unite them in a common identity. These stoneworkers, although occupationally identifiable as Buddhist stoneworkers, had a unique identity by group and person, by origin, lineage, language, customs, and personality. And only in the skilled craft of stoneworking would they share a commonality with the modern Islamic Javanese restorers of Borobudur. Similarly, the "boat peoples" of Canton, Vietnam, the Maldives, and the Southern Philippines differ more from one another than from their respective land-based neighbors.

Geographic contrasts. When Japan tightly closed its frontiers to ingress and egress, the sea was its protective wall. When Commodore Perry's "black ships" breached that wall, the opposition between land and sea disappeared, and the sea became Japan's highway to the wide world outside. Arabia's sea of sand and Central Asia's sea of grass were both homeland and barrier until asphalt or railroads traversed them. Some rivers acted as national boundaries, yet, like the Euphrates and the Amur, they guided armies, floated merchandise, and sustained migrant peoples.

TABLE 1-1 Independent Countries of Asia

COUNTRY	TITLE OF COUNTRY	POPULATION (IN 1000S)	AREA SQ. MILES	AREA SQ. KM.	MAJOR RELIGION	CAPITAL	DATE OF INDEPENDENCE
AFGHANISTAN	Democratic Republic of Afghanistan	15,328	250,000	647,500	Islam	Kabul	1919
BAHRAIN	State of Bahrain	380	231	596	Islam	Manama	1971
BANGLADESH	People's Republic of Bangladesh	93,040	55,126	142,500	Islam	Dacca	1971
BHUTAN	Kingdom of Bhutan	1,364	18,147	46,600	Buddhism	Thimphu	–
BRUNEI	Brunei Darus Salam	200	2,226	5,776	Islam	Bandar Seri Begawan	1984
BURMA	Socialist Rep. of the Union of Burma	36,166	261,789	678,600	Buddhism	Rangoon	1948
CHINA	People's Republic of China	1,055,304	3,691,502	9,600,000	Various[a]	Beijing	–
CYPRUS	Republic of Cyprus[g]	642	3,572	9,251	Christianity	Nicosia	1960
INDIA	Republic of India	723,762	1,178,995	3,136,500	Hinduism	New Delhi	1947
INDONESIA	Republic of Indonesia	157,595	735,268	1,906,240	Islam	Jakarta	1949
IRAN	Islamic Republic of Iran	41,203	636,659	1,647,240	Islam	Teheran	–
IRAQ	Republic of Iraq	14,034	167,924	445,480	Islam	Baghdad	1932
ISRAEL	State of Israel	3,916	7,992[b]	20,720	Judaism	Jerusalem	1948
JAPAN	Japan	118,519	142,900	370,370	Shinto	Tokyo	–
JORDAN	Hashemite Kingdom of Jordan	2,391	37,741	96,089	Islam	Amman	1946
KAMPUCHEA	People's Republic of Kampuchea[c]	5,882	69,898	181,300	Buddhism	Phnom Penh	1953
KOREA, NORTH	Democratic People's Republic of Korea	20,586	46,540	121,730	Buddhism, Confucianism	P'yongyang	1948

Country	Full name				Religion	Capital	Year
KOREA, SOUTH	Republic of Korea	41,092	38,022	98,913	Confucianism, Christianity	Seoul	1948
KUWAIT	State of Kuwait	1,553	7,780	16,058	Islam	Kuwait	1961
LAOS	Lao People's Democratic Republic	3,577	91,428	236,804	Buddhism, Animism	Vientiane	1949
LEBANON	Republic of Lebanon	3,177	4,015	10,360	Christianity, Islam	Beirut	1943
MALAYSIA	Malaysia	14,661	127,239	332,556	Islam	Kuala Lumpur	1963
MALDIVES	Republic of Maldives	163	115	298	Islam	Male	1965
MONGOLIA	Mongolian People's Republic	1,759	604,247	1,564,619	Buddhism	Ulaanbaatar	—
NEPAL	Kingdom of Nepal	15,715	54,362	141,100	Hinduism	Katmandu	—
OMAN	Sultanate of Oman	948	82,030	212,380	Islam	Muscat	—
PAKISTAN	Islamic Republic of Pakistan	93,106	310,403	803,000	Islam	Islamabad	1947
PHILIPPINES	Republic of the Philippines	51,574	115,830	300,440	Christianity	Manila	1946
QATAR	State of Qatar	258	8,500	10,360	Islam	Doha	1971
RUSSIA (in Asia)	Union of Soviet Socialist Republics	71,500	6,469,360	16,760,000	Various[d]	Moscow	—
SAUDI ARABIA	Kingdom of Saudi Arabia	9,975	830,000	2,331,000	Islam	Riyadh	1932
SINGAPORE	Republic of Singapore	2,472	224	618	Buddhism	Singapore	1965
SRI LANKA	Democratic Socialist Republic of Sri Lanka	15,398	25,332	65,500	Buddhism	Colombo	1948
SYRIA	Syrian Arab Republic	9,423	71,498	186,480	Islam	Damascus	1946
TAIWAN	Republic of China[e]	18,456	13,885	32,260	Buddhism	Taipei	(1949)
THAILAND	Kingdom of Thailand	49,823	198,445	514,820	Buddhism	Bangkok	1946
TURKEY	Republic of Turkey	48,105	301,412	766,640	Islam	Ankara	—
UNITED ARAB EMIRATES	United Arab Emirates	1,240	32,278	82,880	Islam	Abu Dhabi	1971

TABLE 1-1 (Cont.)

COUNTRY	TITLE OF COUNTRY	POPULATION (IN 1000S)	AREA SQ. MILES	AREA SQ.KM.	MAJOR RELIGION	CAPITAL	DATE OF INDEPENDENCE
VIETNAM	Socialist Republic of Vietnam	56,430	128,408	329,707	Buddhism, Animism	Hanoi	1954
YEMEN (ADEN)	People's Democratic Republic of Yemen	2,022	111,086	287,490	Islam	Aden	1967
YEMEN (SAN'A)	Yemen Arab Republic	5,490	75,290	194,250	Islam	San'a	—
OTHER POLITICAL UNITS IN ASIA						Bagawan	
GAZA STRIP	Egyptian Military Administration [f]	467	146	378	Islam	—	—
HONG KONG	British Dependency	5,272	399	1,036	Various	Victoria	—
MACAO	Province of Portugal	289	6	16	Buddhism	Macao	—

Data from government and United Nations sources. Population figures as of July, 1982.

Dates are supplied for countries attaining independence after World War I.

[a] Religion in China repressed; traditionally Buddhism, Taoism, Confucianism.

[b] Figures for Israel—and Jordan—vary over claims to the West Bank.

[c] Also known as Democratic Kampuchea.

[d] Religion in Russia repressed; Islam, Buddhism, Animism, Christianity still present.

[e] Taiwan commonly viewed as an independent country, but status is indeterminate.

[f] Still occupied by Israel.

[g] Northern sector has become a Turkish enclave.

The mountains of Southeast Asia, traditionally international barriers, have also acted as pipelines for countless tribal peoples moving southward.

Economic contrasts. Contrasts of wealth and class between the rulers and the ruled have been traditional in Asia. The price of the rich man's feast would have built the poor man a house. Yet the wealthy and the noble patronized the technicians, artists, philosophers, and administrators who contributed to the culture and science of Syria and Persia, India, China, and Japan, that amazed the early European visitors. The economic contrasts have been modified with the rise of a middle class of merchants, professionals, and higher-paid workers. Japan, Israel, Singapore, Taiwan, and Hong Kong represent three-class societies. India and some Persian Gulf States are on the way.

ECONOMIC ASIA

Trade, Transport, and Communication Networks

Some trade routes began at the dawn of history. The Amber Route traders brought this fossil resin, used for ornaments and healing, from the Baltic Sea to Anatolia (modern Turkey) before and after 3000 B.C. Caravans traveled from India and Central Asia to the Mediterranean coast before Darius I of Persia (circa 558-486 B.C.) set couriers galloping along his 1,500 mile (2,400 km.) Royal Road from Susa to Sardis. Genghis Khan in the A.D. 1200s and his grandson Kublai Khan in the 1300s also established "pony express" systems in their far-flung empires. And the Asian caravans continued to traverse the Silk Route from Peking through the Golden and the Khorasan Roads to Damascus for a total of 6,500 miles (10,400 km.), bringing goods for Venice and Rome, and for Zanzibar and Timbuktu. The only difference today is that great double trailers substitute for camels, and steamships and airplanes have replaced Chinese junks and Arab dhows to link Japan on the Pacific to England on the Atlantic. (Some of the exchange goods are listed in Table 1-2.)

Eurasian Interchange

From 500 B.C. to the A.D. 100s bronze, silver, and gold coinage and letters of credit enabled Eurasia to function as one vast intercontinental trade network. This era of peace during the time of the Pax Romana (27 B.C.-A.D. 180) roughly coincided with two other prospering empires: China's Han dynasty (202 B.C.-A.D. 220) and the Andhra dynasty of South India (c. 100 B.C.-A.D. 200). For many centuries Afroasian turmoil and Arab conquests disrupted Eurasian overland trade, benefitting the Venetians in Europe. Communications reopened in the A.D. 1400s, this time by sea, and, just as the 1500s B.C. saw the expansion of the Aryan peoples, so the 1500s witnessed the expansion of European interests worldwide. These priceless seaborne Asian cargos so stunned the avaricious Europeans that the flow of trade was stifled and almost destroyed. Only from the mid-1800s on did the volume and variety of intercontinental trade pick up and develop to the stage where Asian nations today compete successfully on the world markets in purchases and sales of modern equivalents of the traditional quality goods.

TABLE 1-2   TRADITIONAL ITEMS IN EURASIAN TRADE NETWORKS

ITEM	PLACE OF SUPPLY	ITEM	PLACE OF SUPPLY
Amber	Baltic	Ivory	Africa, India, Syria
Beads	Rome	Jewelry	India, Asia Minor
Beryl	S. India	Jewels	India, S.E. Asia
Brassware	S.W. Asia	Lacquerware	China, Japan
Bronzeware	Rome, Central Asia	Lapis lazuli	Afghanistan
Cameos	Rome	Leather	Spain
Cereals	Egypt	Linen, gossamer	Egypt
Cloisonne	Egypt	Metals	Etruria (Italy)
Cloth, cambric, muslin	Damascus	Oils	Mesopotamia
Cloth, linen	Egypt	Papyrus	Egypt
Coins	Rome, Greece	Peacocks	E. Asia
Copper	Cyprus, Spain	Pearls	Persian Gulf, Sri Lanka, S.E. Asia
Coral	Sri Lanka	Perfumes	Egypt, Arabia, Persia
Cosmetics	Egypt, India, S.W. Asia	Porcelain	China
Cotton	Egypt, India	Pottery	Rome, Greece
Cowrie shells	Sri Lanka	Rag paper	E. Asia
Drugs	Byzantium	Sandalwood	India, S.E. Asia
Dyes	India	Silk	China, Japan
Ebony	India, Africa	Silver	Asia Minor, Persia, Spain
Enamel work	Egypt	Slaves	Africa, S.W. Asia
Fruits, dried	Arabia, Cen. Asia	Spices	Arabia, S.E. Asia
Furs	Russia	Statuettes, bronze	Rome
Glassware	Egypt, Rome, Syria	Swords	Syria, Russia, Japan
Gold	Lydia, Siberia, Scythia, Africa	Timber, cedar	Lebanon
Horn, rhino	Africa	Tin	Spain, Britain
Horses	Ferghana, Persia	Tortoise shell	S.E. Asia
Inks	East Asia	Woolens	S.W. Asia, Afghanistan

The Face and Pace of Progress

Just as the Indus Valley civilization built a new port at Lothal on the Gulf of Cambay around the twentieth century B.C., so in the twentieth century A.D. new ports handle, not the wooden clipper ships or iron-hulled steamships of the 1800s, but cargo-and-passenger efficiency ships and 500,000 ton bulk cargo behemoths of the 1980s. Similarly, although the mileages of roads and railways have trebled since World War II, Israel, Jordan, Iran, India, Japan, the Philippines, and other nations operate domestic and international air routes. Air transport has also proved most efficient in man-hour-work terms in desert Arabia, in mountainous Nepal, in Siberia's vast distances and frozen tundras, and among the 7,100 islands of the Philippines.

Asia has ample resources of oil, tin, manganese, tungsten, antimony, chromium, and aluminum, but these often occur isolated from transportation facilities or matching minerals. Turkey, for instance, has coal and metals but almost no oil, while the Persian Gulf region contains vast oil reserves but few minerals, and Israel must depend upon imported materials and oil fuel. Indigenous advances in technological skills have enabled Japan, India, Taiwan, Singapore, Hong Kong, and South Korea to garner lucrative competitive contracts in the world's markets. The deciding factor, then, is neither the possession of resources nor the lack of them, but the driving initiative of the people.

Chapter *2*

The Many Faces of Asia II

This chapter continues the consideration of some of the larger patterns of life in Asia, specifically religion, geopolitics, and language.

RELIGIOUS ASIA

It is in Asia that the world's major religions originated (see Table 2-1). Of these religions, Hinduism and Shinto are restricted to Indians and Japanese, respectively, Taoism and the Confucian ethic are Chinese. Judaism and Zoroastrianism are propagated through in-group marriage. Christianity, Buddhism, and Islam are broadly international in scope and appeal.

Religion concerns mankind's relationship with the two universes of the natural and the supernatural. Religion also is a catch-all word for such different things as folk beliefs, holy day rituals, and worship of Deity, as well as the articles used, the full-time practitioners, the worshippers and the places where they worship. (Some typical components of religion are set out in Table 2-2.)

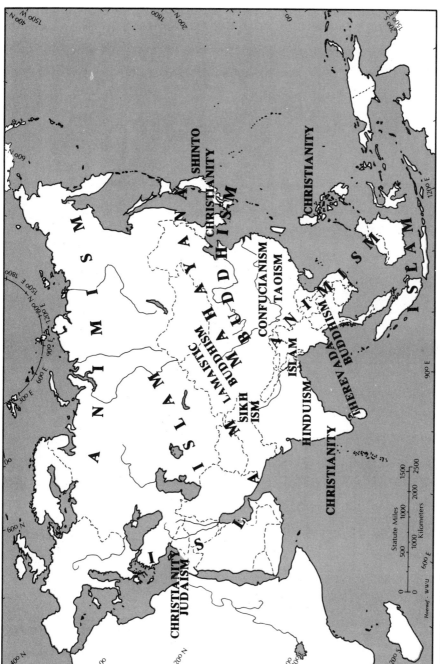

FIGURE 2-1 Distribution of traditional religions in Asia.

TABLE 2-1 MAJOR RELIGIONS OF THE WORLD

RELIGION	FOUNDER	DATE	EVENT, ETC.	COUNTRY	SCRIPTURES	LANGUAGE
		—B.C.—				
Hinduism (550)[a]	Aryan speaking peoples	1500s–1200s	Expansion into India	India	Vedas, Brahmanas, Upanishads	Sanskrit
Judaism (15)	(Moses)	1290	Exodus from Egypt, Law at Sinai	Palestine	Pentateuch, Old Testament	Hebrew, Aramaic
Zoroastrianism (.18)	Zoroaster (Zarathustra)	628–551	(Dualism, animism, ethics)	Persia	Zend Avesta	Persian
Buddhism[b] (225)	Siddhartha Gautama, the Buddha	c. 528	The Illumination under the Bo tree	Nepal/ India	Tipitaka	Pali
		—A.D.—				
Christianity (1,000)	Jesus of Nazareth, the Christ	26	Beginning of public ministry	Palestine	New Testament	Greek

RELIGION	FOUNDER	DATE	EVENT, ETC.	COUNTRY	SCRIPTURES	LANGUAGE
Shinto (63)	Ancient Yamato lineages	pre-400s	Ancestor veneration, ethics, animism	Japan	(Kojiki and Nihongi)[c]	Japanese
Islam (700)	Muhammad	622	Hegira flight to Medina	Arabia	Koran	Arabic
Baha'i	Baha'u'llah	1863	Self-announced prophet	Iran	(General writings)	Persian
PHILOSOPHIES						
Taoism[b]	Lao Zi (and Zhuang Zi)	c. 604–400s 369–286	Philosophic Taoism Religious Taoism	China	Dao De Jing	Chinese
Confucianism[b]	Confucius (Kong Fu Zi)	551–479	School of disciples	China	Yi Jing	Chinese

[a] Estimates of adherents in millions.

[b] Confucianism and Taoism are philosophic systems which, over the centuries, developed characteristics which resulted in a quasi-religious status. Although not permitted on the Mainland, these, and Buddhism, are practiced on Taiwan and abroad.

[c] Ancient Japanese histories.

TABLE 2-2 TYPICAL COMPONENTS OF RELIGION

PARAPHERNALIA	FORMS	CONTENTS
Temples, vestments, altars, utensils, items to be sacrificed.	Rituals, ceremonies, incantations. Sculptures, images, pictures. Sacred texts.	Stable tenets, doctrines. Experiental faith. Relations with spirits and deities.
STRUCTURE	PRACTITIONERS	GOALS
Philosophy, Foundational principles.	Shaman, priest, pastor; believer	Transcendental state; Nirvana; heaven. Association with Ultimate Reality, Deity.

GEOPOLITICAL ASIA

The Expansion of Europe

Since at least the 1500s, as European interests expanded eastward into commercial confrontation or military conflict with Asian nations from India to Japan, the fluctuating fortunes of the nations in Europe mirrored themselves in events in Asia. The Portuguese commandeered ports as way-stations and store cities for trade. The Spanish gripped the Philippines (and the islands of Guam and Belau). The operations of the East India Companies of England, the Netherlands, Denmark, and France led eventually to colonial regimes in India, Burma, and Malaysia under England, the Dutch East Indies (now Indonesia), and the French coalition of local states into French Indochina (now Vietnam, Laos, and Kampuchea). Germany took over northeastern New Guinea, and joined with England, France, Italy, Russia, and Mexico in gaining treaty ports or other privileges in China. America took a very minor part in these transactions, but, under Commodore Matthew Perry and Ambassador Townsend Harris, was largely responsible for opening Japan to the modern world. Always to the north were the Russians applying their expansionist pressures. However, by the mid-twentieth century almost all these colonial relics had disappeared, or were radically transformed.

Bottlenecks and Borders

Geographical bottlenecks, whether on sea or land, often are communication channels through which flow people and goods. They frequently become political hot spots. Control of these passageways implies taxes, wealth, power, empire, confrontation—and war. In addition to the Strait of Gibraltar and the Suez Canal, other narrow sea lanes are found at Aden and the Bab al Mandab (Gate of Mandab), the Persian Gulf, and the 20-mile (32-km.) wide Strait of Malacca. Shouts of victory or defeat have reverberated around the fortress mound of Megiddo in Israel, the Cilician Gates into Turkey, and the Khyber Pass in Afghanistan. Countless troops have squeezed through the rocky defiles of the Pamirs, through the Dzungarian

Gates into Kazakhstan, and past the Jade Gate separating China from the desert sands of Xinjiang.

Control of border territories has always been critical to national defense. From Jordan and the West Bank to the passes in the Himalayas and the icy waters of the Amur in northern Manchuria, disputes have ended in fighting. In the case of Afghanistan, the whole country has been regarded as a border territory for hundreds of years, a buffer zone between Persia and India and pressures from Central Asia. The most recent episode was the culmination of at least ten years of international jockeying—the occupation of the country by 100,000 Soviet troops.

Treaties and Trust

Following World War II and the end of the colonial era, when the French, British, German, and Dutch empires fell apart, many new nations were suddenly born. Fourteen Arab states formed the Arab League in 1945, established a Treaty for Joint Defense and Economic Cooperation, and set up the Arab Development Bank. The new Southeast Asian nations made several attempts to bolster their identities and security. The Southeast Asian Treaty Association (SEATO), the Association of Southeast Asia (ASA), and MAPHILINDO (intended to signal an end to the territorial squabbles between MAlaysia, PHILippines and INDOnesia), were tried and discarded before settling comfortably and efficiently into the

FIGURE 2-2   The five regions of Asia: a diagrammatic chart.

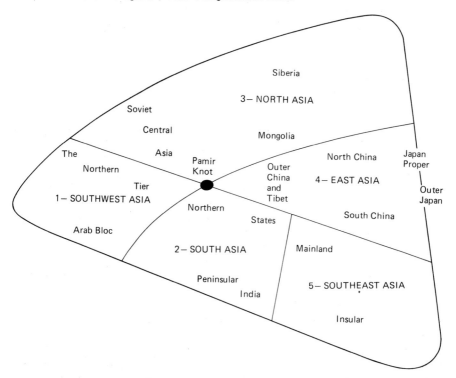

BOX 2-1 *SOCIOPOLITICAL REGIONS OF ASIA*

The five geographical regions of Asia correlate closely with the political boundaries of the nations. The characteristic placed in parentheses following each number indicates the criterion used to establish the subdivisions within that region.

1. *Southwest Asia* (ethnic)
   Arab bloc: Syria, Lebanon, Jordan, Saudi Arabia, Yemen (San'a), Democratic Yemen (Aden), Oman, United Arab Emirates, Qatar, Bahrain, Kuwait, Iraq
   Non-Arab bloc: Turkey, Cyprus, Israel, Iran, Afghanistan

2. *South Asia* (religious)
   Hindu bloc: India, Nepal
   Non-Hindu bloc: Pakistan, Bangladesh, Bhutan, Sri Lanka, Maldive Islands

3. *North Asia* (political)
   Soviet Asia
   Mongolia

4. *East Asia* (ideological)
   Communist bloc: China, North Korea
   Non-Communist bloc: Japan, South Korea, (Taiwan)

5. *Southeast Asia* (geographical)
   Mainland SEA: Burma, Thailand, Laos, Vietnam, Kampuchea, Malaysia, Singapore
   Insular SEA: Indonesia, Brunei, Philippines

Association of Southeast Asian Nations (ASEAN). Turkey, looking west, joined the North Atlantic Treaty Organization (NATO) in 1951.

It hardly matters whether geopolitical power in Asia is viewed in terms of (1) control of the World Ocean, (2) control of the "impregnable" Asian Heartland (vitiated by its paucity of transport facilities, local food, and other resources), or (3) control of Asia's Rimlands—the real key lies elsewhere. David Ben-Gurion, Israel's first president, placed it squarely before Israel's leaders, saying Israel's permanent security lay not in military preparedness and control of defensible borders but in amicable relations with the surrounding Arab peoples. Here is the key in Linden Mander's five words: "International relations are personal relations" (Mander 1942). Trust, not Curtains (Iron, Bamboo, or other), is the guarantee of security. And who will inspire it? Governments look to nationalism; corporations look to internationalism; presidents look for the emergence of a world leader; several religions look for the return of a prophet and savior. Whichever it is, dynamic forces at work in Asia will certainly contribute critically to world war or to world peace.

LINGUISTIC ASIA

Asia is a continent of languages. Nearly three billion people speak thousands of languages and dialects belonging to eight major stocks (see Figure 2-3). Most of

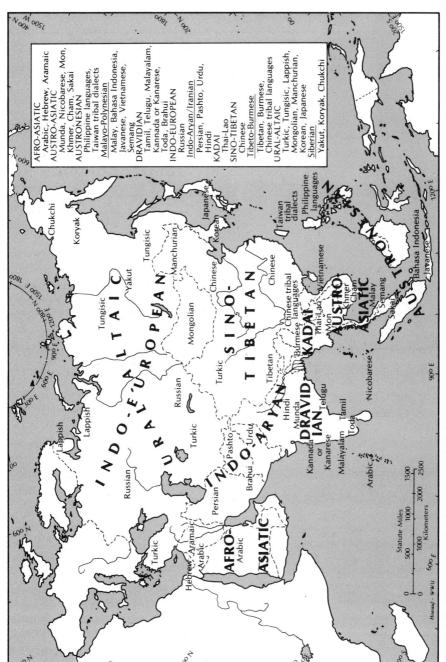

FIGURE 2-3 Distribution of major languages in Asia.

BOX 2-2 *LANGUAGE AND DIALECT TERMS*

Phylum, stock	A major language or group of languages having no known relationship with any other phylum or stock.
Family	A major group of languages within a phylum more closely related to each other than to those in any other family.
Language	An internally organized body of speech forms (including spoken, written, and other representations) common to a community which is unintelligible to those who have not learned it.
Dialect	A variant form of a language, a sublanguage, which is more or less intelligible to speakers of other dialects of the same language.
Communolect	A subdialect characteristic of a subgroup within a community.
Ideolect	The form of speech peculiar to an individual.
Jargon	A restricted body (corpus) of speech forms peculiar to a particular group for a special purpose (for example, market bargaining) or as a secret code for in-group use only.

these languages are ancient, a few are comparatively recent. Language, culture, and personality are inextricably intertwined, mutually illuminating each other.

Looking Through the Lens of Language

Language and identity. We learn, we know, we live, we grow—through language. Each new language learned is like entering a new world. When the Sikkimese Council of Ministers were sworn in in 1979, four were administered the oath of office in English, two in Nepali, and one each in Tibetan and Lepcha—revealing the wise distribution of representation in a multiethnic and multicultural country (now incorporated into India). To bolster national identity, governments promote a unified citizenry by the use of a single national language. Hindi is the goal for all India, Tagalog in the Philippines, and Russian is required throughout Soviet Asia.

Language has a forked tongue. Language is both a uniter and a divider of people. From the residential enclaves of merchants in ancient Anatolia 3000 years ago, to Arab and Persian quarters in medieval China, to Tamils and Chinese in Malaya, the unifying aspect of language fostered the establishment of language-related groups, including the various European "foreign concessions" in China, and the Chinese in Xinjiang, in the 1800s and 1900s. But, in the 1970s when India's leaders decided to enforce Hindi as the national language, several hundred million non-Hindi speakers protested against losing part of their own linguistic identity, fearing they would become second-class citizens to the Hindi speakers. In 1983 the Tamil-speaking third of Sri Lanka's population rebelled, partly for the same reason.

Languages are born, develop, and die. To promote communication between speakers of about a hundred languages and major dialects, the government of Indonesia developed simplified Malay as its new national language, Bahasa Indonesia. Similarly, the Israelis brought their ancient Hebrew out of its time-stopped cocoon and transformed it into a new and vibrant modern language.

Over the centuries some languages tend toward a simplified grammar and a vast expansion in vocabulary, as has happened, for instance, in English, Chinese, and Tagalog. In other cases complexity is added. *Urdu zaban* or camp Urdu, developed when the Mughal court and its Muslim army added Persian vocabulary to spoken Hindustani to form a *lingua franca,* and used the Arabic alphabet to write it. The Hindu population around the same time took the textbook material in Hindi, prepared at the College of Fort William in Calcutta for the use of English officials, added Sanskrit vocabulary, and wrote it in the devanagari script, thus forming modern Hindi.

When peoples move, they take their language with them. The Aryan speakers spread Aryan languages throughout Persia and North India; the Magyars in the 900s took their speech from Asia into Hungary; and the Thai, Khmer, and Burmese took their South China languages to Southeast Asia by the 1300s. From the 1600s on Russians brought their Slavic language to Central Asia, just as millions of Chinese took theirs to Oceania, Europe, and the Americas. Europeans introduced English, French, Spanish, Dutch, and other languages to South and Southeast Asia.

Other languages die, or expand. After the fall of Sumer about 2800 B.C., its language was no longer spoken, but its written language continued as the language of diplomacy for another thousand years. Classical Latin ceased as a mother tongue but has continued as the *lingua franca* of the Roman Catholic priesthood. When dominant languages expand they devour minor vernaculars, as in the Philippines, where Ilocano, Cebuano, and Tagalog all are spreading at the expense of extinguishing minority languages. Samaritan, spoken by a remnant of about 450 persons in Israel, represents a language that has refused to die.

Writing Systems and Social Change

Literacy is the key to political and technological progress. As illiterate peoples enter the modern world, their languages are reduced to writing and are usually recorded in the Roman alphabet. To signify the change from the social attitudes of a medieval empire to those of a modern republic, Kemal Ataturk abolished the Arabic script for writing Turkish and employed instead the Roman alphabet. The Malay language, first written in an Indian script, was changed to the Arabic script following the adoption of Islam and today uses the Roman alphabet. Because the Chinese characters and their associated phonetic values did not fit either the sounds or the syllable structure of the Japanese and Korean languages, these peoples invented their own scripts: the Japanese *kana* syllabary before A.D. 776, and the Korean *hangul* alphabet in the 1300s. However, in both languages today the key ideas (content words) in a sentence are represented by Chinese characters, and the rest of the sentence is written in the local script.

Scripts also live and die. Some scripts, such as the Egyptian hieroglyphics and the Sumerian wedge writing (cuneiform), are dead. The ancient Aramaic script of 700 B.C. was written horizontally. Copied later by others in Syria, Iran,

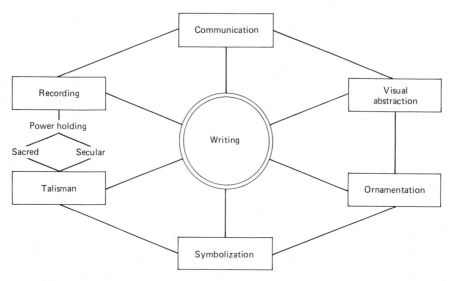

FIGURE 2-4 The many functions of writing.

and Central Asia, it was transformed during the Middle Ages into the vertically written alphabet of the Mongols and Manchus, who still use it. The classic Indian alphabet, *devanagari* or "script of the gods," was borrowed and changed in Tibet and Southeast Asia, where it was diversified into a variety of syllabaries written on leaves in Indonesia and carved onto bamboo cylinders in the Philippines. Other widespread scripts include the Arabic alphabet, Chinese characters, the Russian Cyrillic alphabet, and the Roman or Latin alphabet. The curious thing is that any given script may or may not really fit the phonetics of the next language, the letters or signs being either too many, too few, or just unsuitable. So scripts may change, and children in school may be frustrated. Numerous native scripts and derivatives of Sanskritic scripts have flourished in Southwest China or the Philippines and have perished with but few traces left to record their existence.

The Social Use of Language

Asian societies are societies based on respect. Courtesy talk between persons and diplomatic language between nations enable people to hold violent differences, yet still talk to the other parties. Age and seniority, host and guest, caste and class are facts represented in Asian speech forms, and the rules of etiquette constitute the lifelines of communication. All such verbal behavior involves choices between different levels of grammatical form, words, and even languages.

Respect as a Verbal Role

Everyone knows the word *sheik* as the head of an Arab clan, and the word *emir* as the ruler of an Arab state. But, depending upon the character of the person, the terms may apply to the head of a large household or the governor of a whole community. But the Arabic *sahib* meaning "master" or "lord" becomes just "sir," or "a gentleman" in Hindi and Bengali, as in *daktar sahib,* the doctor. Bengali

नियतं सङ्गरहितमरागद्वेषतः कृतम् ।
अफलप्रेप्सुना कर्म यत्तत्सात्त्विकमुच्यते ॥ २३

(1)

KESUSASTERAAN LAMA MELAYU

(2)

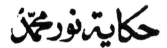

(3)

Хөгжимд шингэсэн хүн

(4)

1. Devanagari (writing Sanskrit language)
2. Latin (writing Malay language)
3. Arab (writing Malay language)
4. Cyrillic (writing Mongolian language)
5. Cuneiform (writing Assyrian language)
6. Mongol (writing Mongolian language)
7. Chinese (writing Chinese literary language)

(5) (6) (7)

FIGURE 2–5 Some Asian scripts.

recognizes social hierarchy, or social distance between people, and verbalizes the distinction by three pronouns for "you": *apni* toward superiors and honorable persons, *tumi* toward equals and ordinary people, and *tui* toward inferiors or one's intimates. To a Chinese the courtesy speech word for "my country" is *bi guo*, my humble country, and that for "your country" is *gui guo*, your honorable country. Hindi, with its twelve levels of terms of address is paralleled in codified effusiveness by both Japanese and Javanese. In all three countries this speech differentiation represents the legacies of royalty, nobility, free men, and slaves. Hosts in most countries consider it courteous to use the language of the foreign guest as much as possible. Alternatively, the guest may switch to a prestigious international language to establish his or her status as an educated person.

Just as the rejection of courtesy signals the breakdown of communication, so the erosion of respect signals a society's imminent disintegration. The loss of the cohesive force of an energy-laden respect system preceded the fall of Rome, the French and the Russian Revolutions, and the fall of the Manchus and the Nationalists in China. The collapse of South Vietnam and of Cambodia, and the ouster of the Shah of Iran, followed similar patterns. The establishment of respect for some ideal, some leader, some purpose, signals the rise of a society, and this cultural dynamic will then be enshrined in the vocabulary and integrated into the identity of the people concerned.

CHANGING ASIA

Then and Now

Cultural and political variables affect geographical and historical constants. Genghis Khan's Mongols prized the Heartland of Asia (see Chapter 11) for its grasslands; today's Chinese government values its isolation for a nuclear testing site. Through that area ran the ancient trade corridor called the Silk Road; today the armies of Russia and China compose its bristling fence 1,500 miles (2,400 km.) long. For hundreds of years the sea was Japan's protective barrier; today the sea is its highway for commerce with the wide world beyond it. Until the 1900s the journey from Shanghai to the northwest province of Xinjiang took months by river boat and caravan; today a few days by rail is sufficient. For millenia the Southeast Asian jungles were isolated as seemingly endless resources of timber and wildlife. Today pressures from lumbering, hunting, and farming interests threaten to destroy what remains of the forests and jungles and bring about ecological catastrophe.

Other changes have taken place. For two centuries mass-produced goods have been supplanting traditional handicrafts, and a money economy has radically altered the age-old face-to-face exchange system. Electric lights illumine town and village, and Western clothing is found in the cities and Western implements in the farmlands. Western art and music have influenced native styles (and vice versa), sometimes constituting a new blend as in the Philippines, sometimes competing as in Japan, and sometimes frowned upon or muted as in Muslim and Communist lands. Islam and Christianity, secularism and atheism, have vitally affected Asia's religious and political arenas.

New languages and literatures have been added to the Asian repertoire. English has become the language of intercommunication between and within

India, Pakistan, Malaysia, and the Philippines. French, Dutch, and Spanish were introduced into Southeast Asia. The Roman or Latin script is widely recognized, and the Arabic alphabet is current not only in the Arab world but also in Iran, Afghanistan, and Pakistan, and elsewhere where the Koran is read. The Russian language and its Cyrillic script have been made a requirement for the peoples of Soviet Asia. And various scripts derived from a Sanskrit original have spread throughout India and into many countries of Southeast Asia. Bahasa Indonesia and Standard Malay have been developed from a trading language, and then codified and implemented as *lingua francas* for the region of the Indonesian archipelago.

Despite the impact of radios, movies, television; relatively easy motor and train transportation; factory jobs, and so on, many aspects of traditional life have continued in recognizable forms: among them the Arab's preferred marriage to one's paternal first cousin, and the farmer's daily routine on the same farm even with some new seeds and tools. Village clothing and the familiar feasts and festivals have been preserved, together with vernacular languages that articulate the intricacies of etiquette and courtesy speech in the presence of older or more prestigious persons.

Communications

The various mounted courier systems, some in use for 2,500 years, have given place to modern postal services, telegraph stations, and satellites. Cargo ships and bulk carriers have made the speedy Arab dhow literally a museum piece. The Arabian-American Oil Company (ARAMCO) ran the first east-west train from Dammam on the Persian (or Arabian) Gulf to Riyadh in 1951, as well as laying a 950-mile (1,520-km.) transpeninsular motor road to Jiddah on the Red Sea. In the decade from 1962 to 1972 about 6,000 miles (9,600 km.) of paved roads were asphalted between the oilfields and ports of Saudia Arabia and the border points of Syria and Jordan. India and China likewise have greatly expanded their rail, road, and airplane systems, as well as progressing with their space programs, and blanketing their countries with radio communications. Instead of coolie labor handling goods from ship to barge to shore in Japan, mile-long conveyor belts whisk cargo directly from ships in the harbor to factories on shore. In return those same conveyor belts export miniaturized computers, robots, cameras, automobiles, silks, and high grade steel. Most of the Asian nations welcome free exchange of news and information together with their products, thereby maintaining useful communications on the world scene. For this purpose air services and satellite communications now link the most remote areas of Island Asia.

Prospects

The destiny of Asian nations today, and consequently that of their peoples, is inextricably bound up with the destiny of the world. By the same token, events which occur in Asia will affect the fate of the world. Like peoples everywhere, Asians have their hopes and joys, their sorrows and miseries. To look at these many Asias, and the people who comprise them, is to look deeply into humankind, for each individual human being and nation has a dignity and importance which should be respected.

Welcome to Asia!

PART II

Lands of Fervor, Fuel, and Feuds:
Southwest Asia

Chapter 3

"In the Beginning":
History, People,
and Events

GEOGRAPHICAL FOUNDATIONS

To visualize the area of Southwest Asia, look at a map and focus on the two arms of water embracing the Arabian Peninsula. To the east the Persian Gulf reaches into the heartland areas of Iraq, Iran, and Saudi Arabia—the oil region. To the west the upper fingers of the Red Sea nip hold of the earthen peg that joins Africa to Asia— the Sinai Peninsula. The extensive area north and northwest of the Arabian Sea constitutes the continental portion of Southwest Asia. The Black Sea and the mountains and plateaus in the north curtain it off from the Soviet Union, fertile valleys moisten its center, and the south bakes in the searing heat of the Arabian deserts. The wedge of the Sinai and the Eastern Mediterranean shores form the western limits of the region.

The turbulent history of Southwest Asia has left behind a complicated maze of names on the map, as well as complex problems for the modern world. Many places have (or have had) several names, which are used in this book according to context. For example, the region of ancient Sumeria and Assyria is also known as Mesopotamia and Iraq. Canaan, Palestine, and Israel are roughly equivalent. Persia became Iran, Parthia is old northeastern Iran, and Gandhara is now Afghanistan. (All these names are marked on one or another of the maps.) Since experts differ regarding many dates, we have tried to be conservative and consistent.

Even the region as a whole has many names, of which four are in common usage.

1. *Southwest Asia.* This locational term, consistent with other regional names used here, covers southwestern Asia from Turkey to Afghanistan and from Cyprus to southern Yemen.
2. *Middle East.* This World War II term was coined to designate a strategic area roughly from Morocco to Afghanistan and from Turkey to Yemen.
3. *Near East.* This obsolete term was used by West Europeans looking eastward into Asia. The "Near" East took in the southwestern sector of Asia. The "Far" East for some writers began at India, and for others was restricted to Asian countries bordering the Pacific Ocean.
4. *Levant.* This term for the eastern Mediterranean shore originated with the Medieval European traders in the Mediterranean as a designation for the direction from which blew the Levanter, a strong easterly wind.

Similarly, two additional terms have been used for the peninsular region now occupied by the country of *Turkey. Asia Minor* developed from the name of the Roman province of Asia, now part of eastern Turkey. *Anatolia*, a somewhat dated term, refers to the peninsular area only.

Terrain and Climate

Southwest Asia acts as a huge hinge upon which the continents of Europe, Asia, and Africa both join and interact. This bloc of two million square miles (5.18 million sq. km.) of dry land lies midway across the arid belt that runs from West Africa to Mongolia. Its surface features vary from the barren highlands of the Sinai wedge and the 700-foot (213-m.) high sand dunes of Arabia to the rain-drenched slopes of Lebanon and the irrigated river valleys of Iraq. The sunbaked northern highlands of Turkey and Iran also share their winter snow with the icy terror of the Hindu Kush (Hindu killer) mountains and the frigid Wakhan corridor of northeastern Afghanistan.

The surrounding waterways have been frequented by international shipping from the days of galleys and dhows to modern tanker leviathans and missile cruisers.

The regional extremes of temperature and humidity demand cultural adaptation such as the Bedouins' flowing robes which conserve body moisture by day, in temperatures over 100° Fahrenheit (37.8° C), and maintain body heat in the chill of night. Similarly, long wool and fur garments preserve body heat in the icy mountains. In Kabul, nearly 6,000 feet (1,795 m.) above sea level, the subfreezing winter temperatures and an annual rainfall of 13 inches (33 cm.) contrast sharply with summer heat and 100 inches (2.54 m.) of rain in northeastern Turkey. It is within these circumstances that the mosaic civilizations of Southwest Asia have arisen.

Water and Survival

At the same time that rain is one of the region's greatest needs, snow is one of its greatest resources. Human survival depends on the limitations set by the natural resources of the area, as modified by climate and technology, for only 5 percent of the region is good agricultural land. The potential productivity of large areas of marginally arable land suffers mainly from water loss by both evaporation

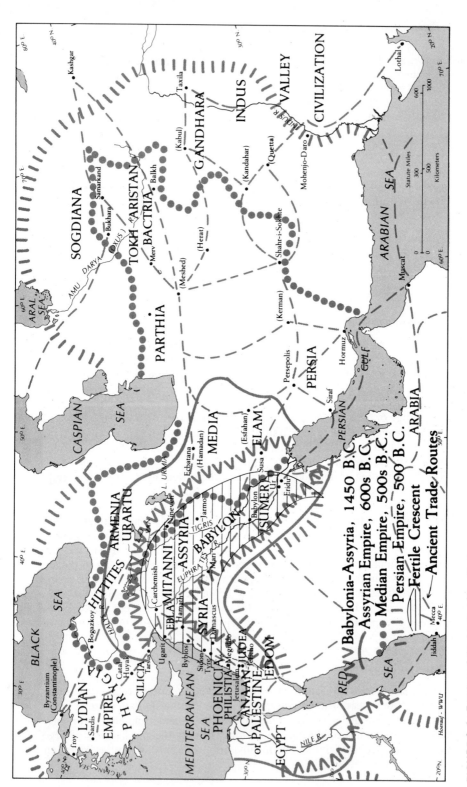

FIGURE 3–1 Empires of the Ancient Near East.

BOX 3-1   *ASIA'S ARID LANDS*

True though it may be that "Only Antarctica is drier than Asia," (with interior Australia a close second, and the Saharan sands of northern Africa shimmering in the heat), 6.5 to 9.8 million square miles (*msm*) (16.9 to 25.4 million sq. km.—*msk*) of Asia, one third of the whole area, is either desert, arid, or steppeland, depending upon the definitions used.

1. A *meteorologic* definition: rainlessness; for example, where Syria lies in the rain shadow of the Lebanon mountains, and Xinjiang in that of the Tibetan Massif; minimal rainfall affects nearly whole area.

2. *Climatic*: evaporation exceeds precipitation; on only 3 msm (7.7 msk) of semiarid land can even dry farming raise a few crops.

3. *Ecologic*: bare ground with sparse, discontinuous vegetation cover; barren 1.1 msm (2.8 msk); desert flora 3.6 msm (9.3 msk); steppeland 2.3 msm (5.9 msk).

4. *Geomorphic*: weathered and eroded basins of gravel, sand, and wind-blown silt cover 30 percent of Arabia and Xinjiang, 25 percent of Pakistan, 5 percent of Iraq, Syria, Jordan, Israel, and Mongolia.

5. *Hydrographic*: Central Asian drainage areas, where drainage never actually reaches the oceans; 6.4 msm (16.5 msk).

6. *Geographic*: areas minimally suited to human habitation; water must be secured by special techniques; 5.5 msm (14.2 msk).

NOTE: The areas given above refer to the 6.5 to 9.8 msm (16.9 to 25.4 msk) total area of arid lands.

Adapted from George B. Cressey, *Asia's Lands and Peoples,* 3rd ed. (New York: McGraw-Hill, 1963), pp. 39–43.

and seepage. Evaporation stimulates the vertical circulation of air, adds to the amount of airborne dust, and limits the amount of precipitation available for use, causing self-perpetuating aridity. Shortages of precipitation and groundwater limit Southwest Asian agriculture.

Some peoples have survived these limitations. Eighteen hundred years ago Nabatean experts in the Negev constructed smoothed hillsides and rock-cut channels to collect runoff in dams, ponds, and cisterns. Israeli settlers have demonstrated that such runoff farming can support one good crop and extensive orchards on 4 inches (100 mm.) of rain annually. A single half-inch shower of rain has resulted in a runoff catchment of 5,838 cubic yards (4,457 cubic meters) of water into terraced fields and cisterns of 262 to 526 cubic yards (200 and 400 cubic meters) and larger capacities. On the semiarid Anatolian plateau the Turkish farmer who finds a spring of water is socially obligated to build a stone trough to make the water available for village use. Elsewhere in Iraq and Iran underground tunnels called *qanats* or *karez* conveyed mountain waters to fields five to thirty miles (8 to 48 km.) away. However, in flat and sand dune areas where such catchments and agriculture are all but impossible, some form of nomadic pastoralism remains the most efficient use of land and resources.

The Fertile Crescent

The "Fertile Crescent," the river-based arc of plenty between Arabia's deserts and Turkey's stony plateau, forms a slanted semicircle from the Nile valley of Egypt northward across the Sinai peninsula and up the Jordan and Orontes river valleys to northern Syria. The Crescent then bends southeast down the Euphrates and Tigris valleys and plains to the Persian Gulf. The adjacent areas of the Mediterranean coast and the nearby mountain slopes of Turkey, Iraq, and Iran form the Crescent's outer boundaries. Here in the torrid wedge of Sinai—that military shoot-the-chute between Asia and Africa—lived Amalekite shepherds, Egyptian slaves in the copper mines and in Roman times the Arab Nabatean farmers. To the north, Phoenicia and Syria grew rich as exchange marts for seaborne and camelborne merchandise. Over the northern borders lived the empire-building Hittites and the Scythian horsemen of the distant grasslands of Central Asia.

The southeastern leg of the Crescent saw the flourishing of a triad of empires —Sumer, Assyria, and Babylon—whose strategic situation on vital caravan routes with a relatively abundant agricultural base, coupled with their ruthless cupidity, made them the terror of early Southwest Asia. A glance at the map shows that this region was the connecting link between trade routes from China through Kashgar and Samarkand, and from India through Taxila and Persepolis, thence through Hittite and Lydian territory to Europe and through Arabia and Sinai into the coastlands and far interior of Africa.

Today asphalted motor roads follow ancient caravan trails, and rivers from the Jabbok in Jordan, the Euphrates in Iraq to the Helmand in Afghanistan have been dammed for irrigation and electric power. Oasis waters have been conserved, thousands of hectares near Riyadh irrigated, and the Jordan drastically reduced to make parts of Israel's Negev "blossom like the rose." The Jordan valley is Israel's and Jordan's most intensively fruitful area, and the productivity of Lebanon's Beka'a valley is overshadowed only by its sensitive strategic value.

To understand these developments we need some background history.

CULTURAL DEVELOPMENT
IN ANCIENT SOUTHWEST ASIA

Humans first occupied Southwest Asia over half a million years ago, and fully modern humans (*Homo sapiens sapiens*) began living an advanced hunting-gathering life there some 60,000 years ago. Seen on this scale, all that follows is but a brief period fraught with change. Around 12,000 to 6500 B.C. occurred the agricultural transformation which would ultimately mold the world as we know it today. At first, farming was simply an adjunct to hunting and gathering; but with increasing population, settled farming became the primary mode of life. This entailed profound changes in all the physical and material aspects of life, and led to new religious and world views.

By 5000 B.C. organized and fortified towns inhabited by several thousand people sat astride strategic crossroads or beside key points on river and coastal waterways. Already well established was the basic pattern which remains today: a large rural population provided the food needed to sustain the city; a small merchant and artisan population traded and manufactured the supply of necessary and luxury goods, many not available locally; and a few ritual and governmental specialists maintained the earthly and divine order needed for the city and its vicinity to survive. This period of early urbanism flourished around 4000 B.C. Urban amenities included woolen rugs, obsidian mirrors, copper utensils, and two-story gabled houses. Security systems of social control provided militia for regional defense and the protection of shipping.

By about 2400 B.C. the early nation-states had a complexity of sophisticated living which included the basic family, social, and intercommunity relationships as we know them today. Social stratification also had become well established. Complex political organizations of interregional trade exchanges (see Table 1-2) accompanied the growth in population and the increasing size of the cities. Although dates and details differ, the general pattern of changing lifeways from

TABLE 3-1   Developing Culture and Economy in Southwest Asia

DATES	ASPECTS OF CULTURE AND ECONOMY	LOCALITY
B.C.		
10,000	Neolithic Age: communal living; simple agriculture; herding of sheep and goats	Southwest Asia
8000	Organized cities of three thousand persons; cereal cultivation; elaborate mixed economy: hunting, farming, tools, pottery; trade; early use of native copper	Jericho, Tarsus
7500	Expanding cities, up to 30 acres (12 ha.) in area	Mesopotamia
7000	Shrine worship; wheat crops, copper and lead crafts; weaving	Anatolian plateau, Jarmo
5700	Burnished and painted pottery	Southwest Asia
5000	Trade networks; hybrid cereals; stamp seal heirlooms; gabled houses for extended families. All basic patterns of livelihood and settled social life	Egypt, Byblos, Mesopotamia, Cyprus
4700	National administrations; international trade networks by land and sea; flood control systems; class distinctions; cities with sectors for government, residential, and industrial buildings; empires; political patterns	Sumer, Mesopotamia, Syria, Phoenicia
3600	Bronze utensils; repeated invasions into S.W.A.	Anatolia, Troy
3400	Fortified cities up to 6 miles (9.6 km.) perimeter; trade networks with Afghanistan, India, Africa; pictographic writing; temples and priests; scribes; copper-tin alloy	Sumeria (Warka or Erech), Syria
3000 to 2200	Bronze Age empires and city states: Sumer, Elam, Ebla, Ugarit; back and forth migration movements; successive eruptions of Semitic peoples from Arabia	Southwest Asia, Sumeria, Syria
1500	Iron Age weaponry (Hittites, Hyksos, and others); increased large scale interregional warfare for control of territory, intercontinental trade routes and satellite states; advanced professionalism, archives, and libraries	Mesopotamia, Persia, Syria, Egypt, Phoenicia; Europe

hunting-gathering to agriculture and city life, as described here for Southwest Asia, was paralleled in principle throughout Asia, except in the tundra and forest regions of the north. And, just as farming provided the initial basis for change, so writing made possible the final complexity of societal life.

The evolution of the Mesopotamian cuneiform (wedge-shaped) writing began as a pictographic system around 3000 B.C., then appeared in the wedge form around 2500 B.C. Pictographic forms merged into ideographic symbols (that is, representing ideas or concepts), and later as syllabic and logographic symbols to represent syllables and whole words. Both the time and the sequence of development of the cuneiform system was paralleled by the Egyptian hieroglyphics (sacred [picture] script) and a little later by the Chinese characters. During the two-millenia-long effective lifetime of the cuneiform script, the original two thousand or more symbols were gradually reduced to 600, and then to an alphabet of thirty symbols. Cuneiform writing was still being impressed on clay tablets until shortly before the first year A.D.

The invention of writing made possible the growth of an elite class of professional scholar-scribes who kept dynastic records in national archives, as in Nineveh, Susa, Ebla, and Ugarit; transmitted imperial edicts in 120 languages and scripts in Persia; and balanced credit accounts at Shahr-i-Sokhte, west of Kandahar.

The 200,000 burials at Sokhte bear mute testimony to the city's 1,500-year history to 1800 B.C. as an east-west trade mart for its alabaster and lapis lazuli products. To the south the coastal waters were alive with shipping between India and the Persian Gulf. Similar land and sea trade routes functioned well into the 1800s A.D.

The hardy men and women of Southwest Asia represent the end product of the influx of many peoples over the last four to five thousand years. Semitic Canaanites and Amorites swept out from the desert after 3000 B.C., followed by Hurrians and Hittites, Cimmerians and Scythians, and Greeks from the northeast and the northwest. Then in the present era Muslims and Crusaders, Seljuk and Ottoman Turks were added to resident Lydians, Armenians, Kurds, and finally a sprinkling of modern Europeans. The history of a single city, Tarsus, epitomizes the history of Southwest Asia.

Life History of Tarsus

Tarsus, which has survived several millenia of tumult, peace, and war, reflects the advantages and hazards of a strategic location. Situated between Antioch (modern Antakya) and the Cilician Gates, on the major highway from Syria to Anatolia and Europe, Tarsus served as a river port, a fortress, and an agricultural center. Following invasions about 2600 B.C. the city was dominated by Hittites, colonized by Greeks, and captured by Sennacherib the Assyrian (705-681 B.C.). Tarsus watched the Persian armies pass by, also those of two famous Greeks, Xenophon and Alexander the Great, and of the Roman generals Pompey and Caesar. It was here that another Roman general, Mark Anthony, had his fateful meeting for the first time with the intriguing Egyptian queen Cleopatra. By the time Saul of Tarsus (later known as the Apostle Paul) was born there, this university city had been endowed by Rome with free citizenship. The Abbasid caliph of Baghdad, the celebrated Harun al-Rashid, fortified Tarsus as a base from which to raid the Byzantine domains around A.D. 787. Captured by the Crusaders after a long siege in 1097 and by the Mamluks in 1359, it came permanently under Ottoman rule about 1500. Following a long decline in interregional trade, Tarsus became prosperous again in the 1920s after its swamps had been drained by the planting of a eucalyptus forest. Today's rolling thunder is that of huge trailer trucks traveling southeast along the nearby Turkish trunk road into Syria and beyond.

The Established Social Patterns

It is now clear that the basic patterns of organized government, trade networks, warfare, specialized crafts, and literate elites, supported by a large farming population, are five to seven thousand years old. One of the remarkable early achievements of Southwest Asia was the codification of law under Hammurabi (c. 1792-1750 B.C.). This justly famous Code of Hammurabi enshrined and shaped the customs of the Near East for centuries, covering rents, runaway slaves, rights and punishments in criminal and civil situations, inheritance, transfer of property, obligations of fief holders, etc. (Few legal enterprises match its greatness, compare *The Law* of Moses, Plato's *The Laws,* Justinian's *Digest and Code,* the *Code Napoleon,* and the *Constitution* and *Bill of Rights* of the United States of America.)

Known throughout the ancient Near East by both desert nomads and urban literati, Hammurabi's *Code* has a modern literary parallel in the knowledge and influence of the *Koran.* The *Koran*'s verbal charm makes memorization easy, and its practical injunctions guide the public and private conduct of Muslim behavior.

FIGURE 3-2 Major Asian migrations.

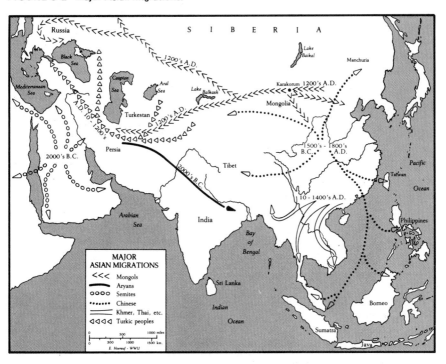

The Ebb and Flow of Peoples

Southwest Asian history is speckled with the continuous flow of peoples and the rise and fall of empires. Triangles of power are not new. Notice the one between Egypt on the Nile, the Hittites in Anatolia, and Assyria or Babylon in Mesopotamia in the 1300s and later centuries B.C. This has been mirrored in the Egyptian-Seleucid-Roman wars of the 100s B.C. and in the Muslim-Byzantine-Persian wars from the A.D. 600s on. Indeed, the Egypt-Israel-Arab wars and confrontations of the 1960s and 1970s seem to follow a very ancient model!

It was in the days of the first triangle, when Ugarit was the queen city of the Levant (c. 1450-1170 B.C.), rich with its trade with Mycenean Greece, Minoan Crete, Cyprus, Egypt, and all interior caravan points, that Palestine was invaded by considerable forces of shepherd nomads. These people, called *habiru,* while not objectively identified as the Hebrews of the Old Testament, came during the generally accepted period of the Hebrew's exodus from Egypt (c. 1290-1260 B.C.) and entrance into Canaan (c. 1250-1220 B.C.).

Soon afterwards (c. 1190 B.C.) the people known as the Philistines, probably one of the marauding Sea Peoples from the Aegean region, established five city states in the prototype area of "the Gaza strip." They eventually disappeared from the record of history, but not so the tenacious and prosperous Greek colonies on the Aegean and Black Sea coasts of Asia Minor, including Byzantium. From about 825 B.C. on, these settlements survived the empires of Persia, Greece, Rome, and Turkey, until the one-sided exchange of Greek and Turkish populations in 1923 culminated in the violent expulsion of 1.25 million Greeks from Izmir (Smyrna) and other Turkish cities. Only a few Greek merchants still reside in Turkey.

THE NEAR EAST TO MODERN TIMES

Empires and Eras

The last two thousand years in Southwest Asia may be viewed as periods of imperial control by Persians and Greeks, Romans and Byzantines, Muslim Arabs and Turks. Only the Persians and the Turks retained permanent controls, but over greatly reduced territories. Probably the most significant outcome of these years is that local communities retained much of their inherited identities, which still are perceptible in the present nations and their territories. The main exception is the state of Israel because, although upwards of 60 percent of its population represents Jewish communities which have resided continuously in the Middle East, the state itself is a new and modern entity.

The *Persian Empire* (559-331 B.C.) of some thirty major satrapies (provinces governed by a satrap) joined contiguous territories in Europe, Asia, and Africa into one huge domain stretching two thousand miles (3,200 km.) from east to west. The *Hellenistic Age* ran for 300 years, beginning in 331 B.C. with Alexander's conquest of the Persian Empire, spreading Greek culture, language, art, philosophy, and coinage through Western Asia and much of the Roman Empire. Alexander's vision of a unified world enriched by Greek culture led him to mobilize "a vast organization" of technical experts (as Napoleon would do in Egypt in 1798), including surveyors, architects, engineers, scientists, and historians.

The *Roman Period* of 500 years (27 B.C.-A.D. 476) witnessed the inter-weaving movements of vast numbers of peoples, armies, slaves, and traders. The Romans spread their Latin language, codified laws, multiplied slavery, and united the area from England to the eastern edges of Persia. Divided in half in A.D. 395, the Western Empire staggered on until 476. The better-organized Eastern Empire, commonly known as the *Byzantine Empire,* continued for almost 1,000 years longer until 1453. As the cultural center of Eastern Orthodox Christianity, Byzantium shielded Europe from Arab and Turkish Muslims until the mid-1300s.

The Byzantine empire paralleled the *era of Muslim Arab rule* (600s to 900s, and see also Chapter 4), and overlapped the beginning of the Ottoman empire. The inception of the *Turkish era* began with the Seljuk empire of the 1000s, which briefly extended from the Indus to the Mediterranean, and was destroyed and supplanted in Persia and Afghanistan by the Mongol Il-khan empire (1256-1335). At the same time other Turkish people established the Ottoman empire in Anatolia, lasting just short of 600 years from 1326 to 1922. Some Turkish communities such as the Turkmen and Azerbaijanis settled in their own niches in and around Persia. (See Chapter 6 for further details.)

FORMATION OF THE MODERN NATIONS

When the rambling Turkish empire was dissolved at the end of World War I, a region little-known to most Westerners stood revealed. There were a few organized nations (Turkey, Iran, and Afghanistan), several small Arab states on the Persian Gulf (Bahrain, Qatar, and Oman), Cyprus and Aden governed by the British, and an Arab region of uncoordinated tribes and sheikdoms. The League of Nations placed some Turkish territories under a system of "mandated territories," to be administered by Great Britain (Mesopotamia; Palestine, including Jordan), and France (Syria, including Lebanon). By the end of 1947 when the mandates terminated, a group of independent nations had been born. Mesopotamia had become Iraq; Syria had been divided into Syria and Lebanon; and Palestine had been divided between Israel and Transjordan, later renamed Jordan. Moreover, most of Arabia had been welded into the new kingdom of Saudi Arabia, and ancient Yemen again was a nation. Over the years the scene was filled in with the independence of Kuwait (1961), the People's Democratic Republic of Yemen, often referred to as Southern Yemen (1967), and the United Arab Emirates, previously the Trucial States (1968).

While these new national alignments have not historically come full circle, there is considerable significance in the territorial distributions. Iraq encompasses the areas of the ancient Sumerian, Babylonian, and Assyrian kingdoms; Syria retains much of its ancient boundaries; and Lebanon in part reproduces historic Phoenicia. Israel covers most of the core realms of Israel and Judah; and Jordan amalgamates the territories of Edom, Moab, and Ammon (perpetuated in the name of Jordan's capital city Amman). The states located on the Arabian peninsula reflect the locations and peoples of the last three thousand years.

So, in closing this all-too-brief survey of the past, we are reminded of two of the themes of this chapter: first, the tenacity of community identity despite the trauma of alternating victory and defeat; and second, the ability of individuals and communities, as they move into new areas and environments, to both retain some-

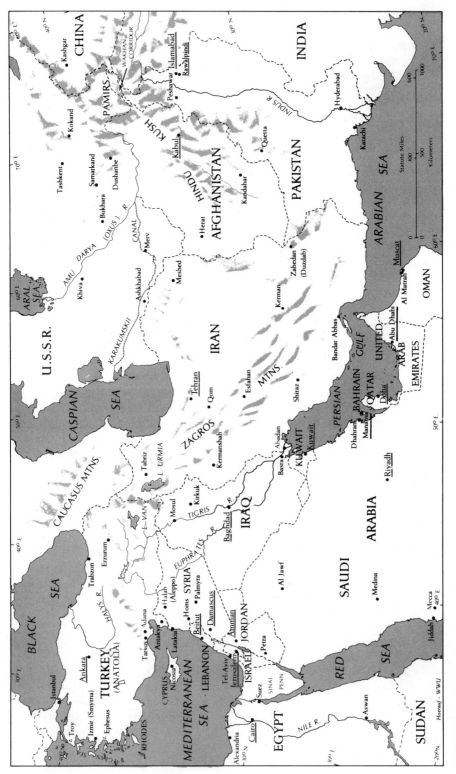

FIGURE 3-3 Modern Southwest Asia.

thing of their heritage and blend into fresh configurations, with new destinies and responsibilities. Realizing these new destinies and responsibilities in today's world has been complicated by the presence of superpowers and nuclear technologies, new fashions and philosophies, new religions, leverages and communications. In each case the impact of these new situations is forcing the reevaluation of the community's essential nature, its goals, and the methodology of adjustment.

THE PARADE OF CAPITALS

The efforts that humankind has exerted to survive in this hard land have produced Southwest Asia's modern sheikdoms and nations. United by lineage and language, dignified by art and science, toughened by millenia-long exposure to sand and sword, each community has graduated from the grim pages of history to merge successfully into the maelstrom of our mechanized modern world. The amazing progress these countries have made during even the last fifty years can be seen through a brief description of their capital cities.

One ex-capital city of great size and importance is a city of many names: *Deri-Seadet* to the Persians and Arabs; *Cospoli* to the Levantines and Italians; and *Tsari-grad* to the Bulgars; *Byzantium* to the early Greeks and the Romans; *Constantinopolis* to the modern Greeks; and *Constantinople* to Westerners. Today it is called *Istanbul* ("into the city") by the Turkish people. Istanbul sits at one of the most strategic crossroads in the world, where the principal land routes connecting Asia with Europe are only half a mile apart across the Bosphorus (Greek for "oxford"), and the Black Sea begins its traverse to the Mediterranean. After 1100 years as the capital of Byzantium and 470 years as the capital of Turkey, its place as capital was taken by Ankara in 1923. But Istanbul remains the center of Turkish education, culture, industry, and religion.

Beneath the shadow of an ancient fortress *Ankara's* modern buildings service the needs of the people on the central Anatolian plateau. Said to have been founded by king Midas of Phrygia (c. 700 B.C.), it was chosen by Kemal Ataturk to be the capital of modern Turkey after the abolition of the 600-year-old Ottoman Empire.

Just off the south coast of Turkey, Greek settlers set up small city states on the island of Cyprus about 1200 B.C. and commenced the civilization known in Roman times for its salubrious climate, wines, and fruits. The capital city, *Nicosia*, nestled in the central valley, has had a checkered history as Romans, Venetians, Genoese, Mamlukes, and Turks took turns plundering it and passing on. This modest but beautiful city, once the professional and educational center of all Cyprus, became in 1974 the capital of only the Greek section of the island. On February 13, 1975, Turkey proclaimed the Turkish-held northern third of Cyprus an autonomous but not completely independent state with Famagusta as its capital.

Damascus, thriving in its luxuriant Syrian oasis, is perhaps the oldest of all the ancient large cities. It has been continuously occupied since before 2000 B.C. and has been a caravan entrepôt since 1000 B.C. Among its attractions are the Great Mosque of the Omayyad caliphs, originally a Byzantine church, and the Street called Straight. There also is the tomb of Islam's mightiest warrior, Saladin, the Kurdish sultan of Syria who held at bay England's soldier king Richard Coeur-de-Lion during the Third Crusade in 1192.

FIGURE 3-4   Bedouin camped outside trading city.

For at least 3,500 years, the galleys and ships of *Beirut* on the Phoenician-Lebanese coast have roamed the Mediterranean. Beirut functioned as the western connection of trade routes that extended eastward over the caravan trails (and now railway lines) to Damascus and all points east. North and south trade from Ethiopia, Egypt, and Libya to Ugarit, Antioch, Tarsus, and the Black Sea also passed through or transshipped at Beirut. The massive destruction caused by the 1976-84 internecine fighting, and Israel's invasion of the 1980s, put a temporary end to Beirut's glittering role as the Paris of the Levant.

Moving south from Beirut, we may note that, before king David captured Jebus about 1000 B.C., the city now known as *Jerusalem* already had a two-thousand-year existence. Taken and retaken more times perhaps than any other city in the world—27 times up to 1244—Jerusalem is a holy city to the members of three major religions. It is sacred to Jews, for the altar to Jehovah stood in the city of David and Solomon; to Christians as the site of the death and resurrection of Jesus Christ; and to Muslims as the place from which Muhammad ascended to heaven. As the city of three Sabbaths—Friday for Muslims, Saturday for Jews, and Sunday for Christians—the future for its 400,000 people may be as troubled as its past.

If we pass eastward across the Allenby Bridge over the Jordan river, we shall come to *Amman* (ancient Rabbath-Ammon). It was called Philadelphia when it was one of the cities of the Decapolis (the district of the Ten Cities) under the Seleucid rulers of Syria (305-64 B.C.). It became the capital of Transjordan from 1921 to 1950, when the new name of Jordan was adopted. Sitting on its seven hills, this busy city of a hundred modern gold shops and a huge Roman amphitheater built in the second century encloses everything from bazaars for the desert dwellers to machine shops for the latest jet fighter planes. Amman became home to the royal Hashemite family in 1921, and in 1977 celebrated the silver anniversary of King Hussein's reign.

Riyadh is a forty-square-mile oasis of brick-and-concrete, gardens-and-greenery in the central desert of Saudi Arabia. From the palace square, four broad asphalt streets radiate outwards: north past modern administrative buildings to the airport, east to the railway station, south to residential areas, and west to the magnificent royal palace. And the asphalt strips continue on east to the Persian Gulf, and southwest via Mecca to the Red Sea at Jiddah. Capital of booming Saudi Arabia and goal of aspiring social climbers, Riyadh reflects in its staidness the strict Islamic moral code of the Wahhabi sect to which its ruling family belongs.

Located in the southeast corner of the Arabian peninsula, and probably highest of the capitals in altitude at 7200 feet, *San'a* has walls and minarets which overlook Yemen's plateaus, cliffs, and coastal plain. So well watered is this land of five million people, that it is called Arabia Felix ("Fortunate Arabia"). Inside the city walls, Republican soldiers mingle with tribespeople, some still loyal to the deposed Imam as their spiritual leader. With or without rifles slung on their shoulders, they peacefully share the narrow streets with peasant coffee growers, and master craftsmen in textiles, leather, and glassware. Old though some of them are, none of San'a's two- to six-story brick and stone houses belong to the days of Bilgis, Queen of Sheba (and friend of King Solomon), who ruled the Yemenis around 950 B.C.

In contrast to San'a, *Aden,* capital of Southern Yemen, occupies a narrow, hot, mountain-girt valley into which the British used to import and plant roadside trees that lasted six months before shriveling up. From ancient times Aden has been a port of call for both pirates and traders on routes stretching from Egypt to India and from Basra to Zanzibar. Aden became even more important as a coaling station for steamships after the opening of the Suez Canal in 1869. Herdsmen, farmers, and fishermen mix on the broad business streets and in narrow residential lanes, and meet with businessmen who are likely to have a family member as a merchant as far away as Indonesia.

Muscat, capital of the sultanate of Oman, has had an up-and-down history. Held by the Persians in the 500s B.C. and the A.D. 500s, it was intermittently small and independent. Muscat was the capital of an empire which included Zanzibar in East Africa and territory to the north on the Baluchistan coast in the A.D. 1600s and 1700s. (The capital was moved briefly to Zanzibar from 1832 to 1861.) During the 1700s Oman's dhows carried ivory and frankincense as far as China. Now astir with radios, motorbikes, and multinational business and advisory personnel, Muscat today is still in the entrepôt transshipment business. Still small and hot, the city seems destined to remain near the center of any activity involving the Persian Gulf.

Seven small sheikdoms along the dusty southeastern shores of the Persian Gulf, which had been under British protection as the Trucial States since 1835, were united to form the United Arab Emirates in 1971. *Abu Dhabi* was selected to be the capital. A modern city has been built around the Emir's palace, between the desert and the sea, to house the administrative and business needs of these enterprising and oil-rich minimonarchies.

If a Qatari boy with telescopic vision were to sit on the rim of the 40,000-

TABLE 3-2 The Capital Cities of Southwest Asia

NAME	DATE OF FOUNDING	COUNTRY	POPULATION (THOUSANDS)	PRODUCTS
ABU DHABI	Ancient	United Arab Emirates	264	Petroleum products
ADEN	Ancient	Southern Yemen	88	Shipping trade, oil refinery, handcrafts.
AMMAN	pre-1300 B.C.	Jordan	600	Light industry.
ANKARA	800s B.C.	Turkey	1,461	Market for regional agriculture and manufacturing products.
BAGHDAD	A.D. 762	Iraq	1,500	Petroleum products, grain, fruits
BEIRUT	pre-2500 B.C.	Lebanon	475	Banking, trade, educational facilities, tourism.
DAMASCUS	pre-2000 B.C.	Syria	837	Metalwork, brocades, mosaics.
DOHA	post-2000 B.C.	Qatar	100	Petroleum products, pearls.
*ISTANBUL	Early 500 B.C.	Turkey	2,376	Educational, banking, and trade center.
JERUSALEM	pre-2600 B.C.	Israel	344	Chemicals, leather goods, machinery, pottery.
KABUL	pre-500 B.C.	Afghanistan	318	Handcrafts, textiles, cement
KUWAIT	c. A.D. 1740	Kuwait	700	Petroleum products, banking, flour, and fertilizer.
MANAMA	Ancient	Bahrain	88	Petroleum products, fish, pearls.
MUSCAT	pre-536 B.C.	Oman	10	Transshipment trade, dates, fish.
NICOSIA	c. 1200 B.C.	Cyprus	115	Textiles, cigarettes, footwear, fruits.
RIYADH	1824	Saudi Arabia	450	Nerve center of Saudi Arabia; no factories.
SAN'A	c. 1400 B.C.	Yemen	120	Handicrafts, coffee, fruits.
TEHERAN	4th c. A.D.	Iran	4,000	Automobiles, cement, sugar, armaments.

*Capital of Turkey for 470 years until 1923.

spectator stadium in *Doha,* he probably would be able to see fifty miles north and west and south over the whole Qatar peninsula and to the once pearl-rich waters of the Persian Gulf beyond. He would see mammoth tankers in the Gulf and at the city wharves, while at his feet would lie the new University and the ancient fort, the schools and fisheries, the Great Mosque and the oil refinery. He also could pick out the imposing buildings of Government House, the museum, hotels, airport, and the parabolic antenna of the satellite station, and some of Qatar's nearly 200,000 energetic people.

To 80,000 of Bahrain's robed citizens of *Manama,* this capital of Bahrain's four-island archipelago is also harbor and home for pearling and fishing fleets operating in the Persian Gulf. Variously occupied by Portugal, Persia, and Great Britain, and independent since 1971, Manama on the one hand retains three-thousand-year-old Dilmon's ancient pride, and on the other exploits today's riches in oil.

Near the head of the Persian Gulf, the palm-lined six-lane roads of *Kuwait* city are shaded by its modern buildings and residences. Prominent among these are the palatial government rest house and maternity hospital complex. The telecommunications center is faced across the city by other sumptuous-looking "low-income" housing. Only men sailed the lateen-rigged dhows of 5,000 years ago, or handle the 300,000-ton oil tankers loading here today, but modern Kuwaiti women are taking an unusually active part in the everyday life and business of the bustling high-income population.

Proceeding another 350 miles (560 km.) northwest, *Baghdad* on the Tigris lies near the end of the Berlin to Basra railway. The city straddles the crossroads of transdesert motor and caravan traffic and of east-west airlines. Seat of the Abbasid caliphate of the just and able Harun al-Rashid, the sultan of the *Arabian Nights,* it was razed by Hulagu the Mongol in 1258. Restored by the Ilkhan governors Baghdad was next conquered by the Ottoman Turks in 1534, and seized from the Turks by the British in 1917. Modernized since 1958 as the capital of Iraq, it is a bustling and brittle center of Islamic fervor and radical politics.

Northeastward over the Zagros mountains in Iran, the 110-square-mile (285 sq. km.) city of *Teheran* sprawls on the southern slops of the towering Elburz peaks. This beautiful city is the thirteenth century successor to the city of Ray, the ancient Ragha known from a prehistoric site dated circa 2000 B.C. Teheran profited when Ray was destroyed in 1220 by the Mongols, and in classical times, as the capital city of Persia, it was rivaled only by Damascus and Baghdad. Later it lay rather quiescent until the official enthusiasm of the twentieth century accelerated the growth of spacious buildings, manufactures, rail and air connections, and universities.

Kabul, the last capital in our eastward journey through Southwest Asia, straddles the Kabul river nearly 6000 feet (1,830 m.) above sea level, and only a few miles from the famous and bloody Khyber Pass. Thirty-three miles (53 km.) long and previously only ten feet (3 m.) wide at its narrowest point, the Khyber Pass remains the major land gateway for caravans and armies going southwest from Greece, Persia, and Central Asia, into the Indus Valley and India, and for spices, silks, jewels, and religion (Buddhism) going west and north. Today Kabul's universities and institutes train teachers and technicians for the country's multilinguistic peoples.

Both Teheran and Kabul have had their recent troubles: Teheran with intra-Islamic feuding and bombing, and a dragged-out war with Iraq, and Kabul as the headquarters of a Marxist government bolstered by 100,000 ruthless Russian troops.

ARE YOU WHAT YOU THINK?

Is it true that, "As a man thinketh, so is he"? Look at one aspect of Asia: kingdoms and sheikdoms on the Arabian peninsula, military dictatorships in Iraq, Pakistan and Bangladesh, civil dictatorships sporadically in Indonesia, South Korea and the Philippines, and Communist regimes in Mongolia, China, Afghanistan, North Korea, and Southeast Asia. To a greater or lesser degree they have a common social factor embedded in the language and vocabulary, in the levels of social structure and etiquette, and in community expectations—an authoritarian form of government. By contrast, a modern trend is toward republicanism, the sharing of authority freely throughout the nation. Other trends are toward individualism in contrast to group solidarity, and toward equal citizenship under law applied impartially to everyone, in contrast to a hierarchy of privilege and responsibility. Moreover, industrialism, since it pays individually earned wages, operates against family and lineage cohesion and mutual sharing.

Every aspect of modern life seems to nudge both person and group away from religious faith and nudges values towards secularism. The present most forceful form of authoritarianism, Communism, applies authority to every aspect of life, from governmental, social, and personal to spiritual, mental, and verbal conduct, together with a denial of all aspects of religion. It is in this environmental maze that Muslims, to preserve unsullied their Islamic identity and heritage, have reacted in several directions. One is the affirmation of their faith by stubbornly perpetuating their Muslim way of life in Soviet Asia. A second is by spreading their faith abroad, including to Great Britain, Japan, and the United States. A third is the attempt to recreate in the 1980s the purity and fervor of precept and practice they believe existed in the early days of Islam 1,300 years ago—statedly a major objective of the Ayatollah Khomeini in Iran in recent years. Furthermore, to the economic philosophy of profit making, in increasing the price of petroleum, the Arab countries have added the philosophy of social concern: by the end of 1979 their unfettered financial aid to about 50 countries had totaled about U.S. $20 billion. If we equate the philosophies we adhere to with the personal and social values we live by, then to that extent we are what we think, and what we think becomes immediately vital to the well-being of the world around us.

SOME GLIMPSES OF THE RESULTING MOSAIC

Tribal, territorial, religious, and economic factors are major components of group identity, along with sectarian, kinship, occupational, and linguistic differences. All are age-old and very tenacious. Sometimes they are weakened by equal citizenship and a growing sense of nationality, as in the new nation of Israel. Sometimes they are intensified by modern situations of pressures from within and without, as exemplified by the factional and international aspects of the bitter fighting in

Lebanon beginning in 1977. Explosive antagonisms broke out between Arab leftists (mostly Muslims) and Arab rightists (including Muslims, Druzes, and Christians of the Maronite (Syrian) church), as well as Arab Palestinians and Arab Syrians.

Anatolian villages may appear to be "the same," yet one has a patrilineal kinship system and the other is matrilineal, suggesting different origins back in the years beyond their counting. In Baghdad you may find an Iraqi official stamping your passport, an Armenian changing your money, a Kurdish porter shouldering your luggage, and an Arab taxi-driver delivering you to the airport.

The listing of the component parts of the Middle East mosaic seems as endless as it is exciting and meaningful: Druze and dervish, Sunni and Shi'ite, Israeli and Iraqi, Al Fatah and fellahin, prince and Ph.D., mountaineer and plainsman. There are conservatives advocating religious law as the law of the land, and liberals promoting secular law. Always there are the old and the young, the rich and the poor found among peasants, students, and state administrators. All combine to preserve the distinctiveness of this land in the face of change.

Chapter 4

Islam, Arabs, and Southwest Asia

PRE-ISLAMIC ARABIA

The Region

Arabia, a seemingly endless sea of land and gravel, ringed by established settlements and washed on three sides by the salt seas, in the A.D. 500s was home to the nomadic Bedouin, still solidly loyal to the *sunna* or customs of their ancestors. The Byzantine and Persian empires were the world's great powers, although the empire of Kindah to the southeast of Mecca shone briefly.

Although the centuries-old transit trade between the Orient and eastern Africa, Egypt, and Europe now passed them by, Mecca and a few other towns had the good fortune to sit at major Arabian crossroads. Mecca grew rich. Throngs of travel-weary caravaneers flush with cash turned Mecca into an Arabian Corinth, a center of licentiousness. There was no regionally accepted religion with moral and ethical standards to act as a social stabilizer. The fear of *jinns* (nature spirits or demons) and the worship of idols—the central shrine, the Ka'ba (Kaaba) was surrounded by three hundred images—were no help. Although most Meccans and other Arabs worshipped a particular tribal or family deity, many thoughtful persons sought better alternatives to the current forms of religion and conduct.

It may seem strange to some Western readers that, generally speaking, Asians live by the dynamics of religion and behave according to its guidelines, or would if they were permitted. But this is so; and herein lies the importance of the following brief introduction to religion and Islam.

52

Contemporary Religion in Southwest Asia

Three major religious systems were represented in Southwest Asia before the rise of Islam: *Judaism, Christianity,* and *Zoroastrianism.* The Jew could look back about two thousand years to the Patriarchs Abraham, Isaac, and Jacob, and 1,800 years to the budding of *Judaism* at the time of the Exodus of the Israelites from Egypt. Jewish communities in Mecca, Medina, and northern Arabia were among Muhammad's early contacts during the troubled years of his preaching. Christians believed that the Aramaic-speaking Jewish prophet who was crucified by the Romans—Jesus, who is called the Christ—was the Son of God Incarnate, and that He rose from the grave and ascended to heaven, whence He had come. The Eastern Orthodox form of *Christianity* was dominant in the Byzantine Empire in the A.D. 600s.

Zoroastrianism, named after its founder, Zoroaster (originally Zarathustra, c. 628-551 B.C.), venerates Ahura Mazda (The Wise Lord) as the deity of light and truth in contrast to Ahriman, the essence of darkness and lies. Penetrating and underlying all the above, there existed the veneration of multiple deities, images, and nature spirits, and the spirits of one's ancestors, which comprised a packet of beliefs and practices commonly designated as *animism.* All these beliefs were more or less current in Arabia in the A.D. 500s.

Links with Ultimate Reality

Three links between Man and an Ultimate Reality have been suggested: a mediator or prophet, a key concept, and a revealed scripture.

Southwest Asia has produced many prophets: Zoroaster on the mountains of Persia; Abraham in the desert near Beersheba; Moses receiving the Ten Commandments on Mount Sinai; Jesus tested and approved after fasting forty days in the wilderness near Jericho; and Muhammad called near Mecca to be the Prophet of Allah.

By our present definition religion is "other-worldly," usually leading humankind toward some definable relationship with Ultimate Reality, whether in this world or the next. Each religion and people selects the link through which the goal is to be attained. To the Greek intellect this link was rationality, to the Buddhist this link is the denial of self, to the Christian the person of Christ the Mediator, to the Taoist quietude and the way of Nature. To the Hindu the practical link is ascetic dedication, but to the Communist it is the Party's social program. Discipline was the designated link for the Stoic, but to the Hebrew the atoning sacrifice alone gives assurance of acceptance before Deity and humankind. To the Muslim (and to the Confucian Chinese) the link is righteousness. For the Muslim the central theme of religion and life is the will of Allah, which is always unitary, that is, both spiritual (other-worldly) and practical (this-worldly) at the same time. The Muslim's reward in heaven depends upon his or her submission on earth.

The Koran and Other Scriptures

The four major religions in Southwest Asia each have their own scriptures: the Zoroastrian *Avesta* or *Zend-Avesta* (Zend, interpretation); the Jewish *Torah* and other writings; the Christian *Bible*; and the Islamic *Koran.* The Hebrew, Christian, and Islamic scriptures each claim to be the revealed "Word of God," and to their respective believers therefore are sacred, authoritative, and inviolate.

The Koran provides for recognition of the members of the other three religions as "People of the Book," saying that "God is one to them and to us." These "other" people, called *dhimmis*, include two groups: (1) the non-Arab Zoroastrians, Jews, and Christians, and (2) the non-Muslim Arabs, called Hanifs, who sincerely worship only Allah and not pagan idols. The Koran's ninety early surahs, written during the grim struggles at Mecca, are pithy, impassioned, moral themes and warnings of judgment; the twenty-four surahs received at Medina are long and legislative, and include stories of the earlier prophets.

MUHAMMAD, THE PROPHET
OF THE WILL OF ALLAH

Muhammad, honored by Muslims as the Prophet of God and the founder of Islam, was born in Mecca about A.D. 570 and disciplined himself to become a man of unusual moral excellence. As a trusted caravan leader at age twenty-five he married his wealthy employer, the widow Khadija, then forty years old. Soon after age thirty-five, in response to his spiritual yearnings he was given revelations through the angel Gabriel concerning the person and purpose of God, and his messages for humankind. His wife, his cousin Ali, his uncle Abu Talid, and a rich Meccan merchant named Abu Bakr believed the messages. Soon Muhammad proclaimed them

BOX 4-1   *WHAT IS ISLAM?*

Let us listen to a conversation under the awnings of the shaded *suq* or market. To an inquirer's question "What is Islam?" different people gave different but reconcilable answers. A Sufi mystic said that, conceptually, Islam represents a state of being, a close relationship with Allah. Everything in this state—trees, rocks, animals, and humans—was created or born harmonious, that is, in a "muslim" relationship to the whole. To be a Muslim, then, is to participate in this harmonious relationship with Allah and His created universe. The *imam* (teacher) standing nearby added to this that, socially, Islam is a community (*ummah*) in which the religious and the secular aspects of society are united in one interweaving system. An educated businessman, overhearing these two replies, hastened to point out the all-encompassing nature of Islam. Islam, he said, is a fourfold movement: Islam indeed is a religious faith, and an organized religion with a political base; it also is a day-by-day way of life, and a system for the interpretation of history. Several men passing by on their way to worship at the mosque stopped to say, very simply, that Islam provides a form of worship and a code of conduct for the man in the street and the desert. They said that when the *muezzin*, the mosque crier, sounds the call to prayer, then, "Wherever we are, we face towards Mecca and pray in the prescribed manner. We also observe the principles of Practical Religion, and the simple but strict restrictions upon diet and conduct." In giving the above answers each man in his own way contributed towards a fairly complete summary of Islam.

publicly and was vehemently opposed by his Quarish clanspeople and the Meccan gentry. The outcome of considerable persecution was that Muhammad and his followers departed for refuge to Yathrib (or Medina) in 622.

The flight (*Hegira*) to Medina is counted as year 1 in the Islamic calendar, and marks the beginning of an expanded following. Muhammad called this new way to worship God (Allah) *Islam,* which, derived from *salm,* "peace," means entering into peace, and is used in the sense of submission (to the will of God). Submission in this sense is the essence of man's dutiful response to the Will of Allah. Followers of Islam, then, are *Muslims,* those who, having made peace with God, submit to Him. This simple and austere message and its corresponding manner of life contrasted sharply with the turbulent warfare, commercialism, and idolatry prevalent in Arabia at that time. During the next few years almost all of Arabia was converted to Islam, and in 630 Muhammad and his army were welcomed back to Mecca where the pagan idols in the Ka'ba sacred shrine were destroyed. With the consecration of the whole shrine as a *mosque* or "place for prostration" and worship and prayer, the meteoric Black Stone in the Ka'ba became the symbolic focal point of Islamic unity. The revelatory messages, intermittently received by Muhammad from about 610 until his death in 632, were compiled into a standard text in 656 and called the *Qur'an,* or *Koran,* meaning "the reading" or "the recitation."

THE CHARACTERISTICS OF ISLAM

Islam as a Fourfold Faith

A rigorously monotheistic religious faith, Islam recognizes no co-sharer in the attributes of deity, just as in the first of the Ten Commandments of the Old Testament: "I am Jehovah your God . . . You shall have no gods except me" (Exodus 20:1-3). Islam is also positive in relating the obedient believer's experience and behavior to this life as well as to a cosmic environment.

Since Islam means submission and a Muslim is one who submits, political authority and leadership are to be expected. The Koran gives instructions concerning submission to the supreme and unchallengeable will of Allah (from which derives the concept of *nasib* or appointed fate), and for worship of His sole and unique Being. Leadership is provided by the *'ulama,* the learned interpreters of the sacred Koran. Strong religious leaders may claim Koranic authority and assert a combined religious and secular (political) authority, as did the Shi'ite Ayatollah Khomeini in Iran in 1979. On occasion strong secular leaders may curtail such claimed authority, as when Mustafa Kemal Ataturk separated religion from the state in Turkey in the late 1920s, while still preserving intact the faith itself.

Islam provides an identity for an individual, and, under the rubric "the brotherhood of Islam" the sense of belonging to a group with a shared history. To understand the nature of this identity it is necessary to know something about the fundamental tenets of Islam and its ritual (see Box 4-1).

Public Worship and Its Meaning

In Islamic procedure, men and women worship separately. Let us follow a man into the mosque.

As the Muslim leaves the mundane world and enters the mosque precincts for worship, he first washes ceremoniously and, as he enters the foyer, removes his shoes as an indication he is entering holy ground. Inside, the central hall is empty save for mats or carpet on the floor and perhaps a raised pulpit from which the *imam* or other appointed person will read the Koran and deliver a short practical sermon. At this *salat,* or public worship, he joins a growing line of fellow worshippers who are already facing the niche in the wall which indicates the direction of Mecca and its holy Ka'ba shrine. After silently meditating on purification, he stands with the other men as they follow the *imam* in front to recite in unison verses from the Koran, and then bow forward in praise to Allah. The men then kneel smoothly with forehead touching the floor and, while kneeling upright, chant the rhythmic syllables of the *shahada* creed: "La-'i-la-ha'-il-la'-llah, Mu-ham-mad-ra-su-la'-llah"—"I witness that there is no God but Allah, and that Muhammad is the messenger of Allah." After again prostrating to the floor in adoration, the whole group stands erect and repeats the ritual a second time, before rising to their feet to pass through the foyer to the outside street.

The external forms of Islam consist of exercises to remind the individual and the society of the goal of Islam—the state-of-being relationship with Allah—and to maintain this state amid the social contacts with a material world.

THE CREED OF ISLAM

Every Muslim or Muslim-to-be has to recite the *shahada,* the confession of faith: "I witness that there is no God but Allah, and that Muhammad is the messenger of Allah." This "Word of Witness" is as much a verbal bond to the Muslim as the Cross is a visual symbol to the Christian. To the Muslim his creed is both fact and faith, proclamation and performance, political and personal. This definitive decisiveness is one secret of the spread of Islam. Moreover, this simple statement of faith is amplified in the Six Articles of Faith and applied in the Five Pillars of Practical Religion or Conduct.

The Six Articles begin with (1) the shahada: *There is no God but Allah and Muhammad is his Prophet.* Allah is solitary in his Person, singular as Creator, unique as the Judge of all men, and the only source of life, wisdom, and power. Muhammad is a man, the Prophet through whom came the last and final revelation of the will of Allah. (2) *Belief in the Koran as the Word of God.* Revealed directly or through the angel Gabriel, a standard text of these revelations was adopted during the Caliphate of Uthman. (3) *Belief in angels as the instruments of the will of Allah.* They are messengers to the peoples of this world and guardians of the world beyond the grave. (4) *Belief in the Day of Judgment, and reward in paradise and punishment in hell.* (5) *Belief in the prophets and their teachings.* Of the twenty thousand prophets, as stated in the Koran—one for every people throughout the world—special mention is made of the five great prophets who preceded Muhammad: Adam, Noah, Abraham, Moses, and Jesus. (6) *Belief that Allah has determined the good and evil that shall befall a man.* Nevertheless, man is responsible for obedience in purpose and act to the will of Allah, dutifully responding to his lifelong *nasib,* "appointed fate."

The Muslim Way of Life

The Five Pillars of Practical Religion or Conduct include: (1) *Faith,* embodied in the *shahada* creed. (2) *Worship: salat* or public prayers facing Mecca five times daily, and *du'a,* or private prayer. (3) *Alms:* obligatory *zakat* dues and voluntary *sadaqa* contributions. (4) *Fasting:* the ninth month, Ramadan, is to be observed by complete abstention from food, beverage, and sex from dawn to sunset. (5) *Pilgrimage:* the *hadj* (or *hajj*) or pilgrimage to Mecca is one cardinal feature that unites all branches and sects of Islam. The returned pilgrim is entitled to be called *haji.*

Detailed instructions have been added: (1) prohibitions against alcohol, gambling, pork, idols, infanticide, and usury; (2) inculcation of the virtues of courage, industry, justice, humility, and temperance; (3) the elevation of social behavior to stress honor to parents and elders, respect for women, kindness to slaves, the equality of all men before God, no color bar, and protection and charity to all persons impartially.

Yet within the seeming monolith of Islam deep divisions exist.

THE MAIN BRANCHES OF ISLAM

The great majority of Muslims, the Sunnis (from *sunna,* "way"), view the revelation and law of the Koran as authoritative and final. The *Sufis* emphasize the transcendent, the eternal aspect, the love rather than the power of God, and purity of soul more than correctness of behavior.

A political event precipitated another major division. The *Shi'atu 'Ali* (Party of Ali) supported Muhammad's son-in-law Ali as the fourth caliph, and his son Husain (by Muhammad's daughter Fatima) to be the sixth caliph. Husain and his entourage were slain at the battle of Karbala in 680, and the grieving faction developed into a religious sect (*shi'a*), now numbering over 40 million Shi'ites. Shi'ism is the majority faith in Iran and Iraq, and is scattered elsewhere in the Near East, India, and Pakistan. Ali's descendants have an honored status as *sayyids* (lord, master) and *sharifs* (prince, chief). Sects and peoples derived from the Shi'a include the Ismailis and Baha'is, the Druzes and Alawis of Syria (see Chapter 6), and the Sikhs of North India (see Chapter 10).

The Aga Khan IV is the forty-ninth Imam of the *Ismailis,* numbering about ten million adherents from Morocco to India. The Aga Khan lineage of Muslim rulers claims descent, and therefore authority, from Ali and his wife Fatima, Muhammad's only recognized descendant. Ismaili doctrine, tinged with Greek rationalism, has adopted a liberal attitude toward the traditional Koranic teachings. In 1863 a Shi'ite Persian nobleman, claiming to be the last prophet of God, called himself Baha'u'lla (Glory of God) and founded the *Baha'i* faith. Baha'is believe in one God and the unity of all revealed religions, and attempt to fulfill in practice what they claim other religions have failed to do. A modern missionary sect based in Pakistan, the *Ahmadiyya,* has sent proselytizing representatives who have won converts all over the world.

However, regardless of which branch of Islam a Muslim belongs to, or which of the various Islamic schools of legal interpretation guides his community, once he commits a serious offense he will be treated according to Islamic law.

THE LEGAL SYSTEM OF ISLAM

The Muslim offender will find himself subject to the institution of the Shari'a and the jurisdiction of the qadhi. The Shari'a, meaning "the clear path to be followed," is the law of Islam, stemming from four main sources. First, the *Koran* (or *Qur'an*) itself. Second, the *Hadith,* the traditional records of the Prophet's words, deeds, and assumed opinions. The Hadith includes the more practical *Sunna* or Way. Third, the *ijima'*, scholarly "consensus" on questions not covered in the Koran and the Sunna. Fourth, the *qiyas,* meaning "measuring" or "comparing" —that is, reason—enabling the principles already established in the above three sources to be extended by analogy to still further questions. These are the four bases (*usul*) of the formal faith of Islam and its application to practical conduct.

In addition to the four orthodox sources of the Shari'a, there also are the

BOX 4-2 *THE QADHI AND THE COURT*

In this hypothetical case, as the defendant and the plaintiff sit side by side on the same bench, to symbolize the equality of all persons before the law, they view a court arrangement analogous to the informal circle where the lineage sheik sat among the tribal elders to hear complaints. As the dignified qadhi (judge) enters to sit behind the table, they recognize him as basically a religious leader, who has undergone nine years' training for appointment as court apprentice before he could assume full responsibility as qadhi for this occasion. As the statements are presented and the lawyers and advisors speak for their clients, the qadhi asks for the defendant's second witness required to corroborate the previous evidence. In this case the defendant has only one witness, and he has the option to substitute himself for the missing witness by taking the oath to tell the truth. He understands fully that such an oath, with its religious as well as its legal connotations, is so solemn and binding that refusal to take the oath, if challenged to do so, will result in an automatic sentence of guilt, while taking it means probably exoneration. (The antiquity of this oath is attested by its use about 1260 B.C. as part of the Mosaic Law of the Hebrews (Exodus 22:7-10 and Deuteronomy 19: 15-21). Since our case is not one simply of "honor" (for instance, pulling a Muslim's beard), but of alleged theft, in the general category of serious crimes such as gambling, assault, and murder, the defendant elects to take the oath. He is acquitted. If he had been found guilty, the qadhi would know from the Koran that one standard punishment for theft was amputation of the hand. Recently in an actual case of aggravated assault, a policeman was challenged to state his innocence on oath. Knowing himself to be guilty, and knowing the consequences of refusing to take the oath, he refused anyway rather than tell a lie. He was indeed severely punished with eighty lashes, six months imprisonment, and a substantial fine.

'adat law based on tribal customs, and the *qanun,* written legal codes of other nations such as Egypt, Persia, and Turkey. The modern laws of Turkey do not include the Koranic laws as such, but are based selectively upon the French code, plus the German commercial code, the Italian penal code, and the Swiss civil code. The modern Asian nations still operating under the Shari'a legal code are Saudi Arabia and Yemen, with Pakistan and perhaps Indonesia tending toward the same standards. Saudi Arabia can provide an example of the operation of the Shari'a (see Box 4-2).

As already indicated, Islamic countries today face two fundamental problems. Internally, they must decide to what extent they will adhere to the traditional tenets and original practices of Islam, and thereby retain their exclusive identity as Muslims. Externally, to survive as nations in today's technological world of contrasting philosophies and conflicting goals, they must make some practical adaptations. For example, their qadhis must be, and in Saudi Arabia are, further trained to cope with the legal impacts of modern technology, business, politics, tourism, etc., so that justice and order for all persons within their borders may be preserved. These questions will arise again in later chapters, for the conflicting claims of tradition and change exist throughout Asia.

TERRITORIAL EXPANSION
OF MUSLIM CIVILIZATION

The Crucial Decision

The expansion of Islam hinged upon a simple but momentous decision. After the death of Muhammad the new caliph (successor), Abu Bakr, and his fellow leaders (including the three men who were to follow him as caliphs, Uman, Uthman, and Ali) considered the complicated situation of deteriorating tribal independence. They finally faced the single question: was the fledgling faith to flutter to its death in the sand, to remain a localized sectarian faith, or was it to become a vital and expanding religious community? The decision was made to continue the faith in the form of the community (*ummah*) of Islam. This fateful decision vitally affected the future of the world.

The decision had several bases. The Medina Suras blended administrative injunctions with religious imperatives and devotional precepts. The restless desert tribes needed and desired wealth as much as the rich merchants did. Muhammad in his later years had fulfilled the multiple offices of leader and prophet, organizer and benefactor. As successor to Muhammad, Abu Bakr found it necessary to continue handing out largess to the tribes by providing material as well as spiritual incentives to this new community. Since Mecca and the other cities were now part of the movement, their caravans and pilgrims could no longer be raided. Wealth had to be found elsewhere.

The Near Eastern Campaigns

The location of this wealth was well-known—it was where the air was cool. While food and water were chronic shortages in sweltering and sun-baked Arabia, only a few days' camel ride away were running streams, fertile fields, and seasonal

TABLE 4-1   The Expansion of Islam

A.D. 570	Muhammad born in Mecca.
622	The flight to Medina; the Hijra or Hegira. Beginning of era of Islam.
630	Mecca occupied; the Ka'ba becomes the central shrine of Islam.
632	Death of Muhammad. Abu Bakr becomes the first caliph (successor).
633–670	Conquest of Syria, Iraq, Persia, Egypt, and North Africa.
634–661	The next three caliphs: Umar, Uthman, and Ali.
661	Mu'awiya establishes Umayyad caliphate at Damascus (661–750).
680	Massacre of Husain and party at Karbala; Shi'ite/Sunni split begins.
691	Dome of the Rock erected at Jerusalem.
711	Invasion of the Indus Valley.
711	Conquest of Iberia (Spain) (711–1492).
732	Charles Martel defeats Muslim army near Poitiers in central France.
738	Muslim colony reported at Canton, China.
740	Muslim colony at Kilwa in East Africa.
750	Abbassid caliphate established (750–1258); capital at Baghdad in 762.
825	Invasion of Sicily.
970	Seljuk Turks become Muslims and occupy Persia.
998	Mahmud of Ghazni annexes eastern Persia and northern India.
1000	Gujarati Muslim merchants bring Islamic faith to Malaya.
1010	Ruler of Gao on middle Niger river converted.
1087	Timbuktu built as prestigious center of Islamic commerce and learning.
1292	Marco Polo finds Muslim kingdom on Sumatra.
1410	Prince Parameswara of Malacca converted, renamed as Iskandar Shah.
1526	Babur and Akbar establish the Mughal empire in India (1526–1858).
1683	Islam entrenched in the Philippines, Celebes, and Moluccas.
1683	Muslims fail to take Vienna; Ottoman territories in Europe begin decline.
1900	Important Muslim communities in the United States, England, and the West; Muslims retain faith in Soviet Asia.
1970–1980	Islam resurgent; intensified concern for Koranic precepts; missionary activity.

rains that made the air crisp and cool. Many desert dwellers had moved already in that direction, to tribal areas bordering the cities and territories to the north and west of the desert. These and other non-Muslim tribes—for some were Christian and some were Jewish—were often bound by tradition and lineage to various ancestral bases in the peninsula. Beyond these borders lay the territories of the Byzantine and Persian empires, both exhausted after a century of confrontations and wars with each other. The plums were ripe for the picking, and the pickers were ready.

The orders to march came shortly after Muhammad's death in 632. Abu Bakr ordered the advance in 633 and gathered up the Arab border communities to further his aims. In 634 the whole peninsula was secured to the Muslim cause, and the only one surprised in 636 was the Byzantine commander, Theodorus, when his dust-blinded army was annihilated. Syria and Iraq were taken by 637. The conquest of Egypt between 639 and 642 made available its wealth and particularly its food. The doors to Africa and Asia stood open.

Plunder for the living and paradise for the dead constituted powerful incentives for the troops, whose potent morale led to greater victories than their initial military mediocrity deserved. Booty led to tribute and tribute to empire. Philip

Hitti sees a three-part process in the conquest, "the last great Semitic migration." First, the march of Arab arms was military and political, as when the treasures and territories of Persia became part of the Arab dominions by 644. Second, about 300 years of religious change followed, as most of the subjugated peoples in the empire converted to Islam. And third, the slow and reluctant process of linguistic change took place as Arabic replaced the various native languages. "Apparently men are more ready to give up their political and even religious loyalties than their linguistic ones" (Hitti 1964: 139).

Conversion to Islam

As already noted, the early Muslims were themselves a group of converted Arabs, an in-group constituency, and the propagation of Islam assumed a conversion process, first of other Arabs and then of non-Arabs. In its more benign aspects, the conversion process was promoted by the simplicity and directness of the tenets of Islam, and by the exhibition of a remarkable degree of equality and acceptance among believers. In addition there were the attractions of acceptance into a wider commercial orbit, and the relief from an undesirable political yoke. In Egypt and Persia, for instance, the Muslim armies were welcomed as liberators from the oppressive rule of Byzantine governors. The Bengali speakers of today's Bangladesh, and the peoples of Malaysia and Indonesia, are among those who turned to Islam as a free, civil choice. But the conversion long ago of multitudes and nations in North Africa, the Near East, and Central Asia was, in fact, under the political shadow of conquering armies.

The *dhimmis* (the non-Arab, non-Muslim followers of protected religions) were tolerated and they paid a poll tax. Converts (*mawalis*), while never accorded equality with Arabs, paid a lighter tax than non-Muslims. So many peoples turned to Islam, and thereby qualified for the lighter taxes, that in the end the national exchequer was seriously affected. Mawalis were allowed to fight only as foot soldiers with a lower rate of pay, a status they resented. This discontent in time gravely weakened the vital esprit de corps which had so successfully animated the early expansion.

Islam's Golden Age

As the caliph Mu'awiya and his Umayyad successors merged into the new cultural milieu of Damascus, they developed poetry, minted new coinage, established horseback postal routes, and put irrigation canals back into productive use. This was a beginning. Islam's Golden Age was that of the famous caliph Harun al-Rashid, the central figure of the Arabian Nights, during his twenty-three-year rule from 786 to 809. Located at Baghdad, the dynasty became enormously wealthy through the shipping and caravan trades, and was enriched by the superior art, science, medicine, architecture, and standards of majesty of Persia. The resulting bureaucratic and mercantile stimulation led to such fiscal concepts as letters of credit and checks, and a widespread banking system.

The contacts with and then immersion in the non-Arab world under the Abbasid caliphs at Baghdad affected both Islam and the Arabs. Arab religion and language indeed were retained, but the culture was considerably persianized. Persian mothers bore most of the thirty-seven Abbasid caliphs, and gradually

FIGURE 4–1
Rug weaving in Persia.

Persian and Mawali salaried bureaucrats largely replaced the Arab aristocracy. Turkish slave troops (Mamluks) replaced Arab soldiers, who then lost their pensions. Perhaps even more significantly, the caliph changed his role as the Successor to the Prophet to become the Deputy of God, thereby signaling the erosion of religious doctrine. In the intellectual realm Greek logic and rationality collided with traditional adherence to the Koran.

Golden Ages neither last forever nor do they bless equally all parts of such a far-flung empire. Regional dynasties continued through most of this period. Following the defeat of the Muslim forces by Charles Martel (the Hammer) in 732 at Poitiers (Tours) in France, an Umayyad dynasty was founded in Spain by Abd al-Rahman in 756. Other regional Muslim governments were established in Morocco and Tunisia, as well as in Persia, Egypt, and Syria. At Baghdad in the 830s, Turkish exslaves were appointed over the palace guards, and soon proceeded to control the appointment of the caliphs—the phenomenon of court intrigue which has plagued imperial politics from Rome to Japan. By 945 these Turks were replaced by the Persians, to be ousted in turn by the Seljuk Turks in 1055.

The House of Wisdom

The Arabs were assiduously engaged in translation for the hundred years between 750 and 850 (Hitti 1964:140). The "House of Wisdom," built at Baghdad in 830 to be a center of learning, poured forth such a flood of translations into

Arabic that by 850 Arab readers could discuss the philosophical treatises of Aristotle and Plato, the medical works of the Roman physician Galen, as well as the science of Persia, India, and even of China. Individual authors flourished, including Hunayn (ophthalmology), Razi (a monumental encyclopedia of medicine), and Ibn Sina (Avicenna) who wrote an encyclopedic *Canon of Medicine* that remained a standard medical work in European universities and southwest Asia for six hundred years.

These researches soon found practical applications. Doctors had to submit to examinations and pharmacies to inspection. Hospitals were set up with different wards for specific diseases, also with an insane ward, and outpatient department. Advances in mathematics, algebra (Arabic *al-jabr,* "calculation"), and the use of the Greek astrolabe (with which Muslim scholars were able to measure the size of the earth), were later matched by Ibn Khaldun, who illuminated history with the dynamic facts of climate and politics, logical laws, and moral choices.

The Muslim Legacy to Europe

The Muslim occupation of much of Spain lasted for nearly five hundred years. The Muslim rulers, partly Arab and mostly Berber, formed the elite aristocracy. In classes successively below them were Spanish converts to Islam, Spaniards who remained Christians but adopted Muslim culture, then Jews, who found Muslims more tolerant than Christians. At the bottom lay the embittered Spanish Roman Catholics. However, the Muslims allowed free choice of religion and, significantly, free employment of competent men at all levels of government.

Muslim Spain became a major center of learning. From there, from a busy translation center in Marseilles, and later from the Kingdom of Sicily, a new wave of learning spread into Europe. Arab scientific developments, Persian economic and administrative practices, and the stored legacy of Greek and Roman culture were all transmitted. Sufic ideas of experiental religion entered–that Allah could be known as the Beloved and Friend only as accompanied by renunciation of worldly attachments. Europe gained hundreds of Arabic words, many beginning with "al-," as *albatross, alcalde, alchemy, alcohol, alcove, Aldebaran, alfalfa,* and *alkali.* The ultimate legacy of this Muslim heritage was the intellectual ferment which became the Renaissance, from which has developed the European and American culture of today.

Later Muslim Empires

The Muslim Golden Age ended, and change came to the Muslim world. The Crusades from 1095 to 1291 opened Europe's perspectives to include the Eastern world, but to the Muslim caliphs were only another version of the continual border wars on the periphery of their empire. The invasion which altered everything came from the East: Turkish tribes from Central Asia converted to Islam and revitalized the conquest. Five centers of Muslim power spread the influence of Islam.

First, the Seljuk Turks overcame the decadent Abbasid empire and defeated the Byzantine army in 1071. Turkish exslaves, as soldiers and administrators in Egypt, overthrew the later Abbasid caliphs and established the Mamluk sultanate of Egypt and Syria (1250-1517).

The second Muslim center lay in the Eurasian steppes where the Mongol Khanate of the Golden Horde in southern Russia and the Chagatai Khanate in

Central Asia held sway. Both lasted from the mid-1200s to between 1580 and 1599.

A Turkish confederation under the Ottoman tribe consolidated their hold on Asia Minor in 1326 and gradually appropriated all the Balkans and Central Europe as far as the Danube. With their capture of Constantinople in 1453 they set up the third center, the Ottoman or Turkish Empire which lasted almost five hundred years (1453-1922).

The fourth Islamic center emerged in Iran (1499-1722) under the Safavid dynasty, during which time Shi'ism was made the state religion, and the capital at Isfahan became one of the world's most beautiful cities. Babur (1483-1530), descended from both Genghis Khan and Tamerlane (1336-1405), was the ruler of Ferghana and Afghanistan. He overran northern India to establish the fifth center at Delhi as capital of the Mughal empire lasting from 1526 to 1857. From centers in Arabia and India Islam spread to Southeast Asia.

The decade of the 1490s saw two momentous events: the discovery of America in 1492, and the discovery of the sea route to India in 1497. From these came the Age of Exploration and eventual European influence and dominance in most of the world. The sixteenth century Reformation brought new impetus to Christianity, while much of Islam lost its spark and became sterile. Today the tide of Europe has crested, and other tides are rising.

The Spirit of Renaissance

After a dormant period of several centuries, a new spirit of renaissance (*nahda*) is spurring Islam's leaders, mullahs, and laity towards closer conformity to the precepts of the Koran in social, religious, and political life. Seeing this as a single interacting package—the opposite of the American concept of the "separation of church and state"—Iran has rejected totally the modernizing programs of the ex-shah, and established itself late in 1979 as the Islamic Republic of Iran. Popular Iranian defiance of the non-Muslim world, in the spirit of martyrdom of their Shi'ite background, has contrasted sharply to the way Saudi Arabia and some other Islamic states have combined the essence of *nahda* with oil technology, asphalt roads, foreign investments, and modern university education for their young men and women.

ARABS, ISRAELIS, AND SOUTHWEST ASIA

The Human Mosaic

When the banners of Islam's armies first waved over Southwest Asia, the peoples' Nilotic, Roman, Syrian, Babylonian, Persian, and other roots and memories were well known. Transportation and banishment brought from Mesopotamia the various peoples who became the composite group we know as Samaritans, to replace Syrians and Jews transported east. Over the centuries the ebb and flow of other armies also added military and civilian settlements to the mosaic. From Gaul in the west (now France) came Gauls to Galatia (Gaul-land); from the south came Arabs; Circassians arrived from the north; and various bands of swarthy Turkish invaders swarmed in from Central Asia. Migrations also introduced Turkomen into

Iran, Arabs into Iraq and Iran, and Uzbeks, Persians, and others into Afghanistan. And in the 1900s Jews returned in large numbers to their ancient homeland from their widely scattered domiciles abroad.

The resulting linguistic medley encompasses hundreds of distinct languages and dialects, each jealously preserved by one or another community. The traditional social webs of customs, occupations, values, kinship ties, and resources that have enabled each distinct community to survive are guarded with care. The ruling elite have formalized their philosophies of government in the forms of monarchies, sheikdoms, democratic (Western type) and Marxist republics, or military dictatorships. Economically wealth and poverty have always existed; today some are oil rich, some still are nearly destitute of natural resources. All are proud and independent: only on this basis have they survived at all.

The mosaic exists because all these varied peoples have made Southwest Asia their home, living side by side, yet retaining their own separate cultures and identities over long periods of time. Most of them are united by their Islamic religion, and many also by the Arabic language. Omitting Israel and the Northern Tier nations (Turkey, Cyprus, Iran, and Afghanistan), the remaining vast majority are cultivating a growing sense of a common ethnosocial identity as "Arabs." Nevertheless, each community is identified largely on the basis of its traditional place and function in the mosaic. However, this characteristic identity may be drastically changed if the community's defenses are broken down. For example, the present Yemen Arab Republic resulted from eight years of warfare leading to victory of the Sunni republicans on the coast over the ruling Imam's Shi'ite forces in 1962. After much local fighting the adjoining ex-British protectorate of Aden and Hadramaut was taken over by a Marxist faction in 1969 to become the People's Democratic Republic of Yemen (often called simply South Yemen). When the integrity of Kuwait was threatened by Saudi Arabia in 1912, and by Iraq in 1956, Britain intervened in each instance to preserve Kuwait's independence. Underneath the blanket of religion and language in Southwest Asia lie tensions engendered by deepseated desires to preserve, extend, or suppress the identity of each component community. Even nationality may be a secondary consideration. This tension-fraught situation is evidenced by the armed conflicts of the 1970s and 1980s between Iraq, Syria, Jordan, and the Palestinians; between Iran and Iraq; between Turkish and Greek Cypriots on Cyprus; and between the militant factions in Lebanon.

Israel and the Palestinians

For upwards of four thousand years the Jews (or Hebrews) have been continuously present in Palestine as tribes, nations, or scattered remnants. During the past 1,400 years Arab peoples have been increasingly dominant there, especially during the Ottoman period. But under the impetus of the Zionist movement in the 1890s and the Nazi persecutions of the 1930s, Jews began flocking into Palestine, which then was Turkish and, later, mandated territory. The very success of their *kibbutz* system of communal farm projects led to broken relations with the resident Arab population. Finally the United Nations divided Palestine between Israelis and Arabs on the basis of population majorities.

The day Israel was declared independent, May 14, 1948, the armies of Egypt,

Iraq, Jordan, Lebanon, Syria, and Saudi Arabia attacked Israel. The Arab residents displaced by the Arab-Israeli wars of 1948-1949, 1956-1957, and 1973, the Palestinians, have multiplied to about five million persons, and comprise significant proportions of the populations of the surrounding Arab states.

The terrorist operations of the militant Palestine Liberation Organization (PLO), together with the ruthless retaliatory actions by Israeli forces, have fomented trouble far beyond the regional boundaries. The human tragedy lies in the thousands of war-scarred children, and armed adults who have come to accept this violent existence as a way of life. The two edges of the Damoclean sword hanging over the region represent the strong possibility of all-out war among the nations over the Palestinian question, and the fact that a wholly satisfactory solution is unlikely.

The Core of the Problem

Some of the elements of the problem may be briefly if inadequately summarized as follows: (1) During the last three thousand years Israelis, Arabs, and others have alternately occupied the land of Palestine. Israelis and Arabs each have some kind of legitimate claim—either ancient or modern—to the territory. (2) Turkey, Israel, and all the Arab nations except some on the southern fringes of the Arabian peninsula are equally modern entities, having been carved out of the disintegrated Turkish Empire following World Wars I and II. (Cyprus was detached from that Empire in 1878 by action of the Congress of Berlin.) (3) The nation of Israel was created and its territory assigned by official act of the General Assembly of the United Nations in 1946. (4) The displaced Palestinians are an internationally orphaned group embittered by their ouster from Israel and by the neglect of their neighbors, amongst whom they still are distinguished from the indigenous national populations.

The strife is not over the price of oil but the possession of land. The equations are quite simple: land and its water equal food, and food equals life. Out of this competition for life came the struggle among Bedouin tribes for land for pasturage and water for irrigation, and among Israel, Syria, Jordan, and the Palestinians for the West Bank and for the waters of the Jordan river. Indeed, the focal point of negotiation from 1977 on has been the occupation and control of the West Bank of the Jordan. Land, food, and security for all of these contestants hinge to some degree on this one central issue. If a Palestinian Arab state were to be established on the West Bank, the question would be how many of the over three million expatriates could be absorbed in that area, where between one and two million Arabs already live in this Israeli-occupied territory. It should be noted that the Sinai peninsula, a desert with few exploitable resources, was returned by Israel to Egypt with hesitation, and this with only strategic defense considerations at stake. In this atmosphere of mutual distrust, lasting for more than thirty years, the negotiations with Israel initiated by the late President Anwar al-Sadat of Egypt represented at the time probably the single greatest ray of hope for permanent peace. His tragic death left the area as volatile as ever, and just as far away from an end to the violence.

Chapter *5*

The Patterns of Life

MANY PARTS, ONE PATTERN

The separate and distinct group identity of every Southwest Asian is a blended collage, almost an amalgam, of the group's history and heroes, songs and skirmishes, language and lineage, residence and religion. Such a collage of group identity reveals to the individual the mystique of belonging, rooted deep in his or her inner being. The religion of Islam is also an ostensible bond of unity throughout the region, as is the Arabic language.

Some parts of the collage present quite a contrast. In addition to the religious distinction between Sunni and Shi'ite Muslims, cultural gaps also exist between the urban bureaucrat and the struggling farmer, the professor in a classroom, the sheik with bejeweled dagger, and the sabra (an Israeli born in Israel) on the Tel Aviv beach. The oil-rich Arab buying a hotel in London is far removed in culture and outlook from the smartly uniformed Turkish soldier on parade in Istanbul, and from the Kurdish mountaineer watching the Iraqi government pipe the petroleum from his land. Yet all of them are intrinsic to Southwest Asia.

The intricately interwoven strands of occupations, economies, religions, and organizations form a web of interdependence that in peacetime is region wide. But kingdoms and empires have been founded, won, and lost in countless wars waged to capture or control the strands or the whole web. This is the recurring theme of Southwest Asian history (see Chapter 3). This chapter begins on the local level where nomads and oasis dwellers and settled villagers have mutually protected,

67

sustained, and exploited each other down the ages. Modern environmental and political pressures on nomadism have enhanced the role of villages as the basic unit of economic concern. The village, then, interacts with the nomads and even more directly with the market town, and the towns with the regional cities, as part of the central web of national organization.

RELATIONS WITH THE ENVIRONMENT

Environmental Limits
to Occupational Preferences

A theoretical experiment will help us understand the meaning of relations with the environment, using representatives of basic occupational categories in a monitored environment. The five generalized categories of occupations or livelihoods are hunter-fisherman-gatherer, pastoralist or herdsman, slash-and-burn cultivator, plow-using agriculturalist, and urban technician. The area of the experiment is a region with varied terrain: Southwest Asia. Let us monitor the treatment of the environment by members of each of the five categories of occupations.

Hunters-fishermen-gatherers found animal and vegetable sources of food and livelihood on or near the surface of most parts of the region. Conforming to nature as they found it, they adapted their tools and procedures for efficient garnering of chosen resources. It is many millenia since such harvesters roamed freely in Southwest Asia, though some still function in parts of Southeast Asia.

Pastoralists first took stock of a variety of animals, and herded them all according to their capabilities and feeding habits: pad-footed camels on the flat arid plains and hard-hoofed horses, sheep, and goats elsewhere, including the high mountain valleys. Pastoralists did little to alter the terrain, for they needed the balanced variety of grassy growth, water sources, and climatic variations. Constricted by nature, they utilized what the environment made readily available. In Southwest Asia, for instance, they traditionally herded camels in desert and arid lands, or migrated annually with other animals to and from the mountains and plains.

Slash-and-burn cultivators, whose principal tools were a digging stick, a machete, and a hoe, cut down the trees, slashed and burnt the brush, and used a digging stick to make holes in the soil for seed planting. After a few years the soil was exhausted and some of the clearings reverted to forest, while others were taken over by ineradicable coarse grasses and thus lost to further agricultural use. Although they cooperated with nature, slash-and-burn farmers also altered the environment. Slash-and-burn farmers, like hunter-gatherers, have vanished from Southwest Asia but still remain in Southeast Asia. (See Figures 14-1 and 18-3.)

Agriculturalists or plow farmers looked over the plains, hills, and mountainsides for any place where the surface features could be transformed into arable land. Manipulation of this process made possible the increase of food supplies for the world's expanding population, but at the price of contravening nature, resulting in barren mountains, silt-clogged rivers, and flooded plains.

Urban technicians or engineers carefully scanned the observable features of the whole region and then dug beneath the surface to ascertain what might be found there. The insatiable appetite of their 'omnivorous' society required every kind of resource. Because urban technicians put so little back and polluted so much of what was left, their activities amounted to a confiscation and destruction of nature. Although urban people's useful activities have built and sustained twentieth-century society, we must face the consequences of our negative actions.

Technological Options

The occupational preferences exhibited in the preceding section indicate the level of technology of the community as a whole, the more powerful and complex tools giving the user a wider range of options. Digging tools made possible the long underground water conduits, called *qanats* in Iran, to bring mountain water into the water-hungry lowlands. Modern drilling rigs pipe deep-lying water to irrigate large areas of dry but fertile ground in Iraq and Saudi Arabia. Israel has channeled water from the upper Jordan valley via the Jordan Conduit to the almost waterless Southland or Negev 130 miles away. Oil and ores brought by modern machinery from deep underground have made both possible and necessary the industrial towns built nearby to handle them. Floods are being controlled largely by dams on the Euphrates and other rivers, which provide water for irrigation and the generation of electric power. The potash, bromine, and magnesium salts washed into the Dead Sea by the Jordan river are being retrieved for industrial use.

Essentially these activities mean that in various parts of Asia the habitats suitable for hunters, cultivators, and pastoralists are more and more restricted, being taken over by agriculture, industry, and housing settlements. On the other hand, lands previously barren may become irrigated oases, and thereby the agriculturalist has achieved another conquest of previously unproductive land. Dams have saved from devastation areas earlier subject to floods and erosion, just as the planting of millions of trees and the covering of sand dunes with grasses or with grids of straw have helped in some places to stay the march of the desert. Not only Southwest Asia but also Pakistan and India, China and Central Asia, all have shared these and similar benefits—and some damages—from such impacts of technology upon the environment. In these improved areas hundreds of people live per square mile where before only a handful could survive.

Society and Environment

Societies still occupationally dependent upon their environments adjust in such matters as clothing, group size, and types of leadership. Among some of the nomad tribes, loosely called Arabs, who conduct an irregular search for pasture on the rather inhospitable plateau north of the Persian Gulf, their small mobile bands have developed no strong leadership pattern.

West of them, in the mountainous area around Shiraz, the more numerous Basseri camps operate on the consensus of the larger household heads as they plan the day-by-day movements of herds and people up and down the mountain migration routes. The need to withstand pressures from national authorities and from the surrounding sedentary villagers, and to preserve pasturage rights over the course of their transhumance migrations, has led to the development of a hierarchy of leadership.

The nearby Qashqai occupy a richer pastoral terrain with shorter migration routes than the Basseri, so that their larger population lives in a more restricted area. This situation necessitates a strong and unified leadership to organize and control relations within the community and to plan their movements within their area of migration. In passing it may be noted that the term "Arab" above is partly political, partly linguistic (some speak Arabic and some Turkish dialects), as is the appelation "Turk" applied to the Turkish-speaking Qashqai. The Basseri speak a dialect of Persian and have been called both Arab and Persian.

Among the Bedouin in Arabia, the numbers of sheep and horses kept had to be restricted, for they need water every day. So, with the coming of modern technology, everyone tried to purchase a pickup, then a truck, and finally a big tank truck to haul in the needed water. These changes bring their own employment opportunities, which are part of the government's plans for modernization. Similar changes are taking place on the plains of Mongolia where animal power and transportation are gradually giving way to their mechanical counterparts.

NOMADS AND NOMADISM

Types and Techniques

Of the five types of nomadic pastoralism found in the vast arid belt stretching from West Africa to the Arctic tundra of Siberia, four are found in Asia. (The *cattle cultures* of sub-Saharan Africa with their millet and sorghum food bases, lie outside our consideration here.) The *camel culture* of North Africa and Southwest Asia is the most extensive zone, and relies on wheat or rice for the main cereal and on dates as the distinctive auxiliary food. Wheat and barley sustain the *sheep herders* of the mountains and high plateaus of Anatolia, Iran, and Afghanistan. Central Asian *steppeland pastoralists* need a supply of summer hay as fodder for cattle, sheep, and horses during their harsh and frigid winters, spent in regular winter quarters of some sort. The northernmost sub-Arctic zone, extending from Norway to the Bering Strait, is a *reindeer herding* region where meat and milk are supplemented by the products of hunting and fishing.

The key technique in pastoralism is the care of indigenized animals in a specific environment, slot, or niche in an area marginal to agriculture. Although most pastoral people know the general principles of agriculture, they live directly on the unimproved natural environment. Since cattle, horses, and sheep prefer to graze, goats both graze and browse, and camels are browsers, the type of environment and nomadic movement for each can often be predicted. Camel country is arid and flat with some brush and grass; cattle and horses utilize rolling hill country with grassy pastures and plenty of water; sheep need grass and regular water; while goats are hardy wide-ranging eaters in almost any terrain. Sheep and goats often are taken up and down the mountains in what is called *transhumance nomadism,* as among some of the Kurds, Lurs, and Pushtuns (see Chapter 6). By contrast, relatively level ground nomad travel as among the Bedouin, some of the Mongols and reindeer herders of Siberia, and the Dhangars of Central India, is called *migration.*

BOX 5-1 *A SIMPLE MODEL FOR NOMADIC PASTORALISM*

1. Nomadic pastoralism probably originated in a mixed agricultural economy in response to an increased ratio of population to current technology and resources, so forcing the use of nonagricultural territory.

2. The fluctuating conditions created by a variable climate in an intractable environment will result in instability of numbers and composition of both herds and herders in order to maintain optimal efficiency under all circumstances.

3. This threefold instability will necessitate flexibility in social structure and leadership at the local band level.

4. Compensatory stability will be found (1) at the total community level of tribe or confederation: socially in structure and leadership, and culturally in norms of behavior, value systems, and religion; (2) around the periphery of the nomad territory: in beneficial economic and political interaction with agricultural villages and urban trading and governing centers.

5. The community's persistence depends on three vital factors: (1) self-sufficiency in resources and technology, (2) self-perpetuation by replacing personnel, and (3) self-government for internal peace and external independence.

Nomad Independence

Nomad independence is a fragile independence. Nomad communities must be self-sufficient for the replenishment of resources vital to their mode of life, together with supportive technology. They must be self-perpetuating in replacing necessary personnel either by an adequate rate of fertility or by adoption. And they must be self-governing internally for social control and externally in repulsing enemies. This self-sustaining cycle and the very existence of the tribe may be broken up by restriction of their foraging territory, by lack of personnel, or by loss of livestock. Undue dependence upon fixed outside sources of basic foods and materials, and required residence at fixed locations and times can be equally damaging to their freedom. The first three dangers would probably arise from within the environment, the latter two from outside political pressures, as is the case in Tibet and Mongolia. In these regards their situation exactly parallels that of other "endangered species."

THE OASIS: RESIDENTS AND VISITORS

Ecosystem and Way Station

The oasis, isolated by the desert sands, is a single ecosystem, a fragile yet self-sustaining and self-regulating life system. Plants within the cool haven of an oasis have an indigenous relationship with climate, water quality, foods, competitive vegetation, insects, and animals—and pests. In the Arabian oases the prized plant is the date palm, which suffers no great damage from scale insects, rhinoceros beetles, and other borers under normal conditions. Modern changes, however, have made the oasis highly vulnerable. Roads have introduced trucks, people, animals, pests, and worst of all, chemical insecticides. In these ways, a minor nuisance may become a major pest, and thus threaten survival.

Oases vary from Damascus and its rivers of plenty, to the single wells of a Bedouin tribe. Palmyra (or Tadmor), while not an oasis in the ordinary sense, performed the same function by serving as the major way station on the desert transit between Damascus and the Euphrates. Once the capital of the imperious and lovely Queen Zenobia who reigned from A.D. 267 to 272, but known in Arab history as the murderous queen Al-Zabba, Palmyra alternately acted as a Roman administrative center and as a vital, independent kingdom.

In contrast, the so-called "heat oasis," a form of oasis in reverse, occurs where dark soil patches amid the arctic tundra of Siberia absorbs solar radiation. Here, as in the desert oases, are found the greatest varieties of local plants, vegetation, and protection from the freezing winds.

Population and Use

Maps showing types of terrain and climate closely correlate with maps show-ing population and types of livelihood. While desert and mountain areas will be al-most empty, the wetter coastal strips, the river basins, wadis, and oases will be inhabited with hundreds of people per square mile. This contrasts with about forty for each square mile of Southwest Asia's 2.7 million square miles (7 million sq. km.).

As an illustration of a seasonal visit to an oasis, we could consider Jabrin, one of four small oases of the nomad Al-Murrah Bedouin in the northern part of the Rub' al-Khali or Empty Quarter. Jabrin's watered area spreads palms and grazing pasture over an area about fifteen miles long by two to three miles wide. Contrast such lush greenness, for instance, with the *'erg* sand dunes of the Rub' al-Khali. These dunes run in parallel lines in a southwest-northeast direction for a distance of twenty-five to one hundred miles (40-161 km.) each, and are from several hundred yards to two miles (about .3-3.2 km.) in width. Their sharp crests rise 100 to 200 feet (30-61 m.) above the base. On the desert there is little brows-ing for the camels save the *abal* shrub, which remains green for up to four years after rain. What a relief to leave the baking desert and enter the cool arena of the palm-studded oasis to find pasture, leisure for social companionship, the exchange of news, and the renewal of kinship ties—maybe even to find a marriage mate!

The Al-Murrah know about agriculture and tree farming, but agriculture is not their way of life. They always have seen themselves, and have been regarded, as the ideal type of free-moving aristocrats of the desert, the opposite of village *fellahin* (farmers) tied to the land. In desiring to remain free they differ from practically all other Bedouin tribes who today, as seminomads, have up to half of their number permanently residing in their larger oasis settlements.

These semisedentary Bedouin mix nomadism with agriculture as an adapta-tion to necessity. The illiterate village fellahin, restricted to their often miserable plots of semiarid land, never received any respect from people of either the desert or the town, but when irrigation provided an oasis situation the fellahin's plentiful crops, palm groves and fruit trees, and steady income made them the respected economic equals of many of their earlier detractors.

INTERGROUP RELATIONS

Interaction on the Local Scene

The desert and oasis people interact with the villagers around the edges of the desert in many ways. The villagers may care for nomad-owned date palms while the nomads pasture the settlers' animals. Both participate in barter exchanges: grain for goats, watermelons for wool, rifles for rugs, and daughters for sons. Nowadays the truck, as well known as the camel and a lot quicker, carries dates, hides, animals, and local wares produced by nomads and villagers to the town, and returns with household goods, foods, arms and ammunition, clothing, and metalware. Trucks will also pick up every possible hitchhiker along the way.

Even tent cloth can be the catalyst for interaction. In only a few Jordanian villages today do the older women still spend the evening spinning goat's hair wool to weave into the customary Bedouin tent cloth. Most households now use the Syrian factory-made strips of black wool cloth, the cash price of which only begins to pay for this easily acquired convenience. Though made of wool, the factory cloth is shoddy and lets the rain through despite the futile addition of patches of burlap sacking or sailcloth. Near such cities as Kuwait even those tents kept for alternative use in the spring disappeared along with the shanty-town huts when the Kuwaiti authorities provided low-income housing.

Interaction on the National Scene

The wide-spread armed insurrections in 1979 and 1980 by the Azaris or Azerbaijanis, the Kurds, the Baluchi, and others have brought into the open their smoldering resentments against Iranian government efforts to deny them their individual identities. In such cases governments perhaps have three options: one, to crush by force all such separate individual and group identities. This apparently was the policy of Turkey, the U.S.S.R., and China in this century towards some of their minorities. Two, to grant them autonomy as independent nations, as when Pakistan was compelled to grant the independence of the Bengali peoples of East Pakistan to become the new nation of Bangladesh.

The third procedure is to institute dignified relations among the various mutually self-respecting groups within the nation. Traditionally the mobile Bedouin were the military specialists of Arabia, screening not only their own territories but also the oases within them, and such unarmed villages adjoining their borders that asked for protection. The Saudi Arabian government, recognizing both their tribal identities and their military capabilities, and probably also the average household's need for cash, recruited Bedouin men into the Saudi Arabian Reserve National Guard. The salaries and pensions paid these men, along with some wage labor, have since provided the main cash income for many camp and village households throughout the nation. Looked at from another angle, service in the armed or civil services, as in Israel and Iran, has helped to integrate the minorities.

FIGURE 5-1 Turkomen rug merchants in Iran.

VILLAGE DWELLERS

Tradition in a Bedouin Village

In contemplating a look at village people in Southwest Asia it is important to remember that, just as nomads and oasis dwellers and town residents differ from each other and from community to community, so also it is difficult to find a "typical" Arab or Southwest Asian village. We can begin with a village in southern Iraq that displays a common three-class structure. This village of five hundred or so people is located on the edge of the desert but has a road linking it with the railway to Baghdad. A canal and the bridge over it both separate and join the section occupied by the officials and upper class of merchants and others around the market, with the section occupied by the tribal people on the outskirts of the town.

Walking through the village, one can see the tree-shaded homes of the mayor, the doctor, the irrigation engineer, some of the schoolteachers, and others of the more educated and well-to-do people. The houses in this neon-lighted street are made of fired brick with tiled floors, set amid spacious gardens. These upper-class people often dress in Western-styled clothes and their women appear in public unveiled. Considering that their role in society requires an aloofness and culture conformable to their urban upbringing, this elite company obviously constitutes a world unto themselves.

Moving on down to the *suq* or bazaar part of the village, the contents of the shops clearly indicate considerable variation in the affluence of their owners. Housing is similar to the common Asian style of mud brick one-story buildings, often plastered in white, clustered around one or more work-and-play courtyards of tramped earth. Here and there groups of men gather at the coffee shops, graded somewhat according to their pretensions to social connections. Here each man's respectability and acceptance is registered by his presence in the relaxing atmosphere of warm smoke and warmer friendship. Both these sections of the village are on the "right" or communications side of the canal.

Leaving the neutral meeting-place area of the markets, one can cross the canal to the tribal settlement, which adjoins the open country of cultivated fields, and looks out over the more arid land of the Bedouin beyond. Here the high blank walls line dusty lanes, their hidden doorways opening into clean-swept courtyards rimmed with low housing, one for each nuclear family of parents and children. The men might be away in the fields or at the *mudhif*, the community house of the tribe to which all of them belong. The building itself, vaulted and huge, looms invitingly to one side of the dwelling area. The few women who pass slip silently by, cloaked from head to foot in the black *abayah*. They are expected to be seen only by their husbands and sons, to cook and tend the family chores, and to rear obedient children. Once or twice each year, usually at the three-day feast celebrating the end of the *Ramadan* month of fasting, the men of the tribe will come with boisterous gaiety to renew their allegiance to their chieftain, and to eat his salt.

Modern Impacts

The desert as an area of isolation is contracting. A system of paved roads is lacing it together, and bulldozers and asphalting machines are making the earlier balloon-tired trailer rig less necessary. So also the occupational and social world of camp and village is being permeated with the leaven of modernization. This means that the thousands of young men who hitch a ride to a town job may return later with wage money that makes them independent of the elders' largesse, and replaces the close loyalty to the sheik with a partial loyalty to the employer. Technology is replacing tradition. Young women hear news of the outer world over the radio, see new styles of dress and deportment, and wonder whether current restrictions on their participation in society are not, after all, arbitrary. Whereas in the 1920s, Turkey by legal compulsion abolished the man's fez and the woman's veil, today's incentives to change are found on radio and television, and in the Arabic language newspapers and magazines. Here they see portrayed with implied approval both men and women in Western attire and with considerable freedom in public conduct.

Yet age-old values remain deeply embedded in the web of everyday speech and in the accepted norms of social conduct. Kinship terms are used to call forth or express certain expectable responses in attitude and behavior. For instance, when he was in the hospitable home of his professor and wife, a lonely graduate student requested and was readily granted permission to address them as "Father" and "Mother," as an expression of his response to the cordial relationship. In some groups pride of lineage may result in women remaining single for life because there were no available paternal first cousins for them to marry.

Even residence away from the home area carries no automatic exemption from tribal and village values. A woman from a tribal-related village, employed in Beirut together with her lawfully wedded husband, may be severely ostracized. She was condemned because, by Bedouin custom, she had married lewdly by marrying outside the lineage, without the consent of her father, and in an unholy (that is, unveiled) situation (in the city). Of the many possible criteria to symbolize the honor of the group, Arabs have emphasized the decision-making role of the man, his bravery and competence, and the purity of the woman. If the honor of either is besmirched, the whole tribe is ashamed until recompense has been exacted. Other aspects of Southeast Asian life are seen in two Lebanese villages.

Kin and Conflict in a Druze Village

The dominance of the senior male is a prominent consideration in Southwest Asian society. In a Druze village in Lebanon major family relationships revolve around the father. Son and daughter would trace their ancestry through the male line (patrilineal descent), the son would seek his bride among his father's kinsfolk (lineage endogamy), and would bring her to reside at or near the father's home (patrilocal residence). The bride would quite likely be his father's brother's daughter (patrilineal first cousin), that is, his *bint el 'amm.*

For conflicts arising within the lineage, clan, or tribe, the first settlement procedure involves intralineage adjustment, that is, reconciliation through compromise. When necessary a middleman or woman is called in to mediate. He does not arbitrate or judge, let alone pass sentence, for these last three adjudications are the prerogatives of the courts. Since court actions destroy the role of the face-to-face mediator, everyone within the lineage endeavors to avoid referring disputes to the courts, unless outsiders are implicated. In this village the fact that the majority in it are Druzes is also important, for the Druzes pride themselves on maintaining isolation from other socioreligious groups, and on preserving inviolate the details of their religious beliefs.

Crops and Classes in a Shi'ite Village

Quite different is a village located amid precipitous mountains in southern Lebanon. The village of 1,200 people acts as the market center for four other settlements. This location, and the Shi'ite sectarian status of the villagers in a mostly Sunni Muslim region, serves to isolate them. Although the terraced slopes receive fifty- to sixty-inch annual rainfall from the moist Mediterranean air mass, the hot dry summers underline their crops' dependence on irrigation from high-altitude springs. On the lower and more fertile terraces vegetables, oranges, and quinces grow well, and on the upper terraces a booming growth of apple orchards brings unexpected prosperity to the owners. Plums, pears, and pomegranates, as well as walnuts, olives, grapes, figs, and sugar cane add to the value of useable and exportable products.

Social terracing (stratification) takes the form of four categories of families: the Learned Families, the shopkeepers, the peasants, and the Christians. Four fifths of the Learned Families are Sheikhs and wear white turbans. These educated gentry comprise almost one fifth of the population, officiate in social and legal affairs, own half the land area (there are no absentee landlords), and claim lengthy genealogies. The rest of the gentry, the Sayyids (descendants of the Prophet), wear green turbans and officiate in religious ceremonies.

Western-style suits and the red fez on the head identify the shopkeepers and petty traders. In one or another of their twenty small stores the householders purchase what they do not otherwise acquire through barter among themselves. The numerous peasants, three fifths of the population, are expert farmers who dress differently from the other groups. Their preferred attire includes felt hats, shirts, and trousers with baggy seats and narrow cuffs. Surprisingly, for peasants usually are both culturally and religiously conservative, their women are unveiled, unlike those in other villages. The fourth group, the Christians, constitute a static minority of some twenty-three persons who own only one and one-half acres between them. A unifying feature of the village is that all groups participate in local affairs, as well as in the import and export trade with towns in the valleys below.

A REGIONAL ECONOMIC NETWORK: MAKING RUGS IN IRAN

An Occupational Web

Already we have seen that a necessary connection exists between the various occupational groups utilizing different niches of a geographical region. Nomads occupy terrain-climate areas unsuitable for agriculture, and supply animal-based products to the villages, and purchase from them foods, cloth, metal, and retail goods. The villages in turn are suppliers of agricultural products to the towns and receive from them manufactured goods. The towns mark a sort of meeting point between the urbanization of the city and the ruralization of the countryside. The following case study of a regional rug-making industry in Iran indicates typical economic and administrative linkages which tie the different social, occupational, and residential segments of a region to its strategic center, the city.

Herders and Villagers

Herders. The seminomadic herders of the region, because they are widely dispersed, and because they herd partly their own sheep and goats, and partly those financed or contracted by absentee owners, have been unable to form any useful organization such as that of the weavers. Somewhat like a sharecropper, the shepherd receives an annual wage of around fifty dollars, and a percentage in money, lambs, or milk according to the number of animals herded; grazing privileges and housing are provided by the contractor. Very seldom do the shepherds receive any of the wool, since wool enters directly into the weaving and rug-making business so central to this region.

Farmers. Contracts for sharecropping farmers are more rigid. The landlord usually provides everything except labor. In return 50 to 70 percent of the crop is exacted. Here also the percentage varies, according to five factors of production: water, seed, oxen, land, and labor. However, before even these shares are divided, deductions are made by the landlord for the carpenter, bathkeeper, water bailiff, field warden or "crop watcher," and others who contribute minor services.

The role of the village. The role of the village depends upon the extent of the contracts with local herders and farmers, the size of the village, its nearness to a city, and to the *qanat* (underground water canal) or other water system upon which it depends. Village administration deals with maintaining the *qanats* and regulating the water supply to farmers, and with coordinating dates for plowing and sowing. Its responsibility also includes rotating and protecting crops, appointing village officials, and levying water dues and national taxes. The water bailiff supervises the critical balance between the type and amount of cropping and the expected actual flow of seasonal water. The field warden takes care of security in the fields. Within the village are various guilds regulating the weaving industry, controlling apprenticeships, settling disputes, and mediating between weavers and city contractors.

Village and Town

A complete establishment of forty or more weavers, dyers, draftsmen, and designers is kept busy by the few city carpet merchants who are wealthy enough to control the whole process. Lesser establishments controlling only parts of the system are found in the smaller towns, and only individual weavers and the local guilds are present at the village level. Because of the time and skill involved in the production of a quality rug, contracts specify the design, colors, density, and knotting of the desired carpets. Some contracts are with individual weavers, more often with middlemen or brokers in touch with ten to a hundred city and village weavers and their guilds. Most of the actual weaving is done by women and children under supervision of a master weaver. The remuneration is based on whether or not the contractor supplies the loom, wool, dyes, or spun and dyed thread, and on a master weaver's average daily output of 16,000 standard knots of two warp threads each. For 100 rows of 160 knots each he used to be paid about eighty cents, though doubtless somewhat more today.

The inhabitants of small villages of four hundred or so persons are mostly peasant cultivators, interrelated by marriage and served by traveling peddlers and barbers. The only professionals are the schoolteachers. The larger villages of a thousand persons and over have a bathhouse, shrine, mill, and some shops. A few professionals and artisans serve the tenant farmers and weavers who usually have no financial surplus with which to help each other. Everyone tries to produce for his or her family as many of the basic necessities as possible by tending gardens, collecting firewood, keeping animals and chickens, and working at two occupations.

Town and City

The regional towns of 1,000 to 1,500 households are simplified editions of the city. Two-thirds of the population of the towns are guild craftsmen and service workers: artisans, weavers, *qanat* builders, shopkeepers, and professionals.

The remaining one-third is composed of farmers and herders. The upper and middle classes include the mayor and town councillors, also the wealthy landowners, managers of banks and carpet factories, the professional doctors, teachers, mullahs, and the tax-collectors, all of them carefully observing the cardinal rule—to ensure frictionless relationships within the system.

In such towns great wealth is unattainable, so education, lineage, and religious piety become important factors in local prestige. Farmers dressed in the blue cotton trousers, long shirts, and felt caps of the peasant comprise the basic occupational group in the environs of the town.

The City

Iran. The city is the administrative center of the governor and the power elite of landed aristocracy who finance and control the key activities and resources of the province. Traveling mendicants, robed and turbaned tribesmen, and carpet buyers from the capital mingle with farmers and moviegoers and carts and donkeys on the crowded streets and bazaars of this regional metropolis. Having paid the local transit tax on goods, the people bringing fruit, grain, firewood, and handi-crafts find their places in the market, and slow the pace of bid and counter-bid in order to banter gossip and swap the latest news. When their goods have been sold by barter or for cash, there still is time for visiting relatives and friends, and for worshipping at the mosque, especially if the day is Friday. After purchasing salt, sugar, tea, or cloth, the marketers board the bus for the five- or thirty-mile ride home. This whole economic web is a two-way communication network: purchases are made primarily in the city, and control by contract is exercised from the city.

The modern class structure is also interesting. A governing and wealthy elite forms the top 5 percent of the city population, the criteria for membership based on land ownership, lineage, money, and power. A small middle class of younger or less affluent bureaucrats, merchants, religious leaders, doctors, etc., occupies a 10 percent position between the elite and the 75 percent of commoners who constitute the bulk of the population. These are the artisans, clerks, servants, sharecroppers, and vendors. Vendors include water carriers whose donkey-powered carts carry tanks of water. Rather curiously carriers of water from a spring outside the city see themselves as superior to their fellows who tote only local city water. Since women are greatly restricted to the home, swarms of peddlers bring to their doors every variety of purchasable small items. At the social ground level are the Gypsies. Gradations of prestige and wealth are changing as improved public trans-portation facilities give greater opportunities for better prices, and for mobility in residence and job-seeking outside the village.

Other Occupational Webs

Afghanistan. The same situation exists on a smaller scale at Aq Kupruk, a town of about 1,500 men (census figures often omit women) in Balkh province of northern Afghanistan. As the market center of a ring of villages, with a screening of seminomadic herders in the surrounding mountains, its minor place in the provincial government system had changed little from the satrapy patterns of the ancient Archaemenid empire (c. 600–330 B.C.), until the winds of "new democracy" blew in 1963. Then came young, educated district chiefs (*alakadurs*), open elections, Indian movie music, and work gangs that cut across kinship and ethnic lines. Previously located on a southern branch of the trans-Asian Silk Route, it was bypassed by the new motor road, but rejuvenated as farmers profited from ownership of their lands.

Kuwait: then and now. The traditional-to-modern metamorphosis of an Asian society and its environment can be illustrated by events in centers such as Hong Kong, Singapore, and Tel Aviv. The exceptional case of Kuwait (diminutive of *kut,* a fort) clearly exemplifies the process. Kuwait's six thousand-year tradition of seafaring was still observable in 1763 when its 10,000 inhabitants maintained a fleet of 800 vessels. In 1929 the harbor was full of dhows bringing cloves, tea, and rice from India and Zanzibar, cut palm fronds for firewood from Basra in Iraq, and locally grown dates, fruits, and green fodder. Local merchants rode to shop and office on large white donkeys or on horses. The Sheik kept fifty beautiful mares in his stables. In the crowded market square Bedouin tent-dwellers could be seen loading their camels with take-home supplies of foodstuffs, rice, spice, coffee, and tins of kerosene. Money for these purchases came from the sale of camels for slaughter, black sheep's wool (all Kuwaiti sheep were black in those days), Astrahan lamb hides, brushwood and palm fronds for firewood, and small mats woven by the women. Nothing came across the desert from Syria and Lebanon; everything from north and west came down the Euphrates and the Shatt-al-Arab through Basra. Pilgrims to Mecca crossed the desert sitting crosslegged in covered basket seats slung on the sides of camels which grazed as they walked.

Today all is changed. Producing about 5 percent of the world's crude petroleum output from about one fifth of the world's reserves, Kuwait's population of 1.1 million enjoy the highest per capita income in the world—around $11,000 (U.S. dollars) per annum. Kuwait's ninefold population increase, from about 122,000 in the 1930s, has been mainly by the immigration of several hundred thousand Palestinians, besides other Arabs, as well as Indians, Pakistanis, and Iranians. Most of these people work in the oil refineries, fishing fleets, and factories manufacturing building materials, chemicals, canned goods, and furniture. Still others are engaged in salt and marble mining, etc. Kuwait supports 19 hospitals with 4,505 beds and educates 30,000 secondary school students. A satellite earth station serves the city's telecommunication center. Other modern improvements include sea water distillation plants producing 62 million gallons of fresh water daily, and an extensive Institute for Scientific Research.

Education for Kuwaitis is free, as is medical care. Working members of the family pay no income tax, and the earlier stark distinction between rich and poor has largely disappeared. Another sign of the changing times are the eighteen modern airlines now operating in and out of Kuwait, while the lateen-rigged dhow is becoming a collector's item. The colors selected for the national flag symbolize something of the dynamic Arab value system: green for fertility of the land, white for outstanding achievement, red for chivalry and swordsmanship, and black for bravery in war. Although this is a rather secular Cinderella story of transformation accomplished by the timely and energetic use of Western technology, the people who fly this flag are staunchly religious.

Chapter **6**

A Mosaic of Peoples: An Ethnographic Survey

INTRODUCING THE COMPONENTS

In the preceding chapters we saw that people may be considered historically and religiously, geographically and occupationally, and also in terms of social class. Now we need to acquaint ourselves with them as specific communities in their various countries. Our first criteria are both genetic and cultural. To the extent that larger aggregations (Iranians, Turks, Arabs) and smaller communities (Greeks, Armenians, Samaritans) marry within the group, this endogamous process reinforces the general physical likenesses of the members of the community, and becomes the genetic side of their group identity. When to these genetic group likenesses are added their distinct preferences in religion, language, dress, and other social customs—the cultural side of group identity—we have the actual ethnic identity of the community, a synthesis of all the influences accumulated in them over the past millenia.

Southwest Asian countries also are linguistically composite, speaking languages both ancient and modern. Turkic languages, which are spoken here and there from Poland to the Pacific and from Siberia to India, are especially obvious in Turkey, Cyprus, Iran and Afghanistan, as well as in Central Asia. Persian dialects are found throughout most of Iran and Afghanistan; and Hebrew, Armenian, Greek, Circassian, Pashto, Baluchi and Kurdish are spoken by significant segments of the region's peoples. Even such an ancient language as Aramaic, once the *lingua franca* of Mesopotamia, Syria and Palestine, is still the daily speech of several villages between Damascus and Mosul, and for several Christian sects in Syria and Iraq it is their sacred language.

In order to understand the present-day peoples of Southwest Asia, such as the Syrians, Turks, or Israelis, it is necessary to look at the ethnohistorical background of the region. This includes indigenous communities, immigrants, and invaders whose operations or depredations have often promoted, upset, or destroyed the delicate balance of civilization.

Successive movements of Asians hammered at the region: the Scythian tribes, the fleeing Cimmerians, the conquering Turks, and the dreaded Mongols. Some invaders like the Cimmerians and Abyssinians disappeared. Some stayed, even for hundreds of years, and then left or disappeared: Philistines, Scythians, Mongols, Crusaders, and the British and French. Others, such as the Turks and the modern Jews, remained to become permanent parts of Southwest Asia's mosaic of peoples. First comes a survey of these uninvited outsiders, and then a look at some of the prominent, the controversial, and the little-known peoples of the region.

INVADERS AND INTRUDERS

Egyptians

Isolated from the surrounding nations not only by desert wastes but also by three thousand years of imperial magnificence, Egypt occupied an almost impregnable position as the military and cultural "Middle Kingdom" of that part of the world. With the rise to affluence of the kingdoms straddling the lucrative trade routes through Mesopotamia and Anatolia—Babylon, Assyria, and the Hittites—Egypt needed a buffer zone against empires hungry for land and loot.

Every few hundred years, therefore, Egypt has made major efforts to control the eastern Mediterranean shore—by the pharoahs, the Ptolemy kings, Saladin, and the Mamlukes—but has never succeeded. Most recently, under the short-lived United Arab Republic of 1958-1961, Egypt and Syria were nominally united. No large Egyptian community has ever remained in the eastern Mediterranean shore region.

The Sea Peoples

The Sea Peoples are one of history's mysterious peoples. Quite likely they were a coalition of coastal adventurers from Sardinia, Greece, Crete, and Asia Minor. They broke the power of the Hittite empire; then, like a human *tsunami*, they harassed Cyprus, thundered in and out of Syria's port cities, and washed up against the coast of Egypt. When turned back from invading Egypt in 1190 B.C., some of them landed from their ships and settled on the maritime plain of Palestine around and north of the present Gaza Strip.

These well-organized invaders, with their long steel swords, kilts, and plumed headdresses, became known to history as the Philistines. The Greeks named the area Philistia after them, hence Palestine. They added to the local technical skills in farming, iron-working, architecture, and social organization, but after Greek and Roman times only lingering traces of them remained.

Two thousand years elapsed before the next invasion by sea, when some of the First and Third Crusade armies came from Europe in the 1000s and 1100s. The latest sea-born "invasion" was that of refugee Jews in the 1940s. Other invaders came by land.

The Scythians

After the Chinese armies set the domino of horseriding Hsiung-nu falling westward about 800 B.C., the next to topple before the Hsiung-nu were the Massagetae or Sakas, who in turn dislodged the Scythian horsemen. The Scythians chased the Cimmerians into Asia Minor and by 675 B.C. had destroyed the Phrygian kingdom of King Midas before the Medes (Persians) forced them back into their home area around Parthia. The Scythian metalworkers matched modern skills for artistry and technique in gold, copper and iron, jewelry, felt applique, and ivory inlay. The Scythians next appeared when they established the Saka and the Kushan dynasties in Afghanistan and India between 80 B.C. and A.D. 400.

It is believed that under the Saka king Gondophares Christianity was introduced into India by the Apostle Thomas, who died there about A.D. 68. The present-day Mar Thoma Syrian Church of Malabar is named after him.

As heirs to the long-lived Greek influence in Western Asia, the Kushan made a critical contribution with their initial sculpting of the image of Buddha. Their greatest ruler, Kanishka, not only facilitated two-way trade between Rome and China by protecting the Silk Road, but also promoted the greatest single change in religion seen in Central and East Asia up to the A.D. 100s—the introduction and acceptance of a new major faith, Buddhism.

The importance of the Scythians in South and Southwest Asia lies not in the few discernible traces of them remaining today, but in the abiding historical and religious changes they made possible.

Greeks

Greek colonies and merchants were already long established in Asia Minor when Alexander the Great burst upon Southwest Asia like a Greek meteor. In a mere eleven years from 334 to 323 B.C. his nearly invincible fighting units, the wedges of spearmen called phalanxes, swept aside the civilizations of Tyre, Damascus, Mesopotamia, Persia, and Parthia. His campaigns opened an expanded Middle Eastern belt reaching from Gibraltar to the Punjab to the art and coinage, thought and language, economy and architecture of Greece and, later, of Rome and Byzantium. Under Greek tutelage the Parthians developed excellent astronomers, physicists, mathematicians, and philosophers. The Graeco-Roman imprint upon the features, postures, and clothing of Buddha's image carried over about two thousand years to the modern temple statues of painted clay in South China. With the advent of the Turkish empire Greek influences gradually faded from the Southwest Asian region, except around the coastal areas of Turkey itself.

Romans

Roman troops invaded Asia as early as 192 B.C. But it was in 66 B.C., when Pompey defeated King Mithradates of Pontus, that Rome acquired the Levantine region of eastern Asia Minor, Syria, and Palestine. Syrian Antioch (now Antakya

TABLE 6-1   Roster of Invaders into Southwest Asia

DATES	PEOPLES	AREAS OCCUPIED	ASSOCIATED EVENTS AND ACTIVITIES
B.C.			
c. 3600	Hittites	Anat, Syria, Leb, Pal	Law, iron weapons, fortified cities, relief carving.
Pre-3500	Sumerians	Lower Mesop.	City and shrine culture, cuneiform writing.
c. 2600	Hurrians (Hivites, Horites)	Syria, Up. Mesop, Leb, Pal, Edom	Mitanni kingdom; art, seals, iron working, Indo-Aryan ruling warrior class, cedar trade with Mediterranean region.
c. 2600	Luvians	Anatolia	Influenced Hittite culture, introduced hieroglyphic script; Luvian became spoken language of Hittite empire.
c. 2400	Canaanites	Syria, Leb, Pal, Jor.	Urban life, pottery, alphabetic script 1000 B.C., ancestors of Phoenicians.
Pre-2300	Amorites	Cen. Mesop, Syria, Leb, Pal	Desert dwellers turned city builders (Mari), principalities, Early Bronze technology.
1300s	Egyptians	Pal, Syria	Military occupation; little permanency.
c. 1290/60	Hebrews	Pal	Gradual exclusive occupation to 537 B.C.; systematic monotheistic religion.
c. 1190	Sea Peoples/ Philistines	Pal	Pottery, iron working monopoly, federation of fortress cities.
c. 1190	Phrygians	Asia Minor	Indo-European kingdom, the Midas kings.
Pre-900	Aramaeans	Syria, Up. Mesop	C. 800 adopted alphabetic script causing Aramaean to become lingua franca of Near East.
721	Scythians	Per, Mesop, Phrygia	Dominated Syria.
333	Greeks	A. Minor, N. Syria	Greek kings of Bactria, Syria, Egypt; Hellenism in N. East, pervasive art, sculpture.
c. 300	Hindus	Gandhara	Little permanent effect.
192	Romans	Syria, Pal, A. Minor	Suzereignty over general region.
95/80	Sakas and Parthians	Gandhara, NW Iran	Helped spread Greek art and coinage; called Pahlavas in India.
A.D.			
50-240	Kushans	Afgh, N. India	Spread Buddhism through C. Asia to E. Asia.
450s	Huns	Afgh, Per	Little permanent effect.
600s-700s	Muslims	SW Asia, NW India, Central Asia	Spread of Islam, Arabic; caliphates.

DATES	PEOPLES	AREAS OCCUPIED	ASSOCIATED EVENTS AND ACTIVITIES
1037	Seljuk Turks	Per, Up. Mesop	Threatened Byzantines; Turkish language.
1096	Crusaders	A. Minor, Syria, Pal	Temporary kingdoms; cultural exchange.
1221	Mongols	Per, Mesop, A. Minor	Defeated Seljuks, widespread devastation.
1326	Ottoman Turks	Mesop, A. Minor, etc.	Mighty empire, Turkish language, invaded Europe.
1430s	Afgh. Mongols	Afgh, India	Moghul empire, Islam in Pak and Bangladesh.
1515	Europeans	SW Asia, India	Portuguese, Dutch, French, English, Russians; trade and empire.

GLOSSARY:

A	Asia	N	North, Near
Afgh	Afghanistan	NW	Northwest
Anat	Anatolia	Pak	Pakistan
C, Cen	Central	Pal	Palestine
Jor	Jordan	Per	Persia
Leb	Lebanon	SW	Southwest
Mesop	Mesopotamia	Up	Upper

in Turkey) was the third city in the Roman empire, and their eastern military base. It remained a Christian center for 1,700 years.

In view of today's Middle Eastern dilemma, Rome's critical action was the destruction of Jerusalem by Titus in A.D. 70, and the wholesale dispersion of the Jewish people. Although remnant Jewish groups continued to live in the area they never regained full political control of their ancient homeland until the mid-twentieth century. Turkish capture of Constantinople in A.D. 1453 eliminated the last vestiges of the Roman empire.

Turks

Moving southwest from Central Asia the Seljuk Turkish horsemen conquered most of Byzantine Asia Minor by A.D. 1071. The Mongols defeated the Seljuks in 1243, thereby paving the way for the Ottoman Turkish empire in 1326. The dreaded Turkish *janissaries* (the best-armed infantry of their day) terrorized Eastern Europe and were turned away from the gates of Vienna in 1683. Although their magnificent mosque architecture, their textiles and poetry, their science and industry continued to flourish, stagnation set in during the 1600s and 1700s. In 1923 Turkey became a republic and entered the roster of modern nations.

Crusaders

Babylonians, Hittites, Egyptians, Muslims, and Turks, and more Muslims— not to mention European nations of the twentieth century—have taken turns invading or occupying the narrow coastal strip of Palestine. Beginning about A.D. 1071 the Seljuk Turks restricted Christian visitation to the Holy Land sites. A motley procession of eight crusades set out from Europe between 1096 to 1270 to liberate the Holy City of Jerusalem from the Muslims, and to promote partisan economic interests. Most of the knights, peasants, and children never reached the desired land, though several short-lived principalities were established in Cyprus, Syria, and Palestine.

However, these prodigious efforts succeeded in breaching the walls of silence separating Christian Europe from Muslim Afro-Asia. New foods and clothing, better ships and maps, prospering trade, and intellectual stimulation were part of a two-way cultural exchange. Crusader kingdoms now have long vanished, but their massive castletowns remain today as tourist attractions in Jordan and Syria. And in some towns Muslim versus Infidel Crusader dramas are publicly celebrated.

Mongols

With the ascendance of Genghis Khan as the Mongol ruler, waves of Mongol cavalry galloped along the prosperous trade routes into China, Central Asia, and Russia.

Ghengis Khan's grandson Hulagu destroyed the Iranian Muslim sect of the Assassins (from *hashshashin*, hashish-eaters) in 1256. Then, proceeding into what is now Iraq, in 1258 he put to death the last Abbasid caliph and piled in heaps the skulls of the slaughtered inhabitants of Baghdad. From these devastations of seven hundred years ago Iran and Iraq have recovered only recently through re-establishing the destroyed irrigation systems. Following his defeat at the borders of Egypt, Hulagu established the Il-Khan empire (1256–1335), centered in Persia, yet extending from the Indus to the Euphrates.

Barren lands and buried cities still bear mute witness to the grim perversity of the Seljuk Turks, the Mongols, and, from 1383 on, of the "Scourge of Asia," Timur the Lame. In the half millenium following the eruption of the Turks, the last Central Asian invaders on the scene, Southwest Asia remained free of major outside invasions.

Europeans

The European "invasion" of the 1800s and 1900s came in the forms of agricultural, political, and technologized changes. The early establishment of the kibbutz settlements was followed in the twentieth century by the occupation and administration of parts of Southwest Asia by League of Nations mandates to Britain and France. The mandates did not last very long, but, in addition to new territorial boundaries, they imprinted upon the region many Western concepts and procedures of government and technology, of philosophy and language, of communications, and even of dress.

AN AWESOME HUMAN MOSAIC

Arabs

The term "Arab" first occurred in an inscription of 853 B.C. wherein Shalmaneser III of Assyria records the contribution of a thousand camels to a rebellion by a princeling named "Gindibu of Aribi" (the Arabian). For the next thousand years the word appears to have referred primarily to the Bedouin of the northern Arabian deserts. As Semites, the Arabs are linguistic kin to the ancient Assyrians, Babylonians, Abyssinians, and Hebrews.

The popular use of the word "Arab" by Arabs as well as by non-Arabs is confusing. The word Arab does not denote a nationality (the individual may be a citizen of Iraq, Lebanon, Israel, Egypt, Saudi Arabia, Yemen, or Iran) nor a religion (he may be Muslim, Alawi, or Christian), nor even one who speaks Arabic (this person may be an Israeli Jew, an Iraqi Kurd, a Lebanese Druze, or a Saudi Arabian Bedouin). While not strictly a legal, cultural, or even an ethnic term, yet "Arab" denotes a living and emotional reality, a concept of "Arabness" claimed by millions of Southwest Asian peoples. An Arab, then, is one who identifies himself or herself with those who cherish Arab tradition and culture, language and land as a personal heritage, and in turn is so regarded by them. By this definition many of the above peoples call themselves Arabs. In this way a concept of Arab identity is produced that is both a basis for mutual acceptance and unity, and also a reason for the pervasive caution in politics and fragmentation in action amongst them.

FIGURE 6-1
Arabia: Bedouin.

During the caliphates, those of Arabian origin became a military aristocracy, and although the administrators and merchants often were Persians, these caliphate periods retained a distinctive Arab character. In the latter half of the twentieth century a somewhat parallel distinction exists between the Pan-Islamism of the Muslim bloc, extending from Morocco to Pakistan, and the Pan-Arabism of the Arab bloc, which excludes the northern tier of non-Arab nations: Turkey, Cyprus, Iran, and Afghanistan.

Amongst other customs characteristic of Southwest Asia is that of paternal first cousin marriage of the woman (*bint 'amm* in Arabic) to her male cousin (*ibn 'amm*) who has definite and in many areas exclusive first claim upon her. The second claim goes to the mother's brother's son (*ibn khal*), and then on down to her sister's husband. The attractions of this system include protection of the lineage and property, control of the persons concerned, and moderate financial costs. But the lineage always takes precedence, because in lineage membership lies the individual's survival and dignity.

Palestinians

Turmoil and fighting preceded the relinquishment of the British mandate over Palestine; and war followed the establishment under United Nations sponsorship of the new State of Israel on May 14, 1948. In the process some 650,000 Arabs were displaced from their homes and farms on Israeli territory. Some fled from fear of trouble, some were coerced by propaganda, and some were forcibly ejected. Those with money, professions, or skills found new homes in neighboring states. Most of those in the camps in the Gaza Strip or in Jordan were farmers, unskilled in other vocations, the very class Arab nations had difficulty providing for within their own nonindustrialized economies.

Unwanted by both Israel and the Arab states, these refugees grew in numbers, suffered privations, and became increasingly bitter. By 1983 the total displaced population had more than tripled to about five million persons. In spite of the numbers still classed as refugees, the Arab states actually have absorbed several times the original number of refugees.

The militant Palestine Liberation Organization (PLO), founded in 1963, by the early 1980s had been granted varying degrees of international recognition, as representing both the Palestinians and the Arabs of the West Bank of Israel. The Syrian invasion of eastern Lebanon in 1976, the Israeli invasion of South Lebanon, the forced scattering of most of the PLO fighters to various Afro-Asian countries, and the use of a multinational "peace keeping" force in Lebanon, further worsened the problem of the "Palestinian State." Peace remains elusive in the Middle East.

Jews and Israelis

The two terms "Jew" and "Israeli" are not the same. The term "Jew" primarily identifies a person religiously. The term "Israeli" identifies a person politically as a citizen of the State of Israel, without regard to religion. The legal question

"Who is a Jew?" has been defined by religious law, and accepted by the State, as a person born of a Jewish mother.

The Jewish settlements, towns, and tribes long established in northern Arabia before the A.D. 600s were later joined by many others. Some Sephardic Jews have been in the land since the A.D. 1000s, augmented by others who had settled in Spain and were expelled from there in 1492. Musta'rabs (Arabic-speaking Jews) have also resided in northern Arabia for centuries. The majority of the European Jews who settled in Palestine from the late 1800s on were Ashkenazim (Jews from Poland, Russia, and Germany). These Ashkenazim founded the State of Israel and established its basic Western character. Contingents of "Oriental Jews"—now about 60 percent of the population—came from countries from North Africa to India, bringing their own languages and customs. A new surge of ultraorthodoxy by Hasidic Jews has added to the existing tensions. The communal *kibbutz* and the cooperative *moshav*, together with common schools and military service have contributed not only to the development of the countryside into productive farms but also to the sociological task of assimilating all groups into a cohesive modern nation. Tensions exist along ethnic, religious, occupational, and educational lines, as well as between Israeli Jews and Arabs of nearly every party and nation. Peace within its borders and with its neighbors still eludes Israel, notwithstanding the aid freely given to many developing nations.

Christians

Christianity began with the birth of Jesus of Nazareth about 4 B.C., while Herod the Great's kingdom of Judea was under Roman rule. After A.D. 313, when Constantine promoted Christianity as a preferred religion in the Roman Empire, Christian Arabs maintained the Byzantine border states of Ghassan and Hira until they were absorbed by the Muslim advance in the A.D. 600s. The major Christian communities in the Middle East, totalling over 3.6 million persons, had their own patriarchs, rites, and languages (Aramaic or Syriac in the east and Arabic in the west) and tradition of self-government. Most Christian groups have some degree of affiliation with the Pope at Rome. The number of Protestants in Southwest Asia is estimated at forty thousand persons.

As a general statement, Christians on the whole appear to be better educated than their Muslim neighbors, to give higher status to their women, and to prefer city life. In Israel Christian Arabs are treated the same as Muslim Arabs; they may volunteer for army service, and in the civil service they are not required to work on their own religious holy days. Shiloh's statement that "most of the provinces of Syria are a kind of ethnic and religious mosaic" (1969:43) is true of the whole region.

Samaritans

When King Shalmaneser of Assyria eliminated the rebellious nation of Israel in 721 or 722 B.C., and deported its people to Mesopotamia, the ancestors of the Samaritans were transported in reverse from that region to Palestine to occupy the land left vacant. These settlers gradually forsook animism and adopted the Jewish Torah, the five books of Moses, as their sole scriptures. Later they built a temple on Mt. Gerizim near Nablus, where their priests still preserve ancient parchment scrolls of the scriptures. Their history has been a depressing calendar of massacres and discrimination.

A tiny yet tenacious minority of some 450 persons clustered around Nablus, thirty miles (48 km.) north of Jerusalem, call themselves *Shamerim* (Observant Ones) rather than *Shomeronim* (inhabitants of Samaria). By means of strictly endogamous marriage laws they have maintained their distinctive religious and cultural identity for 2,600 years. These marriage customs resulted in men waiting until fifty and more years of age before an eligible girl grew old enough for marriage. Recent modifications in this custom permit men to marry earlier, and the decline in population has been reversed.

Lebanese

A different saga is that of Lebanon. Before ruthless warfare blighted this fair land in the 1970s, a Rolls Royce and a donkey could be seen traversing the same Beirut boulevard. At his destination the limousine's rider was received by political friends, banking colleagues, and respectful secretaries. He knew that Beirut's position as the region's financial center rested on the shaky foundation of Lebanon's conflicting community and religious interests. On his way home the donkey's rider was waited on by the alleyway butcher, who cut for him a slice of mutton from the carcass hanging on the wall. He knew that Muslim, Christian, PLO, and other partisans were filling their basements with assorted light and heavy weapons and ammunition. Somewhere in the background their women—whether veiled or unveiled, from housewife to entertainer to university student—provided the subdued but serious social cement that underpinned Lebanese society. All these people knew the political device of a Christian president and a Muslim premier neither disguised nor alleviated Muslim dissatisfaction with a Christian majority in parliament and in the army's corps of officers.

Many Lebanese proudly spoke of themselves as Phoenicians rather than as Arabs, Muslims, or Christians. And no wonder, for here may be found Roman ruins covering even more important Phoenician structures. Amidst the incredible archaeological trove of skulls and bones of warriors from a score of different invasions lie little pyramids of stone balls made for the catapults of Alexander the Great in 321 B.C.

Leaving these historic coastlands, a motor highway winds up over the Lebanon Mountains, terraced with grain fields and fruit orchards, and down into the eighty-mile (128 km.) long Bekaa Valley. Into this lush valley, watered by the Litani and Orontes rivers, the modern Bedouin still lead their sixty to seventy thousand Awassi sheep from the parched eastern deserts. Syrian troops have lined its mountain ramparts with guns and rockets.

In their villages nestled on the steep slopes craftsmen in their tiered houses produce each village's unique specialties: handwoven rugs, cutlery, fried fish, sculptures. Little girls play hopscotch one a piece of 1,500-year old mosaic; the sixty-nine-year old patriarch sitting in the sun may never have been further than an hour's ride from his ancestral village; and the mountain sculptor in iron or wood or stone needs the vista's calm serenity as much as he needs his materials and tools to produce his best work. Nevertheless, under the serene surface lurk smoldering divisions, and rifle shots echo from the hedgerows of villages noted for another ancient specialty—political and family feuds.

Kurds

"Kurdistan" is a word that pleases neither the Turks, the Iranians, nor the Iraqis. About half of the estimated eight million turbulent Kurds live in Turkey, and a quarter each in Iran and Iraq, with some 320,000 in Syria. All are Sunni Muslims living in Kurdistan's 56,000 square miles of contiguous mountains, principally as nomadic and village pastoralists.

These modern descendants of the ancient Medes speak an Indo-Iranian language (Indo-European), and their values include bravery and manly honor, hospitality, friendship, and ingroup solidarity—values essential to the survival of any mountain people. Under the pressures of modern life many young men gravitate to jobs in the cities where their *agha* (leaders) have some influence. Kurdish women are held in esteem, appear amongst their men without the veil, and may even share in positions of tribal authority.

Legends fire the imagination and feed the hope of these hardy people who, having little of this world's advantages, strive for recognition of their inherent dignity. A recent "living legend" was the old teacher credited with having personally taught some 6,500 illiterate mountaineers to read and write in his cluttered clay-roofed cottage. On the other hand, Baba Gurgur, the Old Man Flame of underground gas—also called Nebuchadnezzar's Furnace—no longer claims human sacrifices, or even divines "boy or girl?" for expectant mothers. Baba Gurgur today is millions of tons of oil and gas annually flowing from under Kurdish feet to a gasoline-thirsty world—through Iraqi pipelines.

Other Minorities

The *Armenians* and *Circassians,* the *Druzes* and *Alawis* present different reactions to some broadly similar Southwest Asian circumstances. All have had to struggle to maintain their identities for 750 to more than 1,000 years. While *Druzes* in their mountains of Lebanon and Syria were known as the "Sword of Syria" for their stout resistance against Crusaders, Turks, and the French, the mainly rural peasant population of *Alawis* have found their upward social progress in rather recent years through active participation in modern military life.

The *Circassians,* sold by Genghis Khan as slaves to the Turks, were famous for the fierceness of their warriors and the beauty of their women. Known as Mamluks or Mamelukes, they ruled Egypt for over 250 years until they were massacred in 1811. Near Amman, Jordan, which in 1922 was a small and dusty Circassian town, there still is a totally Circassian village, Wade El-Sier. In all, some twenty thousand Circassians also reside in Syria. Unlike the Druze, who may disguise their identity by adopting the dress, food, and language of their neighbors, the Circassians emphasize their difference, for instance, by wearing city clothes in the rural village. Circassians also reject Arab first cousin marriage, considering it a form of incest.

The *Armenians,* following the collapse of their first century B.C. empire, were almost continually harassed by surrounding peoples even into the 1920s, when the Turks caused the deaths of about 1.8 million Armenians. Converted to Christianity in 301 A.D., Armenians number about 2.5 million in the Armenian Soviet Socialist Republic; about 3.5 million more live scattered around the world. Peaceful and industrious, the Armenians often are city oriented as prosperous merchants and competent doctors, teachers, lawyers, and musicians.

In this region of limited resources, where populations huddle around oasis-style areas watered by rivers and rain, each community necessarily guards its physical and/or cultural boundaries with the utmost vigilance. Displaced peoples are seldom welcome in someone else's territory.

IRAN AND ITS PEOPLES

Demography

About 44 of every 100 Iranians occupy town and city homes varying from the gray-walled village style to modern houses, most being built within high walls around a central courtyard. Here the flowers and trees surrounding a pool of water lend beauty to the family's daily activities. The cities maintain paved streets and tree-lined boulevards where the new schools, hospitals, apartment residences, and government buildings are to be found.

Since Muslim Iran is a man's world, the women's role is correspondingly subdued. While she is the usual controller of the children and of the household's daily arrangements, her emotional release (at least for women in town and city) is found in social contacts at the mosque shrine and in special home prayers. At two special home gatherings—the "chanting in the home" (Rowzeh Khane), and the "spreading of the tablecloth" (Sofreh)—groups of family and friends, rich and poor alike sit in their *chadors* (head-to-foot gowns) on the floor as a female mullah gives an emotional recitation of the Shi'ite saints' lives, particularly of Husain the martyr and of Saint Abbas. It is an intimate time for making and completing vows.

The rural half of Iran's nearly forty million people live in villages whose drab houses line the streets that wind towards the mosque, the public bath, and the flour mills around the city square. Most villages have a school and a store; bazaars or shopping centers are found only in the towns and cities.

The remaining 6 percent of Iran's peoples are mostly nomadic minorities. The following ethnographic sketches complement those in Chapter 5, and concentrate on several of the lesser-known minority peoples, even though their situations may have changed somewhat since the Shah left Iran in 1979.

The Nomads of Iran

Nomads need neither attic nor basement. All they possess must be useable and portable: home and clothing, tools and weapons, utensils and food. They must be as mobile as the horses, sheep, goats, camels, mules, or donkeys they herd.

From the Kurds and Lurs to the Baluchi, men, women, and children must be largely self-sufficient for seasonal journeys that may range 100 to 300 rugged miles (160–480 km.) into the high sierras. They provide themselves with dairy staples, and purchase sugar and tea, dates and fruit at the villages. Wool, lambskins, clarified butter, and some livestock change hands for market goods of cloth and shoes, saddles and jewelry, radios and utensils, rifles and ammunition. The poverty-stricken Gorbati gypsy bands supply handmade mats and spindle whorls, horse shoes and sheep shears, and pot and pan repairs to the nomad bands in return for cash and credibility with other pastoral tribesmen. Disarmed by the government, their pastures nationalized, and their migrations and permanent homestead areas supervised, the nomads exhibit a growing trend toward a more sedentary life-style.

Gone with the Shah was the opportunity for the once independent Lur, Qashqai, and other chiefs to move among the nation's elite. Wealth is reckoned more and more in land as well as in herds. The children study the Iranian language and history in school, and the women, under increasing restrictions, have been forced to resume the veil.

The Gabar Parsis

The "line of minimal identity" that divides one individual or community from another may be extremely fragile and still tremendously tenacious. Such a community are the Gabars of Iran. The term Gabar, arising from Arabic *kafir* meaning non-Muslim or infidel person, like the Turkish term *giaour,* is an obsolete term of contempt once applied to the approximately 20,000 dignified and peaceable Zoroastrians in Iran. Following the Muslim conquest of Persia about 656 A.D. the Gabars had to pay a poll tax, dress differently, and were prohibited from riding horses and bearing arms. Rather than convert and conform they chose to remain a minority by adhering to their separate identity. Purer in ritual than their fellow Parsis in India, they keep the sacred fires burning in temples in Yazd, Kerman, and Shiraz, thus maintaining brightly their traditional integrity for 2,500 years. Prior to the fall of the Shah some were wealthy merchants living in Teheran the capital.

Afghans

As befits one of the important transit areas in the world, Afghanistan has hosted a diversity of peoples: Pushtuns, Tajiks, Uzbeks, Hazaras, Turkmen, Nuristanis, and others who stayed when their forebears moved on elsewhere. The *Pushtuns* were western Asian horsemen who united about 1747 to create modern Afghanistan, and still compose one-half the country's nineteen million people. The Pashto- (or Pushtu-) speaking Pushtuns dominate the government, education, and business, and two million of them are pastoralists who trek back and forth across the invisible frontiers with Pakistan.

Some say the numerous *Tajiks* (25 percent) of the farms and towns north of the Hindu Kush are the original Afghans. They certainly differ from the Central Asian *Hazaras* (9 percent) whose economy includes both agriculture and caring for their flocks which often are snowbound in the mountains. The *Uzbeks* (9

FIGURE 6-2
Iran and its peoples.

AFGHANS	Same peoples as in northwest Afghanistan.
ARABS	Holdover immigrants from across the Persian Gulf.
AZERBAIJANIS	Qizilbash Turks, often bilingual in Turkish and Persian.
*BAKHTIARI	Probably originally Mongol; their Persian dialect contains Arabic and Turkish.
BALUCHI	One million tribal and village people speak Aryan language akin to Persian.
*BASSERI	16,000 tribal nomads tend flocks between the Gulf and the mountains.
BRAHUI	100,000 speakers of a Dravidian language, who, like the Baluchi, live mostly in Pakistan, with some in Afghanistan.
GILANI	Farmers and fishermen on strip of well-watered Caspian coast.
*KURDS	Blend of the ancient Medes with other minorities, live in Turkey-Iraq mountains, speak a Persian dialect. No census; over three million.
*LURS	Primarily tribal nomadic hunters; consider selves a tribal aristocracy.
MAZENDERANI	(See GILANI.)
QASHQA'I	Turkic nomads moving from Esfahan to the Gulf and back. A confederation.
TURKMEN	Mongoloids from Turkmenistan; originally marauders, now settling down.

*These peoples now are ethnically and linguistically similar to the Farsi Persians.

percent), the *Turkmen* and the *Kirghiz* represent the Afghanistan cousins of the greater number of their fellow-countrymen in the Soviet republics of Uzbekistan, Turkmenistan, Kirghizia, and Tajikistan. One small group of 50,000 *Nuristanis* or Kafirs in the almost inaccessible northern valleys have physical features which appear to substantiate their claim to be descended from ancient Greek immigrants. The Afghans' self-sufficiency and fierce independence in a harsh environment, reinforced by their stalwart Muslim faith, have enabled their village fighters and guerilla bands to harass the military might of the Russians.

RETROSPECT AND PROSPECT
IN SOUTHWEST ASIA

Amazing changes have been wrought in Southwest Asia during the vast reaches of 12,000 years of elapsed time. Its peoples have multiplied their numbers from the hundred thousands to more than 150 million. They have created writing systems, organized magnificent empires, and have reached out to lay the gauntlet of war or the robe of religion upon nations from Morocco and Spain to Central Asia and Indonesia. They have advanced medicine and science, and developed their technology from stone tools to today's hand-held computers.

On the mountains of Sinai and the hills of Judea Judaism was born. Christianity arose from the cities of Galilee and Judea, while Islam burst forth in full spate from the desert regions of Arabia.

The region's peoples were diversified by remnant groups from conquest or defeat, migration, banishment, or slavery, and have been sundered by barriers of religion and language, nationality and society. Out of these discords wars have smoldered and flared and are smoldering again. Rivers of oil have been pumped from desert sands and poured out to the ends of the earth, and the resulting cascades of billions of dollars have turned these desert kingdoms into absorbers of industry and financial power. This region of burning sands is now one of the world's hottest centers of political sensitivity.

As of the early 1980s the four Northern Tier countries remained in deep trouble. *Turkey's* government has alternated between military and civilian rule. *Iran,* wracked by years of internal strife and rebellion, assassinations and executions, has been radically changed from a harsh yet modernizing imperial state to a harsh reactionary Islamic republic. A fratricidal and frustrating war initiated by Iraq has helped to unify Iran as a spreader of Shi'ite fervor. *Afghanistan*, for millenia a buffer region between Persia, Central Asia, and India, was specifically bolstered in that position between Russia and the British India of the 1800s. In January 1980, the U.S.S.R. moved some 80,000 Russian troops into the country to solidify the rule of Marxist governments. Unexpectedly stiff resistance by poorly armed *mujahadin* or "holy warriors," and widespread merchant boycotts, disproved Moscow's claim that they came in "by invitation." The incursion has turned into Moscow's Vietnam.

The *de facto* division of *Cyprus* into Turkish and Greek halves has been stabilized outwardly, but the political gap and psychological antagonisms remain unsettled.

Iraq's three-way split, between the Arab Sunni and Shi'ite populations and the Kurdish mountaineers in the northlands, recalls the traditional competition between Byzantine, Arab, and Persian influences of past centuries. Under its Arab Ba'ath Socialist Party leadership Iraq has been the radical odd-man-out in Mideast politics, yet internally they have made the country stable and wealthy, granted the Kurds limited self-rule, wooed their Shi'ite majority, and granted fresh rights to women. *Baluchistan,* with cultural but not political boundaries inside Iran, Afghanistan, and Pakistan, seethes with frustrated hopes of achieving its own autonomous territory. This situation underscores the threat of intervention implicit in the Russian occupation of Afghanistan.

The age-old struggle for dominance of the Arab heartland had its modern phase as Egypt strove for that control with unstable alliances with Syria and Southern Yemen. *Syria* to the north and Libya to the west have had their dreams of supremacy among the Arab States challenged by restive *Iraq,* which envisions a single Arab nation from the Atlantic to the Persian Gulf—with Baghdad at its head. These winds of aspiration are enough to stir the leaves of memory among the long-gone Assyrians and Persians, Romans and Byzantines, and to cause the Abbasid caliphs to stir in their Baghdad tombs.

While the *Gulf sheikdoms,* apprehensive of Iran's Shi'ite fervor, watch the oil flow out and the credits roll in, *Kuwait* has replaced Beirut as the region's financial clearing house. *Saudi Arabia, Jordan,* and various Gulf states have contributed over $30 billion in aid to help Iraq stem Iran's drive to export her brand of Islamic fundamentalism. Alone among the Arab states, *Oman* leads the way for the recently-formed Gulf Cooperation Council to welcome a discreet military presence in the region by the United States, as a counterbalance to the Soviet's potential threat. *Israel,* at peace with Egypt, has returned the Sinai peninsula to Egypt, but has repeatedly invaded *Lebanon* to curtail the military and terrorist activities of the Palestine Liberation Organization. Peace in the region seems at best a distant dream and in hoping for peace there and throughout the world we might well intone the Koranic phrase, *In sh'allah,* "God willing."

Chapter 7

South Asia: The Nations in Space and Time

Largely isolated from massive influxes of peoples for most of the past three thousand years, South Asia's resident populations of diverse cultures and technologies have gradually sifted themselves out by developing many unique patterns of speech and literature, dress and deportment, religion and ritual, philosophies and social values.

South Asia's many facets include sacred rivers and mountain peaks woven into a whole, as in the Ganges region where the climate graduates from tropical in the valley to one of perennial snow on the mountain peaks. Abject poverty contrasts with the wealth of modern moghuls; and the human panorama ranges from millenia-old villages to exploding new city slums. Ancient observatories and modern computers, jetliners and plodding oxen, soaring population and diminishing resources, tigers and plastics, sectarian demands and timeless contemplation, are but a few of the many intriguing facets which represent this land where the secular and the sacred are inextricably intertwined.

South Asia lies suspended like a great exploratory wedge reaching into the Indian Ocean from the mainland. India occupies most of the subcontinent's land mass. The adjacent territories are occupied by Pakistan on the west, Bangladesh on the east, Nepal and Bhutan to the north, and, like a teardrop pendant at the south, the large island of Sri Lanka (previously called Ceylon). To the southwest the Republic of Maldives occupies an archipelago of tiny coral islets. Geologically speaking, however, the Indian subcontinent is in fact thrusting into the Asian mainland, the most visible result being its northern boundary, where the spectacular and icy Himalaya mountains display a unique geologic and religious grandeur.

THE GEOGRAPHIC INGREDIENTS

Terrain

The vast wedge of South Asia, tilting slightly down towards its eastern coast, extends roughly 2,100 miles (3,360 km.) from northern Kashmir to Dondra Head at the southern tip of its pendant island, Sri Lanka (Ceylon), and reaches about 2,150 miles (3,440 km.) from western Pakistan to eastern Assam. The northern mountain ranges severely restrict access from the rest of Asia to the fertile plains below. Watered by the Indus, the Ganges, and the Brahmaputra and their tributaries, these plains support a vast population.

Seen from a space station, the broad Indo-Gangetic Plain is a vast intensely farmed area. Looking westward, sand, gravel, and rock are visible all the way to Arabia. To the north lie the great mountains. The Himalayas (Abode of Snows) and Mount Everest (or Chomolungma, Goddess Mother Mountain) are the sources of the life-giving water necessary for peoples working on the hot and humid plains below. South of the Indo-Gangetic Plain lies a huge triangle pointing into the Indian Ocean. In the center of this triangle lies the Deccan Plateau, partly fertile and partly wooded, which has for millenia separated northern India and its Indo-European speaking peoples from the Dravidian speakers of South India. Rimming the Deccan Plateau are the weathered mountains and hills called the Western and Eastern Ghats. Between the Ghats and the coasts lie the arable lowlands, those on the west being narrow, steep, and well watered, those on the east, fed by large east-flowing rivers, broad and fruitful. Offshore lie the islands; the nation of Sri Lanka; the remote Andamans and Nicobars, politically linked to India, but home to tribesmen culturally linked to southeast Asia; and southwest of India the Lakshadweep (or Laccadive) Islands; and the two thousand coral islets of the independent Maldive Islands. Reaching from the Maldives to the Pamirs, the mountains, plains, arid lands, and riverine valleys of South Asia are traversed and peopled by one fifth of the world's population.

Altitudinal Zones

The terrain of South Asia is extremely varied, and when the factor of a people's technology is added to the environmental factors of climate, soil, and altitude, interesting choices and blends of occupations often emerge.

Pakistan's mountains and plateaus are home to the interdependent economies of sedentary village farmers and of nomad agriculturalists. Other groups shuttle between seasonal niches in the environment which the farmers and agriculturalists do not exploit. Altitudinal residence and occupation distinguish between semipastoral ex-Tibetan peoples on the high mountains of Nepal and the Nepalese farmers in the valleys.

In Assam the Bengali farmers, recent arrivals in the lowlands of the Brahmaputra valley, are separated by forests as well as by language, customs, and religion from the Tibetan, Chinese, and Burmese-related tribespeoples living more sparsely and using a slash-and-burn agricultural economy in the densely wooded hills on each side of the river basin.

South Asia's ultimate low altitude region is found in the nearby Indo-Gangetic Plain. Here, between the Indus and the Brahmaputra, live over 500 million

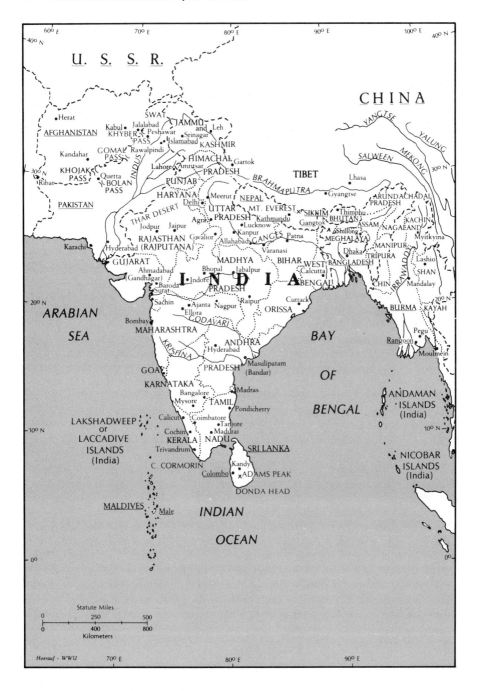

people, mostly farmers, in some of the world's oldest and largest cities and in several hundred thousand towns and villages.

Water and the River System

The geographic ingredient that touches most closely the life of South Asia is water. Water: the gift foaming out from the Himalayan gorges, the gift from the gods as rain, the gift from technology through sluice-gated canals. Water—the precious outpouring from deep tube wells, backyard pumps and rain-fed reservoirs—watched over with loving care from wooden or leather bucket to earthenware storage jar to brass teapot. Sometimes the storm brings too much and the soil along with the harvest is scoured away; sometimes the monsoon rains fail and the last drops merely dampen the desert sands.

Quite predictably, then, the contest for water rights fuels disputes all the way to the international level. Nevertheless, these confrontations also provide bases for conciliation, such as the agreements between India and Pakistan over the Punjab's rivers, and between India and Bangladesh over equitable allocation of the Ganges overflow, in both cases mainly for irrigation purposes.

Another use of water is for transportation. India's major rivers, besides providing for sailboat traffic, have about 3230 miles (5200 km.) of waterways navigable by mechanized vessels. Over one tenth of her 2670 miles (4300 km.) of canals are similarly navigable, and the substantial steps being undertaken to expand water transportation fit neatly into plans for the nationwide expansion of village and cottage industries. South Asia's three major rivers, the Indus, the Brahmaputra, and the Ganges, rise north of the Himalayas. Their very names contribute to the tapestry of life.

The *Indus*, which has given its name both to the country, India, and to its principal people, the Hindus, participates in still another name: the Indus together with its four main tributaries forms the Region of the Five Rivers, the Punjab (from punj- five and -ab waters). Unfortunately, massive irrigation projects without adequate drainage have resulted in the serious salinification of whole areas. (A Harappan water engineer might have commented: "I could have told you so, if you had asked me!") Procedures have been undertaken to lower the water table in an effort to drain off the accumulated salts.

The *Brahmaputra* (son of Brahma), navigable for four hundred of its miles (640 km.) at a bitter elevation of 12,000 feet (3,660 m.) in Tibet, changes its character after it emerges from the terrible gorges into Assam at 1,000 feet (305 m.) above sea level. Here in tropical heat and torrential rains, by slow and measured windings, it is again navigable for 800 miles (1,280 km.), providing new land, fertility, and transportation for multitudes of Bengali farmers. But, after entering low-lying Bangladesh, the river nourishes nature and man for nine months, then for three months spreads devastating floods throughout the jute- and rice-growing lands of the sea-level delta.

The name *Ganga* (anglicized as *Ganges*) derives from the root *gam*, "to go, to flow"; anything that flows could be *ganga*. Even the ocean is *ganga*. "Mother Ganga" together with its parallel tributary the Jumna, is indeed a river of life and is revered accordingly, for it has an identity of its own. Pilgrims converge upon Benares (Varanasi) for ritual purification as they bathe in the sacred waters of

Mother Ganga. Every such pilgrim is a Gangaputra, a "son of Ganga," and those whose remains are cremated on the stone platforms near the bathing ghats are especially blessed. (The word *ghats* means "a place of access," hence a road, stairway, or the scarp of a plateau.) The river touches other facets of Hindu life, for the traditional administration of oaths is by *gangajalam* (Ganges water).

The subcontinent's water cycle is replenished by the southwest monsoon rains sweeping in from the Indian Ocean. They curve northwest along both coasts from Cape Cormorin, where Mahatma Gandhi's ashes were placed in the sea following his assassination in 1948, and then proceed inland. The preliminary "mango showers" may occur in April and May, followed by the full onset of the monsoon season between June and September. By that time the seed grain has been planted in anticipation of the arrival of the rains. But if they come late or are insufficient, famine may result. In some parts of India, three months of warmth and lush growth follow the monsoon, then three months of the hot, dry season that sears the earth and scorches the plants; once again, the subcontinent awaits the rains. In other areas, the northeast or winter monsoon blows cool and dry, between October and February, and brings rain only to the coastal regions.

Communications

Throughout South Asia four channels of interregional communication have been used in the past: (1) overland through Persia to Taxila (near Rawalpindi); (2) by sea from the Indus to the Persian Gulf; and (3) through seaports on the southern coasts, and, in a minor fashion, (4) via the northern passes to Tibet. Oil tankers and cargo-passenger ships now ply the Indian Ocean routes; all-season motor roads now reopen most overland routes to diesel truck-and-trailer rigs; and airplanes leapfrog all boundaries. Moreover, the traditional face to face speech and horse courier post cannot compete with today's telephone, radio, and television communication, let alone with India's space satellites.

Population

The Indian subcontinent competes with China in having the world's densest population in a continuous large area. The extension of agriculture, plus immigrants, increased South Asia's population from about 181 million in the 300s B.C. to 253 million in 1881, and to 970 million in 1983. This means that on the Indo-Gangetic Plain and on some southern coastal districts with a high carrying capacity, the farmer growing rice, millet, or cotton is able to see three or four villages wherever he looks. A Bhutanese shepherd in the mountains, a cameleer in the Baluchistan desert, or a woodcutter in India's forests (one quarter of her land surface), cannot visualize a village of 560 persons in every square mile (216 every sq. km.) in every direction. Yet this in fact would be the effect of averaging the subcontinent's approximately 970 million persons over its area of 1.7 million square miles (4.5 million sq. km.). Depending upon the terrain—fertile plains, desert, or forest—and single or double crops of rice, the population density varies between 39 and 4,000 persons per square mile (15 to 1,544 per sq. km.). Yet the Maldive Islands, which must import all their rice, sugar, and wheat staples, manage to support about 1,217 persons per square mile (470 per sq. km.) on their 215 inhabited coral islets. And the population continues to grow.

TABLE 7-1 Population Density on the Indo-Gangetic Plain: A Comparison

REGION	AREA		POP. IN MILLIONS	DENSITY		COMPARATIVE DENSITY
	SQ. M.	SQ. KM.		SQ. M.	SQ. KM.	
Gangetic Plain[a]	245,000	634,550	500	2,041	788	1 : 1
Norway and Sweden	298,914	774,187	12.5	42	16	1 : 49
State of Texas	266,807	691,030	14.2	53	20	1 : 39
France, Belgium, and Netherlands	238,759	618,386	79.8	334	129	1 : 6
Pakistan[b]	310,414	803,972	85.5	276	106	1 : 7.4
Bangladesh[b]	55,598	143,999	92.6	1,665	643	1 : 1.2

[a] From the Indus to the Brahmaputra, 1,400 X 175 miles (2,240 X 280 km.)

[b] Pakistan and Bangladesh are listed to show comparison with the whole Plain. The western sector of the Plain includes part of Pakistan, and the eastern sector includes all of Bangladesh.

In large-scale perspective, South Asia's high net annual increase in population causes the countries' difficulties in providing sufficient food for their peoples, even with modern agricultural advances. For example, in contrast to the 5.8 per 1,000 increase in the United States during 1975–76, India increased 19 per 1,000, Pakistan 28 per 1,000, and Bangladesh 21 per 1,000. Although in India the birth rate has been considerably reduced from 41 per 1,000 in 1971, as of now some 25 babies are born each minute, or 13 million each year. Thus, the precarious balance between low-level subsistence and periodic famine when the monsoons fail continues unabated.

Looking from the inside, however, one perceives other facets of the reality. Governmental sponsorship of sterilization, contraceptives, raising the legal age for marriage, and other population control measures are set against some practicalities and intangibles. In practice, so many babies die that folk dynamics prescribe as many children as will provide the family with productive workers and male heirs to perpetuate worship on behalf of their ancestors. Children have long provided the peasants' only insurance against a penurious old age. Another intangible assumption seems to be that the children will somehow bring into being their own food, a folk belief perhaps stemming from the distant past when resources abounded.

The Peninsular Region

The peninsular area of South Asia contains several different culture regions. The Deccan plateau for millenia has separated northern India and its Indo-European speaking peoples from the solid block of speakers of the four main Dravidian languages in the south. Space-age activities and much heavy industry share the Deccan plateau with the 2,000-year-old Ajanta and Ellora caves. Extensive forests in the interior still harbor tribal speakers of Munda languages, as well as India's one remaining semi-nomadic pastoral group, the Dhangars, moving annually in a 300-mile circuit through a somewhat arid section. On the Tamil east coast lie the port of Madras and the temple city of Madurai, nourished by intensive double-cropping of extensive rice fields. On the west coast international Bombay contrasts with southern Kerala, the landing place of Phoenician, Roman, Arab, and Chinese merchants, and of Vasco da Gama whose voyage opened South Asia to European shipping.

The Offshore Islands

The palm-fronded islands off the coasts of south India each manifest their own personalities. They include: Sri Lanka, the Andamans, Nicobars, Laccadives, and Maldives.

Sri Lanka, almost joined to southeast India by the islets of Adam's Bridge, forms a gigantic teardrop of palm-fronded beaches, forests, and plantations leading up to a mountain core around 8,000 feet (2,450 m.) high. It lies just north of the equator, and its equable temperature of about 80°F (27°C), together with 40 to 200 inches (100 to 500 cm.) of seasonal and monsoon rains, keep the rivers running from the upland plantations of tea, coffee, and rubber to irrigate the lush ricefields on the coastal plains. Although the distribution of population is uneven, Sri Lanka's sixteen million Sinhalese and Tamils average 632 per square mile (244 per sq. km.) over the island's 25,332 square mile (65,610 sq. km.) area.

The isolated archipelagoes of the *Andaman* and *Nicobar* Islands, near the

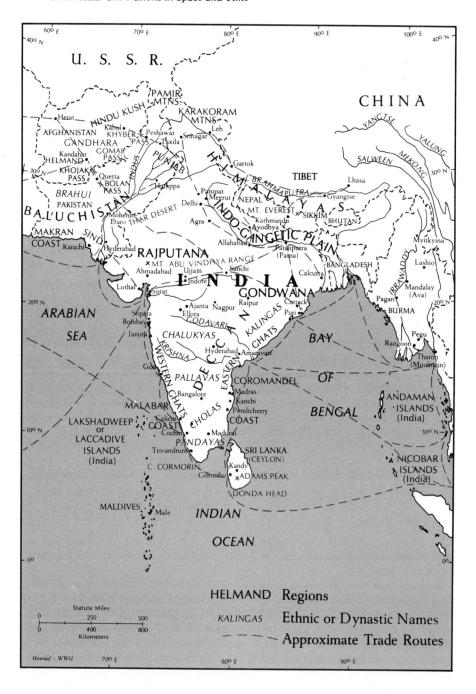

HELMAND   Regions

KALINGAS   Ethnic or Dynastic Names

- - - - -   Approximate Trade Routes

south coast of Burma, form a territory of India. The Andaman population of about 100,000 persons is comprised of a minority of technologically backward negritos and a majority of immigrants from India. The mixed population of some 23,000 Nicobarese, more akin to the Southeast Asians, were known historically for their expertise in the deadly but lucrative vocation of piracy and wrecking. Both archipelagoes are being developed by India, as are the *Lakshadweep* or *Laccadive* Islands to the southwest of India. The latter's 35,000 people, mainly Muslims of Arab origin, live principally by fishing around their ten inhabited coral islets totalling about 12 square miles (32 sq. km.).

Just to the south of the Laccadives the two thousand coral islets of the independent *Maldive Islands* stretch out for 550 miles (880 km.) north to south. The mostly Muslim population of over 170,000 embraces Sinhalese, Arab, and Dravidian peoples who live by fishing, subsistence agriculture, copra production, handicrafts, and tourism. The life-sustaining capacity of a coral island culture is dramatically illustrated here, as in the South Pacific, for the land area the Maldivians have to live on is smaller than the American city of Philadelphia—115 sq. miles (298 sq. km.).

THE HISTORIC INGREDIENTS

The cultural uniqueness of South Asia's regions has origins in the past. In broad terms the prehistory of the area parallels that of Southwest Asia. The Veddahs of central Sri Lanka in the late 1800s probably represented the life-style of South Asia's earliest inhabitants. The Veddahs hunted and gathered in their group areas, lived in rock shelters, and ignited their fires with flint and ironstone. Their quarry included the wolf, mongoose, rhinoceros, deer, and bear. Shamans effected cures, and ritual dances, restricted marriage patterns, and rich oral traditions organized and gave meaning to Veddah life.

The agricultural transformation began by 5000 B.C., and from the 3000s B.C. on, settled neolithic village life merged into the rise of towns and cities. The different scales of life from hunter-gatherer to villager to urban dweller were perpetuated in South Asia, and to some extent in Assam, well into the A.D. 1900s.

Indus Valley Civilization

The Indus Valley (or Harappan) civilization began some time after 3000 B.C., flourished around 2400 to 1750 B.C., and vanished some time after 1500 B.C. The scores of cities for a thousand miles along the Indus, including Harappa, Mohenjo-Daro (Mound of the Dead), and the seaport of Lothal, featured a planned rectangular format with drainage and sewer systems. Organized trade and art prospered. Invasion, floods, soil salinification, or a combination of factors have been blamed for the strange disappearance of this highly sophisticated people and civilization.

Puzzling also is the dominance achieved by the Indo-Aryan–speaking people soon after 1500 B.C. The "Indo-European theory" of waves of Aryan-speaking invaders obliterating the Harappan civilization, and then swamping the Dravidian-speaking inhabitants of the Bronze Age cities and farms on the Ganges plain, is seriously questioned. Some scholars think a slow process of incoming peoples brought about cultural and economic changes. Others think Aryans had been in Bengal and the Indus Valley, alongside other peoples, since about 4000 B.C. Aryans appear to have brought iron tools, horses, social hierarchy, and Sanskrit classics.

Between 1000 and 500 B.C. the Deccan participated in the Ganges culture based on settled agriculture. By 100 B.C. North India was in contact with the South, where enterprising people maintained extensive maritime trade relations with the Mediterranean world and with Southeast Asia. By 700 B.C. numerous small kingdoms existed in the Himalayan foothills. In one such kingdom within what now is Nepal was born Prince Siddhartha, who became the Buddha, the Enlightened One. However, Buddhism as a religion became widespread only under the Mauryas.

The Mauryas and the Kushans

In the 300s B.C. the monarchial system in South Asia made the transition to imperial government with the advent of the Mauryan emperors who ruled the northern plains region. Under Asoka (or Ashoka), greatest of the Mauryan rulers (272-232 B.C.) trade with China and Greece prospered. Asoka greatly expanded his empire through conquest, but ceased warring after converting to the Buddhist concept of ahimsa (nonviolence, kindness to all living things) and tolerance. He sponsored Buddhist monasteries and universities and the spread of Buddhism into Sri Lanka, Southeast Asia, and Gandhara (Afghanistan). Asoka improved irrigation and transportation in his kingdom, and in every important city set up great stone pillars inscribed with the Buddhist *Dharma*, or Law of Piety (compassion, liberality, truth, and respect).

During the five hundred years between 250 B.C. and about A.D. 300, South Asia's international trade with Egypt, Rome, and China flourished; her mathematicians brought to light the so-called "Arabic" numerals, the decimal place, and the concept of zero; and Greek sculptors from the kingdom of Bactria formalized the smooth beauty of the Buddha images. The Scythian king Kanishka of the Kushan dynasty (c. A.D. 78-320) facilitated the spread of Buddhism into Central Asia, and the Silk Road came again into prominence. By sea and land, ideas and customs passed both ways between India, Central Asia, China, and Rome. The inability of the West to match the opulence of the East is manifest in the trade with Rome. In exchange for silk, spices, ointments, and gems, Rome exported pottery, Greek wines, harem girls, and gold coins at a rate of about $4 million annually.

Gupta and Chola Dynasties

The *Gupta dynasty* (A.D. 320-c.500) of northern India saw the revival of classic Sanskritic learning, and the expansion of cities and universities. India became an international center of art, learning, and medicine. The Gupta dynasty was India's first "Golden Age"; and it existed at a time when Europe was in the depths of the "Dark Ages" following the fall of Rome.

India's second "Golden Age" was the *Chola kingdom* (800s-1251) in the south. Chola kings, and those in the half millenium preceding them, established colonies overseas and altered the political and cultural life of Southeast Asia by spreading Indian concepts of statecraft and royal courts to the region. Chola mer-

TABLE 7-2   Some Important Dates for South Asia

B.C.	
3000–1500 or 1000	Indus Valley civilization of Harappa and Mohenjo-Daro. Bronze Age in northern India.
1200–200	Composition of Sanskrit classics: the Rig-Veda (1200–800), Brahmanas (800–600), Upanishads, and Sutras (600–200), Dharmashastra or Code of Manu (c.250); Puranas date from Vedic times.
563–483	Siddhartha Gautama, founder of Buddhism.
c.500	Vijaya invades Sri Lanka (Ceylon).
300s	Agricultural developments lead to population increase.
321–185	The Maurya dynasty; reign of Asoka (272–232).
326	Alexander the Great invades the Punjab.
c.200–A.D. 300	Period of small competing states. Expansion of trade and Grecian-Gandharan art. Emergence of (modern) Hinduism.
200s	Buddhism and cultural arts brought to Sri Lanka.
A.D.	
48–320	Kushan dynasty of Scythian (or Yüeh-chih) rulers.
100s	Rise of Mahayana Buddhism in northwestern India.
320–490	Gupta dynasty.
606	Accession of Harsha (589–647).
600s	Buddhism introduced into Tibet from India and China.
1202–1526	Delhi Sultanate, including many semi-independent Muslim states.
1498	Portuguese captain Vasco da Gama arrives at Calicut.
1526–1858	Mughal Empire; Akbar reigns 1556–1605.
1757	British East India Company gains control of Bengal after battle of Plassey.
1858	British government takes control of India directly.
1920	Mohandas Gandhi leads Indian National Congress (party).
1947–1948	India and Pakistan become independent (1947); Sri Lanka (1948).
1965	Maldive Islands become independent.
1971	East Pakistan becomes independent as the nation of Bangladesh.

chants also traded to Arab ports and to Egypt. South India's cities, architecture, huge irrigation projects, dyes, tempered steel, and textiles placed her on a par with the most advanced civilizations of the period.

During the Golden Ages Hinduism deprived Buddhism of much of its singularity by proclaiming Gautama Buddha to be an incarnation of Vishnu. Thus, by implication the rest of Buddhist teaching and practice was incorporated into the system of Hinduism's all-inclusiveness. Buddhism also suffered two other disastrous setbacks: the wholesale destruction of Buddhist temples by the White Huns in the A.D. 500s, and the desecration of the remainder by the Muslims in the 1000s. From this time on it was only outside its Indian homeland that Buddhism continued to flourish.

The Muslim Invaders

By the A.D. 1000s the north had slumped into fragmented kingdoms and had become ripe for invasion. It did not have to wait long. The Muslim armies pressed in from Persia and Afghanistan and, after defeating Hindu forces in 1192, established the Sultanate of Delhi in 1202. For a brief period around 1330 India was united from Kashmir to Madura (Madurai) in Tamilnadu (Tamil land). But this unity was soon dissolved because Muslim administrative philosophy favored a tribal rather than an imperial form of government. The outcome was that the thirty-three sultans of Delhi belonged to five different dynasties, and independent states took shape in what ostensibly were simply provinces.

Tamerlane's swift (1398-1399) and brutal incursion as far as Delhi paved the way for the fifth dynasty of Lodi Afghans. In the continuing chaos of these fragmented principalities, India again was readied for change. It came in the person of Babur (1483-1530) who, losing his kingdom of Kabul, invaded India and founded the Mughal (from the word Mongol) empire in 1526. Babur's lineage derives from his maternal ancestor Genghis Khan, and on his father's side from Tamerlane. His most famous descendant was his grandson Akbar (meaning "the Great"). Akbar (1542-1605), a successful general and wise administrator, established India as a resplendent world power, and won the loyalty of the dominant Hindu population by religious tolerance. To these magnificent Mughal courts came the Europeans during their "Age of Exploration." Only too soon the vehemently conservative Aurangzeb (1618-1707) reversed the policy of tolerance. His fatally costly wars of inconclusive conquest, together with his oppressive efforts to convert non-Muslims to Islam, so wrecked the twin factors of fiscal stability and popular loyalty that the tottering empire soon broke up.

The European Impact

Waiting to grab their shares of the shattered empire were the European powers, who had gradually gained footholds in the centuries following Vasco da Gama's discovery of the sea route from Portugal to Calicut on the Kerala coast in 1498. Their competition with one another in the Indian Ocean and subcontinent, and elsewhere in Asia, reflected the struggle for power amongst the same nations on the European scene. In South Asia their immediate objectives were the selection and consolidation of trading stations and sailing routes through which the spices, silks, jewels, and handicrafts of the Orient could flow directly to Europe, and the silver and goods of Europe could be carried to the East.

Territorial acquisitions became necessary only as secondary considerations during the phase of consolidation. Beginning in 1600 England and France fought for control of Greater India; by 1819 Britain had become the paramount power in the Indian subcontinent. After the so-called Indian or Sepoy Mutiny of 1857 and 1858, which actually reflected widespread national protest against alien economic and political controls, the British Government abolished the private East India Company and assumed direct control from London under a Viceroy and Council. English was established as the official language of education and government, and of the legal system which was superimposed upon Indian customary and princely judicature. The centuries-old aggressiveness of the Maratha warriors, the militant Sikhs, the restless Pathans, and the neighboring Afghans was controlled only at the cost of a series of wars. South Asia became a whole at peace with itself.

Unfortunately, England and Europe from the mid-1800s were capitalizing on their machine-age technology and mass produced goods, and held India as a hostage market. But the accompanying leaven of new educational and liberalizing philosophies, which described Western-style democracy, individualism, economic freedom, and equal opportunities for all persons, became an intellectual and social ferment. In due course, this ferment would finally remove the rule of England (the

BOX 7-1   *SOME NON-INDIAN RULERS OF NORTHERN INDIA*

Persians and Scythians	500s–300s B.C.	Northwest India
Greeks	327–325 c. 200–130	Northwest India, Punjab
Tocharians (the Kushan dynasty)	A.D. 76–c. 450	Central Asia to Northwest India
Sakas and Parthians	78–320	Western India
White Huns (Hephthalites)	c. 450–533	Northwest India
The Muslims:		
Arabs	711–12	Sind
Afghan Ghaznavids	977–1186	Upper Gangetic plain
Afghans (Sultanate of Delhi)	1192–1526	Northern India
Turkic Mughals	1526–1858	All India
Europeans (British)	1600s–1947	All India

Note: Preindependence India included Pakistan, India, Bangladesh, and Sri Lanka (Ceylon).

British Raj) and would also lead to the subsequent dissolution of the unity of the subcontinent.

Confronted with the twin factors of modernization and Westernization, the Indian soul replied, Modernization—yes; Westernization—no. The emerging middle class of businessmen and upper-class intellectuals organized the all-party Indian National Congress in 1885, and the Muslim League of India in 1906. Mohandas K. (Mahatma) Gandhi, Jawaharlal Nehru, Mohammed Ali Jinnah, and others led the nation through much travail to eventual independence. The historic and current differences between the Hindu and Muslim religions, values, and ways of life led directly to separate national identities. Pakistan proclaimed its independence on August 14, 1947, as West Pakistan (the general region of the Indus Valley) and East Pakistan (East Bengal). India declared its independence on August 15, 1947, and Ceylon (later renamed Sri Lanka) on February 4, 1948. The Maldive Islands retained its connection with England until July 26, 1965. After civil war and war with India, East Pakistan declared itself independent as the new nation of Bangladesh. India, Sri Lanka, and Bangladesh chose to retain membership in the British Commonwealth of Nations.

SOME PATTERNS OF SOUTH ASIA

Social and Cultural Development

Over the millenia South Asia developed several characteristics which have persisted to the present day. Already there was *layering,* the superimposition of one occupation, religion, class, and/or community upon another. Group and areal *identification on the basis of language* existed between speakers of various Aryan, Dravidian, and tribal languages. *Fragmentation* existed because of the very separation of substantial language groups from each other. By 1000 B.C. the various *regionalisms* were established: North vs. South; East vs. West; coastal vs. inland and riverine blocs; and mountains or hills vs. plains. Despite group and regional antipathies, however, a fifth characteristic, a *latent unity,* was present in the actual permanency of the various communities, and the spread of region-wide languages, customs, and skills. These factors continue, and remain today in their national matrices. For each nation today endeavors to cultivate a *national consciousness,* exemplified by India's concept of "Indianness" and by Pakistan's preservation of Islamic integrity.

A Multiple-layered Civilization

In contrast to the societal structuring of the other regions of Asia, South Asia has built up its unique identity layer upon layer into a layered civilization. The following five aspects of culture serve to illustrate this layering:

Locational. Because the successive groups of invaders entered from the north and northwest, the earlier peoples tend to be found towards the south and the borderlands, the newer arrivals in the north and northwest.

Religious and temporal. The religions of South Asia are layered in regard to time of establishment. The early indigenous peoples revered nature spirits and spirits of ancestors (animism). Later came Vedic Hinduism, Jainism, Buddhism, Islam, Sikhism, and European Christianity, in that order. (See Table 8-3 in Chapter 8.)

Social. Caste and class are the principal indices of social rank in South Asia, together with the customary occupation of the group or individual. Caste ranking proceeds upward from the lowest nonvarna castes (the Harijans or Children of God, their 82.5 million in 1978 comprising 15 percent of the population) to the Sudras, Vaisyas, Kshatriyas, and Brahmins. Class is more subtle, since it crosses all caste lines according to degrees of wealth, education, or office. The customary occupations of the groups possess prestige graded upward from the hunter-gatherer tribal peoples, the Dhangar pastoralists, the swidden horticulturalists of Assam, to plow agriculturalists everywhere, and finally to those in industry, administration, and officialdom.

Historical. Invasions and the alternation of native and foreign dynasties have brought into the region diverse peoples and religions, innovations and ideas, and, alas, disruptions and devastations.

Political. Forms of social control have graduated from tribal chieftainship to city states, kingdoms, and empires, and from various forms of autocracy to modern military and nonarchial regimes that suspend their constitutions, and to the parliamentary governments of India and Sri Lanka.

The accumulated effect of all these layerings has resulted in an interesting paradox: although these many peoples, with all their differences, have long been similar in general culture, they have remained fragmented in social structure. Nevertheless, the present situation of seven nations both independent and inter-dependent constitutes hopeful grounds for establishing an amicable future in South Asia.

Chapter *8*

South Asia:
Society and the Sacred

In providing many of a person's basic ideas and principles, religion guides much of his or her daily conduct. So for multitudes of peoples in South Asia and elsewhere around the world, religion is indeed a principal foundation of their societies. Therefore, this chapter first presents in brief outline some of religion's outstanding features as found in South Asia, and then discusses the influence of religions on South Asian society.

WHAT IS SACRED OR SECULAR?

Different peoples have various definitions of what they consider sacred or secular, religious or practical. Whatever these distinctions may be, they are both doctrinal and social, personal and sensitive.

Hinduism, Islam, and Christianity, for instance, are all exclusive in regard to membership, although on different grounds. With a few exceptions, a person wishing to become a Hindu would be told one must be born a Hindu. A person desirous of becoming a Muslim or a Christian would need to demonstrate faith in their respective tenets. The person intending to become a Buddhist would find there is no place in its system for "membership"; one simply worships in the Buddhist way.

While Hinduism has a monistic core, its public manifestation is polytheistic. Hinduism will accommodate within its fold other faiths and manners of worship of any or no deity, will reverence as sacred all living fauna, and readily portrays persons and animals in religious art. Islam and Christianity are monotheistic and are doctrinally exclusive of other faiths. In general they are neutral towards fauna and, while Christian religious art may include every form of life, orthodox Muslims must limit art to flora and geometrical forms.

Delving further, we find that the extremely sensitive caste distinctions (described later in the social section of this chapter) are intimately tied to Hinduism's hierarchical and ritual differences in religious sanctity and social prestige, yet they are irrelevant to the Buddhist, Muslim, and Christian faiths. This is why over the centuries and in recent years large numbers of lower caste Hindus have turned to different religions to escape from the dominance of the caste system. Moreover, when Hindus see a Muslim slaughter a cow their religious convictions are offended, and when Muslims see a low caste Hindu eating pork their social prejudices are revolted. All the convictions discussed above run deep and the concurrent behaviors are deeply embedded, so that reactions to such repetitive contacts tend to run along three lines: (1) communal violence such as flared during the Partition massacres in 1947; (2) compartmentalism, wherein each strictly minds his own business; and (3) apathy, in which probing questions are not asked.

SUPERNATURALISM: THE CORE OF RELIGION

"The term 'supernatural' refers to the area of human experience that lies outside the natural world. It is outside the scope of technological manipulation of the material world, and outside the range of the theories and techniques of the natural and social sciences. By this definition, the natural and the supernatural viewpoints involve two separate areas of human knowledge and experience, and neither is explainable in terms of the other" (Anastasio 1965). This is a Western assessment. Most non-Western societies would accept these "two areas" as interlocking aspects of one whole universe, as distinguishable but not "separate." Each fulfils its allotted function in the total environment.

Belief in the supernatural is a human characteristic common to all societies. However, societies and individuals hold different criteria for what is sacred (or holy), secular (profane, worldly, ordinary), and taboo (to be avoided as polluted or abstained from because "sacred"). Magic, science, and religion add to the complexity of ideas. Magic and science are both used to manipulate the natural world, so some class them as secular. Others say magic uses supernatural means, and so they class magic with religion. The distinctions become blurred, and the practices often overlap. Even scientists are ready to admit that their investigations include questions such as where did the universe and its contents come from, what is to be the end of it all, and what is its usefulness? These are the same questions that philosophers and theologians of tribe and nation have been asking around camp fires and altar fires from the days of cave paintings to the days of nuclear heat and computer printouts.

Religion enters into many facets of individual behavior, family customs, community festivals, and temple worship. Life and death, morality and ethics, values and norms of behavior, even the conscience of the individual, may be illuminated and explained by reference to religion. When sickness strikes, when technology fails to bring relief, when the environment and its useable resources are inadequate to the situation, then supernatural aid may be invoked by means of magic, divination, prayer or rituals performed at home or temple.

Society may also utilize supernatural sanctions to stratify its members into rigid social classes. Even political institutions may be sanctified by supernatural authority, as with the "divine right of kings" (to rule) in Europe, and the once accepted divine descent of the imperial lineage of Japan.

THE SACRED: THE RELIGIOUS UNDERPINNINGS OF SOCIETY

Animism

While many of Hinduism's reported "300 million deities" may be philosophically subsumed under one or two principal deities—as incarnations or emanations of Brahman or of Vishnu and Shiva (Siva)—multitudes relate to prehistoric forms, places, and beliefs. That is, they are manifestations of the ancient and worldwide habit of endowing the phenomena of nature and one's ancestors with some form of life, will, or personality.

From Vedic times and earlier, before 1000 B.C., the common people made images of the godlings they venerated, and of the symbols of sex and of a mothergoddess. The godlings included nature spirits, such as the Muslim *jinns,* and supernaturals associated with animals and snakes, trees and rocks, and spirits of ancestors. These spirits were to be placated rather than adored, and to be appeased with blood sacrifices of bull or goat, pig or chicken, in some cases even humans. Veneration of gods of earth and sky, wealth and sickness, was expressed variously by markings on face or body, and often at wayside shrines with bowls of incense. The attempt to provide protection against malevolent spirits and other misfortunes commonly was represented by medals or silver rings around the neck, by mystic writings, or by talismans in the pocket. Horoscopes supposedly helped the individual watch out for danger.

BOX 8-1 *ANIMISM*

ANIMISM has been defined as a belief in spirits, including the spirits of the dead, as well as those of nonhuman origin. This general definition usually excludes the beliefs and ceremonies of the major organized religions.

Animism includes beliefs in spirit beings, souls, and ghosts, of all varieties, helpful or harmful, ethical or mischievous, together with the rituals and spells, persons and practices, calculated to exorcise them, seek their favor, or manipulate them for public or private purposes. Famous men, vigorous trees, strange rocks, strong charms, the stars, and major phenomena of nature, are considered to possess a desirable and obtainable vital power or life force. Magic, witchcraft, palmistry, divination, and horoscopes are some of the methods used to obtain the desired protections and benefits.

Animism, like all religions, helps individuals to cope with their environment and to reinforce the standards and goals of society.

In animistic practices names can be used like charms and literature like incantations. It has been said that the hymns of the *Rig Veda,* when properly recited by a trained priest and accompanied by proper manual actions, are irresistible—the natural elements, demons, and gods are thereby subdued by "the cosmic power of sound." Astrology and horoscopes are still used almost universally to match Hindu couples for a stable marriage. Shamans, by whatever name they are called, who are possessed by spirits or enter into trance states, act in many religions as intermediaries between the supernatural world and client persons or communities.

The various forms of animism help people in many societies to cope with the otherwise inexplicable and intractable aspects of their environment. Animism, sometimes called superstition, sometimes folk religion, often underlies many of the outward observances of the major religions.

HINDUISM

Most ancient among the major religions, dominant in the world's largest democracy of India, complex in its tolerant inclusiveness, Hinduism has affected the human view of the universe in countless ways. Coming from Old Persian Hind/Hindu, meaning "the River" Indus, and so designating India also, the word Hindu now refers to adherents to the Hindu faith.

BOX 8-2 *HINDUISM*

Brahman the Absolute, the formless and causeless Beingness, gives rise to the operation of the universe, the eternal *dharma* of responsibility. This operation is conceived as the *samsara* cycle of the Wheel of Time, and the rebirth of souls according to the personal activity or *karma* of the individual. Liberation or *mukti* from this cycle to merge into Brahman is termed *moksha* or "salvation."

Humans are considered a "layered being" composed of body, conscious personality, individual unconscious, and eternal being or *Atman.* Human wants include the fulfilment of pleasure, success, responsible duty, and liberation. A program is provided.

The Four Paths to the Infinite include (1) the Way of Knowledge (*jnana yoga,* the self-realization of the Atman-Brahman within one), (2) the Way of Love (*bhakti yoga,* realization of this divinity through unflagging devotion and intimacy), (3) the Way of Work (*karma yoga,* realization through daily duty and intention), and (4) the Way of Meditation (The Royal Way, *raja yoga,* realization through psychological activities of the total person, body, mind, and spirit).

Deities (Brahma the Creator, Vishnu the Preserver, and Shiva the Destroyer) and their multiple incarnations lead the soul from this illusory world (*maya*) to Brahman. Rituals and rules supply guidelines and procedures.

Principal Scriptures: The Four Vedas, the Brahamanas, Upanishads, Code of Manu, also the Bhagavad-Gita, the Epics, and Puranas.

A Set of Premises

The set of premises into which Hindus are born govern their philosophy of life, religion, and society. Central to all is the cyclical, repetitive turning of the Wheel of Time, and the transmigration of souls or the cycle of repeated births of humans and animals. Since both humans and animals are considered to have been humans in some prior existence, their present state is assumed to be the effect of each individual's actions done previously, and actions now taken will in turn reap their effect in the next existence or rebirth.

The Hindu Trinity

In modern times Hindus speak of Brahman as the Supreme World Spirit—eternal and infinite, absolute and neuter—the essence of all things. Without Brahman nothing would exist. Three personifications of Brahman are particularly honored: Brahma the Creator, Shiva the Destroyer, and Vishnu the Preserver or Renewer. Kali, the awesome consort and also the manifestation of Shiva, and two manifestations of Vishnu, Rama the hero of the Ramayana epic, and Lord Krishna the philosopher-driver of Arjuna's chariot, are the three principal incarnations of the Hindu Trinity. Gautama the Enlightened One (Buddha) is said by Hindus to be the third incarnation of Vishnu. The principal literature concerning these matters is contained in the classics briefly summarized in Table 8-1.

Reality and Illusion

The finite realm that humans consider this present observable world of reality is *maya,* an illusion that tricks many humans into thinking it is true and permanent. However, Hinduism does not deny that this *is* the world we live in, and allows that it is to be treated with respect and reason. But preparation should be

TABLE 8-1   Principal Works of Hindu Classical Literature

TITLE	APPROX. DATE	GENERAL CONTENTS
Four Vedas	1000 B.C.	Early period of nature worship and the war god Indra.
Brahmanas	800–600 B.C.	Priestly rituals, sacrifices, prayers, and spells.
Upanishads	600–300 B.C.	Philosophic Hinduism, unity of the universe; only the Brahma is unchanging and real.
Code of Manu (Dharmashastra)	250 B.C.	Legal code for religion, society, women, daily conduct.
Epics and Puranas	400 B.C.–250 A.D.	The epic poems: Mahabharata (Great King Bharata) and Ramayana (Life of Rama). Composed at various dates.
Mahabharata	300 B.C., & various dates	The futility of war; the intrafamily war between the Pandavas and the Kauravas; discussions on religion.
Ramayana	300 B.C.	Story of Rama (Vishnu) and wife Sita and conflict with Ravana the demon-king.
Puranas	Various dates	Creation stories and devotional material.
Bhagavad-Gita	A.D. 200s	Mystic dialogue between Arjuna and Krishna concerning God, worship, and the assigned duties of man. (A part of the Mahabharata.)

made by every person for leaving it and finally merging with the Infinite Reality. There are the "Four Paths to the Infinite" (as shown in Box 8-2).

From Yogi to Sannyasin

Whichever Path *yogi*-followers (with a few exceptions all are male) choose they must be steadfast thereon as they pass through four stages. The yogi-followers begin as students for twelve years. Their second stage is lived for twenty or thirty years as a married householder, being productive in family, vocation, and community. Many stop at this stage and go no further. Those who continue retire from active participation in the home, and develop the potentials of their inner Self, perhaps as a recluse, in stage three. The fourth stage is that of the *sannyasin,* "one who neither hates nor loves anything," and is "identified with the eternal Self." At the end of life the follower participates according to his or her *karma* in the *samsara* cycle of reincarnation. The goal is union with the Infinite . . . the goal is

FIGURE 8-1   General Hindu view of the "self."

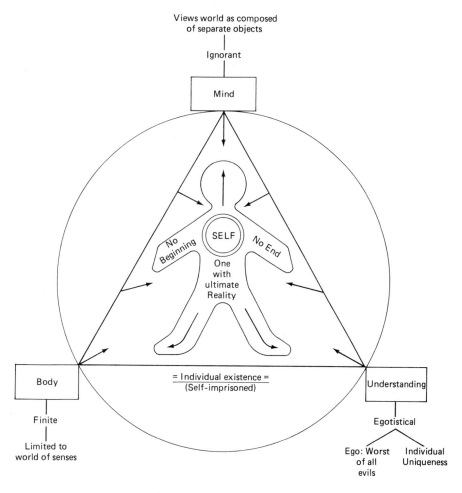

good, the way is benign, the temptations and tempests are but tests, and the Brahman is the ever-present Reality. In orthodox belief only men can find release from rebirth; all women must be born again. But some of the *bhakti* "devotion" movements maintain that women as well as men, of any caste, can through extraordinary devotion to a deity find release from rebirth. Hinduism acknowledges many paths to the same summit, and many deities and spirits and prophets, or none, as guides to the aspirations of humanity for relationship with Deity, by whatever name Ultimate Reality is known. These various aspects of Hinduism are found in its sacred scriptures. Two principal sects have diverged far enough to be considered separately: Jainism and Sikhism.

JAINISM

Affected by the extremely pessimistic view of the 500s B.C.—that this life is a defiled and unpleasant existence—both Gautama and Mahavira turned from belief in a multitude of deities to the goal of perfecting the Self. Both practiced ascetic self-discipline on a rational basis toward this end. Gautama became the founder of Buddhism (to be considered later). Mahavira (Great Hero) became the leader of the Jains (conquerors—that is, over imperfection) as an offshoot of Vedic Hinduism about 570 B.C. Philosophically, Jains consider the Buddhist doctrine that all things are transitory as contrary to the facts of space, time, and matter. Jains maintain that reality and truth are many sided. Belief in the reincarnation of the soul animates members of the Digambara ("sky-clad" or naked) sect who own nothing, not even clothes, and who deny salvation to women. The main body of the three million Jains belong to the merchant castes in Gujarat and Bombay, and stress *ahimsa* or nonviolence towards all living things of every description.

SIKHISM

Sikhism also began as a reform movement within Hinduism. Guru Nanak (1469-1538) tried to blend Moslems and the Hindu castes into one brotherhood, teaching that there is one true, universal God. The myriad deities and images of Hinduism were rejected together with rituals and professional priests, but some aspects of the caste system and the transmigration of souls as part of the progress toward God were retained. Beliefs similar to Islam include monotheism, the equality of believers (the word "Sikh" means disciple), and emphasis upon a disciplined moral life of abstention from practices harmful to the body, such as drinking and smoking. Married life is the social ideal. Social and political pressures resulted in Gobind Singh (1666-1708), the tenth Guru, organizing the Sikhs into a military confederacy. Sikhs were to add Singh (lion) to their new names, and to keep the five Ks: *kesh* (long hair), *kangha* (comb), *kachha* (military shorts), *kara* (steel bangle), and *kirpan* (saber or long knife). Written in the Punjabi language, the *Granth Sahib* embodies their sacred scriptures and is kept in the Golden Temple at Amritsar. When partition took place in 1947 between predominantly Hindu India and Islamic Pakistan, the Sikhs found themselves living on both sides of the new border. Despite their general likeness to Islam in creed and practice they still were non-Muslims, and so joined India. Today some eight million Sikhs occupy their own state of Punjab northwest of India's capital city of New Delhi.

BUDDHISM

Humankind's Sickness and the Buddha's Diagnosis

Buddhism began with a man, "the man who woke up." Siddhartha Gautama, prince of the Sakya clan of Nepal (c. 563-483 B.C.), forsook his luxurious palace when he found that human ways of life were characterized by sorrows and sickness and ended in death. In endeavoring to find an answer through the intensities of philosophic questionings, asceticisms, and bodily mortifications, he concluded that none of these quests were the Way to Reality. About 528 B.C. at the age of thirty-five he experienced Enlightenment: that out of evil comes evil, and out of good comes good. It was from this experience that he was called the "Buddha" (the awakened or enlightened one). His diagnosis of humankind's troubles was enshrined in the *Four Noble Truths.*

BOX 8-3   *BUDDHISM*

Core of Doctrine

The Four Noble Truths

The Presence of Pain: Human life is characterized by pain, sorrow, and suffering (*dukha*), and estrangement from Ultimate Reality.

The Cause of Pain: This twofold condition results from *tanha* (selfish desires for private fulfilment; cravings).

The Cure for Pain: The cure is to eliminate *tanha.*

The Cessation of Pain: The prescription for the elimination of *tanha,* and therefore of the *dukha* "thirst for existence," is to follow the Eightfold Path of right views, right thoughts, right speech, right action, right livelihood, right effort, right awareness (mind control), and right concentration.

Scriptures: The Tripitaka or Three Baskets.

Main Branches

Hinayana, the Lesser Vehicle, or Way of the Elders (*Therevada*), preserves simple reliance on the Scriptures and disciplined life.

Mahayana, the Greater Vehicle, includes temples and images, lifetime priesthood, salvation, judgment, and the hereafter.

Lamaistic or *Tantric Buddhism,* features *lama* priests and *tantra* manuals of instruction, permanent priesthood, and dramatic plays.

Philosophic Buddhism, exemplified by Zen Buddhism in Japan. Buddhism like a ferryboat conveys the believer from this "real" world of sense to the far shore of transcendent and eternal Enlightenment where no dichotomies exist—Nirvana.

Realism and a Solution

This perceptive diagnosis of the human situation led to several simple guidelines for life. First, this approach rendered valueless Hinduism's vast array of spirits, deities, incarnations, and their accompanying rituals and sacrifices. These he rejected because they were irrelevant to his diagnosis of and remedy for the human predicament. It was in this sense that the Buddha has been called atheistic. Hinduism would acknowledge his right to choose such an atheistic view, and still remain a good Hindu. What took him out of Hinduism forever was his rejection of the caste system and of the Vedas as incontestable Truth. Second, the guidelines necessarily included direct action at the root of the problem, that is, intense self-discipline over the aspirations (desires) and the expressions of the Self, whether physical, mental, moral, social, or spiritual.

In these realms of thought and action Gautama could be designated a social reformer, and the ideal man of disciplined integrity. Confucius would have recognized him immediately as the ideal *jun-zi,* the princely man. Of himself Confucius said that as of his older years he was conscious of only a few remaining peccadillos. Christ remained unchallenged when he asked, "Which of you convicteth me of sin?" In a more homely manner the founder of Islam, Muhammad, made no such claims, though he was indeed of unimpeachable personal character. Each in his own way presented a new approach to and standard for life. The record of the Buddha's life and teachings were written down later by his disciples (as was done also for Jesus Christ and Muhammad) in the Three Baskets (*Tipitaka* in Pali, *Tripitaka* in Sanskrit) and other classics in the Pali version of Sanskrit.

In all of South Asia today the most significant numbers of traditional Buddhists are found among the Sinhalese of Sri Lanka, as well as some three million neo-Buddhists in India, and some Tibetan and Sinitic Buddhist peoples living close to the south face of the Himalayan mountains. Religion colors or dominates so much of South Asian life that it is essential to consider some major aspects of the practice and application of religion in society. Prominent among these in South Asia is caste.

THE SECULAR: THE OUTWORKINGS OF RELIGION IN SOUTH ASIA

Caste

The origins of caste are lost in antiquity. Some researchers of Indian culture have found the beginnings of distinctions amongst the incoming Aryans, whose priests were Brahmins, their warriors Kshatriyas, and their helpers Vaisyas. Some believe the beginning of distinctions existed in the separatist relationships assumed to have occurred when the southward-moving Dravidians came into residential contact with the hunting and gathering Veddas of the central and southern forests. The agricultural and urbanized Dravidians differed in occupations, social customs, food, and eating habits from the less advanced Veddas. These points of distinction may have become permanent, and abstention from intermarriage completed the pattern of separation. When the Indo-Aryan–speaking peoples dislodged or assimilated the Dravidians in the Ganges valley, these new "lords" imposed their language (Sanskrit), priesthood (Brahmins), and social superiority upon the region. Gradually, as the Aryan Brahminism took precedence over other facets of religion, and the Aryan conquerors remained in military and governmental control, the social distinctions crystallized into a hierarchy of "color," religion, warriorhood, and service. Ultimately it became that unique and comprehensive system in India known as caste, wherein every person has a divinely assigned place (on the basis of personal *karma*) in the ordered functioning of society. Some of the distinctions and inequities are succumbing to modern ways of life, but the system itself, being based on grass-roots allocation of status and role for everyone, will probably remain relatively intact for a long time to come.

The Varna Categories

Since the two Indian words *varna* and *jati* are both commonly translated into English as "caste" it is necessary to make a distinction between them. *Varna*, meaning "color," designates the four main social divisions of Indian society: Brahmins, Kshatriyas, Vaisyas, and Sudras. These will be referred to as the Brahmin *varna*, etc. The approximately three thousand divisions within the *varnas* are called *jatis*. Within the Sudra *varna*, for example, there are blacksmiths, goldsmiths, stonemasons, and temple builders, etc., all with their own subdivisions. The official term for the non-*varna* people, the "outcastes," is "Scheduled Castes"; the divisions within this sector of society also are *jatis*. For these reasons, the *jatis* will be called castes.

Highest of the varna, the *Brahmins*, are considered ritually pure and so are eligible for *moksha*, salvation in the sense of release from the cycle of reincarnation, and so for union with the Absolute. They alone are formally entitled to expound the Hindu scriptures and to perform priestly ceremonies. The *Kshatriyas* are the ruler and warrior caste, generally including the raja families and soldiers. The *Vaisyas* compose the merchant and trading sector of the community. The lowest of the varna, the *Sudras*, provide the service personnel of farmers, artisans, workers: these are the actual castes and subcastes. The same system of *jatis* and their subdivisions operates amongst the outcastes, that is, the ceremonially unclean castes, who constitute a *de facto* fifth major category. To get away from the derogatory connotations of these two names for them, (and the other common appelation of "untouchables") and by changing the name help to raise their status and acceptability in society, Mahatma Gandhi called them *Harijans, children of God.*

Specific Castes—the Jatis

The word *jati*, which means "type" or "species," may designate any group that has habitually distinctive customs, but usually refers to groups sharply restricting intermarriage, having distinctive dietary practices, essential rituals, occupations, or religions. Each *jati* has a special place in society, fulfilling an appointed and hereditary niche, contributing its own particular activity to the well-being of the total community or nation. In theory, India's caste system provides for the perfect functioning of society, each member filling a designated role. In practice, the foibles and faults of man introduce elements of economic and human exploitation that mar the good intentions, immobilizing men and women and their unborn children in hierarchical classes graded from polluting to sacred. There is a religious

TABLE 8-2   The Varna Castes As Social Categories

THE VARNAS	CLASS OF OCCUPATION	RELATION TO THE VEDIC SCRIPTURES*	ENTITLED TO THE SACRED CORD*	RITUALLY "CLEAN"
BRAHMINS*	Priests	Expositors	Wearers	Clean
KSHATRIYAS*	Warrior-Rulers	Readers	Wearers	Clean
VAISYAS*	Merchants	Hearers	Wearers	Clean
SUDRAS	Service Occupations	Excluded	Non-wearers	Clean
HARIJANS	Low-level Occupations	Excluded	Excluded	Unclean

*The "twice-born" castes relate closely to the scriptures and the sacred cord. The ceremony wherein young males first don the sacred cord constitutes their "second birth," the beginning of their new life as caste members responsible for ritual obligations.

cement that binds the system into a cohesive entity. This cement is the belief that the accumulated characteristics, *karma,* of the person's previous life on earth, coming through the wheel of retributive reincarnation, has ordained the human or nonhuman form of existence being lived in this observable life now. So long as this belief in *karma* and reincarnation is held, so long will the present caste system continue to operate.

VARNA AND JATI IN VILLAGE LIFE

Interaction between varnas and jatis varies considerably, being more formal and strict in South India. Entertainment at a village feast, for example, may mean that the saltmaker invites the guests, and while the shepherd prepares the goat and the farmer carries the cooked food in the pot provided by the potter, the singer provides entertainment. Vegetarians, both Muslims and Hindus, may eat at the same feast, provided they eat from separate dishes and are seated in different lines. Vegetarians—Brahmin landowners and upper-caste persons—are clearly marked out from all castes and Muslims who eat any kind of meat. Marriage partners rarely cross varna lines, and usually are restricted to one's own jati. This often entails securing a spouse from another village up to 100 miles (160 km.) away. In many farming areas there is only just so much arable land, so land acquisition runs head-on into the concept of "limited good," that if one obtains some benefit there is another who is thereby deprived. This means that by hard work any person legally may acquire more land, but in practice a low caste stone worker may be forcibly prevented from buying good land. Residence likewise is often restricted by caste lines and by occupations, so that varnas and jatis commonly reside in clustered quarters in various sectors of the larger villages. One hundred and fifty years of contact with the modernizing world has not radically affected the caste system, although cross-caste contacts have increased and urban industries have created new occupations and opportunities for emancipation.

TABLE 8-3 Dated Overlays of Peoples, Dynasties, and Religions in South Asia*

RELIGIONS	DATES	PEOPLES AND DYNASTIES
Independence	1947	Separation of India, Pakistan, and Sri Lanka
European Christianity	1858	Direct administration by British government
	1763	Expulsion of the French, Britain dominant
	1611-13	British East India Company established first trading posts
	1526-1858	Muslim Mughal empire
Sikhism (in Punjab)	Early 1500s	
	1192-1526	Muslim Delhi sultanate
Zoroastrianism (Bombay)	700s	Muslim occupation of Sind area
Islam	600s	
	650-1206	Rival Indian dynasties
	c. 450-533	White Huns (Northwest India)
	320-500	Indian Gupta empire
Hinduism developed	200-400	
	76/120-c. 450	Scythian Kushan dynasty (Northwest India)
Apostolic Christianity	60s	
	A.D.	
		Greek and Indian dynasties
	B.C.	
	321-185	Indian Maurya empire
	326	Greeks under and after Alexander the Great
Jainism	500s	Indian dynasties
Buddhism	Circa 500	
Vedic Brahminism	1700s-1500s	Aryan dominance
	c. 3000-1000	Indus Valley civilization
	3200?	Dravidians
Animism	Prehistoric	Early hunter-gatherers

*Since this chart indicates the time-related sequence of imposed layerings, it should be read from the bottom up. The two outside columns relate directly to the dates, and only incidentally to each other.

THE JAJMANI SYSTEM

The *jajmani* system of India is a hereditary contract arrangement which provides mutual benefits between the sponsor and the contributing workers. A wide circle of farmers, artisans, and helpers (the *kamin*) provide their distinctive services to a wealthy patron (the *jajman*), who in turn personally looks after their general welfare. Although distinctive to India, the essence of this two-way pattern has parallels elsewhere. Note the interdependent relationships between the Bedouin sheik and his fellow tribespeople, the padrone system in some old-style Latin-American haciendas, and even the Japanese feudal lord and his military and peasant retainers.

In a village near Delhi, for instance, a Nai barber shaving a person once a week may service patrons in several villages. A Dhobi washerman, washing only clothes of high-caste or high-class families, may cater to the needs of a whole village. The kamin's rights to serve a particular jajman are like property, passed from father to son, or perhaps divided between brothers. Reward is usually in grain, preferred because of its high cost, and may be received daily, periodically, or only at harvest time. In these ways the system provides social standing, economic security, and protection from distress for the kamin, and provides for the jajman and his family the array of services needed by the large household of the landowner. The jajmani system functioned best in the preindustrial country villages, where the bulk of India's population lived and worked. Much of the traditional economic stability of each locale depended upon smooth operation of the jajmani system, since the very nature of the system required the cooperation of a wide variety of caste members. Today, more and more the kamin are leaving village service for wage-earning jobs elsewhere; and the jajman are using modern conveniences requiring less personal attention.

ISLAM IN SOUTH ASIA

Islam also has been a powerful organizer in South Asia. The peoples of what are now the northwest provinces had been Muslims for some time before Muslim conquerors entered North India, bringing with them new ideas of art, architecture, and governance, and developing a new language, Urdu. Most of the people of East Bengal (now the citizens of Bangladesh) and large blocs of Harijans converted to Islam to escape from political and caste pressures under Hinduism.

Nevertheless, if the early caliphs in Southwest Asia had been told that in 1,350 years there would be about 300 million Muslims in South Asia alone, they might have replied with a question: Why did it take that long? They expected a rapid military and a spiritual conquest when they raised their banners and set their armies rolling out of Arabia in the A.D. 630s. Estimates assume almost the total populations of Pakistan (92 million) and Bangladesh (98 million), and nearly 12 percent of India's 748 million to be Muslims. This total of about three hundred million people represents nearly 30 percent of the approximately 970 million South Asians, or about 11 percent of Asia's more than 2.7 billion persons.

Islam in India

Islam in independent India has been shaped by its Indian environment towards two views of the Muslim's place in society—one introverted, the other extroverted. The introverted Muslims separate from their non-Muslim neighbors in order to protect their religion and culture. The more responsible Muslims, however, view Islam not only as a privilege to be enjoyed in this world and the next, but as a trust also, a mission to be fulfilled by promoting truth and justice in a universal brotherhood. This includes promoting harmony and goodwill among believers in different religions. Each view in practice is founded on the principle of coexistence, not assimilation.

Since India is a secular state, its constitution guarantees freedom of belief, and the Muslim community has responded academically along two lines. Islamic seminaries train Muslims in theology and the relationship of Islam to life in a secular society. Voluntary associations also concentrate on the religious instruction of their children. Several secular colleges established by Muslim communities bring together both Muslim and non-Muslim students. The Jamia Millia Islamia (Muslim National University) in Delhi, headed for twenty-two years by Dr. Zakir Husain, later President of India, was founded to represent the composite culture of North India. This university, using Urdu as its working language, educates Muslim and Hindu young people in secular subjects and also in the religion of their choice. In addition, they learn the habits of refined behavior characteristic of North India.

Both the Hindu, who views the universe as an integrated whole, and the Muslim, who accepts a dualistic view of a combined religious and secular world, as well as an objective world to come, deserve commendation. Each in his or her own way is adapting a religion-based world-view to the increasing secularism associated with the modern industrialized world.

Chapter *9*

South Asia:
Society and the Secular

THE IMPACT OF MODERNIZATION

Machinery and Moral Values

Modernization is masses of new ideas, manipulative new philosophies, and, from the viewpoint of traditional religion murky new social and moral values. Modernization is also massive new machinery and miniscule new gadgetry. The pervading viewpoint of industry is mechanical and practical, just as its background of science is a data-based analysis of the material universe. In the areas of ideas and ideologies, Barbara Ward some years ago postulated her "Five Ideas Which Change the World": nationalism, industrialism, colonialism, Communism, and internationalism (Ward, 1959). To these a sixth idea must be added, individualism. The activities and effects of these six ideas constitute a continuing ferment in both developed and developing nations. Concurrently with the coming of machines and ideas came instant communications via satellite, films, and television, together with new fashions in dress and music, impressionistic painting and sculpture, and mutual-consent criteria for interpersonal relations.

What nation, looking back into its historical heritage, can find enough alternatives to match these invading changes, and thereby integrate them into a patterned modification of their existing culture? In a region such as South Asia, where the intricacies of interlocking diversities have become traditionally institutionalized, the transition into the modern world often involves soul searching. In cases where

TABLE 9-1   Six Ideas That Change the World

DYNAMIC IDEAS	TRADITIONAL CONTRASTS	DIRECT OUTCOME (*DE FACTO*)	FURTHER DEVELOPMENTS
1. *Nationalism*	Localism, tribalism	Republicanism	Nationwide citizenship and suffrage; Western-type democracy
2. *Industrialism*	Premachine labor	Urbanization	Technology, mass goods, banking, insurance, slums
3. *Colonialism*	Feudal independence	Modern nation-states	Western philosophies; rule of law; monetary system; secularism; impersonalism
4. *Communism*	Feudal peonage; constitutional monarchy; freedom and initiative	Totalitarian-communalism in human relations, politics, etc.	Regimentation; world division
5. *Internationalism*	Separatist states and alliances	Concept of "One World"	United Nations; (supra-)regional pacts; "nonalignment" and "Third/Fourth World" groups
6. *Individualism*	Multiple interlocking loyalties; person-to-person relations	"Dignity of the Individual"	Diversification, entre-preneurism, initiative; atomism; unrest; equalitarianism

Adapted and developed from Barbara Ward, *Five Ideas Which Change the World* (New York: W. W. Norton & Co., Inc., 1959). Used with permission of W. W. Norton & Company, Inc., and Hamish Hamilton Ltd.

religion has cemented together the hierarchy of occupations and the levels of social interaction, these modern occupations and interactions act like a solvent, causing the familiar patterns to become unstuck. Some individuals and some aspects of society merge rather smoothly into the new situations. Some are disoriented. Others are lost.

Problems of Survival

The societies which survive are the ones which are able to develop and manifest attitudes and energies tailored to the impact of modernization upon their self-identity and their self-worth. Long experience in intertribal feuding and competition for resources in Southwest Asia has enabled the Arab and other oil-producing nations there to cope efficiently with the infighting world of modern competition. With their background in group loyalty, the honing of *bushido* (Way of the Warrior) discipline, and of interacting technical skills, the Japanese drove themselves headlong towards the sunlit realms of equality and superiority among the world powers. They would agree certainly with Prime Minister Indira Gandhi's comment concerning the remedy for economic underdevelopment: "There is only one magic which

BOX 9-1   *THE OUTWORKING OF THE "SIX IDEAS"—ASIAN EXAMPLES*

1. *Nationalism*: Nations formed out of the dissolution of the Ottoman Empire, following World War I: Iraq, Syria, Lebanon, Jordan, Saudi Arabia, Yemen, and in 1948 Israel. . . . In 1947–1948 out of 562 princely states and provinces came India, Pakistan, and Sri Lanka; Bangladesh divided off from Pakistan in 1971. . . . Malaysia formed of Malayan and Bornean sultanates in 1963. . . . the island city of Singapore, 1965.

2. *Industrialism*: Singapore: free trade entrepôt, multiple small industries, sea and air transit center. . . . India: Tata Iron and Steel and textile industries, space satellites. . . . Japan: from hermit to industrial Hercules within 100 years . . . . Saudi Arabia: oil technology and revenues transformed desert kingdom to modern nation.

3. *Colonialism*: Modern nation-states of South and Southeast Asia.

4. *Communism*: Non-traditional regimes in China, Soviet Asia, North Korea; Vietnam probing into Laos, Kampuchea, and Thailand. . . . Local Marxist parties.

5. *Internationalism*: Afro-Asian Bandung Conference of "non-aligned" nations. . . . the Indian ocean partly Indian prior to A.D. 1500, then international, then British, now hopefully Indian again, with other Powers pressing in.

6. *Individualism*: Manifested in activities of political parties, labor unions, students; entrepreneurism; equality before the law. . . . Note as examples: Japan, India, Israel, Sri Lanka, in contrast to authoritarian governments.

will remove poverty, and that is hard work sustained by clear vision, iron will, and the strictest discipline." (India News, July 1975).

Afghanistan had an insufficient background of intergroup cohesion and of technological and managerial skills, and its general poverty has been sharply accentuated by the wholesale devastation of agriculture and village life by the occupying Russian troops. Behind their surrounding mountain walls *Nepal* and *Bhutan* have maintained a considerable degree of their accustomed isolation from outside influences and personnel. This isolation has had the benefit of softening the impact of a machine age for which their culture has not prepared them, by slowing the rate of change nearer to the pace of their rhythm of life. Even poverty sometimes turns a profit, for the *Maldive Islands* have so little to entice the modern entrepreneurs that they have been left largely alone. *Sri Lanka's* economy, though tied to the plantation system for its famous teas as well as rubber and coconut products, has been able to diversify sufficiently to maintain a healthy society. *Bangladesh,* bedeviled by floods and storms, still has desperate shortages of finances and foods for its expanding population. Nevertheless progress is being made in agriculture, fertilizer production, irrigation control, and transportation.

Muslim *Pakistan* and predominantly Hindu *India*, as nations with strong religious beliefs, have much in common with Judaic Israel, Muslim Southwest Asia, and Roman Catholic Philippines. Each of these nations is facing head-on the influences of modernization, whose interfaces of friction involve the sacred and the secular.

Each of the above religions deals both with matters of eternity and ultimate truth and with the conduct of daily life. Modernization, on the contrary, brings industry and social philosophies and activities strictly oriented to this present secular world. The expansion of machine-based industry, for instance, together with its insatiable demand for workers, leads to congregations of one-family wage-earners in urban sprawls such as Karachi and Calcutta. Modernization, then, is more than the acquisition of new factories and armaments; modernization is a packet that justifies its characterization as "the modernization of the soul." The essential problem is how to integrate the traditional value systems with the new values of modern progress, in order to promote the better life, in both sacred and secular contexts, that people desire. We turn now to the secular aspect.

GOVERNMENT

Form: Focus of National Identity

A nation's form of government usually is the product of its past history, its social characteristics, and such important considerations as religion, secularism, or some form of authoritarianism. In all of South Asia's seven independent countries the prevailing religions dominate their personal and social lives. So it is intellectually and politically significant that they have adopted quite different legal views of their national administrations. Pakistan is officially a religious republic while India is officially a secular, socialist republic. Sri Lanka established a presidential-parliamentary system similar to that of France. The two monarchies operate distinctively. Nepal's constitution gives the king strong powers, yet provides for a National Panchayat (parliament). Bhutan, slowly emerging from feudal isolation, has a hereditary royal line with a National Assembly and a State Council. The Republic of Maldives was ruled by a sultan from about 1100 to 1968, then by decree to 1978, and now operates with a national legislature.

Freedom: For or Against

A government is a national mechanism for organizing the use of the country's resources and for monitoring the interrelated activities of its citizens. In the universal tug-of-war between the rulers and the ruled, Asian countries have opted historically for monarchies, with clear class distinctions based on wealth, education, and power. The historical pressure of this traditional Asian pattern of government explains why some form of authoritative government—military, civil or religious dictatorships, guided democracies, or other authoritative regimes—spring up so easily whenever nationwide political turmoil or economic stress arises. Events in Pakistan, South Korea, the Philippines, Burma, Iran, and Iraq, from the 1950s on, illustrate the rise, the problems, and the procedures of authoritative governments.

Democracy—wherein the general populace freely chooses and changes its form of government, and chooses its own representatives to administer that government—never grew up in Asia. (The use of the words "Democratic" and "People's" by authoritarian, usually Marxist, regimes is based on their strictly authoritarian philosophies, and does not fit the definition given above.) Nations such as India, Japan, and Israel have striven valiantly to make the Western-type of democracy work. The free elections, for example, which resulted in the decisive ouster in 1977 of the Congress Party of India and its leader, Prime Minister Indira Gandhi, and in the subsequent repeal of her repressive measures by the incoming Janata Party, illustrate the working of a democratic purpose by India's people. Even more startling was the stunning upset victory of the Congress Party (I) in January, 1980, which returned to power the same Prime Minister—assassinated October 31, 1984.

Function: The Rocky Road to Reform by Law

India's Constitution, in assigning the scope and duties of the federal and state governments, made an unusual provision for curbing a state's possible slide into internal confusion or insolvency: the executive functions of the state can be suspended and the state placed under "president's rule" until order and/or solvency has been restored. This provision has been implemented in Kerala and other states on various occasions, apparently with beneficial results. But reform through law may have unforeseen side effects. In endeavoring to slow down the runaway growth of India's population, nationwide family planning, contraceptive measures, raising of marriage ages, and other steps were taken to reduce the fertility rate. When voluntary cooperation was judged too slow, the Congress ordered compulsory male sterilization in some areas. This measure helped precipitate the government's downfall in 1977.

In its concern for equalizing opportunities and benefits for the total population, India's land reform laws limited the *maximum* acreage which could be possessed by one person. Many of the landlords simply distributed their holdings among their family members, resulting in the dismissal of tenants from farms, and a great increase in numbers of landless laborers. Further, in endeavoring to stop division of land into miniscule and unprofitable inheritances, a *minimal* limit of land division was set; so the family members who got nothing also became landless laborers. When the earlier oppressive *zamindar* (landlord) system was outlawed, the previous tenants then had no social sponsor to cushion them in the days of distress and want. On the other hand, the outlawing of social discrimination on the basis of untouchability was a helpful ordinance.

ECONOMY

Unlike the form of government, the economy relates directly to the environment and its natural resources. Several broad topics have been selected for discussion: a general overview, a grass roots view, resources, irrigation, food, industry, science, and the rich and poor nations of South Asia. Most of the discussion centers on conditions in India, the varying situations there being illustrative of parallel or contrasting conditions elsewhere in South Asia.

A General Overview

In twelve months most South Asians earn the equivalent of between $35 and $200 (U.S. dollars), mostly as farmers with mixed results in grain crops. All seven nations concentrate on the production of cereals for their subsistence, yet all import some food grains and specialty foods. In Table 9-2 the principal nonmanufac-

TABLE 9-2 Trade and the Environment

COUNTRY	GENERAL ENVIRONMENT	EXPORTS	IMPORTS
Pakistan	Mountains to subtropical desert	Hides, cotton, rice, textiles	Grain, raw materials, consumer goods
Nepal	Mountains and narrow valleys	Products of forest and farm	Food, textiles, consumer goods
Bhutan	Mountains and narrow valleys	Forest products, rice, dolomite, fruits	Kerosene, sugar, textiles
Bangladesh	Tropical river delta	Jute and cotton fibers, tea, fish, hides	Food, coal, textiles
India	Tropical fertile plains and plateau	Jute, textiles, tea, coffee, cotton, minerals, hides	Wheat, fertilizer
Sri Lanka	Tropical island	Tea, rubber, copra	Wheat, rice, fertilizer, sugar, flour
Maldive Islands	Tropical coral islands	Fish, copra, shells, rope, ambergris, lace	Grain, textiles, consumer goods

The countries are presented from the Himalayas and Hindu Kush mountains in the north to the tropical coral islands in the south.

Manufactured goods and industrial products have been generally omitted as not directly related to the environment. The products listed are those usually reported as major items associated with the named country.

tured exports of the South Asian countries reflect the resources of the various environments from the Himalayas to the sea, and identify the region of South Asia. India also exports heavy steel, electrical and railway equipment, textiles, and precision instruments. Moreover, each nation is busy with its Five-Year-Plan or equivalent program for the development of better agricultural crops and practices, irrigation systems, factories, and the development of road, river, or rail transport to service its internal markets. Government control of the economy of India (duplicated to some extent also in Pakistan and Sri Lanka) led to the division of all industry into nationalized public and permitted private sectors (see section on industry).

A Grass Roots View

Each nation must deal with the question of priorities in its economic development. For example, in days long past the habit of cutting the forest, without reforestation, gradually raised a clear-cut choice of firewood for tonight's supper or timber for tomorrow's house—for too many centuries supper took precedence. This practice led directly to denudation of forested areas, and then brought up another choice: whether to use the cow dung for fuel this week or leave it for fertilizing next season's crops—the dung cakes went from the drying wall into the stove. This practice brought low productivity of the soil, and contributed to crop failure and hunger, sometimes to famine, and always to debt. Yet the farmers know that however faulty the procedures have been, the fact that they are alive today means the community has been preserved, despite the now barren mountains and the silt-clogged streams. What caused some South Asian farmers to change these traditional methods was the demonstration that the new cereals and new techniques of crop management and environmental control actually can yield an excess of food on the table over energy expended. What has happened, then, is that the new technology has enlarged the carrying capacity of the environment, but this still is barely sufficient to cope with a steadily increasing population.

Utilization of Resources

The growth in population—now about 2 percent a year—is running neck-and-neck with the ability of technological expertise to develop new resources necessary for survival. Some gains were recorded by 1978 in cereals with added protein content. This was matched by an adequate production of cotton, lumber, coal, iron, and some minerals which were turned into textiles, paper, steel, cement, and chemicals. Scientific exploration has identified a wealth of strategic minerals, particularly in India, as well as promising reserves of petroleum offshore in the Bombay High area. In the fishing industry better boats and methods have brought more coastal and deep-sea fish into the markets. But the Rajasthan Desert Project illustrates the difficulty of improving resource utilization.

Irrigation

The situation. What happened to India's Rajasthan desert long ago happened to many other deserts. Some 3,000 years ago the entire area of northern and western Rajasthan was fertile and wooded. Today this area of over 132,000 square

FIGURE 9-1
A Hunza girl.

miles (342,000 sq. km.) is mostly sandy desert or thorny scrub land. Centuries of misuse of the land, relentless tree cutting, and uncontrolled cattle-grazing meant that people retreated further and further from a land with no green cover. Even the rivers retreated underground. Similar or equivalent bad land practices reduced to barrenness much of Palestine and Syria, much of North Africa under the Romans, parts of Chinese Central Asia, and most of China's mountains.

Government planning. After laying hundreds of miles of canals India has already irrigated about 100,000 square miles (over 2.5 million hectares) of Rajasthan's arid lands with wells, tanks (ponds), and water outlets. Pakistan has endeavored to irrigate some parts of the Indus valley while lowering the salinized water table in others. Neither country has accomplished in quite the same massive way what Israel and China have done in planting millions of trees to provide timber and stabilize the natural flow of rainwater.

Quite understandably, India's efforts have been directed toward (1) better living through gainful occupations, (2) reduction in the birth rate, and (3) an adequate and permanent supply of food for all. The complexity of the social, psychological, and technological patterning involved led the Indian government planners in their Sixth Five-Year Plan to tackle the ancillary matters of poverty, food production, population control through family planning, and the blending of social advice and welfare with scientific research. Instruction units variously equipped with loud-speakers, posters, nurses, model kitchens, and mass-trained "agricultural experts" tour villages throughout the country holding family planning and farmers' clinics.

Varied responses.   The official urgings towards "induced prosperity" conflict with at least three items of the worldview held in common by most Indian farmers: (1) The concept of "limited good": if *they* are given land then *I* am thereby de-prived. (2) The "limited aspirations": when *I* get more, *they* will take it away. Many peasants simply did not want more than an extra acre or two of land be-cause the extra land would require more effort than they wished to exert, and the landlord and the tax man would just take more of the enhanced harvest. (3) The "limited capacity": *I* can only do *my* allotted task. (This has deep Hindu scriptural backing and ties in with the caste system.) A landless Harijan (outcaste) working for a pittance at a city job may have neither the capacity nor the desire to take up farming, nor may a traditional "scrabble farmer" wish to move, espe-cially since irrigated land and the miracle seeds demand new and different tech-niques and resources.

As a result of the traditional attitudes the government encountered a twofold disappointment in the Rajasthan Irrigation Project. First, there were relatively few takers for the land. Many still in desperate poverty let the water flow past un-touched for the reason that the rains had sufficed for their ancestors, and who were they now to complain against heaven. And second, some of those who did accept land did not use the opportunity to better their long-term socio-economic position. Some of the indigenous population of Bagdis ignored the agricultural extension officials, and, if they had a tractor, hired someone to drive it. They spent their income on clothes and ornaments for the women (such ornaments representing the family savings), and prided themselves that they no longer ate millet, but always ate the rich people's food, wheat! But some people did use the new irrigated land as the government had planned. The energetic Sikh Jats, using the inherited respect for agriculture their caste developed, turned northern Rajasthan into flourishing fields of golden grain by using the canal water. So the Rajasthan Desert Irrigation Project, like many development projects, was a partial success. The already better-off Sikh Jats prospered more, and other farmers remained poor. But grain produc-tion did increase significantly.

Food

South Asia grows rice, wheat, maize (corn), barley, rye, and three kinds of millet in substantial quantities; but rice is king. Rice is the staple food of half the world's people, most of whom live in Asia. Rice ripens in between 80 and 200 days, according to which of the 7,000 to 8,000 varieties is being grown under what climatic conditions—up to three crops annually.

India released two new strains of rice in 1978 with 20 to 40 percent higher yields. India as a producer of rice comes next after China, growing upwards of 53 to 70 million tons (48 to 63 million metric tons) annually. Of the 3.7 million tons (3.4 million metric tons) of rice bran as a by-product over half a million tons were processed as an excellent edible oil, rich in vitamins and low in satu-rated fat.

INDUSTRY

Since India is avowedly a socialist and secular state, much of its industry falls within the public sector of nationalized industries. This sector now encompasses defense equipment, atomic energy, space and satellites, iron and steel (particularly in heavy plants and machinery), turbines, major minerals, aircraft, railway equipment, shipbuilding, generation and distribution of electricity, oil and gas, and the major banks. Some other industries are secondarily included: aluminum, machine tools, drugs, plastics, rubber and certain chemical processes, and digging of deep wells. The private sector in general operates in industries falling outside these governmentally controlled areas. The Hindustan Iron Works and the Bharat Heavy Electricals Limited, two of the most modern and sophisticated firms in Asia, compete effectively for world contracts. In addition to oil being pumped from the Bombay High field, mineral nodules are scooped from the ocean floor, while Indian satellites monitor monsoons and provide television and telephone connections. Moreover, this technical expertise is given free to developing countries.

SCIENCE

India's scientific achievements are not merely modern; they are the lineal descendants of ancient discoveries. India claims credit for the concept of zero, the decimal system, mathematical systems involving algebra and geometry and internal calculus, as well as atomic theory, and plastic surgery by Susruta about A.D. 350. The word "zero" probably came from Latin *ziphirum*, from Arabic sifr, a translation of the Hindu word *sunya* meaning void or empty; compare also the English "ci-

TABLE 9-3 Typical Resources of India

| RESOURCE | AMOUNTS IN MILLIONS | |
	U.S. MEASURES	METRIC EQUIVALENTS
*Minerals**		
Iron	29,000 short tons	26,303 metric tons
Base metals, incl. copper	246 short tons	223 metric tons
Aluminum	230 short tons	208.61 metric tons
Manganese	110 short tons	99.77 metric tons
Lead, zinc	100 short tons	90.7 metric tons
Chromite	14 short tons	12.7 metric tons
Fuels		
Coal	30-66,000 short tons	27.2-59.8 metric tons
Petroleum	130 short tons	117.9 metric tons
Natural gas	78,480 cubic yards	60,000 cubic meters
Hydroelectric energy		
Energy potential	500 kwt	500 kwt

*Other minerals include thorium, titanium, zirconium, and mica.

pher." Also from 350 on, astronomers made important observations, and smiths forged excellent steel.

Today, with about 130 universities and 138 engineering colleges, 45,000 post-graduates in scientific disciplines, 370 "temples of science" staffed by over 100,000 scientists engaged in every field of research from modernizing the bullock cart to designing atomic reactors, modern India has the third largest pool of scientific and technological workers in the world. These vast resources of workers, materials (see Table 9-3), and technological expertise are producing pharmaceuticals and radio isotopes for patients in Philippine hospitals, electricity for India's own teeming millions, laser instruments for eye surgery, industrial diamonds, birth control vaccines, more efficient energy processes from coal, and automobile fuels from castor seeds and ammonia plus methyl alcohol. Special research focuses on the needs of the 400 million persons in rural areas: low-cost housing, smokeless ovens, building materials from rice husks, fuel and fertilizer from algae, biogas, and bamboo tubewells. In particular, methods for conserving moisture in the dry land zones, which constitute three-fourths of the cultivated land, aim at national self-sufficiency in food. Another serious proposal is to link the rivers and canals of the country into a nationwide system giving everyone access to irrigation.

EDUCATION

Inherent in the utilization of technological advances is education, whether formal or informal.

Philosophy

Education and philosophy try to identify facts and ideas and then apply them beneficially to life situations. At least four approaches are used: knowledge, wisdom, reason, and faith. One could summarize it this way: Faith utilizes Reason as far as Knowledge of the evidence allows, and then uses Wisdom to take the further step to grasp the goal inherent in the evidence. The Asian philosopher is likely to start from the holistic viewpoint that man's total universe is a single Reality, of which all the elements of the observable and conceptual worlds are equally valid components. The "scientific" Westerner will probably begin from the observable items, the data, and by analysis and synthesis endeavor to construct a verifiable Totality.

The Indian scholar who addressed the East Asian faculty of a West Coast university some years ago left them completely nonplussed. The chairman finally remarked that, "You leave us completely mystified. We simply do not understand how it is that you, an upper class Indian with a doctorate in sociology from an Ivy League university, can also be a *sadhu* (an ascetic, a holy man) on the byways of India." To these Westerners these two ways of life were incompatible opposites; to the Indian speaker they were but two manifestations of relationship to the one Ultimate Reality.

Libraries

One can visualize Fa-hsien, the famous Chinese Buddhist monk and traveler, poking around the libraries of India during his fifteen years of assiduous research between A.D. 399 and 414, for he wrote vivid descriptions of them. He must have known of the library at Taxila (ancient Rawalpindi), and may have seen copies of the Vedas, and of Buddhist and epic manuscripts treasured in the libraries in kings' palaces and thousand-year-old temples. Quite likely he handled some of the 500-year-old texts prescribed for daily recital by monks and laity that were mentioned in the edicts of Asoka. Naturally Fa-hsien would not have known about the National Library at Calcutta, opened in A.D. 1838 to serve "all ranks and classes without distinction." Nor would he have met the "Father of the Library Movement in India," the Gaekwar of Baroda who, between 1911 and 1939 had both stationary and traveling libraries functioning in town and village throughout his State for men, women, and children.

Traditional and Modern Schools

Education in the countries of South Asia gradually shifted away from the traditional small class tutored by a Brahmin, the temple school taught by a Buddhist monk or the mullah's school at the mosque, where religion and social custom were imbibed along with the elements of reading and writing. The colonial authorities instituted Western curricula taught by French, Dutch, Portuguese or English teachers. Later teachers were nationals trained in the various colonial homelands, or by nationals graduated from local elementary and high schools and universities. Schoolrooms varied from dirt floors in the village to halls with desk and dais in city buildings. The language of instruction was often that of the textbook, the colonial language.

The modern educational system has directed the educated sector of the nation more towards Western than Asian knowledge and literary skills, and produced a surplus of scholastically trained people, whose abilities cannot be adequately utilized; these people become a socially and politically unstable group. It is unfortunate that such education tends to extol "white collar" work. Many governments around the world, like India, are trying to improve the situation by taking steps to upgrade village level education that provides training in farm work, manual trades, etc.

In addition to about 130 universities with 4,500 affiliated colleges, India has 40,000 secondary schools, and 600,000 elementary schools. The budget outlay for 1978 was Rupees 25,000 million (about U.S. $3 billion). Well over 100 million children are in school under some two and a half million teachers, one quarter of whom are women. One college student in six receives a scholarship or stipend, and many of them are underprivileged or Scheduled Caste students. In 1967 over 600 scientific periodicals were published in India alone, where the literacy rate is somewhat over 35 percent. While the present benefits of education go mostly to the top 30 percent income group, the system is being modified to widen the enrollment spectrum, open new types of institutions, and make university education more practical.

Pakistan, with thousands of high schools and hundreds of colleges, still has an overall literacy rate of only 20 percent. At the other end of the subcontinent Sri Lanka with three universities and two national languages has a phenomenally high literacy rate of 90 percent. The greatest drawback in many nations is the speed with which children drop out of school after only one to four years of often intermittent instruction—poor families need their help at home or on the farm.

But even farmers who work fourteen hours a day may be keen critics of or performers in some local variant of literature or music.

ART

Architecture

House and city architecture on the subcontinent certainly goes back at least to the cities of the Indus Valley civilization, Mohenjo-Daro, Harappa, and Lothal. These secular cities with their squared layout of broad streets and intersecting lanes, dating from around 2000 B.C., were lined with shops and booths, and houses with bathrooms. Traditional homes in South Asia vary from flimsy wattle-and-daub huts and the common mud brick two-to-four-room houses on the plains to the fired brick dwellings of the village landlords, to the stone houses inset into the hillside in the mountainous north, and to the unbelievable marble palaces of the rajas. Although the skill of the craftsman and builder was always secular, the aspirations of artist and worshipper between A.D. 1000 and 1500 adorned the temples in "garments of stone and clay."

During the 200s B.C. the polished monolithic shafts 40 to 50 feet high inscribed with Asoka's famous edicts were erected all over India. Artisans hewed temples into the rock at Ajanta in Central India, or cut away the rock face to leave a temple or a statue carved out of the solid rock as at Ellora. Later, the ultimate in perfection was achieved in the uniquely beautiful and balanced Taj Mahal, built by the Mughal emperor Shah Jahan in memory of his favorite wife, Mumtaz-i-Mahal, meaning "Pride of the Palace."

Painting and Sculpture

Asian art has been concerned mainly but not exclusively with religion. Both pictorial and sculptured art in South Asia portrayed by gestures, postures, and conventional emblems of identity and attributes, the devotional and ritual relationships of humans with deity and of deity towards humans. The union of human with the divine was often depicted in South Indian temple sculpture by the graphic and graceful figures of two people in sexual union. In Nepal and Bhutan the highly complex and brilliantly colored art of Tibetan Buddhism conveyed religious instruction; and Indian temple sculptures, like narratives, depicted consecutive scenes from the lives of the Buddha and of Krishna.

Textile art reproduces local stories and epic legends, and the artists of the great Mughal emperor Akbar painted documentary records of actual events and court activities that now are useful for historical reconstruction of Mughal life and times. Realism was not overlooked, for, with the Muslim restrictions upon the delineation of the human figure in particular, birds, animals, and pastoral scenes decorated the ornamental scrolls of flowing Arabic calligraphy. In startling contrast are the wall paintings of voluptuous ladies leading the visitor towards the royal halls of the impregnable rock fortress of Sigiriya in Sri Lanka.

Dance

The art of the dance ranges over some of the same areas as painting. Historical events, the activities of village agriculture, the crises of life in courtship, marriage, and death, and the interactions between humans and gods and demons in the tension-fraught shadows of life were all dramatized. Legends claim that the Lord Brahma created the "fifth Veda," the dance. Rigorous training from childhood was essential to discipline the body and mind, for each motion and gesture—there are 108 finger and hand poses alone—carried its own special meaning to build rapport between dancer and audience. Originally an accompaniment to temple worship, the rajas lured beautiful *devadasis* (temple dancers) to their courts, and the dance became secular and public. While some dances are performed by men only and others by women only, all are accompanied by musicians and often by narrative songs.

Music

The Western repertoire of scales, instruments, tuning system, and emphasis upon a rich vocabulary of harmony is bafflingly different from the emphasis in the Orient upon melody and rhythm, especially when framed in different scales. Asians generally are sensitive to the technique and mood of a few talented performers improving upon known melodies and rhythmic themes. The subtleties of the *sitar* can be appreciated when one knows it is a plucked lute with six or seven principal strings and thirteen sympathetic strings, played against a background of a droning *tamboura* lute, with the accompaniment of one or more *tabla* drums. Music, like literature, has its popular and its highly specialized classical genres.

Literature

In addition to religious classics (see Table 8-1 regarding Hindu literature), Indian poets wrote historical and morality epics in Sanskrit, Pali, Tamil, and other regional languages. Treasured as one of Asia's most famous epics, the *Mahabharata* ("the great (tale) of the descendants of prince Bharata") dramatizes events occurring about 1200 B.C., told in over 100,000 couplets—eight times longer than the Iliad and the Odyssey combined. The second most loved Indian epic, valued in both South and Southeast Asia, is the 24,000 couplet *Ramayana* ("Life of Rama," an incarnation of Vishnu). Tulasi Das (c. 1543-1623) fused the *Ramayana* into 6,300 stanzas and, while including many thousands of words from Sanskrit, Persian, and Arabic, as well as local colloquialisms, produced a moving recital of the adventures of over two hundred characters from gods and humans to monkeys and the lowly spider. A more serious historical poem of about 8,000 verses, the *Rajatarangini* ("River of Kings"), written about 1150, provided extensive dynastic lists of Kashmiri kings covering about 3,050 years.

Today's literature is keyed to modern situations, interests, and needs. The prose and poetry of Sir Rabindranath Tagore (1861-1941) contributed so substantially towards the concepts and organizations for world understanding that he was awarded the 1913 Nobel prize for literature. India's publication of more than 15,000 titles annually represents the social ferment of today's world in the number of languages used and the variety of topics represented. More than one third of these titles are in English, of which 57 percent deal with the various sciences, in contrast to 70 percent of the Indian titles being on general literature. However, the 10 percent of Indian titles on academic and scientific topics is a new and increasingly important sector of literary endeavor. India now is one of the top ten

TABLE 9-4 Government, Economy, and Religion in South Asia

COUNTRY	FORM OF GOVERNMENT	DICTATORIAL REGIMES[a]	RELIGIOUS OR SECULAR[b]	DOMINANT RELIGION	SOCIALIST	NATIONALIZED ECONOMY	BRITISH COMMON-WEALTH
Pakistan	Republic	Military	Religious	Islam	Socialist	Considerable	Withdrew, 1972
India	Republic	–	Secular	Hinduism	Socialist	Major trend	Member
Bangladesh	Republic	Military	Secular	Islam	–	–	Member
Sri Lanka	Republic	Civil	Secular	Buddhism	Socialist	Minor	Member
Maldives	Republic	Civil	Secular	Islam	–	–	–
Nepal	Monarchy	Royal	Traditional	Buddhism	–	–	–
Bhutan	Monarchy	–	Traditional	Buddhism	–	–	–

[a] Either permanent or for substantial periods of modern history.
[b] Refers to the government's legal view of the national administration.

book-producing countries in the world, and third in the publication of titles in English.

LOOKING INTO TODAY AND TOMORROW

Each of the South Asian nations has some difficulty adjusting to the modern world of secular and individualistic competition. In terms of *literacy* only Sri Lanka has a literate electorate, meaning that the people have an opportunity to adequately assess political issues and candidates' personal qualifications. *Religion* also plays a part. Within Hinduism caste still acts as a formalized discouragement to social and occupational mobility. Under the influence of Islam both Pakistan and Bangladesh have areas of variance between the Koranic and the statutory *laws,* and the question of which takes precedence. Koranic law covers areas of religious and personal life not touched by statutory law, and also is harshly specific in some cases (amputation of a hand for theft, for instance), and nonspecific in others (business and industrial concerns).

Pakistan, Bangladesh, Nepal, Bhutan, and the Maldive Islands have in common an *authoritarian* tendency. For most of their short histories, both Pakistan and Bangladesh have lived under military rule. Nepal's hereditary king has used the constitution to dampen elective activity and the National Panchayat (parliament). Bhutan still lives in its traditional agricultural economy, a sort of subsistence cocoon, under its hereditary king. The Maldives preserved for nearly 900 years a sultanate government, only recently becoming a republic.

In discussing the matter of *modernization* in South Asia, Percival Spear (1967:160) pointed out that the attitudes generated by Islam and Hinduism are likely to lead to different reactions. Islam proclaims the equality of all people before God and in great part practices accordingly. Hinduism holds the ideal of equal responsibility to serve society, but in practice the pattern of caste holds people in positions of social inequality. Modernization assumes, and in its outworking requires, a very substantial actuality of equality. Islam accepts the separateness and worth of the individual personality as existing in this world and the next. Hinduism, however, teaches the opposite, that individuality finally is a hindrance that should be discarded. Inherent in modernization is the concept and practice of competition-plus-cooperation, and the idea of one eventually becoming a nonindividual does not easily fit into the scheme of life today. Modernization also is strongly directed towards this present material universe, and here Islam and Hinduism are diametrically opposed. Islam accepts this world as an actual, ongoing entity that provides material benefits to be sought after and enjoyed. The Hindu and Buddhist view is that this world is to be tolerated only in so far as it enables the person to quench desires in preparation for leaving it.

Spear (1967:163) remarks that "The penalty of worldly success may be the end of Hinduism . . . Hinduism may save its soul at the cost of worldly success." Spiritual purity and material affluence may indeed be found together in the lives of some wealthy Hindus, but, since the eternal and temporal goals these two conditions suggest are contradictory in Hinduism's terms, and since modernization is concerned with material affluence, Hinduism stands at a critical crossroads. Hindu India indeed is agonizing in the throes of coping with poverty, illiteracy, undernourishment, and the social stresses of today's changing conditions, and is in no mood to forgo its outstanding industrial and agricultural and social prosperings. Neither will Hinduism relinquish its transcendental aspirations. There is no doubt that both Islam and Hinduism ultimately will find avenues of interpretation and adjustment which will enable their principles and their people to prosper tolerably in this world, and still preserve their concepts of spiritual dignity and of eternity. In a word, South Asia in the years ahead will find an honorable and a prosperous *modus vivendi* between the sacred and the secular aspects of life.

Chapter *10*

South Asia's Regional Peoples

Diversity and unity are both present in South Asia. Because of the kaleidoscopic effect of the interlocking patterns of contrasting diversity, one could almost say of South Asia that diversity is a form of unity. We shall discuss some of these contrasting patterns before taking up descriptions of peoples in the various sub-regions of the subcontinent.

PATTERNS OF INTERLOCKING CONTRASTS

Status and Role

In contrast to the American social customs allowing persons to participate freely in many social roles, the Asian, in general, is restricted to "one status, one role." This means that the manager directs affairs, the typist types, the chauffeur drives the car, the cook cooks, and the baggage carrier does just that. This is an aspect of the pattern that separates the rulers from the ruled. Typically then, the official at the passport office, for instance, will always conduct himself or herself as a person with that status who happens on any given occasion to be paying taxes, buying a watch or sari, counseling a client, or conversing with a guest at the family table.

Asia is a man's world, where women are expected to defer to their men, at least in public. The distinction between the sexes in Asia is likely to parallel in sharpness that between urbanites and ruralites, literates and illiterates, and majority people over minorities and tribals. Always there is some degree of super- and subordination in these relationships. Nevertheless, circumstances and personalities have provided certain notable exceptions. The world's first woman prime minister of a modern country was Mrs. Sirimavo Bandaranaike of Sri Lanka, 1960-1965 and 1970-1977. Madame Vijaya Pandit, sister to India's famous Prime Minister Nehru, in the middle of her distinguished ambassadorial career, was elected the first woman president of the United Nations General Assembly for 1953-1954. Mrs. Indira Gandhi, daughter of Jawaharlal Nehru, was Prime Minister of India from 1966 to 1977 and was elected again in 1980.

The Language Differential

India. The many millions in South Asia who speak only a minority language view all educated persons who speak English, and the elite who speak the national language, as first-class citizens. Viewing also the wide gap between those groups and themselves they understandably fear being treated as second-class citizens. The official reference annual, *India 1974,* states: "The 1961 census enumerated a total of 1,652 mother-tongues" (p. 13). Each of India's twenty-two States may adopt Hindi, the official national language, or its own regional language, as its State language. Then, as part of the accommodation to India's multilingual identity, an English translation is often added to inter-State communications.

Other South Asian Countries

Pakistan has a much simpler problem. Its national language Urdu, together with two major minority languages, Sindhi and Punjabi, are all related to the belt of Indo-Iranian languages across North India. Of the other minority languages in Pakistan, Pashto and Baluchi relate to Persian, and Brahui is Dravidian. Bangladesh is fairly homogeneous linguistically, dominated by the Bengali language. Bhutan is monolingual in Bhutanese. The Maldive Islands with two languages, Sri Lanka with Sinhala and Tamil, and Nepal with Bengali-related Nepali and the Tibetan-related languages of the hill peoples, all have difficulties that are clear-cut and therefore manageable. Many of the peoples in all these countries speak two or more languages as well as English. A common language is always a link which cannot be entirely disrupted, even by differences in writing (Devanagari, Tamil, Arabic, Persian, or Latin scripts) or by class-dividing accents and vocabulary—even though wide social differences continue to exist. Language is a vital link among individuals, and is the filter through which humans perceive, analyze, and seek to deal with the world around them.

THE REGIONS AND THEIR PEOPLES

In nearly every area of South Asia the terrain sparkles with color, from the glistening mineral sands by the blue-green sea in the South, to the green fields and forests on the purple mountains that overlook the yellow and brown of the barren lands. And looking down on the whole magnificent triangle of South Asia, the white mountain wall of the Himalayas nourishes much of it with life-giving waters. This multihued landscape, matched as it is by the gay colors of the women's saris, must not blind one to the drabness of many a mud-brick cottage and the gray tatters that many cottagers call clothes. Nor should it dull our awareness of their dogged patience in guiding the wooden plows behind rail-thin oxen over the grim, dry soils of their parched fields. These, rather than the white-clad townsmen and the politicians, are South Asia's real men and women of courage.

Geographical and other factors have led to the distinction of seven regions: those of the Sri Lankans, the Dravidians and Maharashtrans of the South, the farmers and tribesmen of central India, the Gangetic plainsmen, the varied Northwesterners, the dwellers of the Himalayas, and the Muslims of the Islamic Republics.

The Sri Lankans

Sri Lanka, at various times called Lanka, Serendip (from which comes the word serendipity), and Ceylon, was invaded from north India about 500 B.C., thereby acquiring its Indo-European language, Sinhala. In the 200s B.C. Buddhism and the arts of writing, architecture, and sculpture were introduced. The ethnic and religious layerings since then read like a historical calendar, especially as they are represented by distinctive groups today. (See Table 10-1.) Hindu Tamils, Muslim Arabs, Gujaratis, and Europeans followed one another for trade, conquest, or to work on coffee plantations and quinine and tea estates. In the loose Sinhalese caste system, which used to include royalty and Brahmins, the cultivators are the largest prestigious group, as they also are in China. Fishermen and others whose occupations involve the destruction of life hold only a low rating, along with launderers and grass cutters. Even the once-remote hunting-gathering Veddahs of the interior jungles now do some farming. Since the Europeans came to Sri Lanka, "The Resplendent Isle," a somewhat general social leveling has taken place, and a few fishermen and cinnamon-tree peelers (the bark is used as a spice) have become very wealthy. After two thousand years of self-rule and trade, gem cutting and textile weaving, and the exercise of military warfare and linguistic courtesies, the sixteen million Sri Lankans now operate a solidly parliamentary form of republican

TABLE 10-1   Layering of Ethnic Groups in Sri Lanka

ETHNIC GROUP	PRESENT APPELLATION	APPROXI-MATE DATE OF ARRIVAL	PERCENT-AGE OF POPULATION	RELIGION	LANGUAGE
Malays	(Malays)	Late 1800s	1	Islam	Malay
British	(British)	1796		Christianity	English
Tamils	Indian Tamils	1800s	9	Hinduism	Tamil
Dutch	Burghers	1656	3	Christianity	Sinhalese
Arabs	Moors	A.D. 1500s	7	Islam	Sinhalese
Tamils	Sri Lankan Tamils	100s B.C.	12	Hinduism	Tamil
Sinhalese	Sinhalese	500s B.C.	68	Buddhism	Sinhalese
Veddahs	Veddah	Prehistoric	—	Animism	Sinhalese

government that has resisted authoritarianism. Nevertheless, smoldering animosities between Sinhalese ("People of the Lion") and Tamils (who want their own separate state) flared into armed violence in 1983, resulting in formal exchanges of emissaries between Sri Lanka and a gravely concerned India. It is this same spirit of impatience and intolerance between groups, ethnic communities, and nations that plagues Asia from Cyprus to Vietnam, and creates abrasive lines of friction elsewhere in the world. Next, then, we look at the Tamils themselves.

THE DRAVIDIANS OF THE SOUTH

Considered externally and historically, South India has lain on the East-West sea routes between China and Europe, and also on the periphery of the great Muslim empires. Internally, the mountains, jungles, and deserts which separate the region from North India resulted in the development of a distinctive civilization, as partially indicated in Chapter 7. South India's Dravidian language region, about the size of France and Spain combined, encompasses four nuclear zones: Tamil Nadu, Kerala, Karnataka (previously Mysore), and Andhra Pradesh.

Tamil Nadu

The Tamils. The classical civilization of South India was that of *Tamil Nadu* (land of the Tamils) whose people, relatively unaffected by invaders, retained many aspects of Indian culture in a purer form than Indians elsewhere. Here over the temples of medieval Madurai rise the high gate towers (*gopuram*) with their intricate sculptures aglow with vibrant, brilliant-hued painting that defies description. Here also are found the elaborately costumed female Bharata Natyam dancers, and the highly trained almost trance-like Kathakali male dancers who carry on their ancient traditional art. Two thousand years ago Tamil kingdoms traded with Rome, and today Tamil merchant enterprises are placed throughout Southeast and Island Asia as well as in Fiji in the Pacific.

Centuries ago the Pallavas maintained their own naval base and ruled from their capital at Kanchi, but the Chola capital was inland at Tanjore. Legend recounts that the god Shiva married Parvati, daughter of King Himalaya, and the seven colored varieties of rice thrown at the wedding became forever the seven colored sands at Cape Cormorin. Anyway, a rice diet liberally spaced with hot curry is the mainstay of Tamil fare, and a very intoxicating palm wine (toddy) enlivens many a male gathering. Tamils raise coconuts for toddy and copra and use the coir fiber for matting, besides farming on both dry and irrigated land, diving for pearls, and fishing. Today this densely populated plain is being dotted with modern industries that contribute to the continued growth of its capital city, Madras.

The tribal peoples. Far to the west of Madras lie the Nilgiri Hills of the Western Ghats. The four principal *tribal groups* in the Nilgiri Hills exemplify the interrelationships of environmental niching. Each group filled a separate niche, and contributed to other groups the products of that niche. Long beards and flowing robes distinguish the tall and robust *Toda* men, whose priests conduct rituals centered around a dairying process of making butter from buffalo milk. The cow byres are forbidden to women. Their traditional polyandry (several men, usually brothers, married to one woman) has been modified by a recent decline in deaths of female babies; each young man now may have his own wife. Their speech is the most aberrant of the Dravidian stock, suggesting long isolation of the less than one thousand Todas from the rest of the Dravidian speakers. The largest group in the Nilgiri Hills, the *Badaga* (meaning northerner) came into the area in the 1200s or 1300s, indigenized themselves and speak a Dravidian dialect of Kannada. These approximately 90,000 people use a class system wherein the top two classes are vegetarian, the middle three are farmers and general workers, and the sixth class serves the other five. In recent years the Badagas have taken to education, local and national politics, and high-class Hindu religious practices, and generally have turned twentieth century opportunities to their advantage. The third group in the area, some 1,200 *Kotas,* live in villages dispersed through the hills, and until about 1930 lived in a symbiotic relationship with the Todas, the Badagas and the *Kurumbas.* The Badagas provided grain and cloth to the Todas who reciprocated with dairy products, cane and bamboo articles, and to the Kotas who supplied metal tools, wooden implements, pots, and music. Todas and Kotas cooperated in the same ways with each other and with the jungle-dwelling Kurumbas, who provided jungle products, music, and magical protection. However, after 1930, tools, seeds, and modern know-how led to increased agricultural expertise, and these relationships began to decrease—providing one instance of the continent-wide impact of a largely Western technology upon Asian lives.

Kerala

Kerala is famous for its palm-fringed coast and rain-washed fecundity. The state also presents a cultural kaleidoscope. Situated on the southwest coast of India between the Arabian Sea and the 6,000 to 8,000 feet (1,830-2,440 m.) high Western Ghats, Kerala receives abundant monsoon rains, just as Lebanon enjoys the Mediterranean showers. This state's rugged mountains produce tea and cardamon (named from the Cardamon Hills), also tumeric, ginger, pepper, coffee, and rubber on the lower slopes, and rice on the lowlands.

The people of Kerala (often called Maliali from their Malayalam language) are among the most energetic and best educated in India. They include the Nayars, famed as warriors, whose beautiful women were allowed marital freedom within a matrilineal kinship system that included hypergamy (marriage upward) into the Brahmin caste. Kerala also is the home of the Mar Thoma Christian community. Proud of their freedom and prosperity, today's factory workers prefer to pay bus fare to their small garden-surrounded homes in the country, rather than live in the neat brick housing provided by the company.

Yet with all these amenities, many of the educated Maliali are unemployed and somewhat disillusioned. Maliali voters twice have elected a Communist state government which has created financial chaos each time, necessitating temporary suspension of self-government and the imposition of presidential rule.

One small Kerala export has been very successful. The Nayar martial art of *kalari payattu,* forebear of other South Asian martial arts, was carried by Buddhist monks to other parts of Asia, where it was developed into karate, judo, and kendo-stick.

Karnataka or Mysore

The heart of *Karnataka* or *Mysore* lies inland, on the main western half of the Deccan plateau where live the 29.3 million Kannada or Kanarese Dravidian speakers. The capital city of Mysore and the present administrative center of Bangalore, both lie in the temperate southern section of the state. At Bangalore was built the Indian Institute of Science from donations by the philanthropic steel magnates, the Parsee Tata family of Bombay. Famed for its realistic and exuberant friezes depicting deities, epic events and numerous scenes of everyday life, the great star-shaped temple of Belur compares in importance with other great Asian temples such as Angkor Wat in Cambodia and Borobudur in Java. Contemporary with the cathedral at Chartres (1000s to 1200s), the temple at Belur shares the intent to instruct the illiterate masses in their religion through the visual imagery of statuary and painting. Provision also is made for the expression of devotion at Sravanabelgola where a 57-foot-tall, 1,000-year-old monolithic stone statue of the Jain saint, Gomateswara, is bathed with a solution of sixteen substances at a special festival held once every twelve years.

Karnataka's men and women of education commonly have added a speaking knowledge of Hindi and Urdu to their regional competence in Telugu and their own Kannada languages. The sound of Persian poetry being read in the quiet evening hours can be heard within many a home in town and country. Some Karnatakans, such as those who live in one-room mud houses perched atop rocky hills in the interior, with little of this world's goods, maintain their sense of self-worth through religious zeal. Depending upon the accumulation of sufficient cash and the access to a market, farmers use either a modern plow or one modeled on those used 3,000 years ago. The Coorgis or Kodavas, a minority people who occupy what once was a princely state, live quietly amid their forests, coffee plantations, rice fields, and orange gardens. They have their own traditional language, literature, and culture, and their women enjoy the greatest degree of social equality with men anywhere in Karnataka.

Andhra Pradesh

The state of *Andhra Pradesh,* running south to north for five hundred miles (800 km.) alongside the Bay of Bengal, links the rich and irrigated country of the Tamils with the drier hills, forests, and savannas of Central India. Andhra occupies the lower half of the drainage basins of the Krishna (or Kistna) and the Godavari rivers, which may benignly bless their fertile deltas, or as rampaging torrents can punishingly devastate the crops planted there. Just inland on the Krishna in the first century B.C. stood the flourishing Buddhist center of Amaravati, whose monasteries and universities attracted the devout and the learned from as far away as China. Upstream from Amaravati the Nagarjunasagar dam now stores irrigation water for vast arid areas of the interior, and sustains the five-to-one ratio of rural to urban residents in fertile farmlands. The unifying language of the state is Telugu, (45 million speakers) whose written inscriptions date back to the A.D. 800s.

Tucked away on the coast between Karnataka and Maharashtra, the tiny Union territory of *Goa, Daman,* and *Diu* (population 86,000) was well known as a Portuguese outpost for 451 years (1510-1961). Today it is known for its beaches, Portuguese-style houses, and the marble, jasper, and silver tomb of St. Francis Xavier. From an ethnohistorical viewpoint these early missionaries were among the

FIGURE 10-1 South Indian temple dancers.

few literate persons capable of describing accurately Asian and other cultures to the Western world—counterparts to such eminent writers and travelers as the Venetian merchant Marco Polo, the Arab chronicler Ibn Batuta, and the Chinese monk Fa Hsien.

CENTRAL INDIA

The peninsula-wide belt of rugged mountains and brooding forests—three hundred miles (480 km.) deep—quite effectively shuts off the palm-fringed coasts and the parched plateau of the Dravidian South from the fertile flatlands of the Ganges Plain. One after another the resplendent kingdoms of the South fell before the next aspirant for power and prestige, revenues or revenge. The shout of the victor and the groan of the dying seldom penetrated the thickets where tiger and hunter confronted each other. Moreover, the clouds of dust raised by the thundering hoofs of invading armies, intent on the clash of conquest of the wealthy cities of the Northern Plains, seldom settled here on the hidden villages of the Bhil, Gond or Santal tribesmen.

Here, almost in the center of the Peninsula, live some three million Gonds in the area the Muslims in the 1300s dubbed "Gondwana" (from which was named the primeval Gondwanaland postulated by the geologists). Gondi is a Dravidian language spoken by people whose occupations range from slash-and-burn agriculture to modern farm methods. Their social standings reach from that of forest tribespeople to scions of princely families of their not-so-ancient kingdom.

The mountains, forests, and plains of the region, crowded with over 375 languages and dialects in Madhya Pradesh alone, contain nearly thirty-one of the thirty-eight million members of the Scheduled Tribes of the Union of India. (Scheduled Castes and Scheduled Tribes, comprising one fifth of India's population, are those whose "traditional inabilities" or "geographical isolation" has prevented them from receiving, previous to the 1970s, the full benefit of the country's planned social and economic development [*India,* 1974:97].) In 1921, Mohandas Gandhi heard the tribal people called *kali praja* (black people). He was most indignant, and instructed his followers to work for the uplift of these Adivasis (original inhabitants). Later he included these tribal people with the noncaste Hindus as Harijans (see Chapter 8).

For both mainstream Hindus and many tribal people life in the fertile fields means living in whitewashed mud-brick houses set amid the green croplands. Rice feeds many families; wheat, millet, or other cereals feed others. For those living near urban centers the product from truck farm, sugar cane, jute, or handicrafts provides cash for salt, sugar, oil, cloth, and bangles for the women and girls. Whatever cash is brought in may make the crucial difference which enables the family to survive the late monsoon rains, a poor harvest, the death of a farm animal, or the expenses of a wedding or a funeral. Even a little may save the family from the waiting arms of the moneylender.

An even greater transformation has occurred in the lives of the tribespeople. Many used to practice slash-and-burn agriculture, smelt iron, and make their own tools and weapons. They worshipped their own animistic totems and gods. Now many work in coal mines and steel mills, or as tea-pickers, blacksmiths, or weavers. Some have migrated to the cities, seldom finding much success among the crowded masses of jobseekers. Many have joined the caste system and call on the Brahmins for priestly functions. A few in past years graduated to high caste and claimed status as Rajputs. Hopefully many will benefit from the discovery in the region of vast stores of mineral wealth: coal, manganese, hematite, and other minerals.

THE GANGETIC PLAINSPEOPLE

People of the Heartland

The classical heartland of North India has been the Ganges-Jumna Doab (land between two rivers), and its extension further down the Gangetic Plain. For the millions of farmers the simple upper and lower garments of white cotton, and the women's varieties of ankle-length garments, with or without short sleeves, suffice for daily wear. Upper-class and official men prefer a plain white jacket buttoned to the collar, white trousers fitting tightly from knee to ankle, and a long, black sleeveless vest worn over the jacket. Some politically conscious men wear the small white and narrow Congress party cap. Women's dress includes many varieties of ankle-length garments with or without short sleeves. The whole body is usually draped with a graceful and colorful sari, the loose end falling from the shoulder or turned over the head. Men's turbans come in many styles and weaves according to the locality and affiliation of the wearer. Clothing, then, may denote the sex, class, caste, wealth, and even the ethnic identity and religion of the wearer. On the other hand, in city, factory, school, and many occupations, modern dress may obliterate almost all these distinctions.

In wealthier city homes and larger farm households the extended family includes the married children and their families in several generations. Each nuclear family within such extended households usually cooks on its own hearth, shields its women from male gaze in general, and conducts as much of its daily activities as possible out of doors. In the cities housing and other pressures push the residential unit toward being just the conjugal or nuclear family of parents and children, with perhaps one or two older or related members of the family under the same roof. Urban life is ancient on the Gangetic Plain.

Modern Cities

Benares or *Varanasi,* already ancient when in the 600s B.C. it was known as Kasi, "Resplendent with Divine Light," is a popular shrine to the Lord Shiva. And today it is the most favored place of all for bathing in the Ganges. Millions of the devout come each spring to Allahabad for the Magh Mela or Bathing Festival at the confluence of the Ganges and Jumna rivers.

Calcutta on the Hooghly is India's largest metropolitan area with over seven million people in 1975. A citizen walking the streets could see every type of vehicle from *pushcarts* and *bicycles* to *buses* and *trucks* jostling with *rickshaws,* cows, and pedestrians. Motor vehicles carry everything from coffins to some *pukka sahib* (elegant gentleman), or the latest imported electronic machinery. The itinerant citizen probably would not see all the exquisite embroidery and brassware made and sold in tiny shops along narrow streets. Nor would he or she see the interior of one-family rooms where people take turns sleeping, or the marble stairs in the wealthy mansions of the industrialist and aristocrat. But he or she would see people from every corner of the earth going about their social assignments.

Delhi lies at the other end of this 150-mile (about 250 km.) wide band of fantastic fertility, some four fifths of the way from Calcutta to the Pakistan border, and includes within its city limits over five million people. Heir to the city of Dilli in the first century B.C., even the names of its streets and monuments tell the story of its long and stormy history—often besieged, always rebuilt. Delhi's administrators today handle the strains of internal regionalism, and the pressures of international bloc-ism, more democratically than their royal and viceroyal predecessors in office.

THE VARIED NORTHWESTERNERS

The Sutlej-Jumna Doab encompasses much of *Rajasthan* (abode of kings), homeland of the Rajputs, whose martial and cultural ascendency considerably supplanted the classification of the Kshatriya varna. A pink or yellow turban distinguishes the male Rajput, and an abundance of gold and silver chains, necklaces, bangles, and other jewelry often identifies the female. Hilltop fortifications look down on city and countryside, even distantly upon the grand canal systems that bring water to parts of the Thar and other desert areas.

For five thousand years settlements have existed in the Narmada river valley of *Gujarat,* always a trading center between India and the Persian Gulf ports. Ahmadabad (pop. 1.75 million) is famed as the site of the *ashram* (center for prayer and teaching) founded by Mahatma Gandhi. From here he and his largely Gujarati followers set out in 1930 on his Salt March to the sea to protest the salt tax. Gandhi's policy of *satyagraha* (soul-force, passive disobedience) contributed substantially towards the final independence of India, but his system of basic education and handwork in the village did not prosper. The Patidar class of middle-income Rajasthani farmers are industrious and shrewd, and prosper financially with the aid of new technology and machines. On the other hand, the unmotivated Bariyas and many of the Choudary tribespeople, some of whom suffered with Gandhi in the early years of protest, have made little progress.

Northward are the provinces of the *Punjab* for the Sikh majority and *Haryana* for the Hindu majority, both carved out of the previous single province of Punjab. The tall and muscular Sikhs are perhaps the best known of India's peoples as soldiers and policemen in many major cities of Southeast Asia. Still further north lies the legendary *Vale of Kashmir*—Akbar called it *Bagh-i-Khass* (the Chosen Garden)—encircled by the snow-crowned Himalayas, bathed in peace, and shielded from the strife and heat of the southern plains. Part truth and part nostalgia though it be, the Vale and its people have entertained Indian and foreign royalty. It was the home of the Kashmiri Brahmin family of Jawaharlal Nehru and has been a bone of contention between India and Pakistan since Partition in 1947. This festering conflict seems slowly to be healing with the tacit acceptance of the military dividing line that leaves most of its largely Moslem population and the bulk of the territory of Jamnu and Kashmir under the Indian flag. The seven principal languages spoken in the area point to the diversity of peoples living throughout the mountains that delimit the Indian subcontinent.

DWELLERS OF THE HIMALAYAS

The Process of Embedding

Sikkim, that "little buckle on the Himalayan belt," illustrates the process of one community being embedded in another. Its on-and-off independence has been largely a consequence of its geographic situation. A mountain-girt basin about sixty by forty miles (96 x 64 km.), squeezed between Tibet (north) and India (south), and Bhutan (east) and Nepal (west), it is the easiest entryway from Tibet into India. The maharaja controlled portions of all four border regions during part of the 1600s and 1700s when Tibetan lamaism became the state religion. A Tibetan dependency until 1780 when Nepalese and Bhutanese warriors occupied much of the land, it was temporarily independent, and then became a dependency of British India in 1861. India took over this protectorate in 1947, holding internal affairs under ever closer control until Sikkim's final incorporation into India as its twenty-second State within the Union in 1975.

Annexation as such is simple grabbing; the reasons do not matter. Embedding implies a broad range of preexisting factors favoring union. Seven of ten Sikkimese are Hindu Nepali farmers, which means that most of the people and the dominant language and religion are basically Indian. India had legitimately inherited Sikkim as a protectorate on its sensitive Tibetan border. When Communist China occupied Tibet militarily, India's safety became a political issue. All these considerations led to India's announcement of incorporation. Sikkim's Chogyal (king) and his American-born Gyalmo (queen) became honored citizens of India. The Tibet-related Lepchas and Bhutias in the upper valleys and mountain meadows probably benefitted little from the three hundred to four hundred miles (480-640 km.) of recently constructed roads which have facilitated the export of fruits, spices, copper, and handcrafted textiles from the lower regions. Like Sikkim, the kingdoms of Nepal and Bhutan are also strategically located on the Himalayas.

Nepal and Bhutan

Perhaps it was because *Nepal* formed a buffer state between India and Tibet from A.D. 979 on that Indian Rajputs and others moved into southern Nepal and introduced Hinduism and their Bengali language, now called Nepali. The common surname Chetri still reminds everyone of the leadership's warrior descent from the Kshatriya caste. The Newars, who ruled the country before the Gurkhas came in 1768, now fill the economic slots of craftsmen and government clerks. The Gurkha dynasty ruled through the later 1700s and, after war with the British authorities in India (1814-1816), stable relations were thereafter maintained. However, until about 1951, the Gurkha rulers and the Hindu elite of Brahmins, Thakurs, and Chetris kept Nepal closed to outsiders. Altitude, religion, language, and ethnic stock combine to distinguish the lowland Hindu Nepalese (including some converted Magars) from the mountain Buddhist peoples who speak Tibetan-related languages: Sherpas, Gurungs, Magars, Limbus, and others. With road connections both to India and Tibet, the constitutional monarchy and its elective parliamentary system must watch ever more carefully its jealously guarded identity.

Hanging like a pendant at the southeastern end of the Himalayas, the isolated kingdom of *Bhutan* has had a checkered existence since the Tibetans were driven out in the A.D. 800s. Over these later centuries the misfortunes of war, diplomacy, and dominance have fluctuated between Tibet, Nepal, Sikkim, and, during the 1800s, British India. Bhutan agreed in 1910 to let Britain guide its external affairs, and since 1949 India has guided them. Any representative group of twelve residents of Bhutan would contain eight descendants of Tibetan settlers, three Nepalese, and one person from India or Burma. Each of the mountain-girt valleys is dominated by its massive, white plastered *dzong*—a combination of fortress, monastery, and palace. The dzong is home for the district *penlop* (territorial lord) and some of the 4,500 lamas (Buddhist priests and monks) of the Red Hat Order of Lamas. Led by its energetic young king, the Bhutanese are opening their doors to cultural influences from India and the West.

Assam

The isolated forests and mountains of the region of northeast India originally called *Assam* have been home to at least thirty-six traditionally battling groups of tribespeople. They have come from all directions, from Tibet, China, Burma, and

India. Assam forms a geographic half-cone, its broad end flattened at the delta seashore, which leads the monsoon clouds ever higher to drop 300 inches (762 cm.) of rain annually near the rocky slot from which the Brahmaputra cascades down into the humid valley below.

Until the influx of Bengali farmers took place, Assam was the cultural extension of Southeast Asia. These Bengali farmers cultivated rice in the lowlands, and educators set up modern schools. Many thousands of tribespeople turned from animism to Christianity (and some to Buddhism). Officials divided the region into seven states and territories, including Nagaland and Mizoram. Agitators brought weapons, and only recently have Mizo and Naga dissidents, armed from China, been induced to cease infiltrating into India and Bangladesh. The polyglot pie called Assam, with its crust of modernization, is filled with about twenty million people working at occupations directly related to the environment: rice, cereals, and rape seed (oil) in the lowlands, and tea, lumber, and other forest and cottage products in the hills and mountains.

THE ISLAMIC REPUBLICS

Pakistan

History.   Northern Pakistan, in the northwest corner of South Asia, is the actual *punj-ab* (Persian: five rivers): the Indus, Jhelum, Chenab, Ravi, and Sutlej. Here the *Rig-Veda* was composed, the action in the *Mahabharata* took place, and in the *Ramayana* Rama's wife, Sita, was exiled from here. The five-rivers region contains some of the roots of Hinduism, Buddhism, and Sikhism, as well as residues of influences and invasions from Egypt, Babylon, Greece, Persia, and Central Asia. Muslim rule by one or another dynasty lasted over eight hundred years, until in the 1800s the region became the northwestern wing of British India.

Classes.   The long Muslim occupation resulted in a distinctive social class system. The Sayyids, tracing descent from the Prophet Muhammad, and the Quraishis from a sainted ancestor, are prominent in the learned and religious professions as Qazi (or Qadhi, judge) or Mufti (religious leader). The military and administrative aristocracy, who make the decisions in national and community affairs, maintain a high profile in all aspects of national life. Merchants and other urbanites, many being later converts to Islam, comprise a class to themselves. Rajputs and Jats form the yeomanry of soldiers and farmers. Two other groups live as it were in a world apart: women, and rural farmers desperately endeavoring to wrest a living for their families from the undernourished earth.

Women.   Although the Koranic statements about women raised their status above that of pre-Islamic times, the successive revelations confirmed male superiority in the social and familial worlds. The head-to-foot cloaks (*burqa*) that shroud the women from public gaze in village street and university classroom effectively separate the world of the nation's women from that of the men. Only a minority of the army officers' wives and some upper-class women feel free enough to appear in public in Indian sari or Western skirt. Distinctive attire also sets apart some of the minority peoples.

The regional peoples. Tall and aristocratic in bearing, sharp and neat, the Yusufzai compose the largest and most sophisticated group of Pakistan's seven million Pathans living on the border adjoining their five million brethren in Afghanistan. Besides nurturing their herds they work hard on their freehold farms. Most of the 400,000 inhabitants of the Swat valley are these Pashto-speaking Yusufzais, whose landowning upper class collect up to four fifths of the tenants' crops, and maintain their prestige in the community by reckless largesse to bind followers to their political support.

Passing south through much barren country we come to the fertile and productive *Sind* (from Sindhu, Indus). Many Sindhis, Muslim since A.D. 712 when the Arab general Muhammad bin Qasim overcame the Brahmin ruler, Dahir, may be descendants of ancient aboriginal inhabitants. These include the Mohana fisherfolk of the Manchar Lake, and the camel-rearing people of the Indus delta who today are called Jats. Farmers predominate in Sind, followed by herders of camels, cattle, water buffalo, goats, and sheep. Almost no boats now ply the Indus, but irrigation channels are everywhere.

Baluchistan is sparsely occupied by five main groups: the Makranis on the Makran Coast; the Dravidian-speaking Brahuis ("gypsy" goat herders); the Indo-Iranian Baluchi herders of the vast arid region of the southern Pakistan-Iranian borders; the Turko-Mongol Hazaras, Persian-speaking farmer-herders like their comrades in Afghanistan; and some dispersed elements of the Pathans.

Upon separation from India in 1947, Pakistan had to build from scratch its whole governmental, economic, and social structure. Since the Pakistani concept of the nation is that Islam and the nation, religion, and conduct are parts of an interweaving whole (see Chapter 4), the nation was properly titled the Islamic Republic of Pakistan. While the inescapable will of Allah tends to support centralization of authority, internal protests have sparked violent riots against the continuance of decades of authoritarian rule. Efforts are being made to utilize the benefits of a common Islamic faith, the trauma of several unrewarding wars with India and (the present) Bangladesh, and the products of a modernizing economy, to forge a unifying loyalty as fellow Pakistanis.

Bangladesh

As Vanga, Bang, and Bangla, the new (1971) nation of Bangladesh (country of Bengal) has had its own identity since A.D. 200. The inferior economic and cultural status of the people of East Bengal—the "uncouth" people of Bengali literature—led to their acceptance of Islam when Turki Muslims conquered the land in the A.D. 1200s. As the political scene changed, the constant shifting of provincial boundaries always left the double deltas of the Ganges and the Brahmapotra in the middle.

The Bengali-speaking villagers share real equality in the mosque environment, as part of their class-structured and secular society in which wealth and poverty are the principal distinctions. During the four months of seasonal inundation of much of the low-lying countryside, conversation often centers around life and death, food and health, and the influence of religion and of the *zins* (or *jinns*). *Zins* are regarded as supernatural beings to be judged by God for their deeds in creating fear and uncertainty in human life, and are controllable through the pungent aroma of ritual herbal medicines. Placation of the *zins* may be combined with worship at the mosque in religious practice.

Other villagers are secularly oriented. Also, some Hindu influences persist from the many festivals formerly observed before partition from India in 1947. On the night of Sab-o-barat, the festival coinciding with the birthday of Muhammad, the illuminations indicate a connection with the Hindu festival of Diwali. At Diwali time houses, shops, and other places are illuminated as part of the Lakshmi Puza, the worship of the Hindu goddess of wealth. The two principal Muslim festivals are the Idd-ul-Fitr, the feast celebrating the end of the Ramadan month of fasting, and the Idd-ul-Azha, when an animal is sacrificed and the meat distributed. At all three festivals there are prayers and the generous distribution of food, sweets, and good wishes to all.

The Bangladeshi are people of the rivers, harassed by flood and tidal wave, poverty-stricken and rapidly increasing in numbers. Only two percent are tribal people. The ethos of the Bangladesh populace is bound up with the mighty turbulent rivers and the monsoon rain, where "the beauty of the autumn clouds and smiling paddy fields give him his songs and poetry."

Maldive Islands

Tourists flying in to Male, capital of Asia's smallest country, The Republic of Maldives, would see part of a speckled green mat of coral islets scattered over an expanse of the Indian Ocean five hundred by fifty miles (800 by 80 km.). The biggest island boasts five square miles (13 sq. km.) of land surface, and the cramped space on which the 161,000 Maldivians live totals only 115 square miles (just under 300 sq. km.). Life for these bonito and tuna fishermen in their thousands of 36 foot (11 m.) boats has hardly changed for hundreds of years. These descendants of Sinhalese, Arab, and Dravidian lineages still sail 15 to 20 miles (24-32 km.) from shore to fish with hook and line. Once ashore, the women cook and smoke the catch, and the merchants export the dried fish to Sri Lanka, along with reed mats, copra (dried coconut meat), lacquerware, and rope. Small, slight, and quiet, these Sunni Muslims make a subsistence living that gives them a diet of fish, yams, coconuts, papayas, and pineapples, and provides opportunities for bartering their various products or purchasing their imported staples or rice, sugar, cloth, and medicines.

Two periods of protectorate status of just under 140 years each began with the Portuguese in 1518 and the Dutch in Ceylon in 1656, and a little longer under the British from about 1800 to separation from India in 1948 and full independence in 1965. Islam was adopted in 1153, and for the most part *de facto* local government was under a sultan of the Didi clan, until the republic was proclaimed in 1968.

CONCLUSION

Whether on the sea-girt Maldives, the sunny hills of Sri Lanka, the broad expanses of India, Pakistan, and Bangladesh, or on the high Himalayas, a great immensity and depth of human living fills South Asia. A great dilemma faces humankind today: how to retain hope, caring, worth of being, and a meaningful social life while surviving with modern values and modern technology. How can a society temper life so that the best of its traditional sacred and secular aspects blend with the best of the new to make a satisfying today and a worthy tomorrow. If this dilemma has a solution, perhaps it is in South Asia that the solution will be found.

PART IV

Vastness and Diversity: North Asia

Chapter **11**

Nomads of the North

From the time Ivan the Terrible was crowned czar in 1547, the single whispered word, "Siberia!" often was sufficient to blanch the face of the European Russian, as the place of exile, flogging, starvation, and death. But to the unnumbered generations of its native peoples Siberia was home. Reindeer made life bearable for Samoyed herdsmen-hunters on the frozen or marshy *tundra* in the north, just as varied animals provided furs for the Evenk inhabitants of the somber *taiga* (forest) shadows. The horse, in turn, enabled the Mongol riders of the *steppelands* to herd their flocks, to move their encampments of round felt tents (*yurts*), and to raid their suspecting but unprepared neighbors.

Fabled Karakorum, steppe capital of the Mongols, housed Parisian goldsmiths and Chinese artists; and an express messenger on urgent business for the khan rode relays of Mongol horses and crossed the Eurasian continent in six weeks. But the steppe empire gradually fell apart and the Mongol vision of pastoral nomadism as a way of life for Eurasia vanished with the wind.

Siberia hid within its often icy bosom riches of which its horse and sleigh peoples knew nothing. Within the last two centuries Russians and Chinese have carved out their spheres of national control in North Asia, and have systematically developed the natural resources. In Soviet Asia (Siberia and Central Asia) the modern technology of some 70 million people, mostly Russians, has banded the territory with steel rails, and has carried immigrants east and west to new cities, factories, and mines. Steamboat and airplane have ferried supplies and equipment north and south to supply drillers for gas and oil, miners of bauxite and gold, and workers in textile and steel mills. North Asia now contains everything from sod cabin to Science City. Throughout the region precarious survival and great potentials exist side-by-side.

A LOOK AT NORTH ASIA

Sandwiched between the frigid lands of the Arctic Ocean and Tibet, and between the deserts east of the Caspian Sea and those north of China, lies a vast land spreading from the mineral-rich Ural mountains to the once unknown waters of the North Pacific Ocean. To the Russians in the 1500s it was the land of Sibir. To the readers of this book it is North Asia. (See Table 11-1.)

The term "North Asia" is used as a parallel to the geographic terms which have been employed for the other four regions of Asia. But our interests include not only the permanent geographic features, such as some of the world's mightiest rivers, but also the fluid interplay of peoples and nations as, historically, they moved across or gained control of this or that region. So there will be some overlapping of terms as we discuss peoples in areas to which various authors have given other names recorded in the literature on North Asia. The following definitions should be read in conjunction with the accompanying map (Figure 11-1).

Definitions

North Asia comprises the lands east of the Ural mountains and the Caspian Sea; south of the Arctic Ocean; north of Iran, Afghanistan, Tibet, and China; and west of the Pacific Ocean. Within these boundaries four areas are subject to precise definition (Central Asia, Mongolia, Siberia, and Soviet Asia), while two (Inner Asia and the Heartland) are general and indeterminate at the edges. This vagueness arises rather simply. The trade and caravan routes into and through Inner Asia varied both in their points of origin and destination, and also in their range from north to south. The generalization regarding the Heartland likewise encompasses the changing habitats and migrations of peoples, and the shifting of their political, economic, and military centers of power. The five main areas of North Asia are as follows:

1. *Soviet Asia*: Includes the total areas of Central Asia and Siberia.
2. *Central Asia*: Designates the combined territories of the five Soviet Socialist Republics of Kazakhstan, Turmenistan, Tadzhikistan, and Kirgizia. Administratively, the latter four Republics constitute *Soviet Central Asia*.
3. *Inner Asia*: The general area of the east-west trade and communication conduit from Northwest China to Eastern Central Asia; bordered on the south by Tibet, and on the north by the steppelands of Mongolia and Kazakhstan.
4. *The Heartland*: Even more indefinite than Inner Asia, the main Heartland area includes Mongolia, Xinjiang and Kazakhstan; its fringes touch Tibet, Siberia, and Soviet Central Asia.
5. *Siberia*: The vast northern and eastern expanse of North Asia excluding Central Asia and Mongolia.

Of these five regions, it is Siberia which until recently has been the most remote and isolated. Here humans have faced some of the most extreme survival conditions on the face of the earth—and met them boldly.

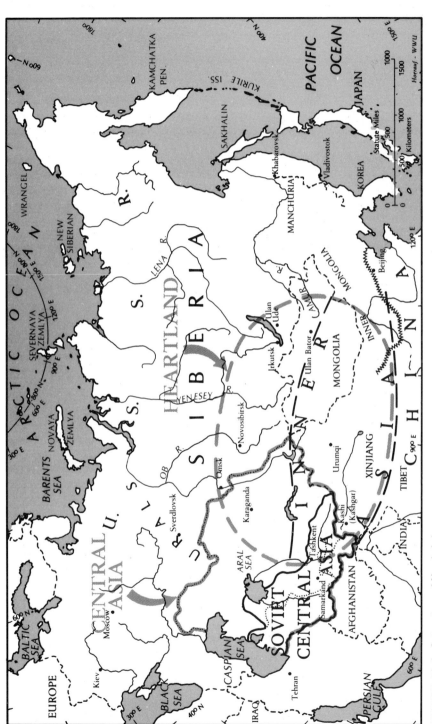

FIGURE 11-1 Subregions of North Asia.

TABLE 11-1   Statistics on North Asia

NAME OF REGION	AREA		POPULATION
	SQUARE MILES	SQUARE KILOMETERS	
Five Republics of Soviet Central Asia	1,542,000	3,994,000	35,284,000
Siberia	5,087,000	13,182,000	35,781,000
Total for Soviet Asia	6,629,000	17,176,000	71,065,000
Mongolia	604,000	1,565,000	1,689,000
Total for North Asia	7,233,000	18,741,000	72,754,000

Figures for Soviet Asia based on Paul E. Lydolph, *Geography of the U.S.S.R.,* 3rd ed. (New York: John Wiley and Sons, 1977). © 1977 by John Wiley.

THE SIBERIAN LANDS

Siberia, for centuries the verbal symbol of a sinister and mysterious land, has earned several nicknames. The Russian novelist, Dostoevski, called it the "House of the Dead," where millions of men have vanished without a trace. Two Tatar words have supplied another name, the "sleeping land," from *sib* (sleep) and *ir* (land). It was indeed a *terra incognita,* unknown and asleep to most Europeans, until after the A.D. 1500s. Another suggested derivation describes its most widespread physical feature: the Mongolian word *siwr* meaning a (damp) forest. This forest zone or *taiga* covers about half the area of Siberia, bordered on the north by the frozen and swampy Arctic region, the *tundra,* and on the south by the *steppes,* or grasslands, and the mountains. *Sibir,* once the name of a small fortress town on the big Irtysh river east of the Ural mountains, still is the Russian term for the whole territory.

Siberia's northern zone is part of the frigid circumpolar region which also includes Alaska and northern Canada with their adjacent islands, Greenland, and northern Europe. Siberia's western and southern areas merge geographically and culturally into the adjacent territories. The environment and cultures of east

TABLE 11-2   Siberia's Principal Rivers

NAME	LENGTH		OUTLET
	MILES	KILOMETERS	
Irtysh	1,840	2,945	Joins the Ob
Ob	2,500	4,000[a]	Arctic Ocean
Yenesey	2,360	3,775[b]	Arctic Ocean
Lena	2,645	4,230	Arctic Ocean
Amur	2,700	4,320	Pacific Ocean

[a] Also given as 5,410 km. by *Soviet Life,* December 1979, p. 17.

[b] Also given as 5,092 km. in same issue and page.

coast Siberia show many parallels with the ways of life of the Eskimos and Indians inhabiting the coasts of northwest America on the opposite shores of the North Pacific Ocean. The interior regions of both northern America and Siberia also have spawned nomadic cultures based on hunting caribou in America and herding reindeer in Siberia.

THE PARADE OF PEOPLES

The Pattern of the Parade

There is some justification for distinguishing between reindeer-herding roamers, horse-borne raiders, and village (and town) residents among the peoples native to Siberia. Nevertheless, difficulty arises in the endeavor to neatly classify many of them as whole units, dependent on any one form of subsistence. Different environments and climates allowed subgroups to exploit several of the many possibilities particular to their local situations. So most of them followed a mixed economy of several occupations in seeking year-round sustenance: hunting regularly, fishing in local rivers, lakes, or seas; and herding whatever animals were useful and available. Agriculture was minimal. Interchange of goods and products prevailed throughout the region, yet became of major importance to only a few groups. However, a generalized classification can be made on the basis of several characteristics: environment or location, movement, activity, and type of residence. Of all the Siberian environments, the tundra is the harshest (see Table 11-3).

LIFE ON THE TUNDRA

Reindeer Herders on the Tundra—The Samoyed

Dark in winter, eerily bright in summer, always underlain by permafrost; the tundra landscape was home to tens of thousands of both wild and tame reindeer, as they migrated from forest edge to Arctic beach and back the whole year round. On the northern Taymyr Peninsula the *Nganasan Samoyeds* kept no large herds of domesticated reindeer but hunted wild reindeer until about 1960. Individual hunters hid behind sleds as blinds, or used tame decoys to entice wild reindeer to mingle with their tame animals for capture. South of the Peninsula, on the treeless tundra and the lightly wooded borders of the taiga forests, most of the 25,000 *Nentsy* (or *Nenet*) *Samoyeds* followed the migrations of their tame reindeer herds. Some Nentsy on the coast hunted sea mammals as well, and others living on the banks of the mighty Ob river became sedentary fishermen. For all these people the reindeer served as the main form of transportation.

The Samoyeds knew their reindeer just as the Bedouin knew their camels and the African Masai knew their cattle. A Nganasan father, for instance, used any one of more than twenty words to tell his son precisely which reindeer to catch. *Tangkaga* indicated a harness animal, *kartaga,* one with many branched antlers, and a six-year old animal was a *sambamta.* A stud was called a *kurie.* In other words, the son knew how to select the right animal according to its function, appearance, or age.

FIGURE 11-2 Siberia: reindeer herding camp.

Move to a new camp. When it came time to move to fresh feeding grounds, men and women set about their respective tasks in preparation for meeting a few days or weeks later at an appointed rendezvous. The men's first job was rounding up the several hundred to two thousand tame reindeer belonging to the household. This was done with the aid of their fluffy and hardy herd dogs, the samoyeds, which had been around for three thousand years. Those preparing to ride a reindeer set the saddle over the animal's shoulders, for the back could not support a man's weight, then mounted and followed the herds. After the departure of the men, the women folded the tent coverings, rolled up the poles, and lashed them to the tent-carrying sleds. Furnishings, utensils, clothing, and toddlers filled the freight sleds to capacity. As soon as the reindeer were hitched to the sleds with a special harness, the women perched themselves on top of the loads and the caravan set off. At this level of technology life on the tundra was entirely dependent upon the presence of the reindeer. Realizing this, the Samoyeds called the reindeer *jilepc,* a word meaning "life," "living."

Arriving at the rendezvous first, the women and children presented a bustling scene as they arranged the poles for the larger tents in a circle with a diameter of about 24 to 27 feet (7 to 9 meters). Reindeer hides sewn into sheets were wrapped in two layers around the circle of poles to form a tipi-style structure. The inner layer had the fur inside, the outer layer had the fur outside, just as they wore the two layers of their own fur clothing. A third wrapping of canvas prevented snow from sticking to the fur. To keep the fierce winds from tearing the tent apart, the women laid poles and H-frames against the tent covers, and tied a binder of rope around the whole. The floor space then was divided equally between the several families occupying each large tent. Some households had their own smaller tents.

Evening in the tent.   The evening scene inside the tent again was permeated by reminders of the reindeer. Clustered around the cooking pots on the iron hearth in the center of the tent, the women prepared several alternatives for supper. Reindeer meat was ready either frozen or partially cooked. There was also sliced frozen fish. One woman would combine rye flour, cranberries, and reindeer blood according to a Samoyed pancake recipe, while another would serve her family with the marrow, which could be either dried, salted, boiled, or chopped up in a soup. On occasion venison, duck, and cooked fish were available. However, the Samoyed did not use the reindeer milk, unlike the reindeer-herding Evenks or Tungus to the east who drank the milk regularly.

On any given evening after the meal the adults laid out their various projects and occupations, if they had the inclination, the materials, and the space. On a typical evening, perhaps, one woman picked up the soft suede leather jackets she had made and began to decorate them with dyed designs prior to adding the fringed borders. Before the winter temperatures dropped to their low of $-76°$ F $(-60°$ C), full length sleeves and hoods were added to the family's fur and chamois garments. One man shaped hides for blankets and tent coverings, another cut strips for a lasso, and a third made needles and arrow heads from the reindeer bones. Antlers, sinews for thread, and other articles lay nearby.

The dogs tied near the entrance gave a staccato announcement of the arrival of a latecomer, who skirted the pile of firewood, threaded his way around the women sewing or smoking, to reach the men now seated around the central fire. Here he too shucked his upper garments, and remarked that the shaman would soon be arriving to treat the woman who was sick. When the shaman came they made room for him to work near the fire. There, dancing uncontrollably, singing his charm songs and drumming on his drum, the shaman sank into a trance to find the cause of the sickness. On awaking, his findings from the realm of the spirits were then communicated to the group in a song.

Chukchi and Koryak

Some two thousand miles (3,200 km.) east across the tundra in the far northeastern sector of frozen Siberia, the forests come quite close to the coasts. This circumstance offered wide environmental opportunities to the peoples residing there. There the 14,000 *Chukchi* and the 7,500 *Koryak* (*koryak* means reindeer people) were divided by residence and livelihood into interior reindeer-breeding groups and coastal fishing groups. The Chukchi and Koryak reindeer-herding sections had more in common with one another than with the coastal section in their respective tribes. Both the inhabitants of the coastal sections and the reindeer herders made a permanent residential adaptation to their own areas. The herder

TABLE 11-3   General Grouping of Siberian Peoples

ENVIRONMENT	MOVEMENT	ACTIVITY	RESIDENCE	NAMES OF TYPICAL PEOPLES
Tundra	Nomadic	Hunting, fishing, (herding)	Tent	Samoyed, Kanti, Mansi, Evenk, Chukchi, Koryak
Taiga	Semi-nomadic	Herding, (hunting, fishing)	Cabin[c] and tent	Ket, Evenk, Even
Steppes[a]	Nomadic	Herding	Yurt	Mongol (Buryat, Kalkha)
Coast and River basins	Sedentary[b]	Fishing	Cabin	Samoyed, Ket, Kamchadals, Koryak, Amur river and Sakhalin island groups
Town and farm	Sedentary	Farmers, technicians, officials	House	Russians

Notes:

[a] Steppes include some mountainous and some semidesert areas.

[b] Sedentary peoples are village (or town) residents.

[c] Cabin refers to log cabins, semisubterranean dwellings, etc., as distinct from tent, yurt, or town house.

groups lived very much like the reindeer-keeping peoples of the taiga forests to be described a little later.

The coastal groups, however, displayed considerable versatility, for they were unique in combining fishing, hunting on land, ice, and sea, and trading. To see the range of their activities we have to follow their annual cycle. According to the migrating and mating seasons of the various animals, they moved to follow the animals in the forest or on the coast. Hunting in the forest they herded reindeer and used them to pull their sleds on land. But on the ice the huntsmen harnessed dogs to their sleds, to return the next day with their kill of seal or walrus. In boats they occasionally hunted whales. So from the animals and fish of their threefold environment of tundra, taiga, and sea coast the coastal Koryak and Chukchi derived their food and clothing, and whale oil for cooking and heating. They traded items such as leather, ivory tusks, and oil with neighboring peoples, including the Russians and the reindeer-keeping groups.

The herder groups, certainly among the Chukchi, necessarily were seasonal nomads, traveling in large parties between separate pastures on the coast in summer and inland in the winter. Wealthy men owned upwards of ten thousand tame reindeer, herded without the use of dogs by the poverty-stricken members of their clan. These large herding groups of thirty to eighty patrilineally related households formed the largest Chukchi communities.

Coastal groups were smaller, including a few Eskimo in the far northwest corner of Siberia. Both the maritime section of the Koryak and the Eskimos hunted in skin boats on the open water between ice floes. Besides chasing the usual sea-mammals, on land the Eskimos hunted arctic fox, polar bear, and hare. It was to be expected then, that just as the reindeer supplied much of the food, clothing, and equipment of the tundra peoples, so the flesh, skins, tusks, and bones, of the sea mammals provided sleds, kayaks, shoes, thimbles, needles, and clothing for the Eskimo and the coastal Koryak and Chukchi.

"Harvesters of the Environment" is a title we might give to these peoples of the tundra and the adjacent forested and coastal borderlands. These peoples merit high praise for their successful adaptation of life and technology to one of the world's most demanding environments. Leaving now the forest and coastal borderlands we move southwards into the taiga forest belt itself.

LIFE IN THE FORESTS

Unlike the actual open skies above the lightly wooded southern tundra, the deep, dark canopy of the dense forests of the taiga protectively sealed people and animals within its somber embrace. Travel time by reindeer sled or horse cart, or on horseback within the shadows of spruce, fir, pine, and hemlock, commonly lagged behind that of the reindeer sled speeding on the firm ice and snow of the tundra. Probably it was faster, however, than the fan of three or four reindeer plowing through tundra snow as deep or deeper than the belly of the animals. The weight of wet snow on tent or sled, and exposure to frostbite, affected travelers during blizzard weather in both tundra and taiga. Yet those in the forest were spared much of the rigor of the tundra's bitter gale in winter and clouds of biting insects in summer. Also, the forest amply provided wood for shelter and fuel, and its animals supplied the finest furs in Asia.

Adaptation

Many of the present peoples inhabiting both tundra and forest, including the Samoyed, Khanti, Mansi, Evenks and Yakuts, moved northwards to the current locations from warmer regions to the south. Leaving behind their occupations in agriculture and horse breeding, they have successfully adapted to the limitations of a radically new environment in the cold northern forests. This has ensured their survival as hunting and reindeer-herding peoples. For example, they now employ reindeer as once they had employed horses, for riding, transportation, and milk. Game abounded in forest, river, and clearing: squirrel, sable, fox, wolf, marten, deer, elk, hare, and bear. The bear usually had a religious significance in addition to whatever practical use was made of flesh, hide, or claws. Salmon, sturgeon, and cod were speared or netted in the streams, while duck, geese, grouse, and other smaller game were shot, netted, or, snared on land.

Situational Adaptation

Situations and hence adaptations varied widely over the 2,500 miles (4,000 km.) west to east expanse of the taiga forest zone. The 21,000 *Khanti* and the 8,000 *Mansi* occupied a bitter blizzard area the size of France in the swamps and forests of the Irtysh and Ob rivers. Just to the east the patrilineal, out-marrying clans of the *Ket* operated fleets of good canoes for their river fishing. The *Evenks* (often called *Tungus*), wide-spread in the Yenesey and upper Lena basins, were a short, stocky and cheerful people. The Evenk reindeer saddle was a prairie horse type, and their open-fronted clothing suited southern climates rather than the coldest winter in the world, which saw temperatures drop to $-80°$ F $(-62°$ C).

Even more interesting as a case of adaptation was that of the early Russians in this area. The swift occupation of parts of Siberia by the Russians in the 1600s paralleled that of Mexico and Peru by the Spanish conquistadors, and that of the American West by the settlers in their Conestoga wagons. The early Russian immigrants to North Asia found shelter in the permanent housing of the Evenks, married the Evenk women, and became fishermen and hunters themselves.

The ancestors of the nearly 300,000 *Yakuts* occupying the middle Lena basin had a similar experience about 800 years earlier. Wending their slow way north from the horse-rearing area around Lake Baikal, they penetrated 2,000 miles (3,200 km.) of dense and almost uninhabited forest into a reindeer-breeding region. Only a few of their kinspeople in the south still remain in a horse and cattle-raising area. The Yakut house, four-sided and substantial, contained plank sleeping benches and other furnishings, and their forts were so well constructed the Russians had great difficulty capturing them. As a forest people the Yakuts tanned leather expertly, but neither wove cloth nor rolled felt. Their mixed economy included spots of agriculture here and there in forest clearings, and their success in utilizing the environment enabled them to refurbish Vitus Bering's expedition of 1724 with the victuals the expedition needed to reach the Pacific coast.

PEOPLES OF THE PACIFIC COAST

Acquainted as they are with life in the forest, for forests were all around them, the Pacific coast tribes were oriented towards the sea and the rivers as fishermen. This orientation made them different from interior groups on the tundra plains and in the taiga forests. The northern Kamchadals, as well as the Chukchi and Koryak, ate sea mammal meat and made durable and waterproof clothing and footwear out of fish skins. Salmon runs provided year-round sustenance for the family, and stockpiled mammal meat meant sustenance for their sledge dogs as well. Furs warmed their bodies and their beds.

The Amur River Fishermen

Many of these Amur river fishermen relate closely—by descent, language, and culture—to the forest-dwelling Evenks and display a technology more advanced than their forest kinspeople. The *Orochi* used sandstone molds for copper castings, and trapped seals in fake breeding grounds. The *Ul'chi* hunted seals in boats made of three boards, which the Cantonese would have recognized as *sampans* (literally, three boards). Their women, like the wives of Chinese river and harbor men, rowed the boats and helped with the netting of fish. The ten thousand *Nanai* near the southern border have been implicated in the centuries-long struggles of the older Korean kingdoms, and were later involved with the Chinese outreach, the Manchu inrush of the 1600s, and the modern Russian take-over. Many well-to-do Nanai wore work clothes of leather, fish skins, and cloth, but for special occasions the men and women arrayed themselves in Chinese styles of silks and furs. Several

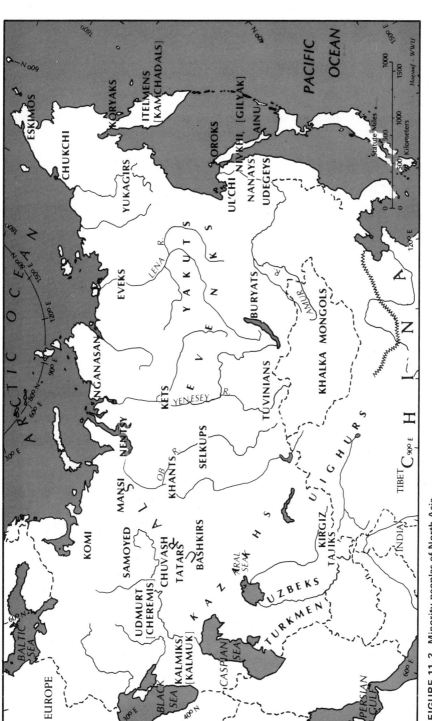

FIGURE 11-3 Minority peoples of North Asia.

groups used an ingenious hunting weapon, a floating harpoon. The harpoon head and staff were secured on a float at the end of a pole nearly one hundred feet (30-meters) long, with which seals or large fish were impaled from boat, blind, or shore.

Sakhalin Islanders

Living both on Sakhalin Island and on the adjacent mainland, the *Gilyak* or *Nivkhi* maintained several distinctive traits in addition to those of the regional culture. As ironsmiths in pre-Russian days they produced massive chains, coats of mail, spear points inlaid with silver and copper, and curved knives for carving wood. Unlike most groups with a two-way marriage arrangement between out-marrying clans, the Gilyak maidens of clan A were given to husbands in clan B. The men of clan A, however, took their wives from clan C. This interesting procedure ensured a three-way system of supportive relationships.

The other well-known people originally occupying the Japanese islands and at least southern Sakhalin and the southern Kurile islands were the *Ainu.* The origins of these people remain a subject of controversy. Under its chief the village was the unit of society, and the well-constructed house was both home and shrine. Stockily built and unusually hirsute, the Ainu were tenacious fighters as well as expert foresters and fishermen. Their assembly-line organization for harvesting the fish runs was so efficient that, as the men caught the fish in the shallows near the shore, the women prepared and packaged them for winter consumption. By the end of the day's effort the day's catch was all stowed away. The Ainu are best known, perhaps, for their ceremonial bear sacrifice, which was the high point in their religious system of placation of the spirits of nature and the veneration of ancestors.

Both Sides of the Pacific

If the Tlingit and other American Indians on the Pacific Northwest Coast had visited their counterparts on the Siberian coasts they would have found so many parallels in their environment, technology, and activities that participation would have posed no real problems. Both areas combined riverine, forest, and seacoast orientations. Both peoples harpooned seals and whales, and both used nets, traps, and fishing spears for salmon, sturgeon, and other fish. Tree roots and twigs were fashioned into baskets, nettle fiber became thread and string, and houses were built with solid planks. Many on both sides built riverine canoes and seagoing longboats. Both also emphasized private ownership of boats and tackle and products of the hunt. Women, who performed much of the chores and drudgery, were usually accorded a dignified and even high position in family and lineage. Artwork ornamentation of canoes, wooden boxes, houseposts and facades, and clothing also were shared traits. However, many other aspects of life and livelihood differed considerably. For instance, the Siberian innovation of the long harpoon was hardly suitable to the stormy profiles of the American coast. Other major differences also concerned the environment. Whereas the Siberian tribespeople had at their backs the readily accessible forests with their abundance of animals for fur and feast, the coastal Indians of northern America were walled off from the forested interior by massive snowy mountains. The reindeer herds available to many of the Siberians had no parallel on the American coast, for the caribou herds of the Arctic northlands of America migrated on the far side of the almost impenetrable ranges. Alternatives for travel also varied. The coastal Indians used neither sled nor ski, reindeer nor horse, although these were very suitable to the Siberian environment.

THE TRANSFORMATION OF SIBERIA

Flames Amid the Snow

Yermak's firearmed Cossacks who roared into Siberia in 1583 were followed by settlers and farmers who established themselves in solid, lighted houses in fortified trading posts. During the 1800s and early 1900s the various forms of the flames of technology—from matches and pressure lamps to factory furnaces and locomotives, automobiles and river steamers—brought to North Asians of every ethnic group fires they never dreamed could exist. And so with the advent of the jet airplane and the helicopter even cosmonauts and space travel could be taken in stride.

Change

Factories, mining settlements, and large cities dot Siberia. The speakers of indigenous languages all have their own newspapers and literature. Schooling is universal and selected students go on to university to become the future specialists of their region.

But many Siberians follow altered versions of the traditional occupations. Reindeer herders and hunters have been organized into collectives which allocate pastures and hunting territories. They are encouraged to farm at their settlements. Fishermen are collectivized and use motorboats. Shamanism is outlawed (but still practiced), and modern doctors are provided. Compulsory study of Russian provides a *lingua franca* for Siberia. Yet still the vast challenge of the Siberian lands remains.

The old unique patterns of Siberian cultures are gradually becoming homogenized. This is the opposite of what happened to the Mongols, where a homogenous group broke up and became separate, heterogeneous cultures.

LIFE ON THE STEPPELANDS

The Mongol Movement

Europe still bears the remnants of the Roman and Latin image and the partial imprint of the Arab and Berber dominance in Spain. At Vienna in 1683 Europe barely shook off the threat of a Turkish conquest. More recent were the devastations of the armies of Napoleon, Hitler, and Mussolini, and the present tensions between the East and West blocs. However, it is probable that few readers know how narrowly Europe escaped massive destruction in 1241 by the nomadic horsemen of Batu Khan, the grandson of Genghis Khan the Mongol. The interesting observation has been made concerning the significance of this Mongol movement

in Europe, that "their's was the supreme attempt to impose nomad domination on the settled peoples of the world" (Phillips 1969: 14). The failure of this attempt meant not only relief for Europe but also signalled the gradual ending of nomadism as the life-style of any great portion of mankind. Nevertheless, for hundreds of years the lifeways of most of the indigenous peoples of Northern Asia continued substantially unchanged, and they still retain elements of distinctiveness in language and tradition today.

The Mongols were one of many horse-riding societies that occupied the vast grasslands which are sandwiched in an east-west environmental zone lying between the *taiga* forests and swamps of Siberia to the north and the more arid and desert areas to the south. Mobility lay at the center of Mongol life.

Stripped for Mobility

Born in a felt-covered "tent" (*ger* to the Mongols and *yurt* to outsiders) the Mongol baby was carried in a portable cradle slung under the mother's arm. Cared for in the average family of four—father, mother, elder sister perhaps, and this baby brother—loved but not coddled, the child grew up hardy, toughened in all weathers by caring for sheep and goats in the lattice pen alongside the yurt. Both men and women dressed much alike in long, loose coats of sheepskin or fur in the winter and cloth in summer. Coats were worn outside the trousers, with sleeves long enough to act as gloves in winter. Men usually wore belts around the coats, and their rather loose, high boots, designed for riding, accommodated several pairs of socks. Their horses, cattle (and some yaks), sheep, goats, and camels—called by the Mongols the "five tribes"—were penned, hobbled, or allowed to graze loose not too far from the several yurts in the encampment.

The Mongolian yurt was constructed around a latticework frame over which were laid heavy felt rugs to form the sides and low domed roof, and was entered by a low doorway. The fireplace lay in the center of the floor space, which often was covered by rugs or furs, with sleeping places beside the tent walls. It contained the household goods, weapons, the shrine, and the few permanent possessions of the family: jewelry, decorated chests, and fine clothing. Nearly everything was, or could be, made by the householders themselves. Only rarely did individuals' ability and inclination, as carpenter, smith, or maker of fine jewelry lead them to become specialists. Nomadism allowed little time for training, and few opportunities to acquire raw materials and tools. Everything was stripped down to the essentials for mobility, and Mongol skills and techniques were honed to the way of life summarized as "living on his horse."

Land, People, and Animals

The shepherding of animals in a grass-bearing region, where rainfall, temperature, and climatic variations necessitate periodically moving the herds from one area to another, is called pastoral nomadism. This was the case with the Mongols, who rode horses, milked cattle, used yaks as load carriers, and herded sheep and goats. In the more arid areas they also kept camels for all these same purposes. These various animals each furnished its own quota of hair (or wool), skins, milk, meat, and dung for fuel. All except the sheep and goats also doubled as pack, draft, or riding animals. The yak, of course, functioned best above 4,000 feet (1,220 m.) altitude. In addition to milk, cheese and meat, the principal items in the daily diet, the animals provided hair for rope and thread, felt for the rugs and tent coverings, skins for clothing and bedding, and hides for leather boots, harnesses, and containers. Each animal was known intimately and was cared for diligently. Nevertheless, because of the perils of drought and snowstorm, the quantity rather than the quality of the animals possessed was important, as margins of a household's security and as the measure of its wealth. The total number of animals in the whole region used to be several scores of millions in the grasslands, and some two million in the desert regions.

The needs of the animals for food and shelter determined the seasonal migratory cycle of movement between a fixed winter home area and the summer and winter pastures. Groups with good year-round pastures moved merely a perfunctory 100 yards (about 30 meters). Others, dependent upon wells and seasonal streams, commonly moved upwards of twenty times annually. But more than care and effort were needed to ensure prosperity.

Intangible Aid for Tangible Needs

Just as other features of Mongol culture related to the environment and to themselves as part of it, so did religion. On prominent hills and mountain passes cairns or monuments of stone, *obos,* were erected, dedicated to the lord or owner spirit of that terrestrial feature, or of the earth itself. The elders seemed to be saying through their ceremonies at the *obo* shrines that, since humans were merely transient beings, the group was obligated to offer sacrifices as an expiation for trespassing on the owner's property. These *obo* spirits, intimately associated with the earth, heaven, sun, moon, stars, winds, and other natural phenomena, were part of the widespread form of Tibetan nature worship, called Bon. This form of animism preceded the introduction of Buddhism into the region.

The Mongols also had two other reactions to the rather unpredictable and all-encompassing world around them, a world which both supplied their needs and limited their options. Both men and women saw that offerings of food and drink were made regularly to gods and spirits. One particular responsibility of the women was to tend to the yurt's representation of the "five elements" of earth, fire, water, wood, and metal—the fireplace and its utensils. On an earthen base several stones acted as a tripod supporting the metal pot of water simmering over a fire of wooden sticks and dried dung; alongside lay the metal fire tongs. The earth god was most important, for upon its favor depended the welfare of the land and of the people and animals dwelling there. Fire, however, commanded the greatest respect from Mongol, Turki, and other nomads.

The crises of life—birth, sickness, marriage, death, and burial—and other important household happenings were met with the aid of thousands of methods of astrology, divination, physiognomy, etc. If the household felt that the occasion warranted special aid, shamans (part-healers, part-seers) of both sexes were available, as well as Buddhist priests or lamas. The shamans knew the procedures needed to cope with relationships with the land, the spirits, and the uncertainties and disasters of life.

Fusion and Fission

A quarrel, for instance, often caused a household to leave a kin-related cluster of households. Replacements had to be compatible. Sometimes these were members of a group dispersed when a previous winter's storms had reduced their four-footed possessions to a couple of horses and a half dozen sheep. Harsh experiences like these formed part of the social training of the younger members of the household. Qualities of initiative and competence were hammered into them for about twenty years by parental precept. They gained practice by the rigors of facing alone, or with a few companions, the biting storm, the lost sheep, the dying calf, the midnight raiders, and the evening wolf. Nonetheless, this capability for independent action was somehow at odds with the basic fact that herding was a group, not an individual, occupation. In the end, teamwork, not individualism, was the essence of survival.

However, if lineage ties were to be perpetuated, children married, and territories protected—if these nomads were to exist as a people at all—then these easily fissionable household clusters had to be fused into larger units of tribe, league, or confederation. This Mongol amalgam of diverse factors had to be preserved, and this raised the further question of leadership.

Leadership began with the father governing the household. Beyond this leadership rested on the preeminence of one among otherwise equally competent individuals. Preeminence depended on wealth, ability, and powers of persuasion.

Additionally there was the ranking of nobility for persons tracing their ancestry back to Genghis Khan, even though this ranking seemed to clash with the practicalities of a mobile democracy. A series of rights and duties bound together these two sets of interests. In return for a month's services and some gifts of animals, cheese, or meat, the noble allocated pasturage, arbitrated disputes, and saw that his followers were neither debt ridden nor in want.

The Circle of Life

Around the core occupation of pastoralism the Mongols, like herding groups in many parts of the world, maintained an outer circle of occupations and communications which were necessary to their continued effectiveness and existence. The Mongol circle of life is diagrammed in Figure 11-5.

The Mongol's much-loved pastime of hunting provided some additional subsistence items of food and fur, and also protection from predators, wolves in particular. Roots and seeds, especially those that substituted for millet and other grain flour, as well as berries, were gathered wherever found. Wood for home furnishings, salt, soda, and bark for tanning hides were also carefully collected. For the Mongols, agriculture was minimal. Among a few groups it was a sideline subsistence project. But in itself agriculture was a sedentary occupation, a different way of life which, if followed, would destroy Mongol mobility, and with that their independence. Some marginal groups near desert areas did just that, first growing wheat and barley and later taking up settled village life.

Mongol trade was essentially a system of bartering based on products of the environment. Large-scale trade required the kind of organization, financial system, capital resources, storage facilities, and so on, which a nomadic culture could not sustain and still remain mobile. This was beyond their capacities. Among themselves Mongols bartered animals, services, metal and wooden articles they had made, as well as imported goods. With the sedentary village peoples on the peripheries of their territories, they bartered their pastoral products for manufactured goods, luxury foods and adornments, cereals, and some metals and weapons.

Relationship to the Land

Mobile and sedentary societies inevitably have different relationships to the land. Sedentary peoples, usually agriculturalists, need permanent possession, ownership, or title to specified sites to carry on their occupations. On the other hand, mobile peoples, commonly pastoralists, require ready access to wide areas with a minimum of restrictions on travel, and on rights of use (usufruct). The Mongol system was similar in some respects to that of the Bedouin of Arabia, in that tribal

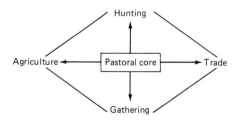

FIGURE 11-5
The Mongol nomad's cycle of life.

TABLE 11-4   Comparison of Elements of Pastoral Nomadism and Agriculture in Asia

ELEMENTS	PASTORAL NOMADISM	AGRICULTURE
Use of land	Extensive; does not destroy natural cover.	Local and fixed; removes natural cover.
Subsistence basis	Animals	Plants
Importance of animals	Paramount; attitude toward animals reflects close relationship.	Secondary; includes different animals, animals used for plowing, treated as commodities.
Relationship of humans to land	Temporary; migratory, right to use land, not private ownership.	Permanent; sedentary, private ownership.
Type of labor	Mounted herding; short, intense periods of heavy labor, long periods of relaxation and ease.	Pedestrian, long periods of hard labor.
Techniques	Herding, riding, stalking, preparation of meat, hides, skins, etc.	Preparation of land, plowing, sowing, harvest, etc.
Foods	Milk and cereals basic. Pig and sometimes pork disliked. Do not eat vegetables.	Cereals and vegetables basic. Milk considered disgusting by Chinese. Pork eaten by non-Moslems.
Material culture	Little, mobile, centered around mobility and life in a tent.	More in total amount and complexity, centered around sedentary life in a house.
Storage of produce	Not possible on a large scale.	Necessary, helps to maintain sedentary nature of agriculture.
Transportation	Horseback, camel for personal use; clothes, boots not adapted to walking or working on foot. Hate walking.	Foot, carts.
Trend to specialization	Not possible to any great extent; not desired; threatens pastoral nomadism as a way of life.	Possible; desirable; need not basically destroy agriculture as a way of life, but incorporate it.

From A. Anastasio, *The Mongols: A Study of Pastoralism in Its Ecological and Cultural Contexts* (University of Chicago thesis, 1952, p. 40).

territory was recognized by other tribes, and was either free to all units in the tribe or was allocated to subunits by tribal authority. Boundaries might vary annually according to the fluctuating needs of the user units or even of the tribe itself. No one owned the land outright, but the Russians and Chinese who moved into and through Mongol land were agriculturalists who sought to own and demarcate the land for their own interests.

THE NEW MONGOLIA

The ultimate result of Russian and Chinese entry into Mongol territory is that Mongolia today stands divided into two political units. Inner Mongolia constitutes a province of the People's Republic of China, called the Inner Mongolian Autonomous Region, where Han Chinese far outnumber Mongols. Sedentarism and agriculture are emphasized and nomadizing strongly regulated and limited. The other political unit, the Mongolian People's Republic, has become a satellite of the U.S.S.R. The capital city Ulaanbaatar has factories, a university, and is the social center for the Republic's 1.7 million people. Since 1958 private ownership of livestock has been prohibited, and nomadizing severely constrained; over half the population live on some three hundred communes. However, a small proportion of the Khalka-speaking Mongols still lead their animals up and down the same seasonal trails as their ancestors. The schools enculturate young Mongols away from nomadism and toward sedentarism. The agriculturalists are finally settling the nomads.

However, this causes problems of over-grazing and land degradation, and leaves unexploited a large ecological niche—that of the grasslands; for to the Mongol the vast steppe was like the sea, beckoning beyond the horizon; with herds one could follow the call.

Throughout North Asia today agriculture, manufacturing, construction, and the extraction and manipulation of resources and rivers are pushing current technology to its limits. Population movements and severe governmental pressures are drastically altering the old ways of life; few indeed are left intact. Yet this vast and still only partly known land remains a place of tantalizing possibilities. When the wind howls across the tundra, rustles through the taiga, and blows along the continent-wide steppe, something stirs.

Chapter 12

Inner Asia:
Corridors of Destiny

Geographic and climatic conditions generally tend to set limits to people's residence and type of life, sometimes very definite limits. Extremes of heat and cold combined with general aridity characterize Inner Asia, and the topography varies from baking desert plain to precipitous icy mountain. Masses of wind-blown sand have caused rivers to flow one way and then reverse direction because of basin areas alternately filled with sand. Uncounted settlements and watercourses have left their shriveled traces in the desert because of these natural disasters.

Human activities also alter the environment. Because they are herders the mountain Tajik (Tadzhik) pastoralists leave undisturbed the mountain valley, the forest, the streams, and the grasslands; the natural resources are needed as is for the animals. Because the lowland Tajiks are agriculturalists, they probably will turn mountain slope and forest, river valley and plain into plow land. Also, urged on by official quotas for grain deliveries, farmers are liable to grow crops on land that is only marginally arable. The Russian townspeople, oriented to industry and trade, tend to turn all available land into house and factory sites, and quite possibly pollute the area with factory wastes. "Progress" sometimes drives a hard bargain. It also affects the core of people's social life, the family.

SOCIETY

The Family

The continuity of the Central Asian family depends upon its men, for the rights of procreation and inheritance go through them. Brides become part of a patrilineal family, where authority passes from elder to younger males. This type of family's stability has an intricate and interlocking foundation comprised of genetic, territorial, economic, legal, and authoritative factors. Finding marriage partners has sometimes presented problems. Among the Turkmens, Kazakhs, Kirgiz, and Uzbeks, a young man and woman could marry only if their lineages were separated as far back as their common great-great-grandfather! The Uigurs merely liked the couples to be from separate villages, the nearer the village the better. The Yakuts agreed, but liked their villages as far apart as possible.

The Turks and Mongols outdid even the Romans in the organized tenacity of their family structure. Within the family no one was equal to another, for each was graded by sex, birth, generation, or other order of precedence. The very rigidity of organization, however, often gave birth to some device for softening the irksome bonds of regulated conduct. Some tenderness could arise between brother and sister, some affection and blood-brotherhood bond between youths of different families, or even through the adoption by an older man of a youth he encountered. A mother's brother could give aid and encouragement to his sister and her children. However, such interest could run counter to other considerations. Among the Kazakhs, Kalmuks, and Kirgiz, their changing laws of inheritance made the daughter's son eligible for part of her father's patrimony, for which she herself was ineligible. Thus, a boy's eligibility could cut into the share otherwise receivable by his mother's brother, his maternal uncle.

Women in Society

Today the position of Muslim women in home and society, and the wearing of the veil and participation in public gatherings, vary from group to group. Kazakh, Kirgiz, and Karakalpak women do not wear the veil and can participate with men in festivals, but the Tajiks, Uzbeks, and Uigurs attach great significance to the veiling and seclusion of their women. These secluded women have their own private religious devotions and exercises. These observances, along with the handicraft artisans, cult of saints, polygamy, child-betrothal, marriage in early adolescence, and the so-called "bride-price" system, are all objects of official antagonism. Nevertheless, up into the 1960s, even some party officials and others belonging to the indigenous nationalities, having Muslim backgrounds, surreptitiously maintained secondary wives or made their wives wear the veil, and stifled public protest against their actions. These practices and many others are hard to discontinue or disrupt whether voluntarily or under official pressure, for Islamic life is a total way of life, from personal habits to family relationships, to community and national life.

THOSE WHO WERE THERE ORIGINALLY: TURKISH, MONGOL, AND SIBERIAN PEOPLES

The Peopling of the Land

A look into any one of the many excellent museums in North Asia will reveal the bone tools, ivory carvings, female figurines, projectile weaponry, paintings from life, and other artifacts left behind by prehistoric people who occupied the region long before the domestication of the horse about 3000 B.C. Certainly by 2000 B.C. there were hunters around Lake Baikal, fishermen along the Amur river, and hunters in the forests and frozen lands to the north. The Tungusic tribes

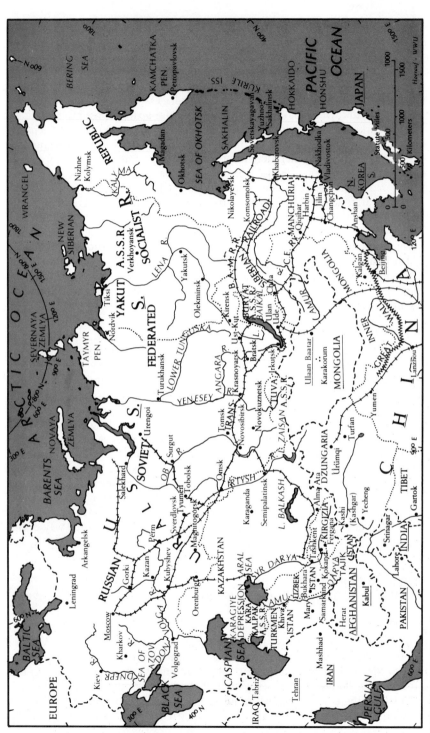

FIGURE 12-1 North Asia.

were herding reindeer by 1000 B.C. and pushing the hunters further northwards. Between the 600s B.C. and the A.D. 100s the spreading copper culture had reached the Ural mountains, and farmers were cultivating irrigation crops north of the Altai ranges. Most importantly, horse-riding nomads occupied the vast steppelands from the Black Sea to Mongolia: Mongols and Manchus, Uigurs, Turkic tribes, and the Turkmen and Tajiks of the southwest.

In the A.D. 700s various religiously oriented peoples entered Central Asia. Assyrian Jews fleeing discrimination in Iraq came to their present residences in the Karakalpak area south of the Aral Sea. Nestorian Christian missionaries arrived from Syria and Palestine, some of them en route through the Corridor to far Cathay (China). Then between 651 and 671 surging armies of zealous Arabs spilled northeast from Mesopotamia; some of their descendants are farmers around Samarkand and Bukhara. During this period merchants and priests brought their Buddhist faith and ritual from India and Gandhara on their way through Inner Asia to China and beyond.

The Repercussions of the Mongol Empire

If the whole Central and Inner Asian regions could be spread out like a living, pulsating panorama we would have seen the Mongol tribes grouping together in the east in the A.D. 1200s. The Uigurs and other Turkic tribes occupied the central areas, Xinjiang, and eastern Turkestan. As the Mongols massed and moved westwards, they swallowed the khanates and chieftaincies which had existed in one form or another for much of the preceding 1,200 years. Inevitably they incorporated these Turkic peoples into their armies under Mongol officers, for they could not leave enemy cavalry in their rear. This swelling empire again pressured the Samoyeds, Evenks, Yakuts, and others to move further north, to become reindeer herders in the forested taiga and the barren tundra. When the Mongol empire disintegrated into several large khanates, the Uigurs still inhabited their old homelands, but a major wave of Turkish conquest rolled west over Iran and Iraq and came to rest in Turkey. The populations remaining in the Central and Inner Asian region were mainly speakers of Turkic languages.

Formation of New Entities

Moreover, by the late 1500s various Turkic, Iranic, and Mongol elements amalgamated to form the new solidarities later known as the Uzbeks, the Kazakhs (Kazaks), and the Kirgiz. Each forged its own new political, linguistic, and ethnic identity, which has continued to the present time. These westward migrations and amalgamations were followed by an eastward migration of ultimately millions of European Russians who conquered and populated Central Asia and Siberia as far as the Pacific Coast.

THOSE WHO CAME OUT: CONQUEST AND MIGRATION

The Coiled Spring

Isolated from the major centers of civilization by massive mountain ranges, water-hungry deserts, endless forests, undeveloped grasslands, and by the Caspian Sea, Central Asia always has been a mysterious and dangerous land shrouded in mystery and sheathed in danger. Seething within its vast lands succeeding federations fought for the food-lands, the market-interchanges, and the rights to levy taxes on the rich merchandise carried in and out of its fabled cities of luxury and languour. Still more intense was the struggle for the men, horses, and equipment, and the lines of supply needed to invade the source areas of that merchandise: Mesopotamia, Persia, Russia, Gandhara (Afghanistan), India, and China. Political weakness in these outside lands, coupled with the internal strength of good crops and augmented manpower (or the sting of famine), set the stage for the thunder of the invading cavalry of scores of thousands of lean and avaricious horsemen surging out of the Asian grasslands.

The Empire-building Cavalry

Nomad horsemen are always unsettled mobile groups, and by lifelong training they are a potential force of aggressive light cavalry. Banded together under war leaders, clouds of grim Central Asian warriors swept into Southwest Asia and Europe. Among them were the *Scyths* (or *Scythians*), the *Hsiung-nu,* and the *Huns.* The *Scyths* set styles of lightning-quick cavalry attacks from their fortified center at Kamenka in the Russian Ukraine. Their curvilinear animal art and metallurgy also spread through much of Asia from the 400s B.C. onwards. About 200 B.C. the *Hsiung-nu,* started westward from north of the China border, and established an empire stretching from north of the China border to the Aral Sea. Their mobile and wealthy chieftains would have scoffed at the Western saying, "Rolling stones gather no moss," for their tombs have yielded rich stores of portable valuables: golden ornaments, costly raiment, inlaid weapons, and luxuries from distant trading sources. After having controlled intercontinental trade between Rome and China, their empire collapsed internally around A.D. 48, but not before dislodging a group of Iranian speakers, the Yue-ji (*Yüeh-chih*) or *Indo-Scyths,* who founded the Kushan empire in India. The *Huns,* whom some historians consider a branch of the Hsiung-nu, crossed the Volga river about A.D. 350 and, under Attila "The Scourge of God," grew enormously wealthy through gold bullion tribute received from Rome and plunder from others. They faded into obscurity in Europe after Attila's death in A.D. 453.

The development of the war chariot and the compound bow in the Central Asian-Persian-Mesopotamian region revolutionized the methods of warfare. This weaponry also affected the borderland peoples to the extent that the Hyksos conquered Egypt, and the Kassites ruled in Mesopotamia in the 1600s B.C. Over the centuries the effects reached into India and the borders of China, and materially affected the fortunes of the kingdoms and empires mentioned in Chapters 3 and 6.

The Phenomenon of Migration

To set into historical perspective the above-mentioned movements of peoples through or around Asia, we must consider in more detail the phenomenon called migration. In Asia especially this phenomenon has been marked by the movement of massive numbers of people, and by the enduring results of such placements and displacements of multitudes of men, women, and children.

Migration inevitably alters the population balance and the cultural mix in

TABLE 12-1 The Incidence of Migration East and West Out of the Steppelands

WHO	WHEN	FROM	TO	COMMENTS
	B.C.			
CIMMERIANS	c. 1000	Caucasus	Anatolia	Disappeared after Scythian onslaught
SCYTHIANS	721	Central Asia	Persia, Syria, Russia	Destroyed by Sarmatians in Crimea
SARMATIANS	500s–200	Central Asia	Southern Russia	Disappeared, A.D. 500s
	A.D.			
SCYTHO-PARTHIANS	50	Central Asia	Afghanistan, India	India's Kushan dynasty
HUNS	170–370	East of Volga	Central Europe, France	Blended with Central Europeans
MONGOLIANS	200s	Mongolia, Manchuria	Korea, Japan	Yamato Japanese?
KHAZARS	600s	Central Asia	Southeastern Russia	Converted to Judaism
KITANS	974	Mongolia?	North China, Korea	Liao dynasty (China)
SELJUK TURKS	1037	East of Aral Sea	Persia to Anatolia	People of Turkey
MONGOLS	1211–1237	Mongolia	North China, Russia, Persia	Yuan dynasty (China), Il-khan dynasty (Persia)
OTTOMAN TURKS	1326	Central Asia	Iraq, Anatolia	Majority in Turkey
TURKI-MONGOLS	1369	Central Asia, Afghanistan	Southwest Asia, India	Armies of Tamerlane; retreated to C. Asia
MANCHUS	1644	Manchuria	China	Qing dynasty
MONGOLS	1600s	Inner Asia	Western Siberia and Volga frontier	Merged with general populations

the receptor area. If, for example, large numbers of Jews had not migrated to Palestine from Europe, (and later from countries in the Middle East), in the late 1800s and the 1900s, there would be no State of Israel and no Middle East problem (in its present form). Peoples may move both ways between the same areas. They will leave traces of their movements in the form of artifacts used, places named, genes bestowed, landscapes devastated, enclaves established, industries developed, or languages distributed. Migration may be intranational, from country to city as in Japan, or international as in the transfer of Indians to Fiji, Arabs to North Africa, Chinese to Southeast Asia, and Japanese to Brazil. Migration may be by land, as the Mongols went through Central Asia and Iran, or by sea, as the Europeans, Muslims, Indians, and Chinese went en route to Southeast Asia. Wars have provoked migrations by sending armies abroad and by settling disbanded soldiers on foreign territories, as the Romans, Greeks, Muslims, and Chinese have done. Warfare also has caused the mass flight of millions of peoples as during the Bolshevik Revolution, the Japanese invasion of China in 1939, the Pakistan-Bangladesh fighting in 1971, and the Russian invasion of Afghanistan in 1980. Government action in driving out or deporting whole communities, as was the practice in the ancient Near East, also has been done in modern times by the Turks, the Vietnamese, and the Kampucheans.

The Lure of Greener Pastures

Having considered migration as a movement of peoples, and having seen that more or less violent pressures may be at work, we should also consider another principle. The law of migration is that the motivation and direction of the movement is determined by the attraction of the richest destination, although the realities of specific migrations may alter the orientation.

If one could scan the faces of the migrants—reindeer herders searching for seasonal mosses, camel herders asking where the rains fell, Qashqai, Kurds, or Kafirs traversing mountain and ravine for goat and sheep pastures—their hope for survival would be obvious. As for the Bedouin and Indian young men drifting to the cities for wage-earning jobs, penurious peasants flocking to Kuwait, Kabul, or Kyoto, or Tamils and Tagalogs seeking plantation or construction work on the islands of the Pacific—their faces are set steadfastly towards a place of richer rewards than those available at their present locale. It can be argued that the same motive and direction governed the massive movements of raiding Mongol armies into Afghanistan and India, and conquering Arabs who settled in Iraq, and Turks in Turkey. This is partly true also for Russia's technologized millions moving into Siberia.

Governments may coerce or force people to migrate either to obtain the resources they produce in their new locale (as was the case for the Japanese in Manchuria), or in order to grab the resources they leave behind (as in Vietnam). During the course of migration or at its end the migrators may alter their perception of what constitutes the greater advantage, and must adapt their economic expectations and techniques to fit the new environment.

WHO AND WHAT WENT THROUGH:
WARRIORS, WEALTH, AND WISDOM

Merchants and Merchandise

Trade may be viewed as the migration of goods; similarly, cultural diffusion may be viewed as the migration of ideas. For example, as the plodding caravans of one or two hundred carts and camels plied the months-long Silk Route (Marco Polo's Golden Road) through Inner Asia, the ideas, habits, and utensils of the caravaneers went along with their merchandise.

The scene behind the closed doors of any of the rich merchants' establishments in the main caravan cities would reveal every sort of package going in at least two directions, east and west. The eastbound caravan brought European goods: metalware, glassware, furniture, precious mechanical knick-knacks, coinage, and cloth. The westbound caravan from China brought silk, brocades and embroideries, tea, ginger, porcelain, paper, fruits (peach, apricot, and persimmon), rhubarb, and gems. Some types of merchandise going both ways were similar in type though different in particulars: paintings, sculptures, coinage, and jewelry. But the most interesting of the exchanges were the intangibles: genes, languages, and philosophies—and secrets. The secrets revealed the identity of the material called silk, the product of the silkworm, and the art of making fine paper. The Eastern caravaneer brought without thinking such ideas as the use of paper for currency and the narrow printed slips of what we would call playing cards. That all happily shared their genes goes without saying. Over the centuries the Asians spread themselves and their languages westward: Turkish, Hungarian (Magyar), Lappish, Finnish, and Mongol dialects. What would become the Korean and Japanese languages drifted very early from Inner Asia to those two countries. Religions such as Buddhism, Islam, and Christianity all went east, as did the modern ideologies of equality, individualism, and communism. Philosophies such as Confucian ethics and Taoist naturalism received careful hearing in the West.

"Ichabod"

Yarkand, Kashgar, Samarkand, and Bukhara are fabled names conjuring up scenes of fruits and fountains, fair arbors and fairer women, of bejeweled amirs and dagger-wielding cutthroats. Most of the tales were true enough. Bukhara's irrigation system, developed over millenia, provided grains, herbs, fruits, fowl, and meat for Bukharan gourmets. The treasures of trade and raid robed merchants and rulers in brocades and furs. Parks and gardens cast a haunting beauty over the

FIGURE 12-2   Eurasian empires of the A.D. 1200s and 1300s.

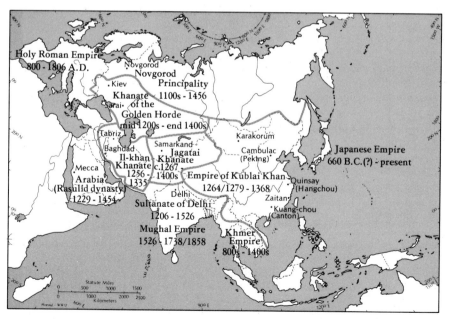

favored quarters of the affluent. Even beggars fared well. Libraries and literature flourished as the University of Bukhara and the famous mosques attracted the world's foremost scholars, artists, poets, and calligraphers.

However, the cultured flower is also fragile. Mongol barbarians not only wiped out the cities and killed their inhabitants, but also destroyed the irrigation systems, and with them the sources of food and life. When the Mongol dust had settled over western Central Asia, Afghanistan, Iran, and Iraq, one word could have been written over them all: *Ichabod,* the Hebrew word meaning "The glory has departed." The four cities mentioned above have survived, but much of Central Asia today remains a huge mausoleum of perished and forgotten cities and civilizations. The Mongols were not the only people to devastate wide areas, but they were the most destructive.

THOSE WHO WENT IN: THE EUROPEANS

The collapse of the Mongol empire in the late 1400s prepared the way for the entrance of Europeans into northern Asia. First, then, a review of the sequence of events.

The Pax Mongolica

Many people have wondered how law-abiding, disciplined and often artistic people can be, on occasion, savagely destructive. Genghis Khan's stringent *yasak* law did not fit the all-too-frequent mass slaughter of civilians and soldiers alike. The *yasak* included provisions such as: (1) no retreat in battle; (2) no looting without permission; (3) no man to desert his assigned task or position; (4) women have rights to property; (5) fraud and bankruptcy banned; (6) honor to be given to the righteous, the innocent, and the aged. With an empire extending across 2,500 miles (4,000 km.) of often wild country, it was hardly an idle boast when the Khan reportedly stated that a maiden could walk the length of his dominions carrying a bag of gold and not be molested. This situation was possible because the punishment for disobedience was swift and merciless, often a cruel death. The key to the puzzle would appear to be that the *yasak* law was designed for and operated within the nation, the in-group. Foreigners, therefore, as the out-group were outside the provisions of this code, and were treated on a different basis of military necessity, or caprice.

Following the death of Genghis Khan and the division of the empire into several increasingly independent khanates, the reality of the Pax Mongolica ("Mongolian peace") gradually faded. The western Mongols of the "Golden Horde" (*ordas*) and of the Il-khan dynasty in Persia became Muslims and gradually blended into the peoples among whom they lived. The Mongols of Kublai Khan's Yuan dynasty in China became Buddhists, as did those of the homeland khanate at Karakorum in Mongolia. While the homeland Mongols retained their ethnic identity, out of the one million Mongols in China when the Ming dynasty came to power in 1368, only sixty thousand went home. The others stayed and blended into the Chinese population. The remaining Mongols in Mongolia submitted to the overlordship of the powerful Manchus around 1644, and for more than two hundred years followed the traditional nomadic patterns of life (described in Chapter 11). The disintegration of Mongol power throughout Siberia and the adjacent western borderlands left a population in a power vacuum.

The Ferment in Europe

At about this same time two very different movements originated at the opposite ends of a politically and militarily divided Europe. One would consign Inner Asia to semioblivion, the other would make it a source of contention. The first movement began in the late 1400s with the discoveries and inventions under the direction of the Portuguese Prince Henry the Navigator. The resulting ship-borne traffic between Europe and East Asia was cheaper, usually safer, and generally took less time than the arduous cross-continent animal caravans—even when in the mid-1800s a voyage from London to Shanghai might take up to six months. Most of Europe forgot about Inner Asia for over two hundred years. The other

BOX 12-1 *PROGRESS OF RUSSIAN OCCUPATION OF NORTH ASIA*

Pre-1500	Fur trade with Siberia; some exiles already in Siberia.
1581–82	Yermak's Cossacks capture Sibir on the Irtysh, capital of small Tatar khanate. Beginning of the march to the Pacific.
1586–87	Fort at Tyumen; and at Tobolsk on the Irtysh.
1602–04	Fort at Ket on the Yenesey; and at Tomsk on river Tom near the Ob.
1628	Krasnoyarsk on the Yenesey; population 800,000 in 1979.
1632	Prison fortress at Yakutsk on the Lena; 150,000 in 1979.
1649	Settlement at Okhotsk on North Pacific Coast.
1700	Mining and smelting of silver, copper, lead, using bonded and convict labor. Systematic development of natural resources.
1800	Russian migrants total about 500,000.
1853–56	Crimean War, Russia defeated; increased migration to Siberia.
1858–60	Huge area north of Amur River and east of Ussuri River ceded by China.
1865–76	Military campaigns overcome resistance of Central Asian peoples.
1900–14	Trans-Siberian Railroad helps mass movement of 4,000,000 persons.
1905	Japan defeats Russia in East Siberian campaign.
1917	Bolsheviks win power in Russia; inception of Communist regime.
1918–41	Immigrants number 6,000,000 additional persons.
1923	Soviet rule exercised over Koryaks in northeast Siberia.
1924	Final elimination of khanates of Khiva and Bukhara; consolidation of Central Asia (Turkestan) into "national" republics.
1939–45	Hundreds of factories and workers transferred to Siberia.
1974	Multiplied cities, industries, oil and mining complexes, and new resources, led to building of the Baikal-Amur Railroad (BAM) across East Siberia, north of TSRR; completed in 1983.
1979	Population of Soviet Asia approx. 66,000,000, mostly Russians.

movement began in 1581 when Russian soldiers, exiles, and traders began spilling over the Ural mountains to gradually seize the whole northern half of Asia in the name of the Czar.

Enter the Russians

It has been pointed out that by A.D. 900 Berlin still had no Germans, Moscow no Russians, Buda-Pest no Hungarians, Ankara no Turks, and that Madrid was a Moorish, and not a Spanish, city. Nor were there any Russians in Siberia. Subsequent population movements altered all this. In 1581 the first Russian adventurers passed over the Urals into Siberia. By establishing fortress trading posts along the river systems, the Russians were gradually able to control tribal peoples farther east until by 1649 they had reached Okhotsk on the Pacific coast. Only the larger groups of Yakuts, Buryats, Uzbeks, Kazakhs, and a few others adjusted and profited from the encounter. The Russianization of North Asia was an uneven process, but it could be averaged at 60 square miles (130 sq. km.) every day for three hundred years, from 1581 to 1881—a total area of about 6.6 million square miles (almost 17.1 million sq. km.). The expanding grasp was relentless. The greatest single event signaling the pending transformation of North Asia into a modern, industrialized region was the opening of the Trans-Siberian Railroad in 1901.

Today Central Asia has regained its strategic importance. Considering the geopolitical viewpoints of the U.S.S.R. and the countries along the southern borders of Central Asia—an area where both the Soviet Union and China maintain nuclear and space facilities—it is apparent why the bulk of their armies are stationed along their 2,500 mile (4,000 km.) border. A large part of the populated areas of the world are vulnerable to whomever rules Central Asia.

THOSE WHO STAYED THERE:
THE TECHNOLOGIZED MILLIONS

The Five Central Asian Republics

The varied terrain. In broad terms, the area of the five Soviet Socialist Republics of Kazakhstan, Turkmenistan, Uzbekistan, Tajikistan and Kirgizia or Kirgizstan comprises a vast desert and semiarid region, part of the great interior drainage basin. The two great deserts, the Kara Kum or Black Sands and the Kyzyl Kum or Red Sands, and the extensive semiarid plains, also include the Betpak Dala, the Perilous Plain or Hungry Steppe. These are surrounded by the steppeland belt to the north, the Altai, Tian Shan, Pamir, Hindu Kush, and other mountains to the east and south, and the Aral and Caspian Seas on the west. Mining and manufactures, mechanized farming and modern water systems have turned into new channels the occupational economies of the greatly increased populations. But mobile pastoralism, that is, seminomadic animal husbandry, remains the most efficient use of much of the fringe lands where the uncertain supply of water prohibits settled farming.

Uzbekistanis and other plainspeople, looking from their sun-drenched lands to the snow-topped ranges away to the southeast, have irrigated their fields with the snow-fed mountain streams for two thousand years. Central Asia's most impor-

TABLE 12-2 The Five Central Asian Republics

REPUBLIC	DATE OF FORMATION	AREA (SQ. MILES AND SQ. KM.)	POPULATION (REPUBLIC & ELSEWHERE)	DOMINANT PEOPLES (POP. IN 1000S)		COMMENTS
Kazakhstan	1936	1,049,000 2,717,000	13,695,000 Kazakhs in U.S.S.R. 5,581,000. In Xinjiang 500,000	Russians Kazakhs Ukrainians Germans	5,807 4,465 986 904	Sixth most populous group in U.S.S.R. Germans were evacuated eastward during WW II from Black Sea steppes and Volga German A.S.S.R. Another pop. estimate: 8,425,000.
Turkmenistan	1924	188,000 488,000	2,159,000 Turkmen in U.S.S.R. 1,525,000. In Iran and Afghanistan 600,000.	Turkmen Russians Uzbeks	1,417 313 179	Traditional aloofness from other Central Asia khanates.
Uzbekistan	1924	173,000 447,000	11,799,000 Uzbeks in U.S.S.R. 9,000,000. Afghanistan 1,000,000. *1,896,000	Uzbeks Russians Tatars	7,725 1,473 574	Uzbeks are largest Turkic group in U.S.S.R., second only to Turkey in the world. Some Uzbeks originally were Kazakhs.
Tajikistan	1924	55,000 143,000	2,900,000 Tajiks in U.S.S.R. 2,136,000	Tajiks Uzbeks Russians	1,630 666 344	Undoubtedly oldest ethnic element in Central Asia, closely related to Iranians and Afghans.
Kirgizia	1924	77,000 199,000	2,933,000 Kirgiz in U.S.S.R. 1,452,000. In Xinjiang 70,000	Kirgiz Russians Uzbeks	1,284 856 333	Varied occupations: mountain pastoralists, lowland farmers, urbanized miners, factory workers, officials.

The population figures of 1970 for the four Republics of Soviet Central Asia, which omit Kazakhstan, show a total of 19,791,000, of which Russians and Ukrainians number 3,285,000, the "titular native groups" 13,933,000, and "others" 2,573,000.

*Approx. figures for 1979.

Based on Paul E. Lydolph, *Geography of the U.S.S.R.*, 3rd ed. (New York: John Wiley and Sons, 1977). © 1977 by John Wiley.

tant natural wealth is that very snow upon the mountains, snow that has spawned some six hundred rivers and streams. Almost all of them irrigate oasis fields as their streamlets fan out on the plain, and, before disappearing into the sands, nourish groves of nut trees and over six thousand varieties of vegetation. Only two rivers, the Amu Darya or Oxus and the Syr Darya or Jaxartes, are copious enough to cross the desert and empty their remaining waters into the Aral Sea. In their courses they provide life not only for the forests and crops but also for snow leopards, antelopes, tortoises, four-foot long monitors, and two-humped camels, not to mention goats, sheep, cattle, and horses. Furthermore, both rivers have been tapped for continuing irrigation-supported communities, and the Amu Darya has given birth to the Kara-Kum Canal, approximately one thousand kilometers long. The minerals found include coal, gold, copper, tungsten, salt, natural gas, marble, and sulphur. The climate alternates blazing summers with freezing winters. But the people are happiest with the abundance of grains and fruits, especially cotton, for "The cotton plant is a child of the sun."

The varied peoples.   The region has not been called Turkestan for nothing. Only the Tajiks represent the earlier dominant population of Iranian-speaking Scythians and others. All the other nationalities for whom the five Republics were

FIGURE 12-3
Mongolian woman milking goat.

named speak Turkic languages, even though they are composed of groups that were originally Turkic, Mongol, Chinese, Iranian, and European. The impact of conquerors coming and going through their territories has had the effect of amalgamating these diverse constituents into the present stable and cohesive national identities. Born and welded together in the crucible of war and hard work, they are in no mood to meekly acknowledge the innate superiority of their present overlords. One evidence—sturdy adherence to the practice of their Islamic faith.

During the 1400s two sets of communities began to coalesce into two separate peoples with similar names. The word "Cossack," from Polish *kozacy* and then Russian *kazaki,* originated from the Turkic word *kazak* meaning freebooter, rebel, masterless man. The Cossacks, indeed, were peasants who left the Ukraine, joined with Turkic and other elements in the general Volga region, and became the Cossacks of history. There are some 650,000 Cossacks scattered throughout Siberia. The other community, the *Kazakhs* of Kazakhstan, composed of an amalgam of Turkic and Mongol groups who speak a Turkic language, were called "riders of the steppe." To distinguish between the two communities the Russians called the first Cossacks, and then for a long time miscalled the Kazakhs "Kirgiz."

The Uzbeks, who took their name from an early Turkish leader, constitute the most numerous non-Russian nationality in the Heartland of Asia. The Turkmen, by holding aloof from neighboring peoples and khanates, have preserved their own distinctiveness. The Tajiks, harassed by waves of conquerors passing back and forth, have been backed up against the majestic walls of the Pamir mountains. They

BOX 12-2 *NOTES ON KAZAKHSTAN*

Steppelands turned into farmlands: 100 million acres (156,250 square miles, 404,690 sq. km., or 160,000,000 hectares)

Potential arable and irrigable land: an additional 200 million acres.

Potential wheat acreage is larger than wheat acreage of the United States, Canada, and Australia combined (as of the 1970s).

Population in excess of 14 million persons, of whom 52 percent are urban, 42 percent are Russian, and about one third are Kazakhs.

Approximately 1.5 million persons are farmers on 2,230 state or collective farms.

Grain output: 1979 record of 34 million tons; 20 percent of Soviet output.

Production of iron ore: 10 percent of Soviet output.

Vast deposits of coal, iron, tin, copper, lead, zinc, also petroleum, gas, and paraffin.

Groundwater under Kazakhstan's deserts estimated to equal the water in Lake Baikal.

About 1960 it was estimated that "The center of population for the entire world lies 500 miles northeast of the Aral Sea, near 62°45'E and 53°52'N," that is, near the town of Kustanai in northern Kazakhstan (Cressey 1963: 595).

deserve commendation for having retained their language and other substantial elements of their ancient Iranian culture. The Kirgiz, too, live tucked into a mountainous reservoir of snowy peaks. Numerous small communities—Baluchis, Jews, Dungans, and many more—are housed in the region, including an interestingly large number of about 213,000 Koreans. Another group are the Uigurs, whose main body of members live in Xinjiang. Perhaps the most harried of all the Central Asians are the Tatars from the Crimea, now numbering about 780,000. During World War II, on unfounded charges of collaborating with the Germans, they were forcibly sealed in foodless cattle cars and transported nearly two thousand miles to their present location in Uzbekistan, and not allowed to return. Deportation still goes on occasionally.

New Paths in the Corridors of Destiny

Russian military controls and subsequent Soviet political and economic programs have altered almost every aspect of life in Soviet Asia. The indigenous types of social control have varied considerably. The Turkmen, for instance, exercised social control within their communities through direction by male elders within the kinship group. They also regulated life according to occupation, that is, according to the differing economic functions of their farmers and pastoralists. The Kazakhs and Uzbeks favored a class system of nobles and commoners to preserve orderliness in society. Whatever were the clan or tribal organizations, all these systems were subordinated to, or were replaced by the orders of the administrators of the communes into which everyone was placed.

Occupations and herding areas were allocated and coordinated by the commune. The traditional herding unit of a household of three or four generations of married kin was replaced by the brigade or other designated work group. In some cases terrain guided modifications. From the icy heights of the Pamir mountains—where three of the Soviet Union's highest peaks peer through the clouds—Tajik stock raisers care for their herds down through the forested and fertile foothills to the jungles (complete with tigers) and plains below. Others in these different levels of elevation cultivate upland wheat, barley, and millet, then fruits and food grains, down to the broad vistas of cotton fields on the plains. Climate also affects the economic calendar of the mountain Kirgiz. Their 60-day summer is the free-from-snow season for manuring, cutting and storing of grass for fodder, and the preparation of pack animals to carry grain and other household needs. Nomadic pastoralism has been replaced by sedentary pastoralism.

Throughout the five Republics economic, educational, and political life is systematized. Among the Kirgiz, for instance, those residing on the lowland communes continue in agriculture as they did before the Revolution, but over greatly extended and diversified areas. About 8,333 sq. miles (21,583 sq. km.) are under cotton, and the livestock population includes six million sheep and goats, and 750,000 cattle. In addition the Kirgiz factories manufacture clothing, sugar, flour, and shoes, and process fruit, cotton, and silk. Mining and exporting minerals, including three million tons of coal annually, utilizes more Kirgiz workers.

The traditional role of the tribal intelligentsia as power brokers is gone. Modern education, however, has created a new proletariat class of intellectuals who represent the various political levels of society, and who staff the teaching, medical, mechanical, and research positions in the appropriate institutions–all strictly within the Soviet political system. Literature, as among the Turkmen, was controlled by substituting the Latin alphabet for local scripts, and then by enforcing a switch to the Russian Cyrillic script. Many aspects of daily living have been improved; feuds and wars have been eliminated, and women generally have equal rights with men. Most medical doctors, for example, are women. In one area these nationalities have made strenuous and not unsuccessful efforts to maintain a measure of independent identity: they have perserved their Sunni or Shi'ite Muslim faith, observing both daily prayers and the fast of Ramadan.

Society-wide organization, then, has ended the hodgepodge of khanate government and tribal authority, and with it that whole way of life. It is evident that, in the five Republics, the 1,500 self-sustaining collective farms (*kolkoz*) and the 850 wage-giving state farms (*sovkoz*) have vastly increased general productivity. The black and brown soils of the vast plains produce one third of Russia's grain harvest. The array of agricultural machines matches the extensive breeding of more than four million cattle and over eighteen million sheep and goats. Nevertheless, a Kazakh poet, seeing the end of the old freedom to roam put it this way (Winner 1958:97):

> Instead of herds, money. From such cattle
> You can obtain no milk.
> How can one put a saddle on it?

PART V

The Self-Contained Civilizations: East Asia

Chapter **13**

China: From Honored Past to Pragmatic Present

One quarter of the earth's people live in East Asia. Their milieu is one of ancient sophisticated cultures, which, until the technological impact of Europe and America, were very much a world unto themselves. In many ways, they still are.

China came of age as the Middle Kingdom. From it radiated a high culture borne by armies for conquest, envoys for peace, traders for exotica, and by scholars bringing literacy, government organization, and Confucian principles of rectitude. The aura and some of the substance of this glory was woven into the developing fabrics of the kingdoms of Korea and Japan, of Tibet and tropical Vietnam. Over the centuries princes and ambassadors of the kingdoms and empires from Java to Rome and from Samarkand to Ceylon traded with or sent tribute to distant China.

Geography has contributed to the isolation of East Asia. High mountains and rapids-strewn gorges block the west of China, jungles the south, and desert and forest the north. Dangerous trails formed the only entrance to the high Tibetan Plateau. Pirate-ridden seas barred entry to Japan and much of Korea. Populations crammed into the limited areas of intensely worked fertile farmland, and groups isolated by mountains and hostile terrain developed their own identities. History and literary tradition have imbued the landscape with historical and poetic meanings, and set patterns of conduct which have lasted through centuries.

The ancient and the modern intermingle today. China forms a key block in geopolitics. Japan and South Korea hold key roles in the development and manufacture of high technology. Tibet, though a part of China, remains a land of mystery and isolation. Even now, East Asia is still a largely self-contained area.

THE SETTING

Mountains, rivers, people, and cities cram into East Asia an immense and varied density of human existence. From desert and forest in the north to mountain, jungle, and sea in the south, from the rugged Tibetan plateau in the west to the typhoon-washed shores of Korea and Japan in the east, the region houses numerous cultures, united in their diversity by participation in, borrowing from, or reaction against Han Chinese culture. Such is the ancestral unity.

The Chinese language recognizes five cardinal directions: east, south, west, north and center, the middle. From ancient times China has considered itself the "middle kingdom" with respect both to geographic orientation (China is in the center and all others lie on the periphery), and to culture (Chinese life and culture are the epitome of what ought to be, others are worthy only insofar as they follow the Chinese mode). By definition, the Chinese thought of everyone as a "barbarian" except themselves, the people of the Middle Kingdom.

The Road to Destiny

China settled into its central role of the Middle Kingdom along three interlacing roadbeds: geographical, intellectual, and institutional (Liu 1972).

Geographically isolated from the rest of Asia and the world by deserts, mountains, and seas, China was nourished within by the agricultural wealth of a unique advantage: the two broad, fertile river valleys of the Yellow River and the Yangtze. Imperial planning and local initiative linked the country into a vast canal and river network of waterborne travel and trade.

The most obvious *intellectual factor* was the uniform written language, which gave China's people a vital link to one another. That so many people of widely differing capabilities learned the intricate system of writing illustrates the Chinese concept that "everyone is teachable." Children were taught through the family lineage at home or in the clan's ancestral hall; minorities were taught through the local schools in the Chinese language, and by the carrot of social approval and the stick of ethnic distinctiveness. In addition to "reverence for the heritage (and) the search for improvement, ... the urge to integrate" was applied also to social and personal dynamics through the "three teachings" (*san jiao*). Confucian teaching impregnated the life of government, society, and the individual with the principles of uprightness (*zheng*). Buddhism inspired a sense of responsibility in this life in view of judgment in the next. Taoism instilled into the personal life a refreshing state of quiet naturalness. At least these were the concepts, always a positive force even though human misapplication of the teachings often muddied the streams of conduct.

The clearest illustration of the *institutional* factor is the central form of government, with its final authority in the emperor, and its functioning through the bureaucracy of scholar-officials. The bonds unifying this elite class of scholar-officials were their common educational training and their upper-class value system. It was Jiang Kai-she's (Chiang Kai-shek) reliance upon old-line, self-serving administrators during the Japanese invasion period (1937–1945) that led in large degree to the downfall of his Nationalist regime. The Communist program called for a new society from top to bottom, replacing traditional social institutions with forms and loyalties new to China's millenia-old institutions.

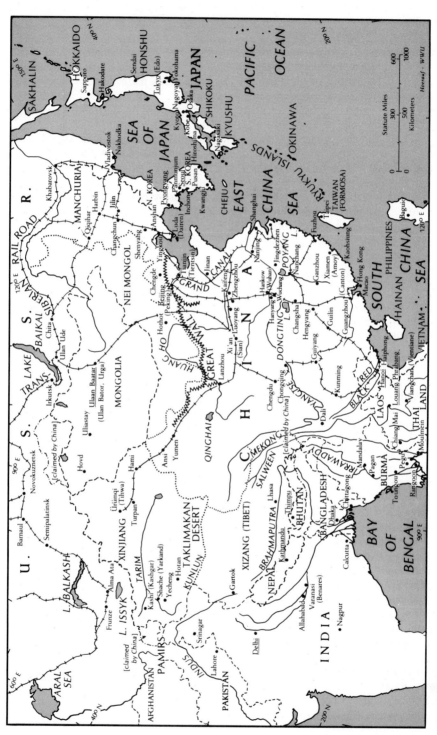

FIGURE 13-1 East Asia.

These three roadbeds were primary factors affecting the broader aspects of China's organized society as a total structure, even though "society" and "culture" overlap and intertwine. Atop the roadbed came the gradual addition, piece by piece, of many of the traditional and modern building blocks that finally composed that enduring entity—today's "China."

HISTORY AND DEVELOPMENT
OF CHINESE CIVILIZATION

The Prehistoric Beginnings

The earliest inhabitants of China were the *Homo erectus* ("Peking Man") of half a million years ago. Dwelling in a cave on a hillside near modern Peking, they hunted, made tools, and used fire for warmth in the extremely cold winters. Subsequent millenia brought later hunter-gatherers, who developed regional cultures. Some time after 10,000 B.C. the Chinese began to farm.

The Neolithic Yang Shao farmers of the fertile plans of North China and of the rich Yangtze valley made distinctive pottery. Their pillar-supported round houses, with internal partitions and tipi-style thatch roof, contained varied burnished bowls and ornamented jars. Their utensils included tools of chipped stone and polished axes and arrow heads. Living in undefended villages, the Yang Shao people ate millet and pork, and kept cattle, goats, and dogs. Subsequent farming groups developed increasingly elaborate social hierarchies and complex trading networks.

From Legend to Early History

Traditional legends speak of the *San Huang* or the Three August Ones—Fu Xi (Fu Hsi), Nü Gua and Shen Nung—who initiated marriage and plow agriculture, and of the *Wu Di* or the Five Sovereigns. The latter, including Huang Di, Yao, and Shun, like culture heroes, are credited with bestowing upon the Chinese people the knowledge of smelting and weaponry, porcelain, cereal transplantation, civic virtues, the solar year, and penal law, as recorded in the *Shu Jing*, the Book of History attributed to Confucius.

Yu, a descendant of Huang Di, is said to have founded the Xia (*Hsia*) dynasty, which traditional histories place variously between 2205 and 1766, 2183 and 1752, or 1989 and 1557 B.C. This rather vague Xia empire nevertheless was filled with multitudinous villages of real farmers living in a market town economy, who owed allegiance to kings who possessed military chariots and bronze weapons.

With the rise and fall of the Xia dynasty begins the cycle of the Heavenly Mandate (*tian-ming*). Briefly, a family provides an outstanding son who demonstrates his capacities by becoming king, thus obtaining the favor of Heaven (*tian*). Heaven then gives investiture or mandate (*tian-ming*) to the king, who thereafter is entitled to call himself the Son of Heaven (*tian-zi*). The Mandate is always provisional and, if the ruler loses hold of the empire, "the Great Happiness (of acquiring the empire) does not come twice!" This waxing and waning of governments has repeated itself at least fifteen times during China's long history. It had its modern episodes in the Warlord Period between the Manchu dynasty and the Nationalist

FIGURE 13-2
Peasant woman harvesting wheat
in North China.

regime, and between the ailing Nationalist period and the inauguration of the People's Republic of China. The present Communist Party, correctly or not, attributes its mandate to "the people."

Whatever records the court historians of the *Shang* or *Yin* dynasty (1771–1122, or 1751-1122, or c.1500-1027 B.C.) deposited in the national archives, very little has been preserved. The recent unearthing of an ancient Shang city at Zhengzhou (Chengchow) revealed affluent art work, and cowrie shells from Canton used as trading currency. The standard term for a merchant, *shang-ren*, literally means a man of Shang. The rise of feudal estates and warfare is known to have coincided with the development of urban government, philosophy, and art in a three-class system of nobles, free men, and slaves (often prisoners of war). Ancestor worship was institutionalized among the rich and the powerful.

The Zhou Dynasty and Feudalism

The feudal stage during the Zhou (Chou) dynasty (1122/1111/1027–256 B.C.) fostered the further development of warfare, ritual, agriculture, artisanship—and intrigue! This also was the "Age of Philosophy" among the small principalities held as fiefs from the emperor. For about three hundred years the dynasty was secure, holding at bay the "Barbarian Ring" of non-Chinese tribal peoples, partly by the device of building stretches of wall to demarcate Chinese territory and dissuade invaders. But from about 770 B.C. on, Zhou imperial control gradually disintegrated into a merely titular prominence among many competing states, a situation having some parallels with the later emperors of Japan and the sultans of Delhi. It was to the dukes and marquises of these principalities—some the size of various European nations today—that the philosophers purveyed their panaceas for peace, usually in vain.

The philosophers of the period (see Table 13-1) emphasized the principles of good government in terms of the nature of man, basically good or evil, pointing out that their subjects' conditions revealed the character of the ruler and of his administration. Some of the populations were dying of famine, some lay wounded in the wayside ditches, and droves of them voted with their feet by fleeing to another state. Some also prospered. These social sermons, and the graphic examples they quoted, are as relevant today as they were then. These rulers as a class predated the *daimyo* lords and *samurai* warriors of one thousand years later in Japan, in that they not only were warriors but also were scholars. As this period overlapped into the *Period of the Warring States* (481/475-221 B.C.) with its strife and turmoil, the efforts of these schools of philosophers shines rather brightly. Three of China's principal classics refer to the Zhou period: the *Shi Jing* (*Book of Odes*), the *Shu Jing* (*Book of History* or *Documents*), and the *Yi Jing* (*Book of Changes*). However, the writings of Wei Yang, Xun Zi (Hsun Tzu), and Han Fei Zi prepared the way for the world's first totalitarian regime the Qin (Ch'in) empire.

TABLE 13-1   China's Ancient Philosophers

NAMES	DATES B.C.	PHILOSOPHIES ADVOCATED
Lao Zi— Lao Tzu	6th century	The "Old Master," reputed author of the *Dao De Zhing* (*Tao Teh Ching* or *Book of the Way*), from which Taoism was named.
Kong Fu Zi— Confucius (K'ung Fu Tzu)	551-479	Preeminent teacher of moral rectitude, official righteousness, and proper relationships between ages and classes of persons.
Mo Zi— Mo Ti (Mo Tzu)	c.470-391	Proclaimed universal love and utilitarianism.
Wei Yang— Wei Yang	?-338	Proposed Legalist conviction that a system of "rewards and punishments" was the true basis of sound government.
Meng Zi— Mencius (Meng Tzu)	c.372-289	A Confucianist, believed human beings are innately good, and that this goodness is the key to human perfectability and good government.
Xun Zi— Hsün Tzu	c.300-237	A Confucianist, taught human beings are essentially evil, yet susceptible to progressive reform through law and discipline.
Han Fei Zi— Han Fei Tzu	?-233	An ardent Legalist, insisted that a harsh totalitarian rule was essential to an orderly nation.
Zhuang Zi— Chuang Tzu	300s	His writings on universal harmony helped establish Taoism, and to shape the Buddhist philosophy of Zen.

IMPERIAL CHINA: THE "FIRST EMPEROR"

King Zheng's (Cheng) assumption of the throne in 221 B.C. inaugurated a radically new era. He is known as Qin Shi Huang Di (Ch'in Shih Huang Ti), that is, the First Emperor of the State of Qin. The name "China" is derived from *ch'in*. The Emperor implemented the Legalist teachings and ordered the burning of all literature except technical works on medicine, agriculture, and architecture. He hoped thereby to destroy the memory of the past and begin a new future. He also took positive measures. He implemented standardized writing (the "small seal" script), centralized archives and bureaucracy, abolished feudal titles and fiefs, and divided the land into "military commanderies" (a sort of provincial system). Enforced standardizations included weights and measures and the length of cart axles (so that all road ruts would be equidistant and any cart or chariot could travel anywhere— important for quick military deployment). In the new society which evolved, soldiers formed a ruling class, and surnames came into use.

More than a million men died in consolidating, fortifying, and manning the 1,500 miles of the Great Wall (said to be the only man-made object on earth visible from outer space). An unforeseen result of Qin's severity and rigid governance, with its mutilation or banishment for minor infractions of the laws, was that China developed no true civil law. Legal concern was confined to the criminal branch, where it retained much of the severity of Legalist practice as advocated by Wei Yang, Xun Zi (Hsun Tzu), and Han Fei Zi. But it must be remembered that Legalist administrative measures, together with Confucian moral principles, preserved China's orderly identity for 2,100 years. (In one sense, the present Communist regime is Legalist in practice.) It was the very severity of Qin laws that led to rebellion and its downfall in 206 B.C., and the subsequent establishment of the Han dynasty.

TWO GOLDEN AGES

The "Men of Han"

The memory of Han's greatness is revived every time an ethnic Chinese says *Wo shi Han ren*, "I am a Han (Chinese)," distinct from tribals, Muslims, etc. In Han times the wheelbarrow was a transportation vehicle, chariot horses wore shoulder collars, and soldiers carried a powerful cocked crossbow to protect the silks and brocades going west along the Silk Road to grace the ladies of Rome, and Persian carpets going east to the palaces of Han. Han documents on newly invented paper contain our earliest knowledge of Japan, and record the appearance of Buddhism from India. The foundations of enduring Chinese culture were firmly established in this empire, which was more than two thirds the size of Europe. The Han dynasty was the first Golden Age of China, lasting from 206 B.C. to A.D. 221/ 219, and the fall of Han brought on three hundred sixty years of disorder, including the *Epoch of the Three Kingdoms* (220-265), later romanticized with tales of the derring-do by statesman and general Zu-ge Liang (Chu-ko Liang), inventor of military strategy and siege weapons. Out of this anarchic Age of Confusion emerged the short-lived *Sui* dynasty (581/589-618) which accomplished the goal of reuniting China. Failure to conquer Manchuria and Korea resulted in the fall of Sui, for people interpreted the failure to mean that the dynasty had lost the Mandate of Heaven. It gave way to the victorious Tang armies.

The "Men of Tang"

In certain ways China's second Golden Age during the *Tang* dynasty (618–907) picked up where Han had left off. Buddhism progressed through Korea to Japan, and Southeast Asian affairs were now recorded in some detail. The maritime counterpart to the Silk Road brought Islamic Arab, Persian, Turkish, Jewish, and Christian merchants to load and unload at Canton. (This enclave of 120,000 persons was massacred in 878 during post-Tang riots.) Tang's capital city Chang'an (now Xi'an or Sian) exuded such a cultural aroma of science, art, and learning that it was internationally known, and so impressed the Cantonese that thereafter they called themselves "*Tang ren*," Men of Tang. The notion engendered during Tang times that China was a unified whole, specifically that of their ethnic identity, is held to this day by both the Mainland and the Taiwan governments, for both parties insist that there are not two Chinas.

The Song Afterglow

After the fall of the Tang dynasty a confused multistate period of 373 years (907–1279) saw Khitan and Jurchen Mongols rampaging and ruling in the north, while South China blossomed under the Northern and Southern Song dynasties. Hangzhou's (Hangchow) population reached one million, police and firefighters protected its people, parks, and palaces, and the poor and aged were nurtured by state relief and nursed in hospitals. Fiscal stability enabled merchants' sons and scions of elite families, by studying books printed with moveable type, to compete in civil service examinations for eminent official positions. However, Mongol and other technicians copied the Song invention of incendiary projectiles, grenades, and cannon, and in the end literally drove the last of the house of Song into the sea off Canton.

THE FINAL DYNASTIES

The Yuan Dynasty's Mongol Khan

After twenty-seven long years of fighting and disorder (see Table 13-2 for demographic effects) Kublai Khan fully controlled the Mongol's greatest prize, China. The nation was again united by various types of networks (1260/80–1368). Military garrisons provided stability; officials and civil service examination graduates exercised government control; and mounted couriers with 200,000 horses ensured speedy communications. Like the Alexandrian grain ships conveying Egyptian tribute wheat to Rome, so convoys of rice proceeded northwards up the Grand Canal to Khanbaliq, the city of the Khan. Long a dynastic capital, the city was rebuilt and enlarged by Kublai, and described in 1275 by Marco Polo as magnificent Cambulac. Quite expectedly, it was referred to by the Chinese simply as the Da Du, the great capital. For most of the last six hundred years it has been Peking (now Beijing), the northern capital.

Even while he was the Crown Prince under Mangu Khan, Kublai had led a Mongol army through the awe-inspiring gorges of the upper Yangtze (where a rocky defile still bears the record of his passing—Tai Zi Guan or Crown Prince Pass) and on into southern Burma to destroy the kingdom of Pagan. Going and coming he abolished the five- to six-hundred-year-old Nan-zhao kingdom at Dali, Yunnan. This became the province of Yun-nan (South of the Clouds), under a Mongol Muslim governor and garrison. The restless Kublai continued to keep his armies busy. Korea was occupied and Annam reduced to vassalage. Maritime expeditions attacked Champa and Java in Southeast Asia, gaining fleeting toeholds, but naval and diplomatic attempts to conquer Japan met with disaster. The Japanese called the typhoon that wrecked Kublai's second expedition *kamikaze* (divine wind), a term later applied to the suicide pilots and planes that attacked American ships in the West Pacific theater during World War II.

The Yuan dynasty, alien and hated as it was, nevertheless unified China as never before, and established patterns of national, economic, and social life that endured for about six hundred years—until the overthrow of the last imperial dynasty in 1911. Out of the many rebellions troubling the Mongol rulers finally arose an illiterate peasant, once a Buddhist monk, who was to establish a Chinese dynasty, the Ming.

Ming China and the Outside World

China finds the outside world.   In contrast to that of other dynasties the Ming emphasis was southward and overseas for prestige and trade (1368–1644). To secure his land base Hong Wu, the first Ming emperor, so dispersed the Mongols that even the conqueror of Western Asia, Timur-I-Leng (Tamerlane) could not hold the old Mongol capital of Karakorum, "where princes and envoys from nearly all Eurasia had knelt in homage a century earlier" (Goodrich 1963:190). Fifty years before Europe's "Age of Exploration" even began the Ming Emperor Yong Luo (Yung Lo) and his successors financed seven huge naval expeditions between 1405 and 1431, reaching countries from Vietnam to East Africa. They brought back navigational information, ambassadors, ostriches and giraffes, and as captives the prince of Palembang and the king of Ceylon. In spite of a prohibition to leave the country many Chinese moved into the Philippines, Malaysia, and the East Indies to establish the commercial dominance they have preserved ever since.

Ming China finds itself.   With the expulsion of the Mongols, Chinese dignity was restored, and highways, bridges, and defenses were improved. Over forty thousand Board of Works projects were completed in a flurry of public works, including the rebuilding of 432 city walls and the construction of 132 new ones. However, in spite of Ming court intrigues, the misuse of executive power by palace eunuchs, and a generally inefficient system of government, there were some excellent administrators among the one hundred thousand civil and eighty thousand military officials in the empire. Southwest China was transformed from the place of exile to an increasingly thriving region by the transfer of scores of thousands of Chinese to settle and consolidate this border region. On the negative side, however, seventy to seventy-five million household hewers of wood cut China's forests for timber and firewood, and denuded the mountains.

TABLE 13-2 Ming Dynasty Contacts with the Outside World

OUTGOING CONTACTS	DATES	INCOMING CONTACTS
Ming armies subjugate all peripheral regions	1368-1398	
Yong Luo sends ministerial representatives to Tibet, Java, Siam, Bengal, etc.	1403-1425	
Admiral Zheng He's seven naval expeditions to S.E. Asia, India, Arabia, Africa	1405-1431	Tribute from Japan, Java, Ceylon, South India, E. Africa, Persian Gulf states, Samarkand, also Vietnam and Burma; some 36 countries in all
Ming fleets roam oceans from Japan to East Africa		
	1514/17	Portuguese arrive at Chinese ports
	1544	Portuguese settle at Xiamen (Amoy)
	1550-1563	Japanese pirates sack coastal cities
	1554/7	Portuguese settle at Macao
Tens of thousands of Chinese resident in Philippines and Sumatra	1560s	
	1565	Spanish traders begin coming from Philippines
	1567/1619	Russians fail to secure a place at Court
	1582	Christian mission work begun under Matteo Ricci
Ming troops repel Japanese invasions of Korea	1593-1597	Languages spoken at Court included: Korean, Japanese, Turkish, Persian, Mongolian, Jurchen, Uigur, Thai, Malay, Vietnamese.
Ming tea becomes known in Europe	1600s	
	1622	Dutch land on Formosa (Taiwan)
Ming lose Manchuria	1622-1624	
	1637	English ships force entry into Canton
	1644	Manchus expel Ming dynasty to conquer China, Russians reach the Amur.

The outside world finds China. Beginning in 1368 some thirty-six nations and rulers sent or brought tribute to the splendid Ming court at Peking. But from 1498 on, when Vasco da Gama returned from Calicut in India to report that the wealth of the Orient was not only fabled but fabulous, Europe went east to get it. The exchanges of goods, ideas, and currency brought both bane and blessing. Contributions from the New World, via Europe, included tobacco, corn (maize), sweet potatoes—and syphilis. The Spanish trade via the Philippines and Mexico brought silk and porcelain to Europe, and in return 400 million Mexican silver pesos poured into China, to remain China's basic currency until the 1930s. Peanuts, sweet potatoes, sugarcane, and corn added vast areas of less fertile plains and mountainsides to the zones of food production, and the altitude line between irrigated rice and upland corn became the residential boundary between the lowland Chinese and the hill tribespeople. Indigo helped the Chinese to designate themselves as the "blue-clad people." Since the Ming period courtesy to guests has meant roasted peanuts and sweet potato flakes accompanying a cup of tea.

Although tea was first mentioned in China just before A.D. 273, it was the 1600s before Ming tea changed Europe's social habits. Loose leaves went to Europe, pressed bricks of tea to Tibet and Russia. The Japanese "tea ceremony" and the English "tea time" developed together with the demand for Ming porcelain.

During Ming times there was a meticulous mapping of Inner Asia and West China, as well as researches antedating those of Europe into lexicography, drugs, famine foods, hydraulics, and other basic interests. But in time Ming faltered, and the once-nomadic Manchus invaded from the north, coming through passes in the Great Wall to claim a new Mandate of Heaven.

The Manchus and Those Who Stayed

The campaigns to establish the imperial power of the Manchu *Qing* or *Ch'ing* dynasty (1644–1911) over the whole country reduced the population from a (probably high) estimate of 150 million in about 1600 to 108.3 million in 1661. (Tax register figures are said to be sixty million and nineteen million respectively.) However, in contrast to the overtly military rule of the Mongol Yuan emperors, the Manchu rulers deliberately espoused a bureaucratic civil government. So it was that the Ming forms of government and social life were continued undisturbed, with a few minimal exceptions. The shaven head and long pigtail or queue, mandated as a sign of Chinese subjection, gradually became sublimated into an emblem of ethnic pride. Dress styles also changed. The Manchu style of trousers and diagonally cut shirt, jacket and robe was ordained for everyone except priests, Koreans, and tribespeople, who retained their separate dress patterns until the late 1940s.

Within the empire much had been stirring. Taiwan was occupied as a province in 1683. In 1720 Tibet was placed under the Dalai Lama, who was designated the secular as well as spiritual ruler, with a Chinese garrison as a guarantee of peace. In the same year, the southwest frontiers were finally stabilized by abrogating the authority of the tribal chieftains, and placing the tribes under appointed Chinese officials. But by 1800 the growing incompetence of Manchu rule had encouraged dissension in the provinces and frustration among the foreign nations endeavouring to bring China into the mainstream of Western trade and diplomatic intercourse. In addition to the troubles of the Opium War there was the trauma of the Tai-ping rebellion of 1851 to 1865. Belying the meaning of their name, Great Peace, the Taipings laid waste to central provinces and caused the deaths of about fifty million people. Their final suppression turned the Manchu dynasty into a caretaker government. Rather curiously, this success gave the dynasty a reprieve—many loyal Chinese officials preferring this alien dynasty to anarchy—while at the same time heralding its ultimate demise.

With the removal of the Ming trade restrictions, exports to Europe and America burgeoned, bringing with them a new crop of unwelcome Europeans. Non-Oriental aliens have been in China for at least 1,500 years. In the A.D. 500s there were more than 10,000 households of foreigners, mostly Arab and Persian, in Loyang city alone. But, after hundreds of years of minimal contact, the Treaty of Nanjing, which closed the infamous Opium War of 1839 to 1842, gradually opened eighteen "treaty ports" to foreign trade and residence. Unfortunately the treaty legalized the opium trade. This trade had arisen largely because of the considerable self-sufficiency of China. There was little Europeans could offer that China did not have already, usually of equal or better quality. Only a few trade items were really welcome, including beche-de-mer (sea slug), sandalwood, and furs from the North-west Coast of America. Always residentially segregated from the Chinese, the in-creasing numbers of foreigners flocking into the treaty ports raised legal questions of jurisdiction, leading to the establishment of the partial autonomy of the various Concessions and the foreigners within them, a condition termed "extraterritoriality."

TABLE 13-3 Social and Political Impacts Upon Population Growth in China

DYNASTY	DATE (A.D.)	MILLIONS	COMMENTS ON CAUSES
Han	2	58/59.6[a]	Of 43 million in North China, 35 on Yellow River plain.
	57	40–45	Reduced by floods, wars, famines, plagues.
	140–160	50–55	Movement southward towards Yangtze basin.
	157	56[a]	
	280	16	After disasters like those of A.D. 57, people at the time believed that only one tenth of the Han population was left.
Sui	609	46/54[a]	
Tang	742	51.5/75[a]	Probably omits Guangxi and Yunnan on the southwest frontiers. 1.8 million in and near Chang-an, the capital.
	c.750	70–75[b]	This peak was followed by rebellion losses.
Song	874	Less than 50[a]	Censuses reported less than fifty; historians' estimates between sixty and seventy.
	980	60–70	Prevalent rebellions and invasions.
	1100	100[b]	Five urban areas with over one million people.
Yuan	1290	58.8	Fearful toll through wars and Mongol invasion.
Ming	1381	59.9	Very slow recovery; mutual slaughter in North China.
	1516–78	64	Introduction of new food sources—maize, sweet potatoes, peanuts, sorghum, squash, beans—plus peace, led to population surge.
	1600	150[b]	
Qing	1661	108.3	Decrease from war of conquest; famine.
	1741	143.4	Extended cultivation of new foods; peace. About 1700 population of all Western Europe (British Isles, France, Holland, Germany, Italy, Austria) estimated at 54 million persons.
	c.1800	300+	Abundant food; internal tranquility.
	c.1850	430	Devastation during Taiping Rebellion soon resulted in about 50 million deaths.
	1900–1911	340	Rebellion, and recurrent famines.
Republic	1920s	400+[b]	Popular phrase: "400 million brothers."
	1950	583	Beginning of population explosion.
	1978	950–989[a]	Estimates vary from 894 million to one billion.

Sources: (Yi-fu Tuan 1969) and (Goodrich 1963).

[a] Census.

[b] Estimate.

The slowdown in estimated population growth between 1978 (950–989[a], with estimates up to one billion) and 1984 (1,048,200,000[b]) represents the stringent government and social pressure to restrict children to one or at most two per family.

Following the Boxer Rebellion of 1900, revenues from the Maritime Customs, the Salt Gabelle (a tax monopoly), and the Post Office, excellently administered by Europeans, paid for war indemnities and national projects. But the elimination of the reform-minded young Emperor Guang Xu (Kuang Hsu) by the ultraconservative Empress Dowager Ci Xi (Tz'u Hsi) revealed a desperate confusion at court. The delusion of the imperial rulers in Peking that they still were the arbiters of their own and other peoples' empires was fatal. The Revolution of October 10, 1911, finally shattered that delusion, and snatched away their Mandate of Heaven.

POSTDYNASTIC CHINA

Indecision and the Warlord Period

The rebellion against the Manchu Qing dynasty which began at Hankow on October 10, 1911—thereafter celebrated as the Double Tenth—led to the inauguration of the Republic of China on January 1, 1912. Its principal architect, Dr. Sun Yat Sen soon resigned as President, and Yuan Shi Kai held the office until 1916. Parliamentary procedures bogged down; competent administrators and the schools to train them were lacking. Military leaders began to carve out their own territories. Stagnation was compounded by regional isolation, since land communication consisted principally of the horse, the sedan chair, the wheelbarrow, and the river sailboat. Between 1916 and 1928 ambitious governors and generals fought for territory and money—maritime and provincial customs, taxes, and levies—as means to power. They were repeating with cannon and rifles instead of bows and spears the same interdynastic turmoil which occurred in the periods of the Warring States and the Three Kingdoms. The closure to this period came from an unexpected quarter.

The Nationalist Achievement

For sixteen years prior to 1911 Dr. Sun Yat Sen toured the world to promote the Revolution, then for ten years afterward despaired of the results. In 1921 he became president of the dissident "republic" in Canton. With funds, personnel, and disciplinary know-how from the U.S.S.R., the only foreign government willing to help him, he planned the unification of China under his party, the Kuomintang or National People's Party. In 1926 the military arm of the Kuomintang initiated the Northern Expedition to take political control of all China. Its Communist and the Nationalist factions soon fell apart.

The Communist faction set up their short-lived government at Hankow in central China. The Nationalist forces under Jiang Kai-she (Chiang Kai-shek), however, securely established the new capital at Nanjing. Within a mere nine years from 1928 to 1937 this Nationalist regime under Jiang as President rid the country of its warlords, and brought to order the nationwide political, administrative, and fiscal chaos. Following the elimination of the Foreign Concessions, China was recognized as a united, dignified, and unshackled modern nation.

A Provincial Illustration of Turmoil

The province of Jiangxi (Kiangsi) will illustrate an instance of the destruction, death, and devastation from war, exile, and disease that for millenia have periodically plagued China. Jiangxi's prosperous years up to 1927 had been disturbed only lately by rifle shots warning travelers to pull up to the nonlegal transit customs shed. However, with the appearance of Communist troops troubles multiplied. Neutral villagers, accused by both Communist and Nationalist soldiers of aiding the "other side" were robbed and killed by both. In isolation each locality fended for itself as best it could.

So-called "people's" regimes were set up in the smaller county cities and markets under the general Communist umbrella of Chairman Mao and Marshal Zhu De (Chu Teh). These local "soviets" condemned tens of thousands of local peasants for passive noncooperation, slaughtered them morning by morning, and threw their bodies into mass grave pits. Other thousands, by now destitute, were forced from their homes in snowy winters and fetid summers to flee to the larger cities held by the Nationalists. Day by day in these crowded and isolated cities malaria, typhoid, and malnutrition reaped their grim harvest, just as death wielded its savage scythe in the rural counties.

Based on census figures Jiangxi's population in 1927 was estimated at 27 million. After the Communist army left on their Long March westward in 1934 another census recorded Jiangxi's population at 16,409,480 persons. Personal knowledge considers the loss of eleven million lives in eight years (1927-1934) to be substantially correct. From this illustration the reality of the estimated fifty million dead during the Tai-ping rebellion, and other interdynastic drops in population, become startlingly apparent.

The China Incident and World War II

Japan began its military assault on China in 1937 allegedly to relieve its own population pressure and to gain both materials and markets for its growing industries. This assault so disrupted China's stabilizing situation that the Nationalist regime's organization, industry, and finances collapsed. Leaving nearly all the industrial and revenue-producing areas behind, one of the greatest migrations in history took place, as about twenty million Chinese moved 1,500 miles into the far western provinces. Small factories were moved bodily, and university faculties and students held classes by the roadside. As in other times of war and deprivation, the government's demands on the populace became increasingly authoritarian and oppressive, and resentment ate like a cancer.

At the end of the war in 1945, when officials were needed to take control of the large northern and eastern cities, Old Guard graft-ridden officials gained these lucrative positions under the Nationalist flag. The populace viewed such appointments with dismay and disappointment. That was probably the political point of no return for the Nationalist regime, just as the military stalemate in Manchuria a little later in 1946, signalled the beginning of the end.

During this period of struggle between Nationalists and Communists for territory, political power, and for the minds and loyalties of the populace, the prize was the total control of all China. The Nationalist regime and its armies crumbled internally, leaving the Communists completely victorious in 1949. By the end of 1950 the political control of the People's Republic of China extended to the far southwest frontier with Burma. However, the greatest change in China was not in the area of political reorganization but in the transformation of its society and the outlook of its peoples.

BOX 13-1   *A NEW PERSON FOR THE NEW SOCIETY*

Introducing Comrade Wang

Let us consider the forty years' experiences of someone we will call Citizen or "Comrade Wang." Age, about 46. Born at Dali in West Yunnan, 1935. Son of a shopkeeper who sold Dali marble. By age 14 in 1949, while still too young to engage in politics, he had traveled extensively with the caravan traders throughout much of the region of the old Nan-zhao kingdom.

During a visit south of Dali in 1950 Comrade Wang saw mountain tribespeople delivering in rice the taxes the Communist propagandists had promised were all remitted. To obtain the rice the tribespeople had to barter their corn, the main food supply for the next six months until the summer's harvest. He also saw the bamboo stakes in the farmers' fields specifying the high proportion of the officially estimated crops that was to be handed in later at the newly opened government depots. On his own home block the usual people's committee was set up to monitor all activities: occupations, family relationships, and even private conversations. Accusation meetings commenced immediately, children against parents, neighbors against neighbors. In spite of the fact that rape, murder, theft, slander, and bodily injury were almost nonexistent in this region, the meetings went on. If the "crimes" were often nebulous—like the charge of possession of firearms against an itinerant peddler who had bought and sold a hopelessly broken pistol five years before —the fires against which the persons slow-to-accuse and those slow-to-confess were pushed were very real.

Certainly there were many rapacious officials and oppressive landlords; they were readily identifiable, nobody defended them, and their elimination was swift. But the continued and relentless hounding of the people nationwide to uncover and convict "class enemies" finally resulted in the execution or suicide of between twenty and fifty million people. This meant the death of every twelfth or thirtieth person in the entire country.

Between ages 15 and 23 Wang finally realized the desire of the Beijing (Peking) authorities was to break down all the existing family ties and social relationships, and to forcefully mold some sort of new situation in which each individual would do what the Party told him without question. He decided to go along with the program.

Being a city dweller he saw but was not drafted into one of the nation's 24,000 rural communes, each averaging about 10,000 acres (40 sq. km.). Some five thousand households provided about ten thousand active workers of both sexes for each commune. Overall guidance and allocation of labor rested with the commune leaders. The production brigade owned its own industries and was responsible for its own programs. The production team, roughly equivalent to the old farming village, had responsibility for tools, animals, and workshops. The early experiment in sex-segregated communal living was soon abandoned, as was the wasteful Great Leap Forward of 1958. Moreover, the theoretical slogan of compensation—"to each (person) according to his need"—was dropped in favor of cash incentives for extra hard work.

Communism's New Society

By the 1960s Comrade Wang had long worn the button seen on photographs of Premier Zhou En-lai, "Serve the People." During the years since 1949 he had seen the complete replacement of the previous social structures. Gone, as such, were the multiple loyalties to country and community, clan and family, parents and elders. The State now was the focus of all loyalty, and the Party was the instrument of change, policy, and government. Philosophy was in the new canonical books—the writings of Marx and Engels, and especially of Mao Ze-dong (Mao Tse-tung). China had turned inward for development, until a conflict arose between the advocates of "Red *or* Expert" (revolution or technological practicality) and of "Red *and* Expert."

Wang watched with dismay as eleven million youthful and undisciplined Red Guards fanned out across China between 1966 and 1969 to carry the revolutionary message of Mao's Great Proletarian Cultural Revolution to its unintended but bitter conclusion. Chinese of every occupation, position, and age rebelled against the destruction of their country's past, against the depressing present, and against the officially opaque future. Factions and feuds among the Red Guards developed into serious armed clashes between Guards, troops, and civilians. Corpses floated down the rivers. Chaos enveloped factory and farm, city and countryside. Only then was the army called in to restore order, and the Guards were repudiated by being exiled to distant farm communes.

During his twenty years as a party representative, Comrade Wang had observed communes which progressed from simple blacksmithing to the use of heavy machinery to build tractors, harvesters, and other machines, and the local manufacture of tools to repair them. Other communes cultivated better strains of rice, wheat, and cotton in their own horticultural facilities, including triticale, a hybrid of wheat and rye.

Wang's itinerary included some of the new industrial cities, whose tenfold spurt in local population has not absorbed enough of the seventeen to twenty million annual births. This meant that the rural communes, although they used some machinery, remained embedded in a labor-intensive economy—hoes and bicycles being more typical than tractors and automobiles. He heard the comment that, in total, China's "muscles produce more energy than machines," and realized that to preserve psychological and social peace it was essential that every pair of hands be busy.

Following the deaths of Zhou En-lai and Mao in 1976, the twice-purged Deng Xiao-ping began the laborious process of rehabilitating China's economy internally and its prestige internationally. Concurrently this was a process of de-Maoification, signaled by the trial and condemnation of the "Gang of Four," consisting of Mao's widow, the radical Jiang Qing, and three other high Party officials, who were blamed for much of the unrest and death toll of the previous years, and for plotting a coup d'etat.

From 1977 on, the pragmatic return to nationwide use of hardearned expertise implied ultimate relief in terms of Zhou En-lai's "Four Modernizations"—of agriculture, industry, national defense, and science and technology.

Science and Progress

In talking with upper echelon theoreticians and planners, Wang gradually understood that China's philosophic goal still was a balance of material and ethical existence for all its peoples. This was the message, at least in part, of the ancient Chinese classic, *The Doctrine of the Mean*. Science and technology, in addition to bringing China into the nuclear club and producing machines and tools, also include special concentrations upon agriculture, energy, computers, lasers, space science, high-energy physics, and genetic engineering. China desires to reach by 1985 the level of Western technology of the late 1970s, and to be a world leader in science by the year 2000. Research and development in such institutions as the Wuhan Hydrology Research Institute and the unit on Molecular Orbital Theory, are directed toward the ultimate welfare of China's one billion and more people.

Comrade Wang has come a long way from the time when officials, traders, customers, and beggars pored over the veined marble trays and bowls in his father's shop. He has recently seen a trend toward freer initiatives for the people, and toward increased family and village life as the rigidity of the commune system has been greatly reduced. He knows that, while most young people have accepted their official work assignments, many thousands fled in frustration to Hong Kong, some are delinquent, and some have found solace in the small house churches. He is well aware that Party regulations and Communist ideology restrict some freedoms of choice; nevertheless, he is a proud member of an ancient civilization which has a dignified position among the nations of the world.

Chapter 14

The Peoples of China

THE HAN CHINESE

The nation and empire of China has long encompassed peoples belonging to many different cultural groups, and has interacted on its borders with many more. But the vast majority of the nation's people are the Han Chinese. Implicit in the designation "Han Chinese" is membership in a cultural group which has certain shared understandings, social patterns, concepts, and patterns of behavior. To understand what this means, we can begin with something quite ordinary: household courtesy.

Household Courtesy

The wood-block prints illustrating the old provincial annals show in black-line drawings the houses, tools, weapons, animals, and living conditions prevalent in ancient China. While the costumes and weapons have been greatly modified, much of the housing, rural husbandry, etc., are recognizably similar today. Entering into the courtyard of a modern dwelling through the street gate in the high wall of stone, brick, or rammed earth, a visitor sees the open double-doors of the main house. One-story buildings flank the courtyard on each side. The large yellow guard dog having been kenneled or tied, the host seats the visitor in the central *ke-tang* or guest hall. The guest's seat is on the left or honor side of the hall as one looks out toward the front door. The formal cup of tea is handed with both hands and, of course, should be received with both hands, like any other gift.

Naturally, visitors do not gape, talk loudly, walk around, eye the women, and usually do not cross their knees. Neither are they invited into the surrounding bedrooms, storerooms, or kitchen. If the group is small, the meal is served at a small square table seating eight persons, usually in order of honor from one to eight (where the host sits), although simplicity, equality, and informality now connote courtesy.

The Local Environment

To gain an idea of China's local environments, let us pay a visit to observe the differences among them. Depending upon where we are, when we step outside the front door or the front gate, we may be on the pavement of a Shanghai street filled with trucks, automobiles, push-carts, and honking taxis. We may be among the multitude of pedestrians, or beside a girl bicycling in shorts, a schoolboy skateboarding, or a workman drinking tea. Maybe our front gate opens onto a footpath winding between flooded rice paddies in South China, or beside a village near Canton where a three-story brick fort stands guardian. Perhaps the front door of our North China cave home opens to the outside world of ploughed fields and barren mountains. Quite likely our "front door" opens onto the corridor of a commune apartment complex, with scores of fellow members to meet every day as we join in the group field work, or the production team in the machine shop, or the children in school and nursery. The days are now past when, in a 900-year-old village in the New Territories of Hong Kong, families whose ancestors had moved in a mere four hundred years ago were still referred to as the "newcomers." Today, in Mainland China, all are equal members of the commune, though Party members are decidedly more equal than others.

Family, Clan, and Community

Family and community have always been close, and through thirty years of commune living are bonded in a new way. Marriages need party approval, and groom and bride are subject to separate work assignments that may send them to different occupations in distant localities. With the partial discontinuance of the commune system, family ties are stronger, but lack the traditional clan cohesiveness. Outside of Mainland China the go-between would ask each family for the *ba-gua* (or *ba-zi,* the eight characters) which state the hour, day, month, and year of birth of the prospective bride and groom—a horoscope to ascertain marital compatibility. If the horoscopes are compatible, then lineage, wealth, education, health, personality, and physical appearance will all be considered. The bride becomes a member of the groom's lineage, though traditionally she also retained her own surname, and her natal family retained the right to intervene whenever they considered her life or well-being to be endangered or compromised.

The much-publicized "tong wars" in overseas Chinatown communities, like the communities themselves, are symptoms of ethnic and clan (*tang* or *tong*) identity and jealously guarded prerogatives. The impenetrable exchange and information systems these communities have developed among themselves have combined isolation and prosperity. They also have led to highly restrictive legal measures in the Philippines, Indonesia, and Malaysia, designed to force an end to these alien enclaves and to break their grip upon the national economies. The social strength of this family and clan cohesiveness stems, at least in part, from the ancient role of the emperor as the *pater familias* of the nation, and today displays itself in the declarations by both Mainland China and Taiwan that there is only one China, not two.

Four Cardinal Concepts

Han society has always emphasized several governing principles, such as orderliness, practicality, self-identity, and integrity.

Orderliness. The Chinese concept of orderliness works down hierarchically from greatest to least: officials, street addresses, book references. In the area of kinship there was the widely used surname, the clan, lineage, family, individual. Social classes traditionally were ranked down from scholars (*shi*), farmers (*nong*), artisans (*gong*), and merchants (*shang*) to soldiers (*bing*), although in practice the ranking was modified by personal character, wealth, and position. In the People's Republic the scholar was to rank below the merchant, while the regular army soldier was respected for his training and discipline. Women have been awarded equal rights in law, in home and work brigade, and in discussion and decision in the commune. The upper echelons of the party and government, however, appear still to be a man's world.

Practicality. Life in an overpopulated and somewhat bleak land required intelligent expertise applied to hard work by all household members. Daily problems, philosophy, and religion were approached pragmatically. Confucian precepts guided acceptable behavior. Taoist teaching provided for a balanced natural life, and Buddhism added provisions for worship of the deities. Psychic and religious extremes never took root here. From some viewpoints Communism's dialectical materialism was not completely alien to Chinese thought.

Self-identity. So deeply ingrained over some 3,500 years is China's concept of self-identity, of being an ethnic unity, together with being the fountainhead of a peerless culture that promoted the well-being of surrounding nations, that pride in being the region's Middle Kingdom was justified. Not unexpectedly, many of these surrounding nations either sent tribute or else tried to take possession of this rich domain. And even though the two sections of a divided China have been operating as independent nations since 1949, Mainland China and Taiwan both adhere to the concept of this ancient unity—to the extent that Taiwan was willing to be excluded from both the Council and the Assembly of the United Nations rather than declare itself independent.

Integrity and respect. Perhaps the greatest insult to a Chinese gentleman would be to say to him, "*Ni mo-you li!*" ("You are unreasonable!"). The Chinese phrase calls into question his uprightness and his capacity for logic and respect, and implies that he lacks the essential qualities of the "princely person" (*jun-zi*). His very identity is impugned. Embedded in language and behavior, such phrases as "*Li, yi, lian, chi*"—good manners and propriety, righteousness, compassion, and a sense of shame—have preserved a healthy social atmosphere for millenia. The successive debacles ending the dynastic, Republican, and Nationalist eras testify that society disintegrates when the respect-and-values system of society is no longer its standard of behavior. The Communist regime denounced Confucianism, and substituted the State and the Party for the six traditional objects of respect: the ruler, father, elder brother, husband, friend, and teacher. But the essential moralism of the once discarded and now partly rehabilitated classics not only has guided the social conduct of the person inside the Mao jacket, it now is officially approved together with wage incentives and free-time occupations.

CHINA'S MINORITIES

The Minority Nationalities

Two small but significant indicators have symbolized China's composite population. First, the early five-barred flag of the Republic: red for the Han, yellow for Mongols, blue for Tibetans, white for the Hui or Muslims, and black for the Manchus. Second, in 1955 the People's Republic printed banknotes in four languages: Han, Tibetan, Mongolian, and Uigur.

The *Common Program* of 1949 and the *Constitution* of 1954 set forth the

TABLE 14-1   China's Principal Languages

MACROFAMILY	FAMILY	BRANCHES AND LANGUAGES	PROVINCE OR LOCALITY
Sino-Tibetan	Sinitic	Guo-yu ("Mandarin")	All China
		Jiangxi dialects	Jiangxi
		Southern dialects: Fujianese, Cantonese, Ke-jia (Hakka), etc.	Southeastern provinces, Fujian, Guangdong
	Tibeto-Burmese	Chuang-Tai: Chuang, Lao, Pu-yi, Tai-Shan	S. W. China
		Miao-Yao: Miao, Yao	S. W. China
		Tibetan: Tibetan, Jia-rong	Tibet, West China
		Kachin: Kachin	Yunnan
		Yi: Lisu, Luoluo, Lahu, Na-xi Min-jia, Tuli	Yunnan
Austro-Asiatic	Mon-Khmer	Wa, Palaung	West Yunnan
Ural-Altaic	Tungusic	Manchu	Xinjiang to E. Manchuria
	Mongolian	Khalkha, Kalmuck, Buriat	Xinjiang to N. China
	Turkic	Uigur, Uzbek, Tatar, Kazakh	Xinjiang to Gansu
Indo-European	Persian	Tajik	

The speakers of all the twenty-six languages other than Sinitic (spoken by the Han Chinese) are among the fifty-four minority nationalities of China. Among the others not listed above are the Mongolians, Koreans, Russians, and Hui—that is, Muslims.

status of minorities, and two national committees care for their overall affairs: the Nationalities Commission and the Nationalities Affairs Commission of the State Council.

As in some other parts of Asia, the minority peoples of China may be identified by their distinctive languages and colorful dress. The fifty-four "minority nationalities," comprising some sixty million persons, or about 6 percent of the population, speak at least forty different languages and occupy about 60 percent of China's total territory. They have been integrated into the national picture, officially described as a "multinational state in which all the nationalities participate on all levels of government and production." Within the jurisdiction of the Central Government these minority peoples in their five autonomous regions and seventy additional autonomous counties manage most of their own internal affairs. These responsibilities include their finances and the regulation of the political, judicial, educational, occupational, health, economic, and cultural characteristics and services of their own nationality. For some time now they have had their own college graduates, literature, and representation in the Party and in Congress.

Examples of the minority groups both inside and outside the country are described here in general or specific terms, including an informational ramble through a tribal environment in Southwest China. This particular environment could be found repeatedly not only in neighboring areas but also throughout the hills and mountains of Southeast Asia, and even as far away as Assam in northeast India.

TRIBES NORTH OF THE WALL

The Northerners

The Han Chinese began as an ancient agricultural people living in "the land within the passes" of the mountains of northwest China. Following the easiest pass eastward towards the vast fertile plains they gradually spread to the distant shores of the East and South China Seas. But north of the Great Wall, west of the Tibetan foothills, and past the mountains, gorges, and jungles of the southwest, the Han Chinese never settled in substantial numbers until colonies were established in the southwest (1600s), in Xinjiang (1800s), and in Tibet after 1950. Rough terrain, small profits, and tough tribespeople acted as deterrents to farmers from the fertile Chinese plains. Historically, the Chinese used the garrison approach to pacification, but during the last century millions of Chinese have been located in the remoter northwest and southwestern regions as peacefully settled agricultural immigrants. In the north, nationality communes care for several hundred thousand Mongol herder-farmers in Inner Mongolia (now the province of Nei Mongol), others being integrated into the general Chinese population in their communes and factories. Thus, China seems to have solved an ancient threat to security—the danger of invasion by the northern "barbarian" tribes.

The traditional northern hunter-herder-warrior horsemen of Turkic and Mongol extraction learned horsemanship and archery along with their childhood milk, meat, and fur clothing. As they moved their herds from one meager pasture to another, they scrutinized weather, pasture, camp, and visitor with equal suspicion.

The male head of a lineage or encampment would count his wealth in herds, display it in silks and furs, and share it with his several wives and their felt-tent households.

Any weakness in the government south of the Great Wall predictably triggered a massive assault by the northern horsemen upon the villages and towns, provoking in return either a punitive expedition or an imperial subsidy to retire peacefully. Many of these invasions turned into successful occupations of Chinese territory. North China suffered the ignominy of barbarous Mongol kinglets in the A.D. 300s, local Mongol dynasties between 907 and 1234, and then the sweep of Genghis Khan's savage hordes. Once in power these conquerors adopted a variety of state policies. The brief and heavy-handed Yuan dynasty of Kublai Khan lasted barely one hundred years in contrast to the nearly three hundred years of the tolerant Manchu Qing dynasty, for the Manchus adopted Chinese culture and utilized Chinese as administrators. A descendant of a Mongol officer ruled Yongning in West Yunnan in the 1920s, and a village of Manchus near Kunming, Yunnan, are two examples of "relict populations," interesting cultural remnants of the occupations of China by northerners.

Xinjiang Tackles the Sands

During the past two thousand years, Chinese and Scythians, Greeks and Muslims, Mongols and many others have driven or pressured each other back and forth in the Xinjiang horse-and-camel corridor. There have been soldiers and merchants, scholars and bandits, ambassadors and mendicants; speaking dialects of Persian and Chinese, Mongol and Manchu, Tungusic and Turkic, Greek and Latin, German and Russian languages. They have traveled by horse cart, been carried in litters, ridden on horses or camels, and trudged on foot. Their homes have been garnished with silk, and their bank accounts with silver; they left their paintings on the cave walls at Dunhuang (Tun-huang), and bequeathed their bones to the desert sands. Most of the movements of Inner Asia's peoples have been westward, but Buddhism, early Nestorian Christianity, and Islam, for example, all came eastward through Xinjiang to China.

The twenty-four or more towns that travelers passed along the Silk Road south of the Taklimakan (Takla Makan) desert lie buried under the sand scores of miles in from the present edges of the desert. Replacing these lost towns and way stations are 17,000 families living in forty new oases up to sixty miles into the desert. Around the edges of these deserts 2,703 sq. miles (700,000 hectares) of good fields have been put into cultivation. In addition to the refinery at the Karamai oil field, the brand new city of Shihezi (Shih-ho-tzu) (pop. 120,000) in the Dzungaria Basin produces diesel engines, tractors, refined sugar, textiles, chemicals, and woolen knitwear. Xinjiang also houses China's nuclear complex. The present developments in Xinjiang illustrate the current concept of the Chinese Communist Party of cultural autonomy, not independence, for their minority nationalities. Seventy-five percent of Xinjiang's twelve minority nationalities are the indigenous, Turkic-speaking Uigurs; the Kazakhs, Tajiks, and the Hui (Muslims) are prominent among the other groups.

In the early 1900s the west to east traverse of Xinjiang still took six to eight months of weary and dangerous travel, but now takes only hours by plane. The 675 miles (1,080 km.) north to south from Ulaanbaatar (Ulan Bator) in Mongolia to the Great Wall in China still takes thirty to forty-five days by camel, but only three days by automobile, and since 1956 less than one day by train. In this Xinjiang is typical of all North Asia.

The Western Borders

To the west of China proper, Tibetans in the eastern and southeastern section of the icy Tibetan plateau have traditionally displayed the extremes of a class society: an exclusive nobility, a segregated monastic community, a tiny middle class of merchants and skilled workers, and a vast and impoverished peasantry of farmers and herders. Prior to 1951 approximately every fourth man was a monastic, whose ranks included disciplined and high-minded scholar abbots and lamas, highly skilled artisans and actors, and coteries of illiterate monks. Other groups in the west of China include the tribes on the Tibetan border, loosely called Man-zi— the Jia-rong, Nuo-su (Nosu), Na-xi (Nahsi), Tibetans, and others–often "pacified" but never subdued. They were only brought firmly into the Chinese orbit during the last one hundred years. Various Arab, Persian, and Uigur traders were prominent in North China from the A.D. 400s on, and the *Muslim* armies that eventually converted to Islam the Turkic peoples of Central Asia also opened the way to free transit between Southwest Asia and China. During the Yuan dynasty Muslims were extensively used in official positions, ranking second in the hierarchy of four social classes. While their major concentration was and still is in northwest China, they dispersed throughout the country, mostly as merchants and meat vendors in the cities, and as a large enclave in West Yunnan. Sinicized in language, dress, and customs, they have retained their Islamic identity by restricting marriage to those of their own faith, and sometimes by outright rebellion.

THE SOUTHWEST TABLELAND

Cobbled roads three to four feet wide led in ancient times from the gates of remote Chinese cities toward the mountain refuges of over two hundred tribal groups in southwest China. "Snow covered peaks, tropical jungles, vertical walled canyons, and inhospitable tribes unite to hold back contact with the outside world." So wrote George B. Cressey (1934:378) of the provinces of Yunnan (South of the Clouds), Guizhou, and Guangxi, where the overall population of this southwest tableland region was estimated at 157 per square mile (60 per sq. km.).

The handsome Tai-Shan peoples still are the most prominent peoples in the three provinces, but others speaking Sino-Tibetan languages include the sophisticated Chuang of Guangxi, the 1.25 million Zhong-jia or Puyi, the Miao, and the Min-jia. Some four million Luoluo (Lolo) people include the Independent Nuo-su (Nosu), Lisu, Tuli, and others. The Tai, who alone were not regarded by the Han Chinese as *man* (barbarians), occupied the Tian and Nan-zhou kingdoms in Yunnan for one thousand years, while multitudes of their people slowly migrated southward to overrun and rule the region now known as Thailand. The Tai were all farmers of irrigated rice and have been literate in five scripts, which the present regime has standardized into two.

All these peoples have maintained their separate distinctiveness during hundreds of years of contact with Chinese and other groups. The Lisu and the Miao are known by outsiders by their dress. The garments of the Hua Lisu and the Hua Miao are of variegated or "flowery" (*hua*) colors. Those of the Bai Miao and Hei Miao are, respectively, white and black (or have these as contrasting colors) while the Han Miao are so called because their dress is similar to that of the Han Chinese. While the Luoluo and Miao peoples have been generally barred from intermarriage with or passing into the ranks of the Han Chinese, the Min-jia, Chuang, and Nuo-su have had considerable social intercourse with the Chinese. In the 1940s the governor of Yunnan was a Nuo-su general, and the ornate homes of the wealthy Nuo-su in the capital city of Kunming were proudly self-identified by goats' horns nailed over their main gateways.

A Chinese official looking today at the current picture of long-standing ethnic identities and modern majority-minority relationships could well ponder the question of how and why they still remain in this condition. The answer lies in the presence of the Balk Line, and its nearly universal application.

One of the last items in a person's identity repertoire that he or she is willing to let go is speech: the special words, intonation, and rhythm patterns, acquired from those around from early childhood on into adult life. These are some of the marks of distinctive individuality still apparent as we move towards the coast of China and its main offshore island of Taiwan.

BOX 14-1   *THE INTERCULTURAL BALK LINE*

Why Minorities Remain Minorities

Let us keep company with a traveler squeezed into a dusty but efficient charcoal-burning bus heading west from the provincial capital city of Kunming, as it passes over the mountain ranges on the Yunnan plateau. This is the western section of the famous Burma Road. Blue-clad Han Chinese farm the fields of irrigated rice and hillside sweet potatoes, and in the towns operate the transportation system, the banks, the merchandising, and the schools. The traveler finally alights at a market town on a small narrow plain in the western mountains not far from the gorges of the Mekong river. The shopkeepers and street stall holders are all Chinese, but carrying firewood, eggs, and a trussed pig are women wearing pleated hemp skirts, and men wearing bright clothes with a cloth bag slung over one shoulder: a Miao woman and Flowery Lisu visitors. The traveler notices groups of men and women setting out their produce on plaited straw mats at the entrances to the market, segregated from the main market area; they are tribespeople.

Visiting among the Tribes

Fortunately, the traveler meets a friend who takes him visiting in and around the market area. In the valley bottom and the terraced lower hillsides are Chinese rice fields. As the traveler and his friend ascend the mountain trail they reach another market where both Chinese and tribal people mingle together as shopkeepers and vendors, buyers and caravaneers. The traveler's friend points down a side ravine to the river bottom shimmering in the haze of the noonday sun, and informs him that Tai and Puman villagers live well on the rich soil there.

Still ascending above the rice terraces the travelers find Luoluo-speaking Tuli plowing their terraced cornfields, and in the forest their turbaned women are cutting and bundling firewood while tending their cattle and goats. Still further up are White Luoluo villages. They too sometimes use the plow; but in their higher fields they plant coffee and fruit trees on the slopes, some wheat in the glades, or just plant vegetables alternately with the corn or millet as the Tuli do. Leaving this midmountain wooded zone the travelers climb on past untended scrub land—used partly as grazing ground for the goats—to the small upper hollows where the bracing climate favors barley and oats. There they meet some of their Miao friends who live in cavelike homes cut into the lee of the mountain top. At this altitude the Miao villages remain serene and secluded both from the Tuli and the Luoluo who broadcast buckwheat on their barren fields on the ridges, and from travelers on the trail below. The traveler asks his friend where the Lisu live (the Lisu language is a linguistic cousin to that of the Tuli). With some amusement his friend tells him that the Lisu live about two weeks' walk west, in the steep canyons of the Salween, perched on the geologic terraces five hundred to one thousand feet (153 to 305 m.) above the dizzying drop to the white waters below. They also often cut their houses halfway into the bank for warmth, to save timber, and as protection from the wind and storm.

As the travelers stop on the way up to chat briefly with these robust and independent mountain peoples, they are entertained with tea or hot water to wash down parched corn kernels, dried persimmons, dried sweet-potato flakes, and fruit. Their Miao hosts provide them with their most surprising refreshment, roasted oat flakes poured into a bowl and mixed with hot water to form a sweet and nourishing evening meal. The travelers learn something else. They have come to realize that these different peoples from the plains to the mountain tops each maintain their own niche in the environment; that is, in occupying the same general area they seldom compete for the same resources, except perhaps for title to land. This ecological niching utilizes the whole environment, avoids confrontation, and provides everyone with the wherewithall to mutually exchange natural and manufactured products to satisfy everyone's needs.

Reaching the pass over the mountain, the travelers are surprised to find an almost tropical monsoon climate prevailing on the southeastern slope. Going an extra day's walk they find a small hillside market full of tribal people, where only a few itinerant peddlers are Chinese. Among the kaleidoscopic assemblage of silver-bangled Luoluo women and Miao men with heavy silver neck rings, the ones who catch their eyes are the tall, slim, almost statuesque women dressed simply in long black sheath skirts, spotlessly white short blouses and tight round turbans. These queens of tribal women, the Shan, stand silently by their baskets of farm produce, pottery, embroidery, and woven basketry. Some have come up from the steaming and malarial river valley with rice, fruit, and vegetables; some are well-to-do farm wives on the plateau. At the end of their journey the traveler and his friend have met the aristocrats of the non-Han peoples.

The Why and the Wherefore

Trudging the long way back to the bus station the traveler thoughtfully remarks to his friend: "Now I have seen lowland and mountain people in their separateness, and in their proximity. But *why* are they separate? Are they only recently in contact with each other?"

"No," replies his friend. "They have been more or less in contact for hundreds of years. They are still separate because each for his own reasons wants to be separate."

"But why is that?"

"Well, like people, each community and nation has its own individuality. If a person or a community loses that, then the individuality—the identity— is lost, and human nature resents this loss."

"I see. So much for the psychological motivation, a part of one's system of values. What, then, is the process, the social mechanism that results in this stalemate?"

"Somewhere down the line of contact and adjustment, after willingly adopting some articles and customs that can be incorporated immediately into one's regular pattern of living, one feels as if pushed against a wall. And sometimes by circumstances or by law one is deprived of many facets of one's life that make it meaningful, and one finds that wall is the wall of lost identity. One resents too much coming in and too much trickling away, and a state of social resistance is generated. When what is left is the minimum necessary for me to be me and to have any valid sense of self-worth, this state I call the *line of minimal identity*. If I yield more I erode the essential core of my very being. So I balk at further change. From the psychological point of view I call this the *balk line*."

"I can readily see your point as the minority person and community would view it. Does the same feeling and mechanism apply to the majority people and their dominant culture?"

"Yes. Part of the dominant people's identity is that very dominance, and they will try to maintain that relationship by whatever means they consider effective. They too balk at certain changes because their identity as domina- tors can only be yielded so far without generating an acute sense of loss."

"What kind of loss?"

"Psychological, the same as for the minority person or community. This is partly motivated and partly reinforced by the desire to perpetuate power over others, for financial gain from cheap labor, or perhaps for the professed altruism of leading the combined community to the utopia they envision. That is, there are political, economic, and philosophic reasonings behind the dominant society's maintenance of *their* balk line."

"So the final result will be a long-term standoff. Would you call this social equilibrium?"

"Yes. My phrase for this is the *state of constancy*, because we now have a set of constant factors on both sides. The process for perpetuating this state is called *boundary maintenance*, for the whole circle of contributing factors must be kept under control. The majority society ensures its grip upon the legal system of social control, the education system, the major means of production and distribution, and the avenues for social mobility. By these procedures the majority makes certain that blocs or categories of minority persons do not upgrade their social status. These maintenance pressures constitute the active side of the balk line. The minorities supply the passive aspects by preserving their own language, kinship system (this, by the way, is mutual to both sides), and some aspects of dress, housing and furnishing, artifacts, religion, and manner of life. Of course, there is another result of separation: the practice of in-group marriage (called "endogamy") tends to reinforce whatever genetic distinctions were present in each group at the beginning. In time, then, the individual members of the respective communities actually may look different. This again reinforces the mutual feelings and state of separateness."

"I have the impression that Marcus Aurelius was stating a human but not a political truism when he said: 'We are born for cooperation, as are the feet, the hands, the eyelids, and the upper and lower jaws.' "

"True enough, this is the role of cooperation. Today you have seen a partial example: these different communities cooperate in their niching development of the total environment. But when cooperation infringes on what each considers his or her identity, plus his or her prerogatives, then there is drawn up a stalemate that often lasts hundreds of years. Too often this stalemate develops into a *line of friction* at the interface of contact. This is why the international borders throughout Asia so often have become such hot spots that they have sparked conflict and war. If wisdom and tolerance prevail, as you have seen it today on the mountainside, then we could each maintain our boundary balk lines in peace."

"May it be so!" With that remark the traveler profusely and sincerely thanks his friend for the trip and the enlightening conversation, boards his bus, and disappears in the usual all-enveloping cloud of highway dust. Each man returns to his own accustomed world.

Other People's Balk Lines

On his way home the traveler considers balk lines and social boundaries. Certainly the massive movement of Nationalist personnel to Taiwan in 1949 was a manifestation of a major attempt to preserve both a real and a fictional identity for those Mainland emigres, as they transported their Nationalist organization there and set up a shadow government to "represent" all China. The caste system in India has very considerably maintained its assigned boundaries and internalized balk lines for two thousand years or so. The Arab-Israeli confrontation, beginning in antiquity, seems to have fluctuated in intensity according as one or another encroached upon the other's entrenched niche. The Communist principles of the Beijing government have established a fresh set of social categories and assigned their boundaries. The "freedom swimmers" to Hong Kong apparently represent the individuals' efforts to shake free from a line of friction that has become personally intolerable. It remains to be seen whether the present policy of encouraging the minority nationalities to develop their own potentials will be able to rise above a mere rearrangement of the majority/minority relationship. With these thoughts in mind the traveler reaches home, hangs his red star cap on its peg and sits down to supper of steamed rice, chili peppers, cabbage, and cubes of pork.

Name	Altitude Above Valley Floor	Terrain	Type of Agriculture	Products and Animals
Miao	4000–6000'	Barren mountains		Firewood Stone
White Luoluo	2000–3000'	Grassy uplands	Broadcast	Goats Sheep Rye Oats Barley Buckwheat
	1000–2000'	Forest and grassy glades Rivulets and cascades	Grazing Arboriculture / Dibble stick horticulture	Firewood Fruits Camellia oil Tea Cattle
Tuli Villages	500–1000'	Fertile wooded hillsides	{ Plow agriculture	Corn terraces Coffee Vegetables
Tuli	200–500'	Lower slopes and terraced fields		Cattle Goats Sheep Dry rice Fruits Corn terraces
—(Chinese borderline area)—				
Chinese	Valley floor — 4000' above sea level	Irrigated rice fields	Irrigation, deep plowing	Wet rice Cotton Sweet potatoes Water buffalo

FIGURE 14-1 The ecology of altitudinal residence. Altitudinal niching is one way to establish a boundary maintenance mechanism and thereby preserve community self-identity. Such niching constitutes a closed system wherein to fulfil the ecologic potential.

COASTAL CHINA AND TAIWAN

Where the Rhymes Don't Rhyme

Philologists puzzled over the rhyming of the 305 poems in the *Shi Jing* or *Book of Odes,* one of the oldest written works in history, dated between the 900s and 600s B.C. The end-of-line rhymes didn't rhyme, at least not in pronunciations known to modern Chinese scholars. Working back from the present by postulating the previous pronunciations which could combine, for instance, a present *s*/*sh* and a *k* into an earlier rasping palatal sound [*x*], they ascertained the probable pronunciation of Ancient Chinese (500 B.C. to A.D. 500) and of Archaic Chinese (prior to 500 B.C.). Turning to Korean and Japanese words for assistance, they found rather solid echoes of the pronunciation at the time and place of borrowing. For instance, the Japanese pronunciation of their country's name is "Nip-pon," which doubtless comes from the South China words *ni* ("sun") and *pun* or *pon* (now written *ben* in *pinyin,* the official romanization system) meaning "root" or "origin."

Moreover, some ancient pronunciations are still present in the speech of peoples living on the (then) fringes of Han civilization along the coast from Shanghai to Hainan. Cantonese has preserved ancient syllable and word final *-p, -t, -k,* and *-m,* which Standard Chinese lost long ago. The Cantonese word for happiness is *fat* not standard *fu,* to study and learn is *hok* not the standard *hsioh*/*hsüeh* (now written *xue,* based on Pekinese dialect). The Cantonese pronunciation for the South Jiangxi city of Kan-zhou sounds like "gam-chow." All these and many other clues led finally to success in reconstructing the pronunciation of ancient and archaic Chinese, a finding of great importance for deeper understanding of the history and dynamics of the many Chinese "dialects"—now in reality separate languages.

One large population in northeastern Guangdong are the Hak-ka (*ke-jia,* meaning "guest people"). Their name suggests they once were Han Chinese in North China. In culture and physical appearance they are similar to the Cantonese, but rate second to the latter in prestige and economic opportunities. Having a penchant for travel their men will leave the farm and cover South China as traveling salesmen and small merchants. Abroad they specialize in building and stonemasonry in Hong Kong and North Borneo, and in shoemaking in Singapore. The men are distinctive in their speech, a blend of the national language and Cantonese and South Jiangxi dialects. Their women also have the distinction of never having their feet bound, the better to work in the fields—as was the custom in many parts of China, from the Sung dynasty until the Republic, especially among the merchant and upper classes.

"Pure" Cantonese is well understood throughout Guangdong province, just as the national language (*guo-yu*) is intelligible throughout the whole country. But the historic resistance of Canton to sinicization by the northern Han Chinese has been expressed over the centuries, and into the Nationalist and initial Communist eras, in mutual coolness, separate armies, and their own political and economic jurisdictions. Keen businesspeople, enterprising travelers at home and abroad, gourmet cooks, warmhearted yet hotblooded, these South Chinese always have had a dash and a charm of their own. Charm, however, was modifiable by circumstances. Nevertheless, each South China village stood out from others in the country—each had its own fortress tower! The province adopted as its name that of the old kingdom of Yue. From this name also came that of the country south of Guangdong, *Yue-nan* (*-nam* in Cantonese), meaning "the land south of Yue." Today we know this country as *Vietnam*.

Hainan

Hainan, the island pendant off the south coast of Guangxi province, provides modern occupations on rubber plantations and irrigated rice farms, and in iron and bauxite mines. These enterprises plus light industry and the cultivation of cocoa, coffee, coconut, ramie, and other tropical products keep about three million people busy. One third are tribespeople living in the mountains and forests of this 14,000 square mile (37,260 sq. km.) island, where their occupations range from hunting-fishing-gathering to slash-and-burn farming to the cultivation of irrigated rice. Few visiting Chinese would fail to find a homegrown companion somewhere among the Hoklo from Fujian, the merchants from Canton and Hong Kong, or among the ex-Republican soldiers settled here from all over China. Cajoled and pressured to return, the Indonesian Chinese repatriates were sent to Hainan to pioneer the opening up of new lands to cultivation. There are even a few probable

FIGURE 14-2 Wet rice farming in South China.

descendants of shipwrecked Arab Muslims to be found there. Together with Party cadres from North China there is no lack of human and occupational variety on this semitropical isle.

Taiwan: Where Everyone Is an Immigrant

The immigrants. When in 1590 the Portuguese sailors named the island *Ilha Formosa* they were calling it what countless people before and after had discovered, that *Taiwan* was and is indeed a "beautiful island." Seemingly all its present peoples are immigrants. The oldest settlers of Indonesian and Philippine origin began to be restricted to the forested mountains from the A.D. 500s when Chinese first landed there. Chinese and Japanese pirates had to yield to massive influxes of immigrants from Fujian and Guangdong in the 1600s and 1700s, some two million of them. Portuguese, Spanish, and Dutch settlements, and visitations by English and (later) the French were abruptly ended when the Ming official known as Koxinga (Zheng Cheng-gong) took over the island in 1661. The Manchu dynasty's officials annexed the island in 1683 and it remained so until ceded to Japan in 1895. Chinese continuously moved across the Formosa Strait until the flood of Japanese civil and military personnel occupied and developed the island and its resources. The Japanese were summarily repatriated at the end of World War II and their administrative machinery replaced by that of the two million or so Nationalist Mainlanders in 1949 and 1950. Since that time a fair number of European merchants, American military personnel, and Western missionaries have lived more or less temporarily on Taiwan—the last stragglers in the 3,000-year procession of immigrant peoples.

People of the mountains. Two thirds of Taiwan island, an area twice the size of Hawaii, are covered by mountains and inhabited by 250,000 to 300,000 tribes-people of whom the *Amis, Atayal,* and *Paiwan* are the most numerous. Between two hundred and three hundred villages are located on mountain slopes between 1,500 and 6,000 feet above sea level. In order to maintain military surveillance the Japanese imposed residence restrictions that caused the traditional one-clan-one-village organization to give way to a cohesive village unit based on residence, not on clan membership. In turn this affected the hereditary chieftainship over clan groups having an identical surname (similar to the Chinese system of clan surnames). These chiefs were replaced by elected headmen responsible to the Japanese and later to the Chinese authorities, but with no executive authority over the villagers for whom they had to answer. Such arbitrary cultural changes loosened the whole social structure, and inevitably paved the way for today's weakened family ties and discipline.

Village size varied from two families with twelve people in poor areas to one having ninety families with 895 members in a mountain area where rice grew. From this large village the Japanese confiscated 229 firearms of various sorts, evidence of the people's earlier hunting and feuding activities. The Japanese speech of the old people still mingles with their native Malayo-Polynesian languages, and with the Chinese *guo-yu* (national language) of their school children. Another outcome of the disintegrating social climate is shown in the decline in use and production of the bright embroidered costumes and the gold and silver ornaments in which the mountain villagers celebrated their festivals. Instead, the acquisition of Chinese language, coupled with the incentives of wage money and the attractions of low-land city glitter, have resulted in a steady exodus of young people from their mountain homes. Roads and electricity and bus transit also have accelerated the demise of unique village life in the once remote mountains.

People of the plains.   On the lushly verdant plains the gray, brown, and white farmsteads and villages cluster thickly, seldom out of sight of the smoke plumes of factory or town. Here the nearly eighteen million Chinese—Fujianese, Cantonese, Hakka, and Mainlanders—have developed peasant ownership of the land, private business enterprises, and government-directed factory complexes strictly for export overseas. Taiwan represents pre-1949 China: clan and family oriented, intensely Buddhist in religion, everyone energetically concentrating on the assignment at hand on farm, in factory, at school, or at sea in everything from motor-driven fishing luggers to modern container ships. While the Mainland has the technology to produce almost the whole range of consumer and technological products, on Taiwan these things *are* produced, bought and sold in the shops, and exported around the world. The political picture remains authoritarian in principle, but touches rather lightly the day-to-day livelihood and habits of the citizens, and is providing gradually for more and more provincial participation in all levels of administration. The end product of numerous migrations, Taiwan today is a dynamic and flourishing culture. But the imposing and seaworthy junks, that once took the immigrants across one hundred stormy miles of open sea to Taiwan, took others to more distant shores.

THE CHINESE OVERSEAS

Peoples on the Move

First, let us compare several migration movements: (1) the aboriginal exodus some five thousand years ago of early Malayo-Polynesian speakers from South China into Insular Southeast Asia and then as far as Hawaii and Madagascar; (2) the movement southeast of Indo-Aryan speakers through Iran and Afghanistan to the plain of the Ganges, and south to Sri Lanka's palm-fringed beaches; (3) the mass migration from South China of the tribal peoples we today call Thai, Kampucheans (Cambodians), Lao, and Vietnamese; and (4) the silent and peaceful, movement from one village site to the next down the mountain spines of Southeast Asia by the tribal Miao, Yao, Lisu, Lahu, and others out of South and Southwest China. The latest phases have been Chinese soldiers and civilians who expanded into Tibet following the opening of motor roads in 1951; and the aggressive military explosion of North Vietnamese into what were South Vietnam, Laos, and Cambodia.

However, in terms both of the numbers involved and of the worldwide extent of the dispersion, the modern exodus from China dwarfs nearly all other migratory movements. Chinese already were settled at Palembang in the Strait of Malacca as freelancing pirates before a Chinese colony called Tumasik (now Singapore) existed in 1349. Admiral Zheng He (Cheng Ho) and his mighty armada threw out the pirates, but Palembang itself was controlled by Chinese for another two hundred years into the 1600s. The Ming and Manchu emperors forbade Chinese to leave the country, but in their new countries they married local women. Then, as now, these marriages were stable, and their descendants fulfilled the wedding wishes written on the paper lanterns, that their progeny be counted in the thousands.

People of the Dispersion

Fujian (Hokkien) speakers went to Java and Malaya; the Hakka developed a powerful political organization in Borneo; and the Cantonese planted permanent "Chinatowns" in many parts of the world. This migration into the Nan-yang (Southern Ocean) was quite welcome both to local populations and to European administrators. Chinese corner stores then and now purveyed local and imported products for local purchase, and the Chinese handled the market trade and import-export distribution of goods. Their activities far upriver in Borneo and Assam usually helped to keep the hinterlands politically quiet. Especially important to the development of Southeast Asia and Oceania has been these people's capacity for sustained hard work because native labor in these areas is task or situation oriented and unsuitable for commercial agriculture, plantation labor, and mining. So the Chinese worked the tin mines in Malaya in the 1700s, nickel mines in New Caledonia in the 1800s, and gold mines in New Guinea in the 1900s. Gold glittered in California (Jiu Jin Shan, Old Gold Mountain) and upcountry from Melbourne, Australia (Xin Jin Shan, New Gold Mountain). The emigres worked mines and laundries in Queensland, Australia, coconut plantations in the Gilbert Islands, and spread a network of stores in every town and barrio in the Philippines. Honest, shrewd, courteous, and reasonable in their prices, Chinese storekeepers have prospered, often to the envy of city merchants and the dislike of local businessmen who want a windfall profit for minimal efforts. The ensuing legal restrictions on Chinese business enterprises affected some two hundred thousand persons in the Philippines, and over 2.5 million in Indonesia. The situation in Thailand is the reverse. Although only some four hundred thousand are registered as Chinese, estimates suggest that there are over 2.3 million ethnic Chinese with Thai nationality, their descendants being Thai in speech and culture.

The Beijing government has discouraged emigration, and has advised overseas Chinese to become nationals of their present home countries, to send money to relatives inside China but to stay where they are. Actually, these well-to-do and sophisticated sons of Han and Tang, not only are far from being the once distrusted Communist fifth column in their host countries, they also could be a potential irritant if they returned to China. Raised to a good life in freedom and economic security, they are unlikely to fit easily into the lower standard of living and the dictated guidelines of a totalitarian state, beneficial though the regime is in some aspects of its accomplishments. They would face an interesting distinction between capitalism, socialism, and free enterprise. Under capitalism people may hire someone to make money for them, but not under Chinese socialism. But if in China people work harder, sell their personal products and garner extra cash, while fulfilling their social obligations, that is quite acceptable as individual initiative.

THE WRAP-UP

Seen from another point of view, this is an instance of the ruling Communist Party's maintenance of its own balk line. The Party is loath to relinquish its dominant status by letting nonparty-appointed individuals acquire economic power by becoming managers. Antagonism toward overseas Chinese has a similar explanation. When the Chinese, as a group, obtain what is perceived as massive wealth, they are then a threat to the political dominance of the ruling group, for in the modern world wealth is strongly equated with power.

Within China today the Cantonese hold steadfastly to their own language as a form of boundary maintenance. And the attitudes and relationships between China and Hong Kong are a century-old line of friction. The concepts of "balk line," "line of minimal identity," "state of constancy," "boundary maintenance," and "line of friction" go far beyond China in explaining the dynamics of the interrelationships among the varied peoples of the world. In countries whose national religion is Islam, pressures for the Chinese and other non-Muslim groups to conform by converting to Islam are stoutly resisted because they would cross over the line of minimal identity. In Thailand, however, a state of constancy exists between the Chinese and the national majority people, whereas in the Philippines, Indonesia, and Malaysia an economic line of friction has existed for decades.

Chapter *15*

Japan: Dynamo with a Purpose

PANORAMA AND PURPOSE

The Panorama

Japan reclines as a large crescent-shaped island arc in the Japan Sea, vulnerable to the many typhoons that blow in from the south and east. Forming part of the Asian side of the Pacific "Rim of Fire," Japan experiences frequent earthquakes. Indeed, Mount Fuji is the snow-covered cone of a volcano, revered by the Japanese for its symmetrical beauty and as the home of many *kami* (nature spirits and gods).

It has been said that Japanese are born as Shintoists, marry as Christians, and die as Buddhists. To this may be added that most Japanese probably think as Confucianists and handle technology as secularized Westerners, while remaining intrinsically Japanese throughout. To round out this sketch of their history, one is tempted to add that both their military feudalism and their modern business have been conducted with the same commendable group-oriented discipline.

Active and dormant volcanoes smoulder amid the winter snows on the mountainous four fifths of Japan's 143,751 square miles (372,313 sq. km.). These forested slopes provide timber (but not enough), hydroelectric power from their short rushing streams, and magnificent scenery—but little else. The scenery is being exploited to attract foreign tourists (again, not enough) and millions of domestic sightseers and long strings of uniformed school children. Balmy summer weather in the south brings vacationers to the exquisite Inland Sea and permits double-cropping of rice and other foods. But harvests, houses, and shipping remain at the mercy of recurrent typhoons, torrential rains, and earthquakes. Bane and blessing do not faze the cheerful and hardy inhabitants, all 118 million of them, crowded well over 4,000 per square mile (1,544 per sq. km.) on the flat and terraced ricelands, and many more in the factory-jammed industrial cities. Such are the general conditions in Inner Japan's four main islands of Hokkaido, Honshu, Shikoku, and Kyushu.

Outer Japan used to include the northern Kurile island chain and much of oil-rich Sakhalin Island, all annexed by Russia as booty after World War II. However, the southern island chains—Bonin, Volcano, and Ryukyu—were returned to Japanese sovereignty by the United States after the war. These island chains and other coastal areas are vitally important, for the cold waters of their rich fishing grounds provide the main source of protein for the Japanese diet.

The Purpose

Five culture traits have helped Japan succeed in a land of scarce resources. Through *emulation* Japan has developed cultural innovations and technical advances garnered from around the world. By means of in-group *consensual discussion* and by *planning for the future* progress has been accelerated to achieve *high standards* in all areas of endeavor. Fierce *competition* within the hierarchy of achieving institutions has also spurred the successful efforts to become the fully recognized equal of the foremost nations of the modern world.

PREFACE TO HISTORY

The Beginnings

The earliest inhabitants of Japan were hunter-gatherers of fifty thousand to a hundred thousand years ago. Little is known of them. The first Japanese to come into clear focus are the Jomon people, who 12,000 years ago made excellent cord-patterned unglazed pottery. Living in communities of three hundred to four hundred houses, they utilized more than three hundred species of edible plants and animals (among them the domesticated dog). Later Jomon developed a society with hierarchical rankings, shamans who filed and extracted teeth, and skilled artisans who made bronze *dotaku*, bell-like gongs. About two thousand years ago rice was introduced, and a typical Japanese variety of glutinous rice has been the favorite ever since.

The origins of the Ainu are problematical. Coming into the region about two thousand years ago these hunting-fishing people were distinguished by their abundant body hair and tattooing. Around 300 B.C. they were defiantly fighting the Yayoi-Yamato invaders to protect their gradually diminishing land holdings. Today some 15,000 to 17,000 Ainu are left, mainly in Hokkaido, of whom about two percent are considered "pure" Ainu.

THE YAYOI AND YAMATO CULTURES

Around 300 B.C. the Yayoi peoples entered through Kyushu. They found an advanced Jomon culture with palaces and temples of enduring aesthetic design. To this the Yayoi added many aspects of what became traditional Japanese lifeways, such as irrigated rice, iron and copper tools, weaving looms, ceremonial daggers, halberds, mirrors, and large bronze bells, as well as cattle, horses, and chickens. Their sacrifices and ancestor worship, box and earthenware coffins, larger communities with headmen, and a matriarchal kinship system, brought additional complexity to the expanding social order.

By the A.D. 300s organized clan communities, *uji*, were driving the Ainu and others to the east and north of Japan. The *uji* that reached the Yamato Plain finally dominated the others, and became known as the Yamato culture. Yamato chiefs were buried in large stone tombs covered by earth mounds (*tumuli*), enclosed within keyhole-shaped moats. It is through the role of Yamato priest-chiefs that the emperor, and, by association, the Japanese people, used to claim descent from the sun goddess Amaterasu. The Yamato emblems of the mirror, the long iron sword, and the curved stone jewels became permanently incorporated into the imperial insignia. During Yamato times craft specialists were obtained from China and Korea, Chinese writing was introduced in A.D. 391, and refugee aristocrats from the mainland were accepted into the emerging class of military nobility.

By this time the outlines of Japanese society were easily recognizable. As the hereditary heads of clan lineages, the warrior-nobles of the Tumulus period became the *daimyo* (lords of castle and manor). The daimyo and the *samurai* (lower armed aristocracy) played the deadly game of "King of the Castle" for the next thousand years. In the sphere of religion, the *uji* shrine system evolved into *Shinto*, "the Way of the Gods." The ranked system of fiefs or grants of land and crops implied the legal confinement of the peasantry to service to the lord whose land they tilled.

With the virtual closure of the country for over one thousand years the concept of a single ethnic unity arose from the blending of people, language, and culture into a homogeneous whole. While China had a series of cyclic dynasties headed by different ruling houses, Japan has had but one imperial house going back some two thousand years. However, Japan's history has developed through a series of different periods.

THE HISTORIC MOLDING OF MODERN JAPAN

The Era of Organization

The Asuka Period (552-710).   The first period to emerge clearly is the Asuka. Emperors ruling from their various home estates still maintained lands and interests in Korea, helped the king of Paekche, and periodically made war on the kingdom of Silla. (This antagonism culminated in the annexation of Korea in 1910.) Paekche contributed to the critical influence of Buddhism in Japan with the gift in 552 of a gold and copper image of Buddha together with Buddhist scriptures, and scholars with their strong concepts of Chinese culture, ethics, and power.

Around the year 600, when credible Japanese history begins, Prince Shotoku Taishi sponsored the acceptance of Chinese patterns of religion and temple architecture, art and politics, scribes, and the sending of regular embassies to the august Tang court of China. All such borrowings were soon "Japanized." The Taika Reform of 645, which in part laid the basis for the system of fiefs and provided for a system of ranked bureaucrats paid from the imperial treasury, was at the same time connected with an edict declaring that all the land of Japan belonged to the emperor. Current owners continued use of the land at the emperor's pleasure. One interesting feature was the prominence given under the succeeding Taiho Code of 702 to the Department of Worship. Although there was great concern for the orderliness of ritual and ceremony, there was no concept whatsoever of a "Mandate of Heaven" which could eventuate in the forfeiture of the emperor's right to rule.

The Nara Period (c.645/710 to 794). Anyone walking through Nara walks through visualized history. Entering the largest wooden building in the world (161 feet or 49 meters high, built in 1708), the visitor is awed by the gigantic Daibatsu or "Great Buddha" (53 feet tall [16 m.]) of gold-covered bronze. Nearby lies the Imperial Repository of the Emperor Shomu, who erected the Great Buddha about A.D. 735, where the emperor's weapons, land and population registers, and Central Asian art objects are on view. During the Nara Period, Japan's two earliest efforts at writing history were compiled: in 712 the *Konjiki*, "Record of Ancient Things," and in 720 the *Nihongi* or *Nihonshoki*, "Chronicles of Japan." Written in difficult Chinese characters both documents blend authentic history with mythology and Chinese legends. Buddhism flourished so militantly that the capital was moved from Nara (and its monastery soldiery) to Kyoto, then named *Heian-kyo*, "Capital of Eternal Tranquility." Left behind in Nara was one of the Fujiwara's ancestral shrines, approachable from Deer Park through an avenue of three thousand stone and bronze lanterns.

BOX 15-1 *MAJOR PERIODS OF JAPANESE HISTORY*

Archaic Period (Before A.D. 552)

Peoples from the Asian mainland and Southeast Asia settle in Japan, which becomes partially unified in the early A.D. 300s: Jomon culture people arrive from the mainland and S.E.A. c.700 B.C., and the Ainu from Manchuria in prehistoric times. The peoples of the Yayoi culture (300 B.C.-A.D. 100) and the Tomb culture (A.D. 250 on) merge with the Yamato culture to establish an imperial primacy during the 400s.

Asuka Period (552-710)

Buddhism is introduced through Korea. Prince Shotoku initiates Chinese style of government (Taika Reform), rule by regents, and embassies to China. The Taiho Code of law is set up (702).

Nara Period (710-794)

Buddhism becomes strong and militant. Gigantic bronze Buddha is erected (735). Kyoto the first permanent capital (794-1868). *Kojiki* records and *Nihongi* chronicles of ancient history written.

Heian Period (794-1185)

Power shifts from emperor to Fujiwara regents. Art and literature flourish. Hirigana syllabary is invented. Feudal society develops concept of *Bushido*, the Way of the Warrior.

Kamakura Period (1185–1333)

Minamoto Yoritomo, the first shogun, operates the *bakufu* military government, centered at Kamakura. Zen Buddhism develops. Kublai Khan's expeditions fail to conquer Japan.

Ashikaga Period (1333–1615)

The nobility, occupational guilds, and general standard of living all prosper. Noh drama and tea ceremony evolve. St. Francis Xavier introduces Christianity.

Tokugawa Period (1615–1867)

Tokugawa Ieyasu succeeds Hideyoshi, founds the Tokugawa shogunate, and moves the capital east to Edo (now Tokyo). Christianity is suppressed. Japan tightly isolates itself; Dutch settlement at Nagasaki only window to outside world. Commodore Perry wins treaty opening Japan to the Western world, 1853 to 1854.

Modern Period (1868 to present)

Under Emperor Meiji Japan adopts Western style reforms and begins territorial expansion. Japan defeats China (1894–1895) and Russia (1904–1905) emerges as a great power. Annexes Korea (1910) and Manchuria (1931). Military expansion into China (1937) and Southeast Asia (1940) and the Pacific (1941) leads to final defeat in 1945. Civil rule under parliamentary government coincides with expansion of trade and technology, making Japan the third largest industrial nation in the world.

Japan's Golden Age

The Heian Period (794–1185).   The Heian Period witnessed both the greatest fluorescence of Chinese-inspired culture and the beginnings of the Japanese feudal system. A series of campaigns between 776 and 803 as far north as Sendai effectively destroyed Ainu power on Honshu island. The Japanese leader, Tamura Maro, was awarded the title of *sei-i tai-shogun*, "Barbarian-subduing Generalissimo," a title military leaders would covet for almost 1,100 years. In 858 Fujiwara Yoshifusa became Regent to the boy emperor, which established the Fujiwara family as the most powerful nonregal family until modern times.

Three new Buddhist sects brought both peaceful contemplation and, later, politicized turbulence. The contemplative *Tendai* sect provided descriptions of heaven and hell. The *Shingon* or "True Word" sect stressed mantras or ritual formulas, such as *namu Amida Butsu*, "Hail to the Buddha of Infinite Compassion." A salvation faith, the *Jodo* or "Pure Land" sect, still Japan's most popular form of Buddhism, appealed to Amida Buddha for entry after death to the Pure Land.

Another cultural innovation led to Japan becoming today's most literate nation: the development of the *kana* phonetic script from abbreviated Chinese charac-

FIGURE 15-1   Japanese Zen temple.

ters. The angular *katakana*, now used by the army and for foreign words, was introduced around 770, and the cursive *hiragana* about sixty years later.

By the 900s the cleavage between the warrior class and the farmer-peasants was clear, the latter becoming a class of tenant peons and serfs. This feudal society was to continue virtually unchanged until the Meiji Restoration of 1868.

While the Fujiwara family upgraded itself through intermarriage with the Imperial family and fostered the crafts, arts, and luxuries at Court—incorporating an aesthetic facet permanently into Japanese culture—the militant Minamoto clans were acquiring power throughout the provinces.

A Time of Disunion

Bushido: The Way of the Warrior.   During the period of the Gempei War, which in 1185 ended about 130 years of sporadic battles between the Taira and Minamoto clans, the martial spirit came to be formalized. The Japanese code known as *Bushido*—The Way of the *bushi* Warrior (*bu-* military, *-shi-* pattern or model, and *-do* way)—emphasized loyalty, courtesy, honor, courage, and frugal self-discipline. The warrior's prized possession, the sword, itself embodied a mystique to its wearer, as did the wavy-bladed *kris* dagger to the Indonesian and the curved *kukri* knife to the Gurkha. Even the smith who forged the multiple strips of variously tempered steel into the unsurpassed two-handed sword had to undergo rigorous purification rites before beginning the work, wearing the priestly white robes.

Bushido has been likened to Western chivalry—and both samurai and knights were horsemen—but the likeness does not go beyond personal discipline and loyalty to one's manorial lord. Bushido, unlike European chivalry, was essentially an in-group code, having no necessary place for consideration of women or anyone outside the specific focus of loyalty. Bushido was not really intended to apply to one's enemies and did not of itself stir the knight to champion an idealistic cause, though some may have done so. The samurai of those times would have found some close companions among the ancient Greek heroes of Homer's *Odyssey*, or even with Arjuna of the *Bhagavad-Gita*, who fought because that was his ordained duty.

Unlike the Chinese military official who was always of inferior status to his civil counterpart, and commonly illiterate, the daimyo and upper-class samurai were trained as warriors, excelled in literature, and in the feudal period of Kamakura many practiced the contemplative forms of Zen Buddhism. *Shinto*, the Way of the Gods, brought together the placation of the animistic spirits of nature and elements of the shamanism of northern Asia with veneration of the spirits of the ancestors, finally adding creation legends which included the divine origins of the imperial family. The combination of Shinto beliefs, the Buddhist gods, and self-examination, joined with the rectitude and morality of Confucian precepts, took care of most aspects of personal and social life.

The Kamakura Period (1185-1333)

Minamoto Yoritomo finally gained complete military and political ascendancy in 1185. Had this been done in China he would have tacitly accepted the fresh Mandate from Heaven to ascend the throne and start a new dynasty. But not so in Japan. One reason for the preservation of the emperor was to provide legitimacy for the wielders of executive power, the shoguns. So Yoritomo waited until the coveted title of shogun was granted by the emperor in 1192. Obviously, there was a difference between ruling and reigning.

In 1268, however, the outside world rattled their swords upon Japan's door. Kublai Khan, the Mongol ruler of China, demanded that Japan submit to him. Japan refused, and Kublai's two expeditions of 1274 and 1281 were repulsed, the fortuitous "divine wind" (*kamikaze*) virtually destroying the 1281 fleet and many of the 100,000 troops it had brought.

A two-pronged danger led the Kamakura *bakufu* ("tent") or military government towards disaster. Internally their land program resulted in more retainers than plots of land to retain them, while at the same time the higher officials absorbed ever greater wealth and power. Externally they lost power to the daimyo in all the outlying districts, and justice was hard to obtain. Finally they backed the loser to the throne and were eliminated by the militarily ascendant Ashikaga clans.

THE SHOGUNATE

The Ashikaga Shogunate (1336-1573)

Chaos and culture. The agrarian disorders of the first sixty years of rule by the Ashikaga clan of the Minamoto escalated into sporadic civil war between the important daimyo. Daimyo means "great name," and each lord endeavored to enhance his reputation by concentrating art, armor, and armies around his own castle, rather than around the emperor at Kyoto or around the shogun's city. Painting, engraving, textiles, and metallurgy flourished throughout the country, as did Buddhism. Followers of the monk Nichiren joined extreme nationalism with the faithful chanting of *Namu myoho rengekyo,* "Hail to the Wonderful Law of the Lotus Sutra." Meditation and enlightenment provided assurance in the midst of uncertainty and strife.

This period of decentralized feudalism resembled the warlord period of the 1920s in China in that power flowed from the end of a spear or a rifle. It differed, however, in that the Japanese period of chaos had a pattern of stability, for each warring lord possessed his own permanent territorial base.

The business communities allied themselves with the militant monasteries or powerful lords, or formed guilds which made such alliances. For instance, the warehouse keepers were also pawnbrokers allied to the powerful Enryakuji monastery on Mount Hiei; the papermakers were associated with the Bojo clan, the Konoe sponsored the craftsmen in gold leaf, and the Kuga the guild of courtesans. Better methods of cultivation on larger feudal estates doubled and tripled the agricultural output and raised the general standard of living. Domestic and foreign trade increased. Some trade with China was legal and official, but it was the smugglers who kept the economic pot boiling steadily. An official embassy to Ming China in 1483 reportedly took 37,000 highly prized swords as well as scrolls, lacquer work, painted screens, and the folding fan—perhaps a Japanese invention.

Art penetrated everywhere—the monastery, the wealthy palace, the humble home. The "nightingale walks" of many Zen dormitories let out a squeak or chirrup that warned of nocturnal prowlers. The Silver and Gold Pavilions at Kyoto, the elegant gardens, the Noh plays, and the panoramic scrolls reached new heights of excellence to reflect the Buddhist view of life. These recollections of examples of courage and discipline, together with concepts of group loyalty, courtesies to avoid embarrassment, and traditions and skills of sensitive artistry vigorously continue in Japanese life today.

The tea ceremony. The one ceremony that epitomizes so much of Japanese cultural values relating to the environment, the etiquette of interpersonal behavior, and harmony with oneself also crystalized at this time—the tea ceremony. Guests are invited to rest at a special shelter and then slowly and meditatively wander through the teahouse garden, stopping to wash at a rustic watercourse. They enter the teahouse through a tiny door that necessitates their bending low (designedly to indicate humility, and incidentally preventing samurai from wearing their swords inside), then sit or kneel on the plain *tatami* rush mats. Every article used, every movement and sequence is prescribed to portray the unity of the individual in his and her surroundings. A simple but tasteful display appears in the *tokonoma,* a large niche where a motto scroll, a flower, or other artistic arrangement is placed. Polite and introspective behavior surrounds the preparation, serving, and consumption of strong, bitter, and slightly frothy green tea in cups whose rustic simplicity is artfully conceived; for the tea set and the cups may be heirlooms of great value. After quiet conversation on appropriate topics while the host or hostess washes up the utensils in the prescribed manner and puts them away, the guests depart gently redolent of the fine incense which has been burning all the while. Ostensibly the tea ceremony deals with the consumption of tea by a small group of friends. But the reality depicted by the symbolism includes human equality, for the specially selected friends represent different stations in life and participate without social distinctions. Formalism is blended with unobtrusive respect, rank is represented by the host or hostess for the occasion, and the ultimate intent is to remind the participants of the sanctity and deeper meanings of life.

The Period of the Country at War (1534-1615)

Massive and magnificent castles dominated the period of the country at war, a time of incessant fighting when muskets and European techniques were added to the native arsenal. Troops by the hundreds of thousands were at the disposal of the nation's lords and leaders—horsemen and bowmen, armed with spear and sword or musket. Three men rose from obscurity during this period to bring unity out of anarchy: Nobunaga, Hideyoshi, and Iyeyasu. Nobunaga fought for and obtained control of the central provinces, only to be assassinated by one of his trusted generals whom he had thoughtlessly humiliated by tapping the general on the head with his fan. Hideyoshi, the small and ungainly son of a woodcutter, by ability, integrity, and opportunity became a groom to Nobunaga, then his best general, and finally his successor. Relying first upon reason and argument, then strategem, and only as a last resort force, Hideyoshi won over or subdued the daimyo, and established the basis for organized government. On occasion he faced alone and unarmed his adversaries, taking care to avoid revenge warfare by not humiliating his beaten foes. He has been called aptly the Napoleon of Japan. His one great mistake was the massive invasion of Korea, with the intention of conquering China, in 1592 and 1597. It was three hundred years before Japanese troops were seen again in Korea. Iyeyasu cooperated with and succeeded Hideyoshi, completed his work of domination and organization, and after becoming shogun in 1605 inaugurated the Tokugawa Shogunate.

The Tokugawa Shogunate (1615-1867)

The stable effect of the Tokugawa Shogunate is reflected in the population figures. Under the simple hunting and farming conditions of A.D. 610 Japan's estimated population of five million was doubtless spread rather evenly over the occupied area of lowlands and hills. Between about 1600 and 1721 the population increased from 20 million to 27 million, and then remained between 27 million and 33 million until 34 million was reached in 1872. The total of 73 million in 1940 grew to 108 million in 1974 and to 120 million by 1983. The relatively stable population between 1721 and 1872 represented saturation of the arable land available to the nonindustrialized society of the Tokugawa Shogunate. The great bulk of the population added since then has filled the booming and congested cities with their teeming millions of factory workers and businesspeople.

Hideyoshi further ensured stability by freezing social status into a hierarchy of nobility, samurai, farmers, artisans, and lowly merchants. Peasants were penalized if they left their lands, and the craft guilds (*za*, as in *ginza*—the silver guild) were dissolved.

The military caste and their retainers were concentrated more and more in the growing castle towns, of which 453 existed at one time or another. The very flexibility in society that had enabled Hideyoshi to rise to power was eliminated both by the freezing of class status and also by the Tokugawa redistribution of fiefdoms: 145 to Tokugawa retainers, 23 to related noble houses, and 98 to the "outside lords" distant from the newly established capital at Edo (Yedo, later Tokyo). The largest fiefs were like castle-states, and the smaller ones were similar in size to the English manor house or the Scottish laird.

Tokugawa rule became an ingenious sandwich of authority above, peace and prosperity below, and in-between a refined blend of arts, drama, craftsmanship, literature, architecture, and metallurgy. Daimyo were required to visit Edo biennially, and to maintain their Edo and country residences lavishly with hundreds of retainers. Key members of their families were held hostage in Edo. These demands steadily drained daimyo resources, and ensured their inability to mount rebellions. Some historians say Osaka grew to 500,000 people by 1690 and Edo to one million in the 1790s, and concurrently nourished the cult of pleasure: courtesans, geishas, sumo wrestlers, Noh and Kabuki theatricals. The country was closed to outsiders, and Japanese were forbidden to leave.

The only crack left open to the outside world—its ideas and technology—was the tiny Dutch settlement at Nagasaki. Overseas trade was practically nonexistent. Internally, government monopolies controlled most major items, laws were enacted to curb the power of the reestablished guilds, and the increasingly impoverished daimyo fell steadily into the financial grasp of the merchants. The senior merchants were literate, cultured, and influential, and the daimyo's samurai stewards gained fiscal and administrative expertise.

But the regime gradually exhausted its financial, social, and administrative alternatives. Satsuma, Choshu, Tosa, and other western daimyo had read Western treatises on medicine and military and industrial progress; they also knew of Britain's successful imposition of open door terms on China following the Opium War of 1839-1842. The shogunate, however, rebuffed advances by Russia, Britain, and Holland to establish trade and diplomatic relations, denying itself these opportunities to acquire fresh alternatives. Tokugawa, in fact, had primed itself for demolition.

THE MODERN PERIOD

The Meiji Restoration

Pressured by external circumstances—Commodore Matthew Perry's ships could easily have cut off Edo's annual waterborne food supply of some two million bales of rice—and by internal exigencies of a troubled economy, grumbling daimyo, and crumbling power, the Tokugawa Shogunate signed a trade treaty with the

United States on March 31, 1854. Treaties with other nations followed. The result of Tokugawa's economic troubles, military weakness, and internal political dissension was that the daimyo swept away the shogunate, and the proclamation restoring imperial rule was promulgated at Kyoto in January, 1868. The 14-year-old Emperor Mutsuhito took the dynastic name of Meiji, "enlightened rule," and moved his capital to Edo, which was renamed To-kyo "Eastern Capital."

The five articles of Emperor Meiji's Charter Oath of 1868 abolished the Tokugawa feudal classes and customs and opened policymaking and progress to participation by everyone. The worldwide search for knowledge and expertise was as earnest as that of Russia's Peter the Great 170 years earlier, but was peaceful and permanent. Meiji Japan adopted Britain as the model for the navy, France for law, Germany for medicine and the Army General Staff, and the United States for education. Students were sent abroad, and instructors welcomed to Japan. The samurai were pensioned off (their niggardly treatment caused much trouble later), and the daimyo were compensated with capital funds in place of their land revenues.

The proclamation of a constitution in 1889 completed the Restoration, and when the newly elected Diet (parliament) met in 1890 the new Japan was headed along the road to eventual parity with the nations of the West.

Crisis Changes in Japanese Sociopolitical Structure

From near the beginning of the recorded historical period, Japan had been ruled in part or in whole by an emperor with theoretically supreme power. Over the centuries the jostling of clans claiming "unoccupied" lands as they drove out the Ainu and other claimants developed into castle-states under the nominal authority of the emperor. After 1185 the scenario changed. The usurpation of executive powers by the shoguns entailed strict control over the emperors, and the tight regulation of nobility and commoners. A monarchial feudal system became a military despotism.

The abolition of this feudal despotism in 1868 turned Japan into a civil society, represented by a constitution and a parliamentary system, public debate, and universal legal responsibility.

Military influence remained strong, and in less than twenty years after Meiji rule began, Japan had won its small war with China (1894-1895), and beaten Russia on land, while sinking most of its Baltic battle fleet in 1905. In 1910 Japan annexed Korea, and pressed its humiliating "Twenty-one Demands" on China in 1915. Japan secured both the ex-German rights in China and the League of Nations mandate covering the Marshall, Caroline, and Mariana Islands in return for minimal participation in World War I. Formosa (Taiwan) belonged to Japan from 1895 to 1945. In 1931 Manchuria was annexed and made the puppet state of Manchukuo. Contrary to the terms of the League of Nations mandate, Japan immediately set about fortifying the Caroline Islands. Apparently it acted on the maxim that "Possession is nine-tenths of the law," and on a saying common in some Eastern countries, "If you didn't want me to keep it, why did you lend it to me?"

World War II

After nearly two millenia of martial competitiveness for power, exemplified by the intense competition between the powerful daimyo clans of Choshu and Satsuma, dissension continued between military and civil organs of government, and between the Army with its Choshu backing and the Navy with its Satsuma tradition. Japan used to be called the "Little Britain of the Far East" but more closely resembled Germany. Between 1937 and 1945 Japan's cherished design for hegemony over East Asia was thinly disguised in the motto on the banners fluttering over Chinese towns and villages, and floating in the sky over each captured city—in gigantic words in Chinese or English—"Greater East Asia Co-Prosperity Sphere." Japan's devastating defeat at the hands of the allies in 1945 ended its dreams of military dominance in the East, and began the process of peaceful growth that has returned it to a position of world prominence.

Social and Economic Changes

Today Japan ranks economically and technologically as No. 3 in the world and is careful to tread softly in international affairs, while energetically utilizing at home the social and political alternatives of a free society. These changes come at the end of a long series of events.

Under the post-Meiji Restoration program, education became universal, peasants became free, and rich and poor alike were liable for conscription into a

FIGURE 15-2 Japanese fishing village.

national army. Using alternatives already available, the daimyo, compensated for loss of lands and revenues, became modern capitalists, and samurai stewards, together with merchants who had become rich on loans to impoverished daimyo, became managers of the new commercial enterprises created for the essential import-export trade. Their increasing expertise was vital to Japan's purpose of surpassing the nations that had not hibernated for some three hundred years. Interestingly, the paucity of managerial personnel and of fluid capital funds meant that the same few individuals appeared in one enterprise after another. These were known as the *zaibatsu* firms or "financial cliques," usually maintaining preferential ties with the Restoration leadership.

As examples of the *zaibatsu* firms, note the house of Mitsui which started in the 1600s by brewing rice wine, then operated a pawnshop and later dealt in rice. In 1673 Mitsui opened a retail textile store in Edo, then branched out to conduct banking business for the shogun and the emperor. It eventually transformed itself into one of the most successful industrial holding companies in modern Japan. After the Restoration a Tosa samurai set up his own shipping line to become in time the giant firm of Mitsubishi operating the famous Nippon Yusen Kaisha (NYK) or Japanese Mail Line. The third largest firm was founded by a well-to-do peasant who later became president of the First National Bank, founded the prosperous Osaka Spinning Mill, and was influential in about one hundred other firms.

Anyone seeking employment had two alternatives: the large urban firms employing college graduates and competent artisans, or the small family enterprises which provided poor facilities and poor pay. Otherwise it was "back to the farm." Farm work was considered drudgery, even though the invention of small machine cultivators to till more fields with better strains of rice under better methods has made the islands self-sufficient in rice production.

Today the key to ultimate employment rests with parents. Those parents who can get their tiny tots into the "right" kindergarten have a better chance of getting them into the right elementary school, high school, and university. The best firms hire personnel only from the "right" universities. Failure at any point means loss of self-worth, family honor, social esteem, and financial security. Reaction to this "examination hell" has spawned a frustrated counterculture of dropouts, and numerous suicides at every age from toddler to adult. Nevertheless, modern education, universal suffrage, a free press, open markets, and foreign intercourse have been reflected in boosted wages and a higher standard of living in a confidently dynamic Japan.

A recent development is the 1978 treaty signed by Japan and China to end thirty years of latent hostility. Official relationships have also been reestablished with the Philippines, trade has been resumed with Indonesia, and sightseeing parties now tour Thailand. The marvelously delicate skills traditionally displayed in the arts, silken textiles, gold and enamel inlays, parchment-thin porcelain and unbreakable lacquer trays, have been sublimated into the top-flight wizardry of sophisticated scientific instruments and technological innovations. Many of the goods produced are sold in Japan, but more are exported, for the slogan "Export or Perish" simply tells the economic truth.

The post-World War II reevaluation of the basis for Japanese self-esteem touched both tradition and modernity. As a symbol of Japan, the dignity of the emperor's status and his worth as a person and scientist were brought out more clearly by discarding the myth of the divine origin of the imperial lineage. And the point was emphasized that the people's self-esteem also is founded on personal discipline and solid achievement, not on the previously supposed inherent and mystic superiority above other peoples, which had been based on the belief that the Japanese alone were descended from the Sun Goddess.

THE DYNAMISM OF SOCIAL VALUES

The Changing Family Structure

Lineage, family, and household, of course, are as different as the words imply. The traditional stem family or lineage (*ie*) consisted of those kin and nonkin who resided together and perpetuated their shared social and economic life. Several *ie* commonly composed a clan (*dozoku*), consisting of a head lineage or house (*honke*) and one or more junior branch houses (*bunke*). The residential unit, irrespective of its kinship composition, was the *setai* or household, which might cease if its members dispersed. The male heads of these social units usually have retained moral responsibility for the conduct and well-being of their members, although the cohesiveness of family ties has diminished under the circumstances of urban life. The distinctions between kin and nonkin in both *ie* and *setai* have been sharpened, because wages or salary must be applied by the male to support first of all the wife and children of his own conjugal family.

However, another problem has arisen. Both respect and support have traditionally been accorded the aging heads of families, and this still applies in most homes. Today, however, tens of thousands of old people are being put out of home to fend for themselves, because the wages earned, and the cramped living quarters of the urban nuclear (or conjugal) family, preclude their continued support. Thus, a fresh moral, familial, and social circumstance is arising, doubly painful because it is in conflict with deeply-rooted systems of social and personal values.

General Values

Values, as we use the word here, are what we would retain while being compelled to give up other treasured ideas, rights, or possessions. Social and personal values constitute the dynamic core of inner motivations that shape the preferences, fashion the attitudes, guide the choices, and finally manifest themselves in actions taken. Patrick Henry proclaimed a personal value when he stated, "Give me liberty or give me death!"

Concerning Japan we have already noted the value given to hierarchical ranking from emperor to merchant, the persisting elements of the *bushido* code, and the emphasis upon leaders and leadership from the shogun to the head of the family. Modern hierarchical values include majority/minority statuses and roles, occupational mobility and ranking, sex distinctions, and employer/employee relations. Harumi Befu, a Japanese anthropologist, has observed that "Japanese sharply distinguish between themselves and foreigners," believing "that only the descendants of Japanese can be truly Japanese" (1971:125). Caucasians, Orientals (Chinese, then Koreans), and Negroes usually rank below Japanese in that order, with the *burakumin* (a depressed class of fishermen and others) somewhere at the bottom.

The concept of purity (pollution is its opposite) is central to this ranking—tied in part to the sun goddess Amaterasu tradition of the mainstream Japanese—and therefore discriminating against various minority peoples. Centuries ago the *Eta* were connected with the care of animal bodies, corpses, and graveyards, and were regarded as permanently polluted. They still are ostracized to the extent that no Japanese would think of marrying an Eta. A prevalent view appears to be that such minorities are part of the natural state of society, and consequently there is no need to do anything to alleviate their predicament. This psychological attitude leads to the identification and low social ranking of such new minority groups as the A-bomb victims, who were wrongly alleged to be susceptible to rare diseases or to produce human monstrosities, and the *ainoko* (children of mixed Japanese and foreign parentage).

Occupational Values

Industrial progress has changed many occupational ratings: service and professional specialists like university professors, physicians, government officials and engineers have gone up and semiskilled and unskilled occupations have gone down. Professionals usually are the sons of professionals, whereas clerical, managerial and semiskilled workers' fathers followed different occupations. The white-collar "salary man" (*sarari man*) forms the new middle class reserved for college graduates, who celebrate new kinds of festivals: birthday parties, Christmas, wedding anniversaries, and the like. Labor laws in the 1880s and unions in the 1900s merged into a system of lifetime employment in stable and face-to-face conditions of employer/employee loyalty. This developed into "managerial paternalism" in large companies with generous fringe benefits in housing and recreation, medical and retirement care, and so on. Cultural emphases are always group oriented, so the Japanese would ask "Where do you work?" rather than "What is your occupation?" as is common in America.

Personal Values

Carried on someone's back from babyhood, the Japanese child is likely to depend on and then presume on the mother's love and indulgence. These dependency expectations and demands are known as *amae.* Another step comes with the granting of a favor by the parent or a gift or benefit by the employer, which creates a situation of indebtedness on the part of the receiver. This benefit-induced indebtedness constitutes an *on* relationship. For example, this relationship of indebtedness of child to parent, student to teacher, and employee to employer is permanent. The *on* relationship, of course, implies hierarchical status between giver and receiver. Whatever the gift or benefit, the giver at that point possesses some degree of superiority, causing acute embarrassment until adequate recompense has been made.

Unlike *on,* which is a passive situation, recompense is a positive activity, such as the exercise of filial piety (*oya-koko*) within the family, or loyalty (*chu*) to employer or emperor. (The concept of *chu* was elevated to a sacred duty to Emperor and Country before and during World War II, stirring the nation to extreme sacrifices.) These two concepts of *oya-koko* and *chu* spur the son, the student, the soldier, and the common people to repay their indebtedness to parent, teacher, emperor, and country. This general or unconditional repayment-in-full, completely subordinating personal desires, is called *gimu.* Other situations also compel the reciprocal gift, favor, or action that appropriately cancels or satisfies the *on* obligation. This specific response or recompense is *giri. On* situations occur also between equals as in gift-giving etiquette, helping one's neighbor, and in maintaining amicable social relations. *Gimu* and *giri,* in turn, are moral compulsions to remove an imbalance in social relations, from a deliberate insult to the proffering of a cigarette. Quite commonly one's personal inclinations and feelings, *ninjo,* must be repressed. *Ninjo* must always give way to the "wearing" of the *on* obligation. If a father slyly purloins the son's savings, or the mother forces the son's beloved wife to leave the home—all should be borne without reproach, and ideally without resentment. If these relationships seem complicated—they are, as the following will show.

The Forty-seven Ronin

The celebrated tale of the "Forty-seven Ronin" illustrates several of these basic social principles. Goaded by shame and resentment against the public and repeated belittling by the shogun's official, the Lord Asano drew his sword and wounded the official. The penalty for drawing one's sword within the palace precincts was death, and Asano duly committed *harakiri* (death by disemboweling oneself). With his death his estate was broken up and his samurai retainers thereby became "masterless men," that is, *ronin.* Biding their time—and knowing well the inevitable penalty—the forty-seven *ronin* broke into the official's residence, beheaded him, and presented the head at their master's grave to indicate the completion of revenge on the insulting official. Unofficially and popularly they were praised for clearing the honor of their dead master, but officially the penalty for murdering an official was death. The forty-seven ronin cheerfully consummated this samurai ritual of *harakiri.*

The Lord Asano owed his fief and title to the country and to the shogun, thereby incurring an *on* obligation towards these as *on jin* or *on* men, which must be unreservedly requited by the obedience of loyalty (*chu*). Both the official who insulted him and Lord Asano himself gave way to their *ninjo* inclinations, which should have been repressed and subordinated to the fulfillment of their obligations. However, in drawing his sword on his tormentor Lord Asano was acting out his rightful *giri* to remove the blotch of an insult. The shogun, on his side, must exact retribution for the offense against the correct priority of obligations over *ninjo* and personal *giri*; so Lord Asano, as a noble samurai, was given the option of self immolation. This death satisfied the *gimu* repayment of obligations to country and to shogun. The insult, however, remained unrequited. So Asano's *ronin* demonstrated social *giri* by remaining faithful to the honor of their deceased lord, and fulfilled his personal *giri* on his behalf by executing the insulting official. Nevertheless, in acting independently and not officially, they ran afoul of their *on* responsibilities to the greater lord, the shogun, and therefore had to pay with their lives the penalty for murder.

That these values are alive today was evident in the assassination some years ago of national leaders who were thought by young radicals to have reneged on their moral obligations to society. Also, as indicated already, by failing his examination, the unsuccessful student is unable to fulfil his *on* indebtedness to parents and teachers. He also is prevented by custom from following his *ninjo* inclinations to take up some alternative occupation (although, of course, some do so). The student then often feels he has no other option than suicide.

BOX 15-2   *A COFFEE SHOP SUMMARY*

> The comments and conclusions voiced in the unquiet corner of the coffee shop down the side street were very real, even though the shop itself is non-existent. Most of those seated or standing in the smoky haze were students engaged in a free-for-all discussion. A young business management graduate was describing Japan's economic and technological successes, and then continued, "The startling thing is that our success, like the parallel but lesser progress in India, has been achieved within a democratic society and under a free economy." An older man commented that this was "a far cry from the strictly regulated feudalism your grandfather knew." His collar-and-tie companion agreed, remarking that "Asian economic progress doesn't require a totalitarian government," and also that "in most Asian countries poverty no longer is necessary." A longhaired history buff added that "Feudalism, of course, was a hierarchy of status, and in essence this still is the basis of our Japanese society." The philosophy major nearby quoted a saying indicating that today's Japanese are the subjects of "The viewless pressure of numberless vanished generations." "This," he said, "is correct; even though today we are breaking down some of these standards by protests, riots, and bloody battles with the police; it is just these inherited influences which have brought us to the top of the heap."
>
> A somewhat subdued sociology girl pointed out the obvious: that each sex in each social level had his and her own style of behavior, or, as she phrased it, "It's a case of 'one status one role.'" Her illustrations were earthy: housewives looked after home and children and did not question the husband's activities; geishas entertained their male guests on a don't-touch-me basis, but prostitutes were there for the money; bosses managed others, and bosses' mistresses were their privilege for personal relaxation. "You know the sort of thing, everything neatly kept in separate respectable boxes." "Of course," spoke up the psychology major, "in our crowded society compartmentalization is the only way that we can protect our few alternatives. It's like our 'Japanese smile'; we use both the boxes and the smile to display our sincerity and to cover up our very vulnerable privacy. We have to tolerate a good measure of dualism."
>
> The older man sitting quietly in the corner turned out to be a veteran of World War II. He said, "You know, there is one thing that ties together both the old days and the present—*respect*; respect for the hierarchy, for our equals in society, and also for everyone simply because he and she are human

beings. As I learned *bushido* in the navy, and I'm just talking for myself, *bushido* meant this kind of respect as well as loyalty to the navy, the emperor, and the country. So I was ashamed of my countrymen when I heard of the brutal treatment many of the army personnel gave to enemy prisoners during the Big War. Everyone should be respected, even if in different degrees." This was too much for an ex-army man, who expostulated that the navy was always against the army. "Let me tell you about an international conference held many years ago. The equality of all peoples came up for discussion, and the Japanese delegate was asked by a Westerner if he thought the Japanese were equal to other more "advanced" nations. The delegate didn't think so, because the Japanese were superior! With that reply, the Westerner considered further discussion rather irrelevant." The army man finished by adding, "Respect, yes; but all people are not really equal."

"Okay, okay!" interjected another student. "Remember we don't respect our parents and family the way we used to. Our very progress in industry is eating away our traditional values as well as our costumes and customs. There's no respect when we fight to get into a bus or a train. This deterioration of our principles and our conduct is one meaning of the saying that 'Snow is falling. Meiji recedes into the distance.'" "Maybe," piped up a new voice, but our rapidly expanding economy and prestige also has its saying: 'The Sun Also Rises!'" "True enough," grunted an auto mechanic, "but remember, 'Nationalism has only one speed here—Full ahead!' Never forget that!" One of the girls whispered to her friend, "Hear that? Never under estimate anyone who is disciplined!" By this time the topic of discussion had turned to the tendency of politicians to show loyalty to a personality rather than to the principles in a party platform; so much so that when a new leader assumed power he brought with him a whole new crew of associates and secretaries.

Since we didn't wish to be involved in politics we made the usual gestures of departure, and left, much wiser than when we had come. If we had learned nothing else we now realized afresh that the Japanese people have made their own unique adaptation of traditional values to their new technological world. These values and capabilities have been carried by the considerable number of Japanese settlers in Brazil, where pride in their heritage will ensure that they make the best possible Japanese-Brazilian adaptation to both rural and city life—just as they have done in other countries. We were reminded of a perceptive comment made in 1914 by the then Prime Minister of Japan, the Marquis Okuma, that the regions of the world would be governed by a few strong nations, and "that it was Japan's duty to prepare herself to become one of these elite few." (Kennedy 1963:217). Japan has become elite.

Chapter *16*

Lands of Mystery and Isolation: Tibet and Korea

Tibet and Korea, lying distantly on China's western and eastern borders, have long been known as Tibet the "Forbidden Kingdom" and Korea the "Hermit Kingdom." Both have been cultural conduits and cultural deadends. Tibet was a minor channel for Buddhist influences coming from India into China, and later closed itself to most innovations from any outside source. Many of China's cultural patterns and artifacts passed through Korea to Japan, and were adapted to the local social surroundings before each country closed its frontiers. Both Tibet and North Korea in the mid-1900s again were closed to outsiders, and although China has set Tibet's door slightly ajar, very little definite information or contact has come out of North Korea since the Red Star flag of Communism has flown over the land.

TIBET: THE FORBIDDEN LAND

"Compel them to turn and go back the way they came." Such were the orders from the Devashung or Holy Council of Lhasa to the two frontier governors concerning the Swedish explorer of Central Asia, Dr. Sven Hedin, and his party, for "It is entirely unnecessary that European men come into the Land of the Holy Books to spy around it." (Hedin 1903:453–455). This was the situation in the first years of the twentieth century. After nearly eight decades it remains much the same, though for a different reason. Then the Tibetan governors could say with some truth, "The Emperor of China exercises no authority whatever in our country"; now, garrisoned by a Chinese army and governed by an authoritarian Communist regime, Tibet is nearly as tightly closed as it was before.

The Countryside

Land of arctic temperatures, blinding blizzards, scorching sun, endless snow mountains and rocky ravines, it is no wonder that Tibet and its peoples have always been isolated and mysterious. If the whole terrain were flattened out in its present area the average height would be higher than that of snow-crowned Mount Rainier in Washington, an awesome 16,000 (4800 m.) above sea level.

Forbidding territory hems in the Tibetan Plateau on all sides. Looking toward the south, the highest mountain wall in the world—1,500 miles (2,400 km.) of ice-sheathed Himalayan peaks—forms the boundary between this great snowy dome and the Indian subcontinent. Just north of the wall lie the upper valleys of the Indus and Brahmaputra rivers, traversed by the major motor highway linking cities and villages from east to west. Gazing westward across the barren and windswept plateau, dotted with salty lakes, our view again is blocked by the desolate and frigid borderland with Kashmir. Turning half right toward the serrated ranges that eventually drop down from the Kun Lun mountains to the Heartland of Asia, we see one of earth's most uninviting regions, the Taklimakan (or Takla Makan) desert. The entire Tibetan plateau from west to northeast is called home by the *aBrog-pa* or pastureland persons, nearly half the Tibetan population, and perhaps the world's hardiest pastoralists. The eastern approaches to Tibet are still guarded by the hazardous palisades and trenches that define the upper courses of three mighty rivers, the Yangtze (Chang jiang), the Mekong (Lancang jiang), and the Salween (Nu).

In recent decades rich deposits of coal, gypsum, iron, manganese, and oil have been discovered in the valleys and rocky mountainsides. Economic zoning is partly tied to the range of temperatures, for even at the lower elevation of Lhasa (11,800 feet or 3,597 m.) the temperature could vary during the day from $-18°F$ to $100°F$ ($-28°C$ to $38°C$). Zoning relates also to altitude: from the dense forests in the southeast, where horse and mule caravans carry tea and wool to the Chinese lowlands, to the farmlands of the central valleys, and then on up to the high altitudes. Here in the highlands yaks are the burden bearers, and wealth is reckoned in "fields on the hoof," that is, horses, donkeys and mules, sheep, goats and yaks, and various cross-bred animals.

Within the valleys and narrow plains of the warmer southeastern sector, the major portion of Tibet's two million people used to be peasant tenants working lamasery lands or the domains of the 170 noble families. Also prior to the coming of the Communists about one in four or five Tibetan males were monks. The monks commonly have been called *lamas*, but the term *lama* really means a superior person or teacher, a guru, of whom each lamasery had at least one or two. Life, the land, and religion were to them part of an indivisible whole, extending from the distant past to the present day.

ENTITY AND REALITY

Out of the dark void rustled the primeval wind and from the wind came the great Double Thunderbolt, and thence the clouds, the flooding rain, and the abounding waters—*Gyatso*, the universal ocean. Born of the churning of wind and ocean the abode of the gods and the outer worlds of the universe took form and character. As some of the gods continued to feast on the delectables of this earth they finally became people, living in a universe of sun and stars, work and struggle, death and infinite hope. Such is the Legend of the Beginning in the Tibetan *Chöjung* classics. (Norbu and Turnbull 1968:19–25)

Picture of a Vigorous Nation

To the surprise of many, Tibetan history reveals a vigorous nation developing from the amalgamation of many chieftaincies into a single organized kingdom about A.D. 569. Seething with life in the 600s, the capital city of Lhasa was founded, and Buddhism and writing came from India through Nepal. The famous King Srontsan Gampo, who reigned between 620 and 650, married two Buddhist princesses: the Chinese princess Bhrikuti in 641, and then the daughter of King Amshuvavarman of Nepal. (From then on, Buddhism was slowly integrated into Tibetan life.) Subsequently he expanded his kingdom into the lands of Nepal, of Bengal in India, and of West China. Further contact with Buddhism occurred when the Muslim Arab incursion into Central Asia in the 700s forced Buddhist monks to flee into Tibet. However, they were blamed for a smallpox epidemic, and were promptly expelled. Also in the 700s, King Khrisong Detsen scored major victories in China, even capturing the Tang capital of Chang'an (now Xi'an). In the West we associate empire-building with large populations based on vast agricultural lands. It is highly intriguing therefore to find that such diverse peoples as the Tibetans, from their citadel of rock and ice, and the Mongols from their grasslands and desert, could also establish extensive empires; but they did. They were skillful, tough, and organized.

In the A.D. 1000s, while Norman England was being put on the map, and the name Mongol was not yet known in Europe, a Buddhist monk named Milarepa filled the core of Asia with his teachings, and left behind "The 100,000 Songs of Milarepa." Towards the end of five centuries of disunity between 842 and the mid 1300s, that insatiable conqueror Kublai Khan attacked Tibet with an unforeseen outcome—the Khan was so impressed by the Tibetan saint Phakpa ('Phagspa) that, at the Khan's request, Phakpa initiated him into the Buddhist faith, which then became the official religion of his court. This conversion cost his son the supreme Khanate of the Mongol empire because, to the other Khans, now Muslims, he was an infidel Buddhist. Phakpa also devised a script for the Mongolian language based on the Tibetan alphabet.

A Religious-political Duality

In the late 1300s the Yellow Hat or Gelukpa sect was founded by Tsongkapa on more strictly moral and monastic lines than the older and rather shamanistic Red Hat sect. One of his disciples, Gentun Drupa (Gedundrub), became the first Grand Lama. In 1577, Sonam Gyatso, the third incarnation of an earlier lama, received from the Ordos Mongol leader, Altan Khan, the title of *Vajradhara dalai lama* "Thunderbolt Holder Ocean Lama" (*dalai* is Mongolian for Tibetan *gyatso*, "ocean," here symbolizing wisdom). Then in 1640 or 1642 the fifth Dalai Lama, Ngawang Lobsang Gyatso, was placed on the Tibetan throne by Gushri Khan, thereby uniting Tibet as one political unity. This appointment, confirmed by the

BOX 16-1   *PRINCIPAL EVENTS IN TIBETAN HISTORY*

A.D.	Pre-Buddhist period	Bon shamanism.
	c.569	Tibetan chieftaincies organized into single kingdom.
	600s	City of Lhasa founded.
	641	King Srontsan Gampo marries two Buddhist princesses.
	700s	Buddhist monks briefly in Tibet.
		Tibetan forces capture Tang capital of Chang-an.
	1000s	Buddhist monk Milarepa (1052–1135).
	842–mid-1300s	500 years of disunity.
	1239	Mongols invade Tibet; Kublai Khan converted to Buddhism.
	Late 1300s	Gelukpa or Yellow Hat sect of Buddhism founded by Tsongkapa.
		Tsongkapa's disciple Gentun Drupa becomes first Grand (*dalai*) Lama.
	1640/42	Fifth Dalai Lama enthroned as secular and religious ruler of Tibet.
	1662–1723	Reign of Manchu emperor Kang Xi.
	1692	Potala Palace completed at Lhasa.
	Late 1600s	Chinese imperial representative (*amban*) permanently stationed at Lhasa.
	1788–1792	Nepalese invade Tibet; Tibet then sealed against foreigners.
	1800s	Intermittent contacts with British India.
	1903–1904	Mission by Colonel Sir Francis Younghusband reaches Lhasa and concludes agreements; Dalai Lama flees the country briefly.
	1914	Southern border defined by the McMahon Line; not recognized by China.
	1950–1951	Chinese Communist armies occupy Tibet.
	1959	Dalai Lama flees to India.
	1962	Chinese forces invade India to "rectify" Tibet's southern borders.
	1960s–1970s	Multitudes of Chinese settlers transferred to Tibet.
	1965	Tibetan Autonomous Region established under strict Chinese control.

first Manchu emperor of the Qing (Ch'ing) dynasty, inaugurated the religious-political form of government which continued down to the Communist takeover in 1950. Soon after the death of the "Great Fifth" as he was called, his stupendous monastery-palace, the Potala, was completed at Lhasa. From about 1727, when the third Manchu emperor reasserted Chinese control over Tibet, a Manchu or Mongol (never a Chinese) *amban* (a vice-regal governor) officially represented the Peking (Beijing) government at Lhasa. From that time on, although Tibet supposedly possessed internal self-government, the *amban* exercised the same guiding influence that the British Resident did in the princely courts of India during the latter part of the 1800s. Never again would Tibet be completely free.

TRADITIONAL CULTURE

Tibetans traditionally worked hard under harsh conditions, eating two meals a day of parched barley flour (*tsamba*) or buckwheat, together with butter, cheese, and yak milk (for the rich) or goat milk (for the poor). The usual beverage consisted of Chinese tea laced with salt, soda, and butter. Houses for most people had one or sometimes two stories of stone with flat roofs, few rooms, little furniture, few

FIGURE 16-1
Tibetan mother and child.

windows, and conserved maximum warmth. The houses of the wealthy had four or five stories: the ground floor for animals, the next for tools and stores, and the upper floors for the family, retainers, and guests.

Clothing also expressed class distinctions, furs and silks for the wealthy and wadding and cotton for the peasant. Both sexes usually wore long robes (*chuba*) with long sleeves and high collars, worn day and night the year round, and often with the right shoulder bared in the daytime. Women's gala wear for festivals included embroidered skirts and aprons, gaily colored and ironed blouses of wool or silk, and dark sleeveless vests. Ornaments of silver and gold, coral, and mother-of-pearl and pearls adorned the wrists, ears, and neck, as well as the women's elaborate two-horned hairdo. Monogamy was (and is) the general rule, for only wealthy men could support more than one wife (polygamy). If it was difficult to supply the requisite dowry for separate wives, several brothers might share one wife (polyandry), working together to support the family, and to preserve their property within the male lineage.

MYSTIQUE AND CONTRAST

Perhaps only in this land of mystery could the sixth Dalai Lama say, "The demons and serpentiform gods squat on my severe and powerful shoulders" (Maraini 1953: plate 35). Perhaps also only in such a land of frigid harshness, where its magnificent mountains were the abode of the gods, could Milarepa state, "In solitary stony fastnesses among the mountains, there is a strange market, where one can barter the vortex of life for boundless bliss" (Maraini 1953: plate 37).

This half-forgotten, half-unknown land was a place of contrasts, all blithely accepted as the normal round of life. Men, women, and babies at the breast, in both bleak misery and bejeweled splendor, crowded to see the terrifying yet instructive demon dramas in the lama temples. Prayers, transmitted perpetually by twirling wheels and fluttering flags, supplied some reassurance both for disciplined and world-denying priests and for rambunctious peddlers, to whom the miraculous is simply the unexpected coming of the expected. Here was a land whose people learned long ago to cope equally with darkness and enlightenment, with disaster and violence, with gaiety, and with chilling winds that could sweep a whole caravan off the high mountain ledges.

WESTERNER AND COMMUNIST

But the Western world finally knocked at the rock girt portals of Tibet. Restless Nepal invaded Tibet several times, and one result of the Nepal War of 1788 to 1792 was the closing of Tibet to all foreigners by order of the apprehensive Chinese rulers in Peking. But the West would not be denied. So the various contacts made by the British in India between 1774 and 1890 finally resulted in the expedition to Lhasa led by Colonel Sir Francis Younghusband from 1903 to 1904. Agreements were made for two-way trade and for the security of Tibet against suspected Russian influences. Treaties between Tibet, (British) India, and Burma demarcating the southern borders of Tibet (in particular the 1914 "McMahon Line," named after the English negotiator), were never recognized by China.

During 1950 and 1951 Chinese armies occupied Tibet, and the controls imposed sparked such rebellions and turmoil that on March 17, 1959, the Dalai Lama fled the Potala palace for India. Chinese tanks and infantry reportedly killed some 12,000 Tibetans at that time, and another 100,000 during a later revolt, perhaps a tenth of the population in all. After 1959 standard Communist measures were instituted: confiscation of radios and weapons, restriction of travel, and vilification of the gentry as capitalists. Ex-officials usually were killed, and monks were called parasites and put to work. Children were made to accuse their parents and servants their masters. The Chinese used compulsory Tibetan labor to construct all-season military roads around all the borders and, with the consent of Nepal and Pakistan, cut feeder roads through the mountain barriers into Katmandu and Islamabad. (India was indignant but entirely helpless to stop them.)

China then invaded India's frontiers in 1962 to "rectify" the McMahon borders to fit Chinese claims as shown on their maps. During the Cultural Revolution of 1966 and 1967 the young Chinese Red Guards smashed religious shrines and created such widespread havoc that the army finally drove them out. Since the 1950s scores of thousands of Chinese have been transferred to Tibet as farmers, settlers, soldiers, and officials, and the commune system of collectivized labor has been established. The country was reorganized as the Tibetan Autonomous Region in 1965, with limited self-government under direct guidance from Beijing. Since 1980 some of the colonists have been withdrawn and pressures to sinicize have been eased.

COLLECTIVISM VERSUS NOMADISM

The population before Liberation consisted of farmers and nomads, townspeople and monks, nobility and officials. Since then the nomad shepherds and herders have been restricted by Communist officials to certain customary grazing areas and to specified winter settlements. This measure controls their movements under the slogan, "Fixed abode and nomadic herding." The incentive in this control system is the provision at the winter quarters of basic food supplies, fodder, shelter, and schooling (indoctrination) for the children. The nomads' flocks and herds comprise for them the equivalent of the farmer's "soil fields," to be joined on occasion by the two-humped Bactrian camel—an authentic curiosity peculiar to Central Asia. The Tibetan yak, however, is unique. A bull yak may be six feet high at the shoulder, built somewhat like the American bison, and has long silky hair overlaying the fur on the rump. It carries loads of 160 pounds (73 kg.) efficiently between the valley bottoms at 10,000 feet and the 18,000 feet passes (3050-5500 m.). Useful both in life and in death, the yak provides milk, butter, and cheese, hair for carpets and tents, meat, hides for shoe leather, saddles, and boats, and transportation for merchandise.

By the early 1960s, the only group still holding to traditional Tibetan mores and customs were the nomads. And it is precisely because these horse-borne people are so staunchly conservative that the Chinese cadres have backed off from an unprofitable confrontation with their way of life. In any case, they are the only ones who can economically utilize the barren territory that covers most of this arctic-like country. The settled sedentary peoples around them need the beef and mutton, wool, furs and hides, as well as the salt and borax these pastoralists produce.

The Tibetan nomad was something new to the agriculturally minded Chinese. What made them *successful* in their age-old adaptation to this unforgiving environment is still further from the psychological mechanism of a totalitarian system. Ekvall has caught the nomad mystique when he speaks of the "peculiarly personal relationship which made separating a man from his animals, and from the personalized care of them, a delicate matter"(Ekvall 1968:96).

Seeing and Perceiving

When Tibet was pacified following the takeover by Communist troops in the 1950s, elements of modernization from many sources in the outside world entered stealthily. They came by air over the mighty rivers that nurture the peoples of China, Laos, and Kampuchea, as well as Pakistan, India, and Bangladesh. They also came by truck through precipitous canyons and over icy mountain passes. By 1982, this modernization included telephone poles, bicycles, Land Rovers, television sets, and posters of Charlie Chaplin, not to mention a cement factory and oil storage tanks. Still the most poignant recollections of some recent American visitors were the thousands of Tibetans thronging the bazaars and prostrating themselves in worship on the cobblestones and in the temples.

Thubten Jigme Norbu, elder brother of the present Dalai Lama, sees his people differing in occupation and culture as urbanites, farmers, and nomads, yet stoutly united in understanding the Eightfold Path that will help them avoid the three poisons of carnal desire, anger, and blind passion (Norbu and Turnbull 1968: 35), and lead them to the Goal of escape from the lifelong suffering of human Desire. He sees them as integrated participants in a single Ultimate Reality, united in unashamed devotion to the Deities they know. Moreover, Tibetan customs, culture, and religious rituals are being nurtured by several hundred thousand Tibetans now settled in India, Switzerland, and Western America.

KOREA: ONCE THE HERMIT KINGDOM

What the Archaeologist Found

What the archaeologists did not find was substantiation of the legend about a bear transformed into a beautiful young woman who, breathed on by Hwanung the son of the Creator, subsequently gave birth to the semidivine Tangun, reputed first king of Korea in 2333 B.C. But they did find evidence showing the local development of flourishing cultures across the vast Eurasian Plain stretching from the Volga River to the Manchurian highlands and Korea. The pit-dwelling and shellfish-gathering first Koreans hunted the hairy mammoth, the woolly rhinoceros, deer, and other animals after the last Ice Age. In the 300s B.C. they faced the hazards of earthquakes and human raiders. During the 100s B.C. agriculture and pottery developed in conjunction with houses heated by the *ondol* system of conduits under the stone floors. Massive stonework, dolmens (megalithic stone chambers), graves, and menhirs (monoliths) exemplified the monumental architecture of neolithic Korea. These impressive relics suggest an elite class able to command considerable group labor.

Korea's historical beginnings, however, are somewhat uncertain. Tangun's dynasty is said to have lasted until the arrival in 1122 B.C. of the Chinese philosopher-general Kija who, with his five thousand followers, established a dynasty at Pyongyang. This incursion drew attention to terrain features that permitted the movements of many equestrian tribes to and from southern Mongolia and North China through southern Manchuria and into northern Korea. Korea really had little hope of stemming the invading armies of Chinese, or Mongols, Manchus, or Japanese; they just had to battle them when they arrived.

The Geographic Setting

Once joined to the mainland during the Ice Age, Korea now forms a partial land bridge stretching southward for 525 miles from the mainland toward Japan. The Manchurian highlands extend into Korea along the east coast, with mountain spurs nudging the rivers toward west and south. Whereas only two or three feet of tide wash the rugged eastern coast, the Yellow Sea tides of up to 33 feet impede navigation on the myriad estuaries and tidal flats in the west. Barely one fifth of the land sustains cultivation, much of it lying in the south where comparatively mild winters permit double cropping to support a dense population. The humid continental climate fosters a pronounced summer rainy season in the south, and a relatively dry winter in the north where most of the minerals and 80 percent of the prepartition industries were located. Despite widespread deforestation and wars, the peninsula supports about twenty million people in North Korea and forty million in South Korea, of whom two thirds reside in rural areas.

The Historic Development

Known to its inhabitants as *Choson* and *Han Guk* (the Han Kingdom; a different "Han" from that of China), to the Chinese as *Chao Xian,* and to the Japanese as *Choson* (both meaning the Land of Morning Calm), the name *Korea* comes from Koryo, one of Korea's ancient kingdoms. About the time that Alexander the Great was conquering Persia, Chandragupta was founding the Maurya dynasty in India, and the Period of the Warring States was disrupting North China, ancient Choson came into being. Chinese warriors and adventurers, whose ruling class rode horse-drawn coaches and used iron swords, transmitted their bronze and iron culture to Korea and Japan. Such a warrior-adventurer was the North Chinese Wei-man (Wiman in Korean) who usurped the Choson throne, and was followed in about 105 B.C. by Chinese troops who made northwest Korea a hub of artistic and linguistic culture for the next four hundred years. This period of the Chinese Commanderies was one of canopied chariots on paved streets, of tribute and trade, and the effulgent glow of Chinese painting, philosophy, goldwork, and government spread throughout the peninsula and across the Tsushima Straits to the Japanese state of Wa.

BOX 16-2 *PRINCIPAL EVENTS IN KOREAN HISTORY*

B.C.	2333	Legendary Tangun founds kingdom of Choson.
	1122–1193	Kija (Kitze) becomes king; introduces Chinese culture.
	154–108	Weiman dynasty.
	57–18	Kingdoms of Silla, Koguryo, and Paekche established. Koguryo's capital at Pyongyang becomes one of oldest national capitals in all Asia.
A.D.	391–622	Japan established colonies in southern Korea.
	300s	Considerable two-way and through trade with China and Japan.
	372	Introduction of Buddhism.
	600	100-volume history of Koguryo compiled.
	612	Sui emperor's invading army of one million men destroyed.
	715–935	Whole country united as the kingdom of Silla.
	700–1895	Period of general Chinese suzerainty over Korean affairs.
	935–1392	Koryo kingdom and dynasty.
	1200s	Devastations by Mongol armies of Genghis Khan and Kublai Khan.
	1392–1910	Yi dynasty of Choson.
	1498–1545	Successive massacres of scholars.
	1592–1597	Hideyoshi's invasions; Korean invention of iron-clad warship; Korea never recovered from these destructive invasions.
	1600s	Beginning of general era of seclusion, which included many countries in East and Southeast Asia, coinciding with expansion of European influence in the Orient.
	1653	First contact with Westerners (shipwrecked Dutch sailors).
	1777	Introduction of Christianity.
	1876	Kanghwa treaty with Japan closed period of cannonading between Korean forts and foreign vessels; three treaty ports opened to trade.
	1895	Beginning of Japanese influence follows Sino-Japanese War.
	1904–1905	Russo-Japanese War fought on Korean soil.
	1910–1945	Japan annexes and exploits Korea.
	1945–1948	Korea divided into two nations, South Korea and North Korea.

THE DYNASTIC STATES

Compared with the score or so of successive and concurrent dynasties in China and the single lineage dynasty in Japan, Korea falls in the middle with a three-kingdom period followed by three dynasties. The beginning date is about 37 B.C.

The Three Kingdoms (c.37 B.C.-A.D. 668)

Tribal coalitions now had graduated into organized kingdoms, though this did not benefit the common people. The dominance of Koguryo to the north, Silla to the southeast, and Paekche to the southwest endured for about 705 years to A.D. 668.

The Kingdom of Silla (668-935)

By means of organized military effort Silla finally secured peninsula-wide dominance for the next 267 years, largely by the political use of three aspects of control. The Bone Rank system of imperial dominance reserved executive power for the king and royal family (the Sacred or True Bone) and the nonroyal elite. Under the Oath Banner system army units had their own banners and specialized in particular aspects of warfare—crossbow, catapults, ladders, or wall-breaching. The third aspect was a sort of pervasive *esprit-de-corps*—the "Five Precepts for Secular Life"—very similar to the Bushido Code of Japan. These Precepts embodied the traditional *taekwondo* Korean military art developed by a large elite paramilitary youth corps animated by the Silla martial spirit. Here are the Five Precepts: (1) Serve your lord with loyalty and (2) your parents with filial piety; (3) communicate in sincerity with your friends; (4) face battle without retreating; and (5) when taking life, be selective. Despite their organization, Silla's driving systems of control finally faltered and lost their grip.

The Kingdom of Koryo (936-1392)

The Wang dynasty, in uniting the whole peninsula and its northern environs, used an abbreviation of the old Korean-Manchurian state of Koguryo as its state title, Koryo. From Koryo comes the anglicized form "Korea." The organizational structure of Silla was tightened, and formed an interesting organizational bridge between China's civil bureaucracy and Japan's military autocracy. In order to undercut the military and economic position of the provincial gentry, and to add to the national exchequer at the same time, King Kwangjong instituted the Slave Investigation of 956. This act liberated most of the gentry's slave pool of free labor, and returned them to the taxable status of commoners. Government service examinations based on the Chinese classics were instituted, libraries were established in the academies for officials, and private schools were encouraged to prepare promising scholars for government appointments. This educational program replaced the static Silla Bone Rank system with one which permitted some upward social mobility. Commoners, chiefly peasants and fishermen, were designated *yang-min*, good people, in contrast to the *yang-ban*, aristocracy, and to the outcastes who to the eighth generation were prohibited from sitting for the service examinations.

A wall uniting fourteen towns along the northern border discouraged raids by Liao and Jurchen horsemen for the next two hundred years. A small but steady maritime trade with Sung merchants in South China was joined by several Arab ships. Iron coins and silver ingots were minted, Buddhism flourished, and cultural activities included sculpture, metal casting, and the preparation of medical textbooks. Printing with incised wood blocks progressed to moveable wood and clay type. In 1234 moveable metallic type was cast to print a fifty-volume work on ceremony and propriety—a revealing cultural priority. As in Japan, armies of Buddhist monks, besides fighting among themselves, fought for the State in every war on the peninsula until recent times. But politically all was not well. During the 1100s and 1200s quarrelsome military rulers allowed the Mongol domination for 125 years, and paved the way for Kublai Khan's callous use of Korean troops and ships for his abortive invasions of Japan in 1274 and 1281.

The Yi Dynasty of Choson (1392–1910)

On August 5, 1392, the general who outlasted his competitors, Yi Song-gye, ascended the phoenix throne, inaugurating the Yi dynasty which ruled Choson for 518 years until its annexation by Japan in 1910. The prevailing international winds dictated a close relationship with China and occasional communications with Japan. So the earlier Yi kings sought validation of their positions from the Ming emperors of China, to whom four embassies went annually, taking thousands of horses. And about 1420 an Ashikaga shogun agreed to suppress piracy on the Korean coast in return for a copy of the Korean Buddhist *Tripitaka*—all 6,467 volumes! The Yi dynasty period produced many accomplishments. Fonts of metallic type, accurate rain gauges and records (200 years before the Europeans), fertilizers to obviate the need for fields to lie fallow, and land surveys, maps, and gazetteers giving geographic and historic details for the towns described, were typical innovations. Korean and Chinese philologists collaborated to produce in 1446 the phonetic *han'gul* (Script of the Koreans), thereby establishing the prospect of nationwide literacy.

A fifty-year purge of the literati seriously undermined the bureaucracy and substantially eroded the royal and official respect system, a malaise lasting until the end of the dynasty. These internal factional squabblings led to fifty years of warfare with Hideyoshi's rampaging armies and desperate resistance to the encroaching armies of Manchu cavalry. Resistance ended on February 24, 1637, with King Injo's submission to the Manchu emperor, and Korea entered a reluctant tributary status to China that was to last for about 250 years. This was the beginning of Korea's closed-door policy of excluding foreigners in order to maintain internal peace.

Two doorways to the outside world nevertheless remained more or less open: those to China and Japan. Information about the West seeped into Korea through its embassies to Peking: maps of the West, the chronometer, major works on geography and astronomy, together with such diverse things as pistols and the Christian religion. Trade and diplomatic intercourse prospered with the Japanese shoguns, with the lord of Tsushima acting as the semi-independent go-between. By the turn of the 1800s the intellectual ferment in those two countries affected Korea, resulting in the production of encyclopedias, and works of great merit in legal, educational, medical, military, agricultural, linguistic, and other types of literature. But politics and power again spiked the wheels of progress.

FIGURE 16-2
Traditional Korean dance costume.

During the mid-1800s social unrest increased at the same time that recurrent epidemics and famines were added to widespread banditry and limitless extortions by local officials. The nation stagnated in the midst of an awakening world outside its borders. Revolts occurred on all levels of society, a critical sign of deep-rooted troubles, yet leaving myriads of "little people" with the daily struggle to survive.

CULTURE AND CHARACTER

Several ingredients typify the Korean character. (1) A willingness to learn from others enriched them with the arts, literature, architecture, technology, philosophy, and political know-how of China, and to a lesser degree of Japan. (2) The massive assaults and several periods of lengthy occupation by outside forces failed to break their tenacious hold on their own territory. (3) The endless feuding and partisanship over the centuries bred a hard-boiled political and military sophistication that often was less than constructive. (4) Physical isolation and threat of outside pressures led to a high degree of developed arts, technologies, and political organization that adequately met all their internal needs. These ingredients, like the forest hidden behind the trees, were submerged beneath the complexities of daily life shortly before the Hermit Kingdom opened its doors to the West.

BOX 16–3 *THE EVERYDAY SCENE*

To visit an ordinary Yi seaside village today we left the main road for the path winding down the wooded hillsides towards the bay, with the offshore islands lying in the blue distance. Blending into the landscape near the shore, the thatched roofs of the houses covered their mud brick or rammed earth walls.

The men wore loose-fitting trousers and jackets of thin white cloth, quilted in winter. The women's clothing of long-sleeved jackets and wraparound skirts, or of white dresses, gathered high on the breast and thence flowing wide and free to the ankles, were cut to ancient patterns, and seemd to make their wearers stand taller. Then several older men came into view, sipping tea at a table, puffing gently on yard-long pipes, and wearing that most distinctive item of traditional Korean clothing: a flat-brimmed stove-pipe black hat, set high on the head and tied with a cord under the chin.

The fishing boats drawn up on the beach, their nets hung out to dry, complemented the plows, rakes, and hoes set under the eaves, and clearly indicated the villagers' dual occupations of farming and fishing. After sitting down to chat with these elders they told us that their main crop and staple food was rice, followed in importance by barley, millet, oats, corn, and potatoes. Cotton, tobacco, and ginseng (a pungent herb used in medicine) brought in some ready cash as secondary crops. They invited us inside to see how the underground stone flues conducted heat from the kitchen stove to warm the whole house.

While we talked, the able-bodied men and women from the various households streamed out to help work one field in particular, for the owner of that field participated cheerfully in the general village projects and consultations. Two households did not participate. One was that of a quiet humble man who had married a wineshop waitress and, having nowhere else to go, had settled in the village five years before. They were gatherers of octopus and shellfish on the beaches, and were rather shunned by the villagers. The other household, really indistinguishable from other comfortable homes, was descended from a minor branch of the royal Yi lineage. They considered themselves members of the *yang-ban* upper class, and simply did not cooperate with fishermen and "commoners." Tensions existed in the village, of course, but the rules of etiquette allowed everyone who so desired to share in the discreetly formal activities of social life.

KOREA: THE HERMIT KINGDOM NO LONGER

The Opening Door

During the late 1800s increased friction with visiting English, French, Japanese, and American vessels led to cannonading, and finally to the treaty of Kanghwa (1876) with Japan, whereby three ports were opened to international trade. Treaties with other countries followed suit. As Henthorn remarks, "The isolation had ended, not for the sake of embracing the new and the unknown, but as an attempt to preserve the old and the familiar" (1971:225). In this, Korea acted like China, not Japan. A century of divisions and rebellions culminated in 1894 with the landing of supposedly peacekeeping forces from both China and Japan. War was inevitable.

The Swinging Door

Korea, no longer able to control its own destiny, was now faced with the question of which foreign state would control it. The Japanese victories in the Sino-Japanese War (1894–1895) and the Russo-Japanese War (1904–1905) quickly settled the matter. Japan assumed command and annexed Korea in 1910, thus bringing to a close both the Yi dynasty and the kingdom of Choson. Japan brought political order and organization, technology, artisanship, factories, railways, and other aspects of the modern world to its Korean colony. Koreans paid the price in suffering the militaristic methods, the arrogant attitudes and harsh procedures of a ruthless and insecure conqueror, bent on extracting from a slave labor country the most economic profit possible. Unfortunately, contempt and resentment still run deep on both sides.

The Two-Sided Barrier

The Allies in World War II had agreed that Russian troops would accept the surrender of Japanese forces north of the 38th parallel and the American troops south of it. So the surrender on August 15, 1945, was the liberation of Korea from Japanese rule, but with a country divided into two parts. This line became the national frontier separating Korean life into two distinct patterns: Communism under ex-guerilla leader Kim Il-sung in North Korea, and nominal democracy under prison-scarred Syngman Rhee (Li Sung-man) in South Korea. The Korean War of 1950–1953 soon bloodied the whole peninsula, involving also Chinese armies for the north, and American and fifteen other members of the United Nations for the south. The truce negotiations at Panmanjum still remain stalemated more than thirty years later.

NORTH KOREA

The Compulsions of a New Society

North Korea started off with the greater part of the peninsula's mineral resources and the industrialization that has developed the production of chemicals, cement, textiles, aluminum, and iron and steel for machinery and tools. China and the Soviet Union have sent economic and technical assistance for industry. Half of North Korea's population are farmers in mainly collectivized agriculture. The years of rigid regimentation have eliminated political opposition, greatly reduced illiteracy, and made available low-cost housing. old-age pensions, and free schooling and medical care. Consumer goods still are chronically scarce and of poor quality, and travel and freedom of expression remain very tightly restricted.

The leaders of North Korea's twenty million inhabitants regard them as members of a socialist society in transition between a "feudal" capitalism and the not-yet-reached state of communism. Twenty-five years after obtaining independence, state planning in 1970 was still developing economic programs and psychological procedures leading to the North Korean ideal situation where "each works according to his ability and receives according to the quality and quantity of his labors" (Kim 1970:92–93)–an interesting deviation from the original ideal of "according to his need." The driving principle of *Juche* (pronounced "chewche") rejects "subservience and dogmatism" and emphasizes self-reliance and creativity in all aspects of life. The membership of the "vanguard party" goes down to the worker and they solve problems together, utilizing ideological and moral stimuli as well as material incentives. Although restricting itself primarily to other Communist nations for trade and aid, North Korea has acquired a solid and varied economy as well as a significant military capability. President Kim Il-sung, who has remained in power since the establishment of the country in 1948, has endeavored to maintain a degree of international aloofness but has not hesitated to build multiple two-lane wide invasion tunnels under the Demilitarized Zone (DMZ) to the border of South Korea. Since he regards South Korea as having been "turned . . . over to plunder and military occupation by U.S. imperialism" (Kim 1970:11), he would like to complete the "Korean revolution" by uniting the two countries under the Communist banner.

SOUTH KOREA

Traditional and Modern at the Same Time

South Korea's thirty-six million people live in a different world, albeit still a Korean world. Their gross national product (GNP) of about $60 billion in 1976 represented one of the most rapidly expanding economies in the world. Unlike the North Koreans, whose cultural heritage has been considerably disregarded since their "liberation" from tradition and "feudalism" in 1945, South Koreans remember that mural painting dates back to the Royal Tombs of Koguryo from the 50s B.C. to the A.D. 600s, that the great bronze bell at Kwangju was cast in the 700s, and that the famous Satsuma pottery of Japan was first made by Korean artists and master potters carried there by Hideyoshi's forces in the late 1500s. Confucian principles of rectitude, propriety, and filial piety are still strong.

MODERNIZATION

Studded with skyscrapers, factory chimneys, and television aerials, the capital of South Korea, Seoul, is a teeming metropolis of 6.5 million people. Department stores, tea rooms, and specialty shops are jammed with well-dressed shoppers in Western and Korean dress, just as the streets are clogged with some of Korea's five million automobiles. Theaters, universities, sports centers, and upwards of two thousand churches have their full quotas of viewers, students, or worshippers. Yet there is an element of tenseness and more than a glimpse of a military presence, for in Seoul one is only 25 miles (40 km.) from the 150 mile (240 km.) long demilitarized zone (**DMZ**), where one million armed men face each other across the 2.5 mile (4 km.) wide strip of neutral ground.

Nearly every form of transportation is used, from plane and train to pack horse and river sailboat. Education stimulates the minds and energies of 150,000 students in South Korean universities (and about 100,000 in the North). Shamanism and intense concern for social status provide a balance to the keen interest in scientific progress, national security, competitiveness with other nations, and the need to relate urban prosperity to rural uplift.

THE PERILS OF POWER

Koreans, especially students, view with misgivings the inefficiency and corruption within the bureaucratic ranks, and the economic gap between middle-class opportunists and their honest and diligent peers who have not acquired such government favors. Perhaps the major difficulty is political. The late President Pak Chung Hi (or Chung Hee Park) failed to learn from the career of Syngman Rhee that dictatorship and repression are always resented, and was shot to death in 1979. This authoritarian pattern is only too familiar in Asia, as indicated elsewhere in this book. However, it must be emphasized that the purposes behind most of the modern examples represent efforts to promote national stability and progress in a world moving so rapidly in economic, technological, and ideological realms, that the traditional sociopolitical systems lack time and expertise to adjust. They tend to break down, leaving nations, societies and individuals stranded in a world they often cannot cope with and sometimes seem not to comprehend. Viewpoints, and the vocabulary to express those viewpoints and values, often differ drastically.

When East Meets West

"My country" or "our country"? The word "individual" connotes different ideas to different people. It has been said that, whereas to an American the word "individual" has good connotations of self-action, self-respect, and confidence, to a Korean the usual word for "individual" (*kaein*) suggests a selfish, uncooperative loner. The American tends to think along linear, optimistic, and activist lines, while the Korean is likely to think cyclically, pessimistically, and collectively. Life and its relationships to the Korean are wholes and parts of wholes. Koreans are not generally optimistic, and therefore problems should be approached by the group rather than alone.

Responsibility also is corporate and moral, in that the superior or officer in charge is responsible for any disaster or accident occurring within his jurisdiction. Western practice agrees in military matters and for the captain of a ship; but otherwise the blame (or praise) is placed on the individual who acted. The American places primary importance on training, qualifications, and experience in making appointments. The Korean, on the other hand, considers such primacy "impersonal" (the same phrase, *pi in'gan chok,* can be translated as "inhumane"!), and neglectful of the greater value of maintaining good relationships with the loyal persons of the ingroup.

The Ingroup

Visitors are greeted within the Korean home with the utmost consideration and graciousness, for on entering the home they become for the time being members of the family ingroup. However, assuming the family and the same people met as strangers, being part of a crowd waiting to board a bus or train, they would be treated simply as obstacles to be overcome as they clamber into the vehicle to grab a seat. In these "outsider" situations everyone not personally known is by definition a stranger, and therefore a sort of nonperson.

When the individual, the family, tour party, or other ingroup becomes submerged in a large crowd they feel isolated, therefore defenseless and, consequently, fearful. Loneliness and especially aloneness (for they are not the same) are to be avoided at all costs. For this reason friends may drop in by day and by night "to keep one company." In such situations the Westerner can forget the word "privacy," and be grateful for the thoughtfulness of those around who by their presence have shown he or she is accepted.

When West Meets East

Korean and Western views of time, space, and order or ranking differ considerably. To the Korean time is a continuity. It has no arbitrary limits. Its simplest illustration is the three or four generations composing the extended family, a single household unit extending through time. Ho Chi-minh reportedly said Vietnam would be unified in a few years, or in his lifetime, or in fifty years, or in x-number of generations; the time length was immaterial. This viewpoint is incomprehensible to the Westerner, whose "long-term goals" may be only five, ten, or twenty years. But it is entirely logical to the Easterner, whose ancient civilizations, in terms of space, have occupied traditional territories for probably thousands of continuous years. The West, America, and even Australia, have a sort of frontier society outlook with an expansionist mentality. Their recent civilizations have occupied vast lands and/or colonies for but a few centuries. Order, in the sense of clearly understood rank and precedence, spells security to the Asian but perhaps only competitiveness to the Westerner. Understanding each other's logic on these points would be a big step forward for all humanity.

PART VI

The Distant Realms: Mainland and Insular Southeast Asia

Chapter **17**

Lands Below the Wind: From Orangutan to Steamroller

EAST OF INDIA AND SOUTH OF CHINA

Land of contrast and paradox, Southeast Asia remains comparatively unknown despite centuries of European colonization and trade, and the convulsive effects of global and local wars. Its agricultural, mineral, and petroleum potentials are increasing in strategic importance. Nor is the region's economic importance recent. Here lay the fabled Spice Islands whose valuable condiments lured traders from ancient India and China, and modern Europe, to risk the perils of sword and storm. Pirates and smugglers stalked the seas—and still do. In seed-bed and paddy-field, plants and techniques are being refined to better feed the world. The ongoing development of the material and human potentials of Southeast Asia inevitably provides a testing ground for the ingenuity of its peoples and the integrity of the rest of the world.

It is interesting to note that water dominates both Southeast Asia, where rains and typhoon bring exceedingly much water, and Southwest Asia, where water scarcity dominates life. Two sea routes link Southeast with Southwest Asia. One extends over the Pacific Ocean, around Cape Horn, over the Atlantic Ocean, and through the Mediterranean Sea to the western shore of Southwest Asia. The other route leads from the southern coasts of Southwest Asia, directly across the Indian Ocean, and so to Southeast Asia—the ancient spice trade sea lane. Once again Asia's past and present tie together, and the great continent of diversity emerges as a complex whole.

Cities and States

Angkor Wat . . . Borneo . . . Bali . . . Manila . . . the names sound a haunting call to the world where yesterday and tomorrow form today, where the differences of culture closely parallel differences of geography. Mainland and Insular Southeast Asia are worlds unto themselves.

The broad and comparatively flat alluvial plains inhabited by the Mainland irrigation rice farmers nurtured the formation of ruling states, each centered on the city surrounding the royal palace. Some of these city-based states became today's modern nations. Hue, the lovely walled garden city of Annam, where literati took the Vietnamese language to great poetic heights. Hanoi in Tonkin and Saigon (now Ho Chi Minh City) in Cochin China betoken the troubled modern world. Once the temple Angkor Wat adorned the city center of a glittering Cambodian empire which encompassed much of Mainland Southeast Asia. Phnom Penh, capital of Kampuchea (formerly Cambodia), is the haunted ghost of a boulevarded city where once the traditional and the modern strove for cultural harmony. Situated on an upland riverine plateau Laos, represented by its present capital, Vientienne, long has been a country shuttlecocked between Vietnam, Thailand, and Kampuchea. In the western third of the Mainland lies Burma's capital, Rangoon, reflecting in its austerity and independence the efforts to remain economically self-sufficient. By contrast the Thai are relative newcomers to the region. When the Burmese destroyed the sparkling, temple-studded Thai capitals of Sukhothai and Ayuthia, the Thai shifted their center southward to the small fortified outpost of Thon-buri—now Bangkok, one of the world's major cities. Manila, once the boast of the Philippines as the "Pearl of the Orient" has arisen again from the devastations of World War II to be a beautiful if expensive city.

A Ball-and-Chain Terrain: The Region's Geography

From north to south a ball-and-chain configuration of lowland plains interspersed between long mountain ranges streams off, as it were, into numberless emerald islands and archipelagoes lapped by the blue-green waters of the Indian and Pacific Oceans. North to south, Southeast Asia extends some 3,000 miles (4,800 km.) and stretches about 3,500 miles (5,600 km.) west to east. The Mainland ranges separate the riverine plains of Burma, Thailand, Kampuchea (Cambodia), and northern and southern Vietnam from each other. The same bands of separation may be observed on a smaller scale in the Insular region—north and south in the Philippines and east and west in Indonesia.

The Wind-Dominated Islands

The seasonal and often stormy monsoon winds which brought Arab and Persian traders to Canton, also wafted Chinese merchants east to the Pacific islands and west to the Indian Ocean countries. Taiwanese fishing trawlers and Japanese pearling luggers followed these seasonal tradewinds south through the Philippines and Indonesia, as far as the oyster beds and bêche-de-mer (trepang or sea slug) shelves of the Great Barrier Reef off the Queensland coast of Australia.

So important were these wind patterns that the coastal kingdom of Brunei in Borneo defined itself as the "Land Below the Wind," because one sailed down on the north wind to reach home. In a broader sense, the term was applied to Indo-

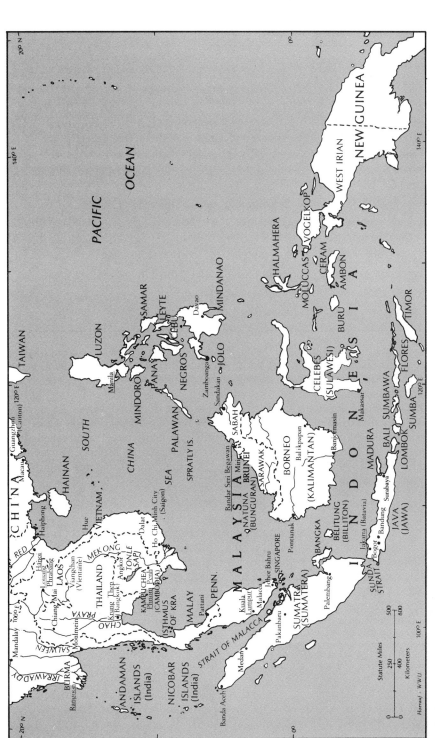

FIGURE 17–1 Modern Southeast Asia.

BOX 17-1 *SOUTHEAST ASIAN DATA*

Nations: Burma, Thailand, Laos, Vietnam, Kampuchea, Malaysia, Singapore, Indonesia, Philippines, Brunei.

Land area: 1,783,426 sq. miles (4,609,048 sq. km.).

Estimated total population: 390,432,867 (1983)

Distance north to south: about 3,000 miles (4,800 km.) from roughly 29° N to 12° S.

Distance east to west: about 3,500 miles (5,600 km.) from roughly 92° to 141° E.

Longest strip of lowland: the Irrawaddy valley, 800 miles (1287 km.).

Largest lowland plus delta area: the lower Mekong area, 100,000 sq. miles (259,000 sq. km.).

Temperatures: average in coastal cities, 78-87° F (C.25.6-30.6).

Temperatures: high in Manila and Saigon, 101-104° F (C.38-40°).

Heavy frost level: above 10,000 feet (3050 m.).

River deltas: many advancing seaward 150-300 feet (46-91 m.) annually.

---

nesia. "Lands Above the Wind" were India and China and other distant realms, because one sailed up (north on) the south and other winds to reach them. Lands Above the Wind were perceived as hostile places, filled with danger, where people had strange customs.

The winds bore communications, fishing boats, trade, and pirates. Even today Brunei medicine men learn a recitation used in attempts to still the winds and towering seas. In the past the more prudent merchants often transhipped their cargoes across the Isthmus of Kra to shorten exposure to tropical storms. The present city-port of Singapore sits as queen of the regional shipping patterns for the same environmental reasons.

Climate

Concerning the tropical forest climate, it has been said that "night is the winter of the tropics," and for good reason. Quite naturally for people sweltering in the humid coastal cities, with their year-round temperatures of 78° to 104° Fahrenheit (25-40° C), a suitable location at 3,000 to 5,000 feet (984-1,640 m.) altitude quickly becomes a resort area. Even native words for frost are rare. Snow twinkles in the sun only on the highest peaks in Northern Burma, Vietnam, and New Guinea. Rain, often torrential, comes with the southern monsoon winds.

HISTORY

Until about 40,000 years ago the area from the Mainland to the Strait of Makassar was dry land. This explains why the Makassar Strait, between Borneo and Celebes, marks the "Wallace line" indicating the eastern boundary of continental Asiatic flora and fauna. The earliest hunter-gatherers could walk to the Wallace line but had to go over water to reach the lands beyond it.

The earliest known humans in Southeast Asia were the hunter-gatherers *Homo erectus* ("Java Man") who roamed Java a half-million years ago. Modern humans, *Homo sapiens,* began entering the region sometime after 100,000 years ago. Archaeologists surmise that they probably used spears, cutting tools, fish traps, baskets, and digging tools and that they lived in shelters raised above ground, roofed with leaf thatch, and entered by a notched log ladder. (This description would have fitted the Mangyan peoples of Mindoro in the Philippines as they lived only seventy years ago.) But of these ancient people's languages, beliefs, songs, and children's toys nothing has remained.

Around 25,000 years ago the sea rose to its present level, and other peoples arrived bringing rice about 18,000 B.C. By 5000 B.C. agriculture was well established with taro, beans, rice, millet, and other crops suited either to swampy ground in coastal areas or to the hills for upland or "dry" farming. These crops, together with exploitation of jungle resources and animal husbandry—including the chicken, which was first domesticated in Southeast Asia—made such a combined pattern of mixed subsistence farming and fishing in the moist heat of hills and valleys, that it still is typical of much of Southeast Asia from Assam to Melanesia. Metals such as copper, bronze, and gold were in use at least by 400 B.C., and for working iron a piston-type blower was used. The simple back-loom typical of Borneo and northern Luzon today dates back to these ancient times, and the basic house-on-stilts doubtless has existed for millenia.

Environment and the Home

For the more than 365 million persons living in the region the realities of a home vary greatly, from stupendous rocky gorges to steamy malarial river bottoms. The Brunei phrase for "home" means a "house-and-ladder," and there are a multitude of shapes to the Southeast Asian house. "Home" may be a three-story city mansion or a leaf and sapling hut in the forest. Home may be a fishing boat bobbing on the sea, or a bamboo and nipa leaf house on stilts over land or water. The family may occupy a cubicle in a twenty-family longhouse by the river or a village dwelling hidden near the hilltop. It all depends upon one's relation to the environment, just as it has from antiquity.

FINGERTIPS ACROSS TIME

The Hunter-Gatherers

Though few in number today, hunter-gatherers are first and foremost gleaners of the products of the earth's surface; they change the landscape not at all. The jungle people, for instance, harvest thirty-nine varieties of tubers and twenty-three different fruits.

Hunting and gathering requires both solitary and group effort. Fishing with spear or arrows is quiet, patient work, but to build a weir or use a large net requires united effort. Typical communities mentally store hundreds of botanical names, each name triggering the knowledge of the item's beneficial or harmful properties.

The small family groups of the Punan of Borneo gather into larger units only for special occasions. Malaria, tuberculosis, accidental injuries, and complications in childbirth endanger their lives. Even the names of the spirits of the dead and of the forest evoke dread. The so-called "timid" *Mangyan* of Mindoro, riding Apache-wise on the lee side of a tame carabao and armed only with a sharp bamboo spear, hunted the dangerous wild buffalo, the tamarau. They also hunted Japanese soldiers hiding in the mountains after World War II. Even more elusive were the *Wild Aeta* of the northeast Philippine Sierra Madre mountains, who preserved their rugged territory with bow and poisoned arrow until about 1960. The most amazing discovery of all was of the vine-climbing *Tasaday* in the southern Philippines, a tiny community of about twenty-seven persons living in two small caves on a hidden mountainside until less than twenty years ago. Once these Stone Age people had been discovered they could never be rehidden.

Until the 1950s, many of these peoples still lived much as their people had for millenia. By road and river, lumberjacks, soldiers, and farmers have infiltrated their territory. Hunter-gatherers today represent endangered cultures, and attempts by the government to relocate peoples such as the Tasaday, and the Punan of Brunei, into subsidized agriculture often are unsuccessful. It is difficult for disintegrated communities to become productive in someone else's social and technological system, whether in Asia, Africa, Australia, or the Americas.

THE PATTERNS OF EMERGENCE

In looking at the peoples of forest and sailboat cultures of Borneo, the Philippines, and perhaps Eastern Indonesia, we see a reasonable facsimile of life before cities, kingdoms, and Europeans appeared on the scene. These ancient patterns of adaptation to the environment, each one different, probably have been perpetuated because of the operation of three "*steady-state*" factors: (1) no drastic change in the environment for many hundreds of years; (2) no significant change in the people's basic technology; and (3) no momentous change in their social, political, and spiritual relationships.

Nevertheless, century by century, a slow tide of newcomers came by sea from faraway India and China, or down the mountain trails and river valleys from South China. These were ripples composed of little flotillas, or the members of a few villages, coming to duplicate in new locations their social organizations and occupations. The newcomers came to lands they considered "empty." This *empty land syndrome* operates whenever representatives of an expanding population of higher technology encounter terrain they consider can be put to more productive or more specialized use than is now being done. To them such an area is "vacant," just waiting for exploitation. The newcomers' innovations disrupt the previous steady state situation.

Four major winds of change blew hard across Southeast Asia in the last three thousand years, altering it radically. They brought new foods and clothing, increased population, enlarged territories, international politics, bigger cities, and memberships in the United Nations. The end result was the emergence of modern Southeast Asia. These four winds of change were Chinese dominance, Hindu influence, Islamic conversion, and European colonization.

TABLE 17-1 Southeast Asia: The Southward Migrations

PEOPLE	PERIOD OF EXIT	PLACE OF EXIT	PLACE OF ARRIVAL	SUBSEQUENT HISTORY
Proto-Malayo-Polynesians	3000 B.C. or earlier	S. China	SE. Asia, Oceania, Madagascar	Mountain groups in SEA; Chiefdoms in Oceania; Kingdoms in Madagascar
Proto-Malays	2500–1500 B.C.	N. Mainland and SE. Asia	Malay Peninsula and Insular SE. Asia	Various kingdoms and sultanates
Mon-Khmer	Pre-Christian era	E. Tibet and SW. China	Burma, Thailand, Kampuchea	Mon States, Burma, Chenla k'dom (Khmer)
Pyu, Burmese	A.D. 200s–800s	E. Tibet and SW. China	Central Burma	Pyu kingdom, Pagan and later dynasties
Vietnamese	214 B.C. to A.D. 1900s	S. China and N. Vietnam	Vietnam, Laos, Kampuchea	Kingdoms of Tonkin, Annam, Cochin China
Chinese	100s B.C. and A.D. 1900s	S. China	Vietnam, Indonesia, Malaysia, etc.	Kingdom of Nam Viet; colonial enclaves
Tai-Shan*	Pre-China era; A.D. 800s–1800s	S. China	Thailand (Siam), Burma	Thai* dynasties, Burmese Shan States
Cham	Before A.D. 100s	S. China?	Central Vietnam	Champa kingdom
Lao*	A.D. 900s–1000s	SW. China	Laos	Kingdom of Lan Xang
(Indians)	1883-4/1900s	S. India	Malaya, Burma	Merchants, laborers)
Small Tribal Groups				
Senoi-Semang	8000–2000 B.C.	Indochina	Central Malay Peninsula	Mountain communities
Karen	A.D. c.1238	SW. China	Burma	Hill and plain groups
Jarai	A.D. 1200s?	S. China?	Vietnam	Mountain communities
Meo/Miao	Early A.D. 1800s	S. China	Vietnam, Laos, Thailand	Mountain communities
Kachin	A.D. 1800s	SW. China	Burma	Kachin State

Information based on Frank M. Lebar, et al., *Ethnic Groups of Mainland Southeast Asia* (New Haven, Conn.: H.R.A.F., 1964); John Cady, *Southeast Asia: Its Historical Development* (New York: McGraw-Hill, 1964).

*Note: "Tai" is used for the ethnic-linguistic group; "Thai" for the people of Thailand. Both Shan and Lao are related to the Thai ethnically and by language.

FOUR WINDS OF CHANGE

Chinese Dominance—Vietnam

From the last millenia B.C. onwards the hardwood timbers of Southeast Asia, augmented by its tropical foods, lustrous pearls, aromatic sandalwood for incense, surplus rice, and exotic spices became irresistible lures to both seafarer and merchant, raja and mandarin. Profitable trade exchanges led to extensive Chinese contacts by 500 B.C., both by highly seaworthy and well-equipped trading junks to the island world, and on land by armies moving south from South China, the land of Yue.

The political fortunes of Vietnam have fluctuated violently. In 214 B.C. the troops of the Qin (or Ch'in) dynasty's First Emperor briefly controlled the area now known as northern Vietnam, meaning "the Land South of Viet" or Yue. Then, after three hundred years of semi-independence, this Vietnamese kingdom of Nam-Viet (Southern Viet, or Southern Land) was conquered by Han Chinese troops in 111 B.C., and a millenium of Chinese domination ensued. Confucian ethics, Mahayana Buddhism, Chinese architecture and culture, and the Chinese government system permeated the whole coastal strip. This strip extended from *Tonkin* (Dong-jing or Eastern Capital) through *Annam* (the Pacified South) to the Cham kingdom of *Cochin China* around Saigon. Trading routes from East Chinese ports, linked with stations along the southern coastlines, followed the often stormy seas to Java, Malaya, and Sumatra, and opened the way to India and beyond.

In A.D. 939 Vietnam threw off for good the Chinese yoke, but not the Sinicized culture which, in modified form, still dominates the region. This history contrasts with that of the Thai and other groups, who migrated south and southwest and thoroughly indigenized themselves. In these southerly areas they came under the influence of Hindu India.

Hindu Influence

Funan (c. 100–600s). Greek accounts describe Indian trade with Malaya and Indonesia by A.D. 70, which brought Indian concepts of government and culture as well as merchandise. So, on the fertile plains of Cambodia, the first-known Southeast Asian kingdom, Funan, used an Indian name for its non-Indian capital, Vyadhapura "City of the Hunters." The capital's brick wall protected rulers and merchants, whose books written in an India-related script have long since disintegrated. Palisades encircling the clusters of elevated leaf-roofed houses guarded the bare-breasted, sarong-clad men, women, and children from unexpected slave raids by Mons from the west or Champa from the east. While cargo boats up to 90 feet (27 m.) long plied the rivers, the king and his retinue traveled on gaily caparisened elephants. Chinese emissaries, and delegates from the king of Murunda, India, were amongst representatives from many countries present at the Funan court in the A.D. 200s.

The name "Fu-nan" represents the Chinese rendering of the Khmer term *bnam* or *phnom* "mountain." The founder-king's Hindu title, Sailendra, meaning "King of the mountain," relates back to Mount Meru in Hindu and Buddhist cosmology as the center of the universe. The king also was the chief sorcerer of

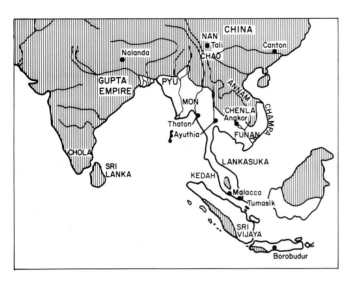

FIGURE 17-2 South and Southeast Asia showing ancient kingdoms and areas under Indian influence (in white).

Adapted from Abd. Rahman Ali et al., *World History for Sarawak Secondary Schools, Book One* (Kuala Lumpur: Longman, 1978), p. 15.

fire and lightning in the indigenous cosmology. Thus, Funan already exhibited two prime features of Southeast Asian empires: Hindu ideology associated with rulership and its potency, plus an undercurrent of pre-Hindu animistic beliefs. Unlike the forcible Chinese conquests of the Red river delta area, the Indianization of the region was a peaceful process concurrent with the Indian merchants' quest for spices, aromatic woods, and gold. Hinduism seems to have been the religion of the ruling group, for Jayavarman, the "great King," worshipped Shiva, and both Buddhism and the worship of Vishnu were the religions of the common people. After the death of Jayavarman in 514 Funan soon declined in confusion, and its role was assumed for two centuries by the successor Khmer state of Upper Chen-la. In time Angkor succeeded Chen-la.

Champa (c. 192-1471).   Contemporary with and outlasting Funan, the kingdom of Champa occupied the area of modern South Vietnam from the A.D. 200s until it was gradually absorbed by Vietnam in the late 1300s. The Chams themselves were identifiable until the 1600s. Living in houses of fired brick, the bellicose and piratical Chams elaborated a social hierarchy marked by differentiated parasols, clothing, and funeral ceremonies which persist as status markers elsewhere in the region today.

Angkor's Wat: Cambodia (800s-1431).   Jayavarman II (802-850) established at Angkor the capital of the most famous of the Hinduized kingdoms, that of the Khmer of Cambodia (now Kampuchea). Whereas Funan had presided over a confederation of Cham, Malay, and Khmer states, the Khmer empire attained its

high point under Suryavarman II (1113–c. 1150) with the conquest of the surrounding Vietnamese, Champa, and Mon states. He built the fantastic mile-square
Angkor Wat (the Temple of Angkor) with its golden towers and carved stone
corridors. He and his successors also built other extensive temples in addition to
hospitals, networks of canals, reservoirs, and roads which covered four hundred
square miles (1,036 sq. km.) of city-settlements and rice fields.

After centuries of intermittent subservience to the Thai rulers at Ayuthia,
a truncated Cambodia became merely the pawn between Thailand and Vietnam,
paying tribute to both. This condition was resolved by the French imposition of
a protectorate over Cambodia in 1863 as part of their multiethnic colony of Indo-
China, incorporating Tonkin, Annam, and Cochin China, with Laos and Cambodia.

The knowledge of these historic factions and fighting makes understandable
the difficulties Southeast Asian peoples have encountered during the later 1900s.
The intrusion into the region of Marxist concepts and programs and of American
interventionist forces has served to reawaken and exacerbate these old antagonisms
and invasion practices.

The third wind of change, Islam, touched merely the southern tip of the
Mainland area, the Malay peninsula, on its sweeping flow through Indonesia (and
the southern Philippines) towards the fabled Spice Islands.

Islamic Conversion

Looked at as broad generalizations, the thrust of Chinese domination was
political, that of Indian Hindu influence was cultural, and that of European colonialism fundamentally mercantile. The distinctive impact of Islam was essentially
religious, even though there were some commercial advantages gained through its
principal carriers, the Muslim merchants.

Arab traders in Southeast Asia predated Islam, and followed an established
pattern of marrying local women, as did their Muslim countrymen from the A.D.
700s on. Gujerati Muslim merchants proliferated in the area from the 1000s and
1300s, communicating their faith to Malay merchants, and thence to the rulers,
whose wealth derived from the prosperity of the merchants. About 1410, Parameswara (Prince Consort), the first ruler of Malacca (Melaka), married a Muslim
princess from Pasai on Sumatra and, as Iskandar Shah, became a Muslim. Subsequently the regional Malay ruling class began intermarrying only with other
Muslims on both sides of the Strait of Malacca. Conversion spread gradually from
the port city merchants to the rural farmers, and from the sultans to the general
populace. By the mid-1400s Islam had advanced throughout Indonesia and northward into the southern Philippines.

In view of the separate cultural orientations of the peoples contacted, Islam
was adopted only by those who could do so without compromising their line of
minimal identity (see Chapter 14). For the multitudes of tribespeople who have
followed their own patterns of spells, ritual, and worship, pressure to convert to
Islam was, and remains, a balk line situation of rejection.

The successive influences of Chinese domination, Hinduism, and Islam, over-
laid upon the environmental and cultural mosaic of Southeast Asia, resulted in an
area of enormous variety and vitality.

THE PRE-EUROPEAN CIVILIZATIONS

Srivijaya

For seven centuries from the A.D. 600s to the 1300s the Sumatran empire of Srivijaya controlled satellite states on both sides of the Strait of Malacca, and became the gateway for Hinayana Buddhism to enter Further India, as Southeast Asia sometimes has been called. In the late 700s the Sailendras of Central Java constructed the tremendous sculptured monument of Borobudur on its seven pyramidal platforms. In the 1200s the state of Malayu (or Jambi) separated itself from Srivijaya, became Muslim, and unwittingly bestowed its name on the "Malay" peoples.

By the 1300s a fourfold threat challenged Srivijaya's profits from its irksome system of transit dues on ships negotiating the narrow strait. The rising Javanese empire of Madjapahit, edging westward towards Sumatra, stripped Malayu of its island possessions while the Thai from Siam appropriated its Peninsular territories. Form the north the Chinese fleets of that restless conqueror Kublai, the Great Khan, threatened the region, and from the west came the increasing economic

FIGURE 17-3
Javanese dancer.

pressures and religious appeal of the eastward march of Islam. A Chinese observer might well have deduced that Srivijaya's "mandate" had run its course. In any case, mighty Srivijaya disintegrated—but the merchant ships continued to pass by.

A look at Malacca. Malacca's meteoric rise to ruler of the Strait as the pivotal port for merchandising in the Orient began when Parameswara, ruler of Tumasik (Singapore), moved up the Strait and founded the town and sultanate of Malacca about A.D. 1400. Ships from every country from the Red Sea to China crowded the harbor. Malacca's cosmopolitan merchants were wealthy enough to finance in gold bars the transshipment of the cargoes of three or four ships at a time. Gujeratis dominated the spice trade going west of Malacca, and Javanese the cloth trade going east. More than sixty countries were represented among the four thousand traders speaking some eighty languages and dialects. The need for a *lingua franca* gave rise to a simplified Malay trade-language, embellished with philosophic, social, and religious terms from Javanese, Buginese, Arabic, and later Portuguese and Dutch.

The Migrants Who Came in Ships

Arabs and *Persians* came to Southeast Asia for spices, jewels, and fine fabrics by the A.D. 300s, and *Indian* refugees found asylum, traders gained wealth, and expeditions garnered booty there. *Muslims* from Arabia and Gujerat first trickled then flooded east for trade and for converts to Islam.

Southeast Asia also attracted Europeans. The *Portuguese* captured Malacca in 1511 and with single-minded zeal introduced to the Orient the ways and customs of the West. The *Spanish* were commissioned to search for gold and spices, to annex lands in the name of the King of Spain, and to convert the local peoples to Roman Catholicism. Following their assumption of supremacy on the seas of Europe, the mercantile *Dutch* threw the Portuguese out of Malacca and settled in Indonesia. Following their victory over Holland in Europe the *English* entered the area to exploit the Dutch sources of income in the East. *France* and *Germany* were the only other European powers which came into the area with any serious impact: France on the Mainland, and Germany in northern New Guinea and Oceania. The stage was set for farreaching confrontations.

THE FOURTH WIND OF CHANGE: EUROPEAN COLONIALISM

The purpose. A colony is an acquired territory or a satellite settlement established outside of and ruled by the mother country. Nations establish colonies to find room for their expanding populations (as Japan claimed in Manchuria), or to control sources of raw materials (as Portugal and Holland in Southeast Asia). Other aims are to find markets for their manufactured goods (as England in India), to secure military advantages (as England in Singapore and Japan in the Pacific), or to increase their national prestige (as Spain in the Philippines).

The enormous caravan trade that nourished the empires of the Middle East, leading for instance, to the Phoenician colonies at Carthage and Cadiz, also set certain expansionist patterns for trade and military security. Rome colonized

TABLE 17-2   Merchandise Exchanged at Malacca in the A.D. 1400s and 1500s

SUPPLIER	GOODS SUPPLIED
Venice	Arms, dyes, quicksilver, glassware
Persia and Arabia	Horses, incense, indigo, amber, pearls, dried fruits, "enormous quantities" of opium
India	Cotton, cloth, leather goods, grain, honey, butter, meat, tapestries, steel
Ceylon	Cinnamon, ivory, precious stones
Pegu, Burma	Rice, vegetables, lac, musk, rubies, benzoin, ships
Siam (Thailand)	Rice, salt, vegetables, arrack liquor
Sumatra	Gold, pepper, aromatic lignaloes wood, pitch, rattan
Indonesia	Rice, slaves, ships, krises and swords, tin, cloves, mace, nutmeg
China	Porcelain, silks, damasks and taffetas, copper and ironware, alum, sulphur, saltpeter, camphor, seed pearls
Liuchiu or Ryukyu Islands	Vegetables, meat, swords and armor, gold objects, paper, special green porcelain ware
Molucca Islands	Spices
Brunei	Hornbill casque, gelatinous bird's nests, gems

Britain for tin, trade, and expansionist prestige, and the Muslim armies cornered practically ever trade route coming to the West from East and South Asia. Because of the rich cargoes constantly flowing through the Strait of Malacca, that waterway had been an arena of trade, piracy, and conflict from at least 200 B.C.—long before the Europeans arrived.

The process. Portugal emulated the Phoenician example by forcibly acquiring strategic trading ports from India to the eastern confines of Indonesia. Spain in turn conquered the Philippine Islands, and thereby linked trade between China and her own fortified centers in Mexico.

In order to permanently secure their trading privileges, the Europeans soon dipped into local politics. They usually took possession of the trading areas and administered them to their own advantage. Such "advantages" commonly involved the subordination, or eventual loss, of the local skills, occupations, and sense of initiative that for 1,500 years had made these Southeast Asian countries equal with or superior to contemporary countries in Europe. The incoming colonial powers cared little for such matters. They required plantation labor and processors of raw materials, and markets for their finished goods.

The product. The end product of these various aggressive enterprises was colonialism. Taiwan (the Isla Formosa of the Portuguese) was briefly held by both the Dutch and English. The Dutch established a settlement at Nagasaki, Japan, which lasted until the Meiji restoration of 1867. Hong Kong was occupied by the English. Spain held on to the Philippines until the American Admiral Dewey bombarded their fleet in Manila Bay in 1898, and America began administering the Islands. The British East India Company, and then the British Government, gradually acquired administrative control over the whole lower portion of the Malay Peninsula, a control which lasted until complete independence was achieved in

TABLE 17-3 Areas and Populations of Southeast Asian Countries

COUNTRY	SQ. MILES	SQ. KILOMETERS	POPULATION ESTIMATES 1983
Burma	261,218	676,552	37,536,400
Brunei	2,226	5,765	209,567
Indonesia	788,425	2,042,005	162,604,000
Kampuchea	69,898	181,035	6,051,050
Laos	91,429	236,800	3,668,920
Malaysia	127,317	329,749	15,171,700
Philippines	115,830	300,000	53,528,200
Singapore	224	581	2,518,130
Thailand	198,457	514,000	51,476,800
Vietnam	128,402	322,561	57,668,100
	1,783,426	4,609,048	390,432,867

1957. France accumulated the territories of the five kingdoms of Tonkin, Annam, Cochin China, Laos, and Cambodia to create the new political entity of Indo-China that lasted until 1954. Dutch supremacy in the Netherland East Indies lasted until 1942, and in 1949 Indonesia became an independent nation.

The post-mortem? "Anti-imperialism" and "anti-colonialism" remain major planks in the national policies of many Asian countries. At the same time, Soviet imperialism has turned Afghanistan into a Russian colony, Israel has occupied southern Lebanon, and French colonialism has been replaced by Vietnamese colonialism in the old area of Indo-China.

THE GAME OF PUSH-ME-PULL-YOU

Travelers have described the Southeast Asian countryside in glowing terms of blue skies and warm sunshine, lush crops and gentle people. No more; the idyll has vanished. Grim shadows of ancient animosities, furnished with new weapons, have fallen bleakly on the land and its people.

War and Its Aftermath

Nationalism pitted against colonialism inevitably ends in conflict. When Ho Chi-minh mated nationalism with Marxist doctrine and implemented it with the Maoist pattern of grassroots terror and organization, the Franco-Vietminh War of 1946-1954 was the result. With this war Western colonialism in Indo-China ended and Vietnamese colonialism began.

After the 1954 Geneva Conference established North Vietnam as the Communist zone and South Vietnam as the non-Communist zone, the governments operated as separate countries. In the 1960s the United States intervened in the fighting between the two countries on behalf of South Vietnam. This disastrous and abortive effort merely delayed until 1975 the unification of the two countries under the

North Vietnamese Communist government at Hanoi. Although the North Vietnamese threw off both Chinese domination and French control, they seem under present political doctrine unable to grant freedom to others. The dominoes of South Vietnam, Laos, and Kampuchea have fallen successively under Hanoi's military and ideological grip. Of the hundreds of thousands of common people who have fled this grip, scores of thousands of "boat people" never reached the desired shores of freedom.

Vietnam's efforts to suppress the remnants of the notorious Pol Pot's Khmer Rouge (the Red Khmer Communist army) have done little to halt the bloodletting during which the Khmer Rouge decimated nearly half of Kampuchea's six million population between 1975 and 1978. Outside the areas of armed conflict the type of "normalcy" found under totalitarian rule appears to prevail in the three countries of Vietnam, Laos, and Kampuchea. These recent events in the power plays of Southeast Asian history are ominous because of the involvement of outside ideologies and foreign support, factors not present in the days when animosities and cupidities were only the whims of individual states.

Peace

Some hope exists in the fact that the region has participated in various international peace pacts. In 1967 a regional and effective pact was entered into by Indonesia, Malaysia, the Philippines, Singapore, and Thailand—the *Association of Southeast Asian Nations* (ASEAN)—stimulating an increasingly close cooperation between the five member states. The *Mekong River Project* for the development of that river's resources was the only pact that continued operations through the first part of the Vietnam War.

Southeast Asia's present uniqueness stems from its environmental setting, the events of its past, the varied cultures of its people, and its drive for development. Starting only ten miles from the port city of Sandakan in Sabah, steamrollers are building airports, roads, and towns through the lands where the orangutan once roamed. From orangutan to steamroller, from mystic past to uncertain future, the people of Southeast Asia have a destiny all their own.

Chapter **18**

Mainland Southeast Asia: A River-Dominated Realm

Southeast Asia is preeminently a water-dominated realm. Oceans constitute the region's major boundaries, except in the north. And the region's rivers have dominated the inner landscapes by draining the rain-drenched mountains and irrigating the fertile lowlands. (See Table 18-1 and Figure 18-2.)

RIVERS OF LIFE

The courses of Southeast Asia's six major rivers—the Irrawaddy, Salween, Chao Phraya Menam, Mekong, Red, and Black—both outline and highlight the outstanding terrain features of the region: its north and south alignments of mountains and rivers and plains. Not far from the upper course of the Yangtze, the Salween and the Mekong flow within fifty miles (80 km.) of each other for about 450 miles (720 km.) while churning south through the Great Trough of the eastern Himalayan massif. They flow within 150 miles (240 km.) of each other for a total of about 1,300 miles (2,080 km.) through almost unbroken mountain defiles. All these rivers, except the Salween, make their greatest contributions as they flow through extensive lowland plains which support dense farming populations. A shallow draft boat (4-6 ft./1-2 m.) can sail up the Irrawaddy for almost one thousand unbelievable miles (1,600 km.) from the delta tip to Bhamo in northern

FIGURE 18-1 River village in Thailand.

Burma. But, whereas the rivers have flowed more or less in their present channels from geologic ages past, the peoples within their watersheds arrived only recently.

Tribal peoples live along the headwater areas of all the principal rivers of Southeast Asia, but, as the rivers slow down on the plains, the tribespeople are located further and further away from the main streams. Transportation follows a gradient of increasing complexity from upstream to downstream. Beginning with the small rafts of bamboo or logs of the upriver people in the shallows and the gorges, we find lower downriver hollowed-out or plank rowboats, then sailboats, motor boats, and finally river steamers. Near the estuaries we meet ocean-going steamers docked at the wharves of the bustling port cities. Technology, agriculture, and sociolegal organization also become increasingly complex as we voyage downstream. Homemade cloth and tools correlate with the slash-and-burn agriculture and the village organization of the tribal forest folk. The mixed subsistence economy of the foothills tribes merges into the market-centered agriculture and trading of the lowland peasantry. Towns and cities nearer the coast are characterized by impersonal officials, money and credit-conscious merchants, and the bustle of transient travelers and merchandise marts.

TABLE 18-1   Principal Rivers of Southeast Asia

NAME	LENGTH IN MILES (KILOMETERS)	ORIGINATES IN	DEBOUCHES INTO	FLOWS THROUGH
Irrawaddy	1,250 (2,010)	SE. corner of Tibet	Bay of Bengal	Tibet, Burma
Salween	1,500+ (2,414+)	N. Tibet	Bay of Bengal	China, Burma
Chao Phraya Menam	700 (1,120)	N. Thailand	Gulf of Siam	Thailand
Mekong	2,600 (4,184)	Xinjiang, China	South China Sea	China, Laos, Kampuchea, Vietnam
Red, Black	Each 700 (1,120)	W. China	Gulf of Tonkin	China, Vietnam

THE PEOPLING OF THE UPLANDS

The following generalized picture of tribal life in Mainland Southeast Asia has been culled from all over the region, and usually portrays conditions as they were prior to the late 1960s.

Most of the peoples entered the region from the north and moved southward. Lowland farmers moved to successive lowland areas, while mountain farmers moved from mountain to mountain. The result was that the geographical configuration of ball-and-chain plains and mountains was paralleled by the migration and settlement pattern of the peoples who inhabited them. The war-time displacement of whole peoples, as well as the purchases of modern gadgetry, clothing, weapons, foods, radios, and so on, have accelerated changes. Even so, their traditional and modified viewpoints and cultural values, embedded deep in their languages and group consciousness, enable them to maintain their separate identities.

Residence and Housing

Tribal hamlets often perch on the lower shoulders and buttresses of the mountains above the 4,000 to 8,000 feet (1,220 to 2,440 m.) deep canyons. The rear of some mountainside homes have been dug into the bank, while the front is scarily supported by long stilts above the depths up to 1000 feet below. The stockaded Karen villages of 10 to 100 houses with 25 to 500 inhabitants indicate that they are psychological kin to Southwest Asia's Kurds, South Asia's Pathans, and others who must defend with their lives their rather inhospitable domains.

The *layout of the villages* reflects the meshing of terrain with religion, family, and sex relationships. Laotian villages may be strung out along a mountain path, but more often are arranged around the central men's club house, where the men and adolescent boys spend their spare time and unattached nights, and where the ceremonial regalia are kept. The most concentrated form of corporate life flourishes under one longhouse roof, where the broad, public veranda, or the fire-pit section running the interior length of some longhouses, forms the arena of common conversation and daily handiwork.

The varied *contents and furnishings* of tribal houses tell the visitor the interests, capabilities, and occupations of the household members. On the veranda are the loom, coils of split bamboo and rattan, chickens in coops, and rain clothes on their pegs. Traps and a bamboo baby-pen lie there also, or are kept under the house. Inside can be seen the wooden boxes containing clothes and valuables, as well as large jars for holding grain, nuts, and foods, covered with lids to keep out dust and vermin. Water in jars or bamboo containers by the fireplace keep company with the cooking pots. Rolled in the corner, sleeping mats lie ready for evening use. Hung from the rafters trophies of the chase nudge smoked hams and baskets of corn.

Thrust between rafter and thatch gleams a parang or bush knife, with nearby a gun, spears, bow and quiver of arrows (some plain, and some poisoned darts in lidded containers). Hoes, digging sticks, and perhaps a plow lean against the house stilts, next to the hollowed-out mortar and the pounding sticks for hulling rice and corn. On the ground are the simple clay retorts for blacksmithing and brasswork. By the stove or in the loft will be the shrine and its offerings. In all, a typical house contains well over one hundred types of items.

House floor plans also differ. There always is a common or family room with slightly raised sleeping places for husband, wife, and the small children. To one side lies the dirt-based cooking hearth with tripod stones, pots, and suspended hook. Often the adolescent girl or girls have a small room partitioned off near the rear door where the boy friend may make nocturnal visits unobserved. Among the Lamet of northern Laos the teenage boy is absolutely required to sleep out at night, either in the men's house or with a sweetheart.

The ramifications of this Lamet custom aptly illustrate the interweaving *complexity of social patterning*. Seven interlinked effects may be noted: (1) This is a pattern transmitted through the generations by parents and relatives of both sexes. (2) The family composition and the household arrangements are thereby regulated. (3) House architecture is affected, for a special room or balcony must be built near the rear door for the family's marriageable girls. (4) The distinction between the boy, the youth, and the man is made formal and explicit. (5) Intersex conduct is directed toward premarital experimentation. (6) It perpetuates a primary use and function of a gender-specific building, the men's house. (7) It touches the system of moral values, for incest must be prevented at all costs.

Land and Occupations

Practically all the tribal peoples of Southeast Asia follow some form of mixed economy, including hunting, slash-and-burn (swidden) or plow agriculture, and the keeping of some farm animals. This occupational mixing indicates *differential use of land*. Hunting-fishing-gathering and pastoral activities leave the land unchanged. Swidden agriculture destroys fruitful forests, often leaving in its place a "green desert" of unreuseable grass-clogged land. Plow agriculture tends to make a permanent transformation of forest or brush land into open arable land. Altitude also affects agriculture and cropping. Buckwheat, barley, rye, and oats are broadcast at the higher altitudes, while millet, wheat, corn, and dry rice are sown on the lower slopes, together with leaf vegetables, legumes, and fruits. Pork, poultry, and occasionally venison provide most of the meat diet. Some populations and some individuals suffer from different aspects of malnutrition, most commonly deficiencies of vitamins, protein, and iodine, resulting in unusually high incidence of goiter, rickets, skin afflictions, and reddish hair.

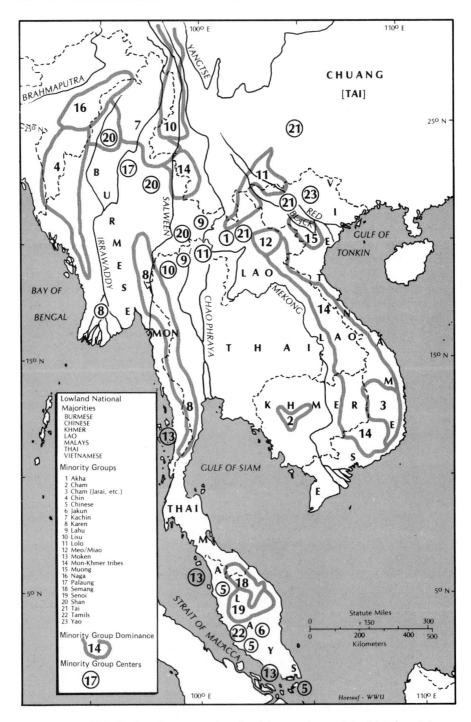

FIGURE 18-2 Distribution of representative minority groups into mainland Southest Asia.

Few communities can support full-time specialists. So the metal worker in iron and brass, the housebuilder and potter, the artisan in silver jewelry, and the shaman usually are also part-time cultivators of their own fields. Occupations are affected by culturally allocated sex roles, leaving the man with the heavier field work and hunting, metal crafts, and itinerant labor in other regions. Women care for the home and family, weave cloth, and participate in lighter field work.

All of these aspects of life—group differentiation, land and housing, family and sex relationships, occupations and trade—necessitate some sort of social regulation.

Social Life and Social Control

Courtship follows two general patterns, the secretive intimacy described for the Lamet, and the open serenading of the desired one by the suitor and his companions. *Marriage*, whether by elopement, capture, or arranged ceremony before a person of status, or even by moving in to live together, is always done publicly according to acknowledged custom. In the end the parents, lineages, and community are involved, because, as elsewhere in Asia, marriage represents the readjustment of society by the transfer of labor, the joining of lineages, and the continuation of society through the raising of the next generation of individual members of the community.

Sicknesses are treated by anyone with herbal or medical knowledge, or by the ministrations of a shaman, a shamaness, or an astrologer to identify and nullify the malignant influence, exorcise the offending spirit, and offer a placating sacrifice.

Religion. The Lamet shaman, for instance, leads the "rice soul" ritually from one harvest field to another, and then to the barn, lest the rice supply soon be exhausted. The spirit "altar" of bamboo and grasses outside the house, anointed with the blood of a chicken offered to appease the spirits, is there to protect the household. Similarly, villages often are guarded by demon arches at all pathway entrances. If that warning is insufficient to exclude unwanted human visitors, reinforcement comes easily to hand—bow and poisoned arrow or gun and bullet. Animistic *spirit worship* and fear of demons fill the mind with foreboding, and govern much of the daily routine. Various amulets and ritual techniques are used in an effort to prevent illness, harm, and hunger.

Social control comes in many forms. On at least one recorded occasion a mountain tribe punished an eloping wife by literally skinning her alive. In another area, the seducer of a tribal girl was tied for three days to a stake in the tribal village square and soundly thrashed. But the most effective controls are the whispers of the peer group. Nevertheless, formal offices and procedures range from group consensus among the *Semai* (Senoi) to the now weakened or lost hierarchy among the *Jakun*, who originally had an absolute chief, councillors, legal experts, and heralds. Among the *Shan*, villages and districts acknowledge the authority of hereditary princes or chieftains called *saohpas* (or *tu-si* by the Chinese; see Chapter 14). In addition to acting as patron and defender of his people, the *saohpa* holds court, rules on crime, and levies fines or other punishment, as necessity dictates.

The changing system of social control among the *Muong* of northern Vietnam brings these traditional patterns up to date. Long ago land tenure accrued to the first developer, from whom those coming later had to seek permission to settle. The end result was a landlord system of elite decision makers guiding the society. Over the later years the system was modified to one of purchase and rental until,

Environment					
Terrain	Water	Crops	Technology	Animals	Peoples
Mountain tops and glens	Springs	Oats, barley, millet, flax, lumber	Broadcast and mixed	Goats	Tribals: Miao (Meo)
Upper slopes	Tumbling cascades	Buckwheat (sweet, bitter)	Broadcast	Goats, sheep	Tribals: Luoluo, Lisu; Kachin, Akha, Miao; Igorot
Middle slopes	Gurgling streams	Forest products, millet, wheat, temperate fruits, tea, coffee, oil trees	Swidden and dibble stick	Cattle, sheep, goats, (horses)	Tribals: Luoluo, Lisu, Naga, Karen; Montegnards; Semai/Sakay; Dusun; Aeta, Igorot, Mangyan
Lower slopes	Running rivulets	Corn, dry rice, millet, legumes, vegetables	Dry plowing	Cattle	Tribals: Tuli, Karen
Terraced hillsides	Controlled terrace flow	Wet rice, sweet potatoes, oil plants	Irrigation, deep plowing	Water buffalo	Lowlander nationals: Chinese, Burmese, Indonesians, etc.
Valley bottom, plains	Still or minimal flow	Wet rice, sugarcane, peanuts, tropical fruits, cotton	Irrigation, deep plowing	Water buffalo	Lowlander nationals: Chinese, etc. Tribals: Tai/Shan, Puman

FIGURE 18-3 Altitudinal zonation of human ecology in Southeast Asia. The lowest point shown is the valley bottom. The other categories are typical of each type of terrain found in Southeast Asia. The details are set out contrastively to show distinctive differences. There always are areas that overlap—some communities live in wider areas than the zone indicates, and not all communities raise all the crops listed for that zone. Finally, this listing is not exhaustive, only typical.

under Communism, government ownership and the state control of products took over. Less drastic transitions also have occurred.

SOCIETIES IN TRANSITION

Two tribal societies at different stages in the process of transition exemplify the manner of change from tribal separateness to integration into the mainstream of national life.

Cooperation and Interaction

The *Palaungs* represent a fairly typical group of about 150,000 swidden farmers in the eastern part of upper Burma. They prepare and export tea, especially pickled tea, and livestock. The men seldom make news, but the women adorn the photographic records, for these women are laden with upwards of sixty pounds (27 kg.) weight of heavy brass coils wound around neck, forearms, and shins. A great amount of interchange of articles and of labor takes place between the Palaung and the surrounding peoples. The Shan provide bags used in tea gathering and cloth on which Palaung women embroider their distinctive colored patterns. Chinese cut timber for them and cast their plowshares. Masonry, carpentry, and painting of buildings is the work of the lowland Burmese. Palaungs do their own blacksmithing and make some jewelry, but their crafts do not enter into trading arrangements. They share the import trade in cloth, kerosene, lacquerware, fish, sugar, canned milk, etc., with the Shan, Chinese, Burmese, and earlier with Indian itinerant peddlers. Situated as they are in the hills between large populations of Shan, Kachin, and Burmese, these peaceful Palaung through their trading connections, have prepared themselves for the next step toward national integration. We see this next step in the developing history of the Karen people.

From Jungle to City

The 1.5 million *Karens* of the hills and plains of south and southwest Burma constitute the largest and most prominent non-Burmese group in Burma. The Pwo Karen are largely plains dwellers, occupying the area around the Irrawaddy delta, while the Sgaw segment of the Karen have distributed themselves widely throughout the whole Karen region, including the mountains. This includes Kayah State where the Karen-ni or Red Karens live. Both groups have outlying communities in Thailand. Subsistence rests mainly on wet or irrigated rice on the plains and dry or upland rice on the hills, augmented by tubers, fruits, leaf vegetables, pork, and poultry.

Although probably present near Pagan since the A.D. 1200s, the Karen came into prominence only after the British occupation of Burma in the mid-1800s. Responding to government and missionary opportunities for education they—and some of the Shan—moved into clerical and petty administrative offices. Quite naturally, the educated Karen and Shan gradually considered questions of nationality and independence. These aspirations achieved at least the recognition of statehood in the states of Kayah and Karen. In a dubious aspect of independent activity Karen insurgents have collaborated with remnants of Nationalist soldiery from China in the growing, processing, and exportation of opium from the "Golden Triangle" area on the borders of Burma and Thailand. The lowland Karens use the house types of the Burmese, whose language, dress, and employment options they share. Nevertheless, enough of the traditional culture and ethos (a group's distinguishing character or "tone") of their Karenity remains constant to mark the Karen as a minority group that has merited and achieved recognition in the mainstream of national life.

The Lowlanders

Because of substantive differences between them, a permanent balk line confrontation exists between tribespeople and the lowlanders, and between lowlander groups themselves. Each lowlander identifies with a nuclear or extended family as his or her basic social unit, especially where agriculture is the economic basis of life. Day after day drudgery in the rice fields forms the rhythm of lowland farming life ... back and forth through the muck behind plow and harrow drawn by plodding carabao (water buffalo)... stoop and bend to transplant seedlings... constantly tend the irrigation ditches and water supply... guard the grain from pests and thieves... then swelter day after day in the baking fields to harvest the grain handful by handful.

The village, town, or city of residence also is an important unit of identity, but the nation-state, often with roots in an ancient kingdom, forms the basic political unit. The ruling hierarchy wields extreme political and economic power, as the genocide in Kampuchea demonstrated. Furthermore, ties of common religion, language, occupation, education, and economic interests cut across many local group boundaries. Even so, the varied range of interests and identities form a total packet of subtleties and patterns, as a brief journey down the Chao Phraya river demonstrates.

BOX 18-1   *TRAVEL ON THE CHAO PHRAYA*

To travel the Chao Phraya downstream on a roaring propeller-driven launch was a captivating education in the panorama of Thai country life and the thoughtful subtleties of Thai courtesy and etiquette. We whipped past field after irrigated field, stopping at countless village wharves, putting people and their market purchases "ashore" on the steps below the overhanging patio-verandas. Saffron-robed monks with their impassive serenity traveled to temple or village ceremony, chattering children with bags and books went off to school, and the sick went to the hospital. One of the monks was son to the lady sitting next to him, who a few minutes before had knelt before him as she filled his begging bowl with rice. As a monk, even if only for the minimum period of three months, he belonged in the category of the sacred as a dedicated follower of the Lord Buddha. A schoolgirl thoughtlessly placed a small Buddha image on a seat to hold down her school papers in the breeze, and was promptly reprimanded: "You don't place that representation of the Buddha down low or use it as a utensil." When we stopped at a temple we noticed that those entering carefully removed headgear and sandals before going in. Some even removed their footgear on entering the cabin of the launch just as they would automatically on entering anyone's home.

Only with the passage of the hours did it become apparent that people endeavoured to keep their heads slightly lower than that of the delightful old gentleman sitting upright on his little cushion; this was part of the etiquette of respect. Also, it gradually became obvious that everyone kept their feet hidden as much as possible. Asked why, a student pointed out that the feet were "low" on the etiquette scale, and it was unseemly to cross one's legs in the presence of a superior or to point the way with the foot, let alone the rudeness of placing feet on desk or table. When the old gentleman finally stepped ashore, those leaving the boat waited for him to go first, and then fol- lowered in the same order of respect as they walked away. The student con- tinued: "It is proper to put "high" things such as hats, books, and flags where they cannot be stepped upon." He added confidentially that it is disgraceful to show affection between the sexes such as kissing or hugging in public; for Buddhists do not do that sort of thing. Going on he quoted the common viewpoint that to be a Thai is to be a Buddhist.

He grew reminiscent. "I studied in America," he said, "and was puzzled by the differences between Thais and Westerners, that is, Americans. Our mothers and sisters breast-feed, cuddle, and carry their babies and little ones by day and by night for years, and the child grows in an atmosphere of per- sonal touch and warmth and security and cooperation. Only after further ac- quaintance with adult American life did their method of child raising make sense to me. They gave the baby a bottle instead of the breast, laid it alone in a crib to cry itself asleep, gave it things not sisters to play with, and only al- lowed it out of its cage at stated times for feeding and cleaning. Perhaps the parents were right to prepare the baby and child for a lifetime of individual- ism and, often, broken homes. We prefer our way."

The propeller droned on as we mulled over the insights into Thai social values gained on a launch trip down the Chao Phraya that sunny day. Here were insights into the world view and formal behavior patterns of vast num- bers of Southeast Asian peoples: the centrality of religion and the practical aspects of relationships between the sacred and the secular; the concept of hierarchy in matters of spiritual, social, and age-related concern; the place of respect as the cement which holds society together, and its outworking in daily conduct.

BUILDING THE NATIONS

Although the majority of the Southeast Asian nations have a constitution, they tend to practice some form or degree of authoritarianism or dictatorship, on the grounds that this accords with present needs and with general Asian autocratic traditions. A brief survey of several of these nations shows something of their diver- sity, and how they came to their present state.

The Burmese

In between the steamy Irrawaddy delta and the dripping northern mountains lies the "dry zone," some five hundred miles of fertile riverine plains. Here for some

BOX 18-2 *BURMESE SOCIAL VALUES*

The Burmese system of social values revolves around four central concepts: *pon, gon, kan,* and *awza.*

Pon signifies charisma, goodness, ability to get things done.

Gon denotes virtue or inherent goodness of character.

Kan sums up the full account of one's conduct, similar to the Indian concept of *karma.*

Awza presents the notion of authority, the right to use power.

The social ideal is that the *man of pon* who possesses inherent *gon,* and therefore is entitled to a commendable *kan,* is the person who should be entrusted with *awza.*

300 years to A.D. 832 the Pyu dominated the valley, to be displaced by the Mon drifting down through Yunnan and Thailand. They in turn were crowded by the Burmese south into their present area in southern Burma.

These Burmese newcomers then established the kingdom of Pagan, where the magnificent scale and the intricate architecture of the gleaming white Ananda temple still awe the fortunate observer. The capture and garrisoning of Pagan by Kublai Khan's Mongol troops between 1256 and 1301 signaled the end of this kingdom. For the next 560 years under Shan and Burmese dynasties, Burma periodically and aggressively expanded to include Assam in India, the Mon territories down to the Kra Peninsula, and almost all of Thailand—or contracted into an agglomeration of petty states, with capitals at Pagan, Toungoo, Ava, and Mandalay. From the 900s to the 1700s the educated and artistic Mon peoples composed the leading elite of many of the Burmese kingdoms.

Burmese advances into Assam alarmed the British in India, leading to three wars and the gradual conquest of all Burma, and its incorporation as a new province into India. Items such as medical practices and a theory of statecraft borrowed from India were acceptably absorbed into their culture, but the wholesale introduction of Indian bureaucrats, heavy-handed tax gatherers, and tight-fisted moneylenders, resulted in their being driven out soon after Independence in 1948. Independence followed the expulsion of the Japanese invaders at the end of World War II.

Typical Burmese villages stretch out along a stream or road, or cluster tightly within the surrounding rice fields, where raised houses of planks, bamboo, and thatch nestle for shade amid trees and towering bamboos. The social and administrative changes brought by the British belonged to the modern world and have been continued by the independent Burmese regimes. The traditional headman-landowner-patron in the village or town setting has been replaced by representatives of government officialdom. Face-to-face bargaining with the local gentry has been supplanted by cold official regulation. The corner store and market emporium have been nationalized, and goods, when available, are to be found at the government's "People's Shops." Turning inward to heal its own financial, social, and political woes has been a frustrating but rewarding exercise in self-identification for General Ne Win's Burmese Socialist Program Party.

The Burmese ideal person, the capable *man of good character* and exemplary conduct, is the one to be entrusted with authority (awza, see Box 18-2). The Western procedure assumes that authority is vested in *an office*, and the appointee is then exhorted to act honestly and honorably in accordance with the dignity of the office. Still further from the Burmese viewpoint (or principle) is the Marxist-Leninist-Maoist program of Communism, as *a program*, by which the self-appointed party hierarchy plans to produce the ideal person and society.

The Thai

Southward in northern Thailand's fan of streams which descend to drain a mountain-girt basin 250 miles (400 km.) wide, the Thai peoples spread out to occupy the whole central portion of Mainland Southeast Asia, thus becoming the Thai of Thailand.

As the areas of Thai farmlands expanded, the tribal peoples were either absorbed or displaced until they were confined to the forests, mountains, and frontiers. The Thai then absorbed the domains of the kingdoms of the Khmer Chenla and of Angkor, and of Langkasuka and Patani on the Malay Peninsula. As an important trading center between two oceans for nearly 1,100 years, Langkasuka formed a major target for naval expeditions from the powerful South Indian kingdom of Chola. Patani also flourished for most of five hundred years, including a century of rule by a succession of queens. These two areas, with their rather uncooperative population of Muslim Malays, still form the southern limits of Thailand.

Provencher (1975:54-55) has pointed out that the Europeans arriving between the 1500s and the 1700s made rather little political or cultural impression on the local imperialist powers—the Burmese and Thai to the north and the Sumatrans and the Bugis of Celebes (Sulawesi) to the south. Moreover, although Europeans monopolized trade with Europe, other monopolies for other goods to India and elsewhere by Indian and Malay traders were not affected. The situation at the end of the 1800s was that Mainland Southeast Asia was controlled by England and France—and Thailand. Having preserved its independence through endemic conflicts with Burma, Vietnam, and Kampuchea, plus interference by Europeans, Thailand has lived up to its proud name of *Muang Thai*, "Land of the Free."

The Lao

Linguistic and cultural cousins to the Thai, the Lao amalgamated with some other hill peoples in 1353 to form the kingdom of Lan Xang (Land of a Million Elephants). Buffeted by both the Thai and the Vietnamese, Laos was freed from Thai suzerainty in 1893 to become part of French Indo-China. The Lao have occupied the narrow flatlands alongside the Mekong, the rest of the mountainous country being the preserve of scores of tribes who used to have Vietnamese as slaves. After twenty-eight years of precarious independence, and of dominance by the users of the Ho Chi-Minh Trail during the Vietnam War, the Communist government of the Lao People's Democratic Republic ended the 622-year monarchy in 1975 by deposing the king. He and part of his family were sent to a relocation center "to grow vegetables and learn Marxist-Leninist doctrine." Hundreds of thousands of tribespeople have fled—100,000 into Thailand—or been forcibly removed from their mountain homelands. The Japanese used to say that Korea was a dagger pointed at the heart of Japan, and for some years Laos seemed to be pointed at the heart of South Vietnam. North Vietnam ended that threat by capturing the whole area. A conservative Lao today might quote the Asian proverb, "It's hard to get one's own sword back when it's in someone else's scabbard."

The Vietnamese and the Kampucheans

The Vietnamese villages in the Red River delta range from 1,500 to 10,000 persons, with public places such as markets, council buildings, pagodas, and temples. The frontage, usually towards sea or stream, or crowning a low hill, is surrounded by farmlands and fruit trees: bananas, papayas, guavas, coconuts, mangoes, persimmons, litchi nuts, and oranges. In the subtropical climate of Tonkin almost everything grows freely except freedom.

The Kampuchean Khmers, like the other lowland peoples of Southeast Asia, have been able to retain their core territory, and in the past often have been described as one of the happiest and most peaceful people in the world. They have a proud heritage from the days of the Angkor empire, an equable climate, and a bountiful land. Many observers, therefore, have been puzzled by the bellicose intensity of the sustained efforts by Pol Pot's Khmer Rouge, the Red Khmer Communist army, to wipe out their own people. Apparently the breakdown of social restraints demanding politeness and respect leads to alienation expressed in extreme violence. Nor has the Vietnamese invasion solved anything; the Kampucheans remain the victims of a glowering and capricious fate.

TABLE 18-2   Representative Cultural-Linguistic Groups in Malaysia

GROUP	RELIGION	LANGUAGE	PERCENTAGE OF POPULATION	ESTIMATED NUMBERS
Peoples of West Malaysia:				
Malays	Islam	Malay	44	6.6 million
Chinese	Buddhism	Chinese dialects	36	5.2 million
Indians	Hinduism, Sikhism	Tamil, Punjabi	8 } 10	1.6 million
Pakistani	Islam	Urdu	2 }	
Europeans	Christianity	English	2	.3 million
Tribal peoples in East Malaysia:				
Iban	Animism	Most tribes		
Dusun (Kadazan)	Animism	speak a Malayo-Polynesian		
Land Dyak	Animism	language or	} 10	1.4 million
Melanau	Animism	dialect		
Murut	Animism			
Orang Asli*	Animism			(25,000–30,000)
Total population approximately 15.1 million				

*Orang Asli is a general term covering aboriginal peoples of West Malaysia, called in the literature by various names: Negritos, Senoi, Semai, Semang, Sakai, Jakun. Senoi is the only term not in some way disparaging.

The Malaysians

Malaysia hums with the activities of its fourteen million people, their cultures as varied as their country's landscapes. The nation's modern history began in the 1400s when Malay chieftains formed their territories into a few small sultanates and accepted Islam as their new religion. Arabic vocabularies added to the earlier loanwords from India special terms for religion, law, government, merchandising, weaponry, clothing, housing, and literature—all now written in Arabic or Latin alphabets. In the 1800s came British colonization, masses of Buddhist Chinese to work in the tin mines, and Hindu immigrants from South India to supply plantation labor. The indigenous Malays were and remained Muslims. Malaysia today protects freedom of worship, but prohibits attempts to convert Muslim Malays to another religion.

Malaysia is a constitutional monarchy. The Paramount Ruler or King, the nine Sultans, the complete executive powers of parliament, the judiciary and police, the medical and health services, and other organs of government at various levels, govern and serve the entire Federation. (Table 18-2 shows the principal languages and the political building-blocks of the nation, as well as representative cultural groups.) While the farming population includes Malays, Chinese, and Indians—all actual or potential Malaysian citizens—the Malays dominate the political scene and the Chinese the mercantile world, a familiar picture in much of Southeast Asia.

A multiplicity of languages, together with the great differences between the sophisticated culture of West Malaysia and that of the tribal peoples of East Malaysia, make a unified sense of Malaysian nationalism a complicated and difficult task. Nevertheless, the common syllabus in education, the open and booming economy, diversified industry, regional and worldwide communications, and a free electoral system of parliamentary representation, all help to ensure an equitable future for everyone.

The Singaporeans

Singapore, the "Lion City," is the crossroads of Southeast Asia, its storefront, and its salesroom. Under the early name of Tumasik, meaning Sea Town, Singapore has a rather blank history extending over seven hundred years. The beginning of the modern city really dates from 1819 when Sir Stamford Raffles set up a small trading post there. The 150 to 200 people Raffles found on the island in 1819 had grown to 10,000 by 1825, mostly South Chinese. In contradistinction to the North Chinese, the South Chinese were seafarers, traders, and colonizers, who set up their business houses or carried their peddlers' packs from the Yangtze to the Philippines, and from Penang to the far Pacific. Today Singapore's population of about 2.5 million retains its Chinese character (74 percent), with Malay (14 percent), Indian and Pakistani (8 percent), and other peoples (4 percent) completing the multicultural blend. Language and religion distinguish the separate groups, as do gait and posture, face and stature, ceremonies and ideologies. But the recognition of common Singaporean citizenship engenders mutual tolerance and consideration of the contribution each makes towards common economic goals.

Geographically speaking, Singapore is near the eastern end of a string of gateways and way stations stretching from the Straits of Dover, past Gibraltar, through the Suez Canal and the Bab (Gate) el Mandeb to Colombo, and threading the Strait of Malacca to Singapore, and thence to Hong Kong and Yokohama. Singapore also stands at the southern tip of the triangle of Mainland Southeast Asia, the pivotal point for a four-way flow of trade of import, export, and two-way transshipment.

As a seaport, Singapore's attractions mirror and magnify those of Malacca of three hundred years ago. Here are modern dock and anchorage facilities in the Inner and Outer Roads, repair yards, ample godown storage and warehousing, banking, hotels, modern Changi airport, and worldwide communications. Singapore is an urban island nation.

Nationhood

The essence of nationhood must be the people's own sense of unity. Constitutions, governments, and other elements of organization exist primarily to confirm this sense of unity and to make it explicit. Whether the people concerned are homogeneous or multiethnic, a common sense of belonging emerges out of their common sufferings, sympathies, and sentiments, often joined to a common religion, language, and geography, all solidified within formal national frontiers. By revolution, design, or agreement, national leadership and administration replaced the colonial powers as the new entities in Southeast Asia. Their proclamation of nationhood was acknowledged by world consensus. The implications of Malaysia's simple motto, *Bersekutu Bertambah Mutu*, "Unity is Strength," carry the globally important message to our increasingly divided world that Unity Equals Survival.

Chapter 19

Insular Southeast Asia: The Enchanted Isles

LOCATED EAST, WEST, AND SOUTH

Introducing the Vanishing World

East of the Indian Ocean, west of the Pacific, and south of the China Sea lie the enchanted isles of coconut fronds and volcanos, spices and erstwhile head-hunters, water buffalo and outrigger canoes, oil refineries and cities with populations in the millions—Insular Southeast Asia.

The Sea-linked Lands

People, animals, and birds of paradise live in a maritime world dominated by large land masses, by the monsoon storms and baking doldrums of the tropical seas, and by the menacing rumbles along the 3,000-mile (4,800 km.) arc of fiery volcanos. Out of the 13,662 islands of the Indonesian archipelagoes, 922 are occupied by about 150 million persons. And just to the north are another 7,100 islands occupied by 50 million more people, Filipinos, who inhabit a region of more water than land, their island terrain being part of the highlands of the vast sunken Sunda Platform. Here in Insular Southeast Asia Indian trader met Chinese merchant a thousand years ago, and Arab dhow followed Chinese junk to the foreign settlements in Canton. Here also some ancient Proto-Malayo-Polynesians turned west to reach Madagascar, while the mainstream turned east to populate the islands of Oceania. Also from here Westerners fanned out over the island world from Java to

Japan, and from Sumatra (Sumatera) to Celebes (Sulawesi) to Jayapura (Hollandia) to New Guinea (West Irian). Centuries would pass before their influence penetrated the jungles and forests of the far interior, for there the different cultures utilized every available ecological niche.

ENVIRONMENT AND OCCUPATION

The Farmer-Hunters

Predominant among economic adaptations is that of farming-hunting. Generally, in the open foothills country, between the higher mountain forests and the lowland plains, the swidden farmers operate their slash-and-burn technique for hoe and digging-stick farming or "horticulture" (a term used here to distinguish it from plow farming).

The land's tree cover is cut down, left to dry out, and then burnt, leaving a plot of ground more or less cluttered with stumps and covered with a layer of fertilizing ash. Either men or women dig a shallow hole with a heavy stick, drop in a few seeds of rice, corn, or other crop, brush earth over the seed with the feet, and hope for rain. After two to four seasons, weeds and soil exhaustion usually require the plot to lie fallow for five to fifteen years to allow the trees to grow again and set the stage for repeating the process. However, if coarse, deep-rooted grasses (*lalang*) take over before the trees grow, the plot will be permanently lost to swidden cultivation—the people have no technique to dislodge the grass, which is good only for thatch. While the plots lie fallow, the community must clear other areas. Swidden farming is wasteful, and only possible where vast tracts of hillsides are freely available. Such clearings are known variously as *kaingin* and *ladang*.

Because swidden farmers live in this well-wooded yet sparsely occupied hilly terrain, they are able to supplement their cropland harvests with hunting and fishing, and they usually keep chickens and some domestic animals, cattle, goats, and pigs. That is, swidden economy is a mixed farming economy, falling between the hunter-gatherer and the plow farmer. When swidden farmers come to an area occupied by hunter-gatherers, the empty land syndrome operates, and the area serves as a migration magnet.

Sumatra. Population encroachment upon their forest and swamp habitat in eastern Sumatra has caused the once seminomadic hunting-gathering people to become squatters around Malay villages. Calling themselves *Orang Darat* (People of the Land) rather than use the derogatory term *Kubu* (primitive), they rather inadequately adopted garden agriculture and claim to be Muslims. Some of them plant small *kaingin* clearings, then go off to hunt and fish, and return to harvest whatever has grown. They represent displaced peoples, who still retain partial control over their former way of life, hunting elephant, wild pig, and monkey with nets, poison, blowgun, and spear. These Orang Darat also managed to retain considerable occupancy of their hereditary area of forest and swamp, but others, like the *Toala* of Celebes, jungle dwellers scattered here and there all over the island, sometimes live in the areas of the peoples who once enslaved them.

Borneo. The *Ibans* of western Borneo are an expanding group who have taken over much of Sarawak during the last few hundred years, raiding, beheading, or enslaving the earlier inhabitants. A riverine and hill people, they were called "Sea Dyaks" because some of them were pirates on the coast during the 1800s. Bright, comely, and energetic, these longhouse dwellers hunt, gather, fish, and cultivate rice on the burnt-over hillsides. The "rice spirit" is central to their traditional thought, ritual, and religious beliefs, and the care of the spirit governs much of their daily activities. Since fire in the wooden planking and thatch of the longhouse is a constant danger, the annual supply of unhusked rice, which keeps well if maintained dry, is always stored in special raised storehouses built away from the longhouse itself.

In a traditional longhouse, household work noisily occupies the daylight hours on the broad, covered veranda: women pounding rice, girls weaving wraparound skirts, men weaving mats and mending nets, making paddles and sharpening parangs (machetes), and the children squealing shrilly as they play or nag the adults for food. Trading expeditions and marriages usually coincide with the period following harvest when food is plentiful and work is light. This was the open season on other people's heads until headhunting was stopped with the imposition of the Westerner's law, under the reigns of the White Rajas of the Brooke family, which lasted from 1841 until after World War II. The timing of the seasons for headhunting and agriculture were regulated by observation of certain constellations and stars.

Modernization has long attracted many of the younger Iban men downriver to compete, though not too successfully, with the more experienced Chinese for jobs. In the 1960s the first Iban university graduates returned from Australia, England, and the United States to take posts in the government and teaching services, thus leading the way towards integration with the modern world. But this same "progress" means that the gap between them and the bulk of the Ibans in the slowly changing environment of the longhouse culture is wide and probably will grow wider.

Celebes. The fantastic view of four hundred miles (640 km.) of mountain peaks along Celebes' northern arm, each peak tipped with pink and gold by the setting sun, looks like the gaily painted spines of a crocodile's tail, an unforgettable sight. Equally unforgettable are the people of Celebes, the largely Christian *Minahassans,* tall, strong and of light complexion, the most Westernized native people of the archipelago. Neat, clean, and organized, each village has its church, and its men supply the professions with clerks and teachers, and the army and police force with many of their recruits. The half-million Minahassans, together with other large groups throughout the island, are perhaps derived from the Toradja people, and all exemplify a typical Southeast Asian capacity to merge an autocratic sultan or raja-type of hierarchy with a relatively simply day-to-day economy.

It is interesting that the *Toradjas* themselves have no tribal chiefs, and that their women are free to choose their own husbands. Culturally they range from mountain-dwelling groups to downriver agricultural settlements of houses set in their own gardens. Over 600,000 strong, the vigorous Toradja illustrate both aspects of a response to contact with modernization: some adaptation to innovations from outside—new crops (tobacco), new house styles, new gadgets—as well as the cultural inertia resulting from the substantial mass of persons to be changed. The interior Toradja have snuggled their fortified villages into the clefts of the forested mountains reached only by arduous foot travel. Here they cultivate millet and maize. Further down towards the lowlands dry and wet rice are cultivated along with vegetables and taro. Sugarcane and tobacco utilize plow technology on irrigated land, itself an innovation.

In time past the Toradja have been avid hunters, owning slaves, buffalos, and other property which was passed down to the children, especially to the daughters. Among outsiders they have been widely known for their elaborate sacrificial rites and huge glazed burial jars. But visitors have been even more amazed at their unique custom of burying their dead in burial chambers far up the sheer walls of caves and cliffs, accessible only by climbing up a ladder of wooden pegs driven into the face of the cliff.

Coastal Fishermen

With gill nets and trawls and hook-and-line, singly or in groups, by day or by night, fishermen of the Southeast Asian coasts brave the seas in everything from one-person canoes to well-equipped "PT-boats" carrying a busy crew of twenty or more. For some in harbors, rivers, or inshore areas, the self-contained small craft is the family home.

For the men of the fishing camps along the island coasts in the southern Philippines work starts at dusk. They fasten one end of the long sweep net to the stationary long boat centered within the wide circle of five or six dinghies, each equipped with two bright pressure lamps. The other motor-driven long boat drags the huge nylon net, several hundred yards (300 meters or so) long by thirty feet (9 m.) deep, under each of the flare boats in turn. Bumper catches of herring may fill both long boats twice in the night. The fish is eaten fresh or is rendered into oil and made into fish paste. The 70 to 80-foot (21-24 m.) long "PT boat," also self-contained, sweeps its net completely underneath the boat when its two rows of 1,000-watt pressure lamps are turned off. Such boats carry their own refrigeration and operate only out of the major port cities.

The specialized lifeways of the fishermen who live in small family boats result in a dialect and clanishness particular to each group. The *Bajau* of the Sulu archipelago in the southern Philippines, who spend their lives on their family craft, are often known as "sea gypsies," and could be classed generally with the *Orang Laut* (Men of the Sea) of the east coast of Malaya. Both groups gradually are making more and more permanent contact with the land, some in houses on piles over the water, and some in coastal villages.

Sailors and Traders

Ancient Southeast Asians pioneered sailboat design, and their descendants ever since have trimmed their sails to every wind around every coast in the whole region. From the days before Vasco de Gama, the ports from Malacca to Manila and from Borneo to the Moluccas have been the scenes of "thickets of masts and acres of canvas." Between 8,000 and 10,000 sloops and schooners relying wholly or mainly on wind regularly carry cargo and passengers to and from the major and minor ports of these more than 20,000 Southeast Asian islands. Timber is the main

FIGURE 19-1   Boat people in the South China Sea.

cargo, but they also sail laden with crates of chickens, baskets of bananas, drums of oil and gasoline, crates of soft and hard drinks, boxes of salted fish, and bales of cloth. Passengers bring their own bedding and sleep on deck, in the cabin, or down in the hold.

Steamship and airplane have squeezed out many of the larger sailing ships that still filled Malacca's harbor up until the 1940s. Nevertheless, without the aid of the sailing ships the interisland trade and travel network would be severely impaired. Gone are the imposing Malay ships, three hundred feet long and with twelve feet of freeboard, that called at Bornean ports. Many of the smaller ships now come with auxiliary motors. But an impressive array of windships not only survives but is constantly being replenished by duplicates fashioned on the various regional models. By palm-thatched huts, under the protective lee of cliffs, alongside river or lagoon, or even on framework in the backyard, ships large and small are carefully and ritually crafted. Some Buginese timber ships rate nearly three hundred tons. Until the coming of the steam and motor ship the Moro *vinta* of the southern Philippines enabled the Moro pirate-smuggler to outrun everything else. The only difference today is that the same smuggler uses powerful twin inboard motors, or multiple outboards in tandem, to successfully evade capture.

Trade unites everyone from the merchant-prince in the capital to the lowly copra grower who loads his four 80-pound (36 kg.) bags on the schooner's dinghy off the remote sandy beach. The merchants at both ends of the route are more interested in their goods arriving intact than in the delivery time. Handling by hand on the schooner is safer than by winches on the "iron-hulled motor ships." The merchants always send their hard liqour consignments by sailboat because the Muslim sailors are unlikely to broach such cargo. Bulky timber finds ample room on the majestic Makassar and Buginese schooners, just as it did on the last of the splendid six-masted schooners running the trade-winds from Australia to England well into the 1900s.

The Sophisticated Lowlanders

Lowlanders of the Indonesian Archipelago share several characteristics: (1) They are plow farmers on permanent lowland plots; (2) a cash economy ties rural markets with city trade; (3) large populations, often in the millions, share common religious affiliations; and (4) historical ties exist with literate, militant empires. These substantial components of the present multicultural nation of Indonesia bring to its political and economic life a bewildering variety of languages and dialects, cultures and provincialisms, competitiveness and general cohesion.

The sixth largest island in the world, Sumatra, is one of the forgotten islands. In the days of Marco Polo, Sumatra was a center of great learning, libraries, universities, and Buddhist temples, to which came scholars from all Asia. The Batak script, now falling into disuse, remains almost the sole legacy of this literary greatness. Until 1961, the educated, aggressive, once opulent, and fiercely Muslim Achehnese, more than two million strong, periodically rebelled against whatever government was in power. The scarcely less aggressive *Batak,* renowned even in Sumatra as warriors, built their eight-family houses with peaks 40 feet (13 m.) high. The rampart which used to surround their villages for protection against headhunting raids has little function in today's peaceful circumstances, for buses in Batakland may be lively with hymn-singing Christians. A quarter million Batak have emigrated to East Sumatra as schoolteachers, clerks, and officials. Toba Batak intelligentsia mingle with the elite in Jakarta, the national capital. Their social peculiarity entails the departure of most of their men to Java to trade, or pursue other lucrative livelihoods to bring back money at the end of the year to their wives and families at home. In the meantime the women manage the home, lands, and the village.

The *Minangkabau* Muslims of west central Sumatra, similarly energetic and ambitious, also participate in the higher echelons of government and army. Religiously they are intensely conservative, and, although the rajas and the slaves no longer exist, the aristocrats and the commoners are still quite distinguishable. Duality is evident in that the village headmen, elected from among the matrilineal clan leaders, represent the pull of *adat* or customary law, in contrast to the status accompanying the religious authority of the *imam.* As among the Achehnese and the Batak, around 85 percent of the Minangkabau are rural villagers engaged in agriculture, trade, and teaching, activities which integrate completely into the networks of which the cities and towns are the centers.

A word should be said about the 220,000 *Niasans* on islands just off Sumatra's west coast. Various remnant groups found refuge there in earlier times, and emphasized headhunting and human sacrifice. Villages of substantial stone and wood dwellings housed thousands of persons, who were governed by an aristocracy of chiefs. Since the influence of Islam touched only the fringes of the port community, the law of the land was that of customary adat, modified by national statutes since the Dutch took control in 1914. Full integration has been slow.

In the area of the ancient Hinduized state of Banten or Bantam (300s–1684), 21 million *Sundanese* occupy much of West Java in villages of 1,000 persons and towns of 7,000 inhabitants. They, and the 11 million *Madurese* of Madura island and nearby Java, have retained a somewhat rural distinctiveness of language and custom in comparison with the more numerous and highly class-conscious Javanese. Two of Indonesia's biggest cities, Jakarta and Bandung, lie in the Sundanese area, and the port of Surabaya lies in the Madurese area.

The two million *Makassarese* and the three million *Buginese* in the southern Celebes, being both plainspeople and seagoing traders, are adept at economics and politics. A striking feature of *Buginese* culture is the duality of their relationship between their bodies, houses, nobility, and the cosmos. The ingroup includes all levels from the conjugal family to the kingdom, centered around a "navel" post in

TABLE 19-1 Glossary of Southeast Asian Place Names

COMMON NAMES	GENERAL LOCATION	HISTORICAL AND MODERN NAMES, ALTERNATIVE SPELLINGS
Acheh	Sumatra	Atjeh [c]
Bangkok	Thailand	Krung Thep [b]
Batavia	Java	See Djakarta
Borneo	Indonesia	Kalimantan [b]
Brunei Town	Brunei [c]	Kota Batu [c]; Bandar Seri Begawan [b]
Cambodia	Mainland SEA	Kampuchea [b]
Celebes	Indonesia	Sulawesi [b]
Djakarta	Java	Jakarta [b]
Hollandia	New Guinea	Sukarnopura [b]; latest: Jayapura
Java	Indonesia	Jawa [b]
Johore	Malaysia	Johor [b]
Makassar	Celebes	Ujung Pandang [b]
Malacca	Malaysia	Melaka [a]
Mindoro	Philippines	Ma-i (Chinese) [c]; Min d'Oro (Spanish) [c]
New Guinea	Indonesia	West Irian or Irian Jaya [b]
Patani	Thailand	Pattani [a]
Penang	Malaysia	Pinang [b]
Sabah	East Malaysia	North Borneo
Saigon	Vietnam	Ho Chi-Minh City [b]
Singapore	Singapore	Tumasik [c]
Sulu	Philippines	Sulu Sea [b], but Jolo for islands and city [b]
Sumatra	Indonesia	Sumatera [b]

[a] Alternative spelling

[b] Modern name

[c] Historical name

the center of the house or a person of good character, such as a noble. Such centers act as spiritual umbrellas and as givers of essential life-energy. The outgroup includes all others, including evil spirits, and confrontation is inevitable. All apertures in the house and gaps in the ingroup must be guarded against bad influences, unless one is within the protective aura of the life-energy of a morally superior person.

Being somewhat distant from Muslim centers and having perhaps a Toradja background, both the Makassarese and the Buginese mingle some traces of Hinduism and animism with their practice of Islam. Self-disciplined and industrious, they are keen traders and have their own literature. And, as suggested already, the Buginese are unsurpassed in Indonesia as shipbuilders and seafarers.

The flamboyance of the *Balinese* storybook culture often overshadows the intrinsic dignity of a sensitive and highly artistic people. Skilled artisans have a high status in the village, and are specialists in forging tools of iron, musical instruments of bronze, ornaments of silver and gold, and in preserving and portraying traditional tales. The deferential use of finely graded titles when addressing members of the gentry class pervades all social life. But, as in many cultures, social alternatives have been devised to avoid being locked into a single rigid system. Many other social associations crosscut this dominant system of social deference: groups concerned with government, ownership of rice lands, temple ceremonies, drama presentations (of the *Ramayana*, for instance), and active teams for work in crafts and agriculture.

THE INDIGENOUS KINGDOMS

The Tantalizing Legacies

Empires and kingdoms have waxed and waned—from early Funan to modern Thailand on the Mainland, and from Srivijaya and Sailendra, to Madjapahit and Mataram, and even Brunei on the Islands—yet little remains to show for much of it all. Some left magnificent architectural masterpieces, some anonymous ruins, some only names. Doubtless whole kingdoms vanished without a trace. The magnificence of Angkor Wat remained concealed from the outside world in the embrace of jungle growth for half a millenium until discovered by the explorer Henri Mouhot in 1860. Other tantalizing hints remain here and there: the stone foundations of a fourth century Hindu temple at a trading center near Kuching, Sarawak; and the earliest known Old Malay inscription in an India-derived script of the seventh century, was found in southeast Kalimantan (Borneo). The stony silence of the intriguing frescoes on the Buddhist monument of Borobudur contrast startlingly with the living spontaneity of Hindu art, dance, and temple ritual on Bali. It is well known that traders and raiders from Borneo spread goods and destruction all around the borders of the South China Sea, but few know that they also spread the art of writing—a form of that same Indian script—around the same area. In many ways, however, the outstanding legacy of Insular Southeast Asia's pulsing shafts of past glories may be seen today in the Sultanate of Brunei.

The Sultanate of Brunei

The thunk! thunk! thunk! of heavy wooden paddles hitting the sides of huge dugout canoes, upwards of 80 feet (25 m.) long, advertised to the townspeople of

Brunei the speedy arrival of spear and parang-wielding tribesmen from upriver. The cloud of sails sweeping in from seaward heralded the fire and sword of the Bajau and other sea-gypsy raiders from the northern coasts. Even the Bruneis' arms and armor and their prestigious bronze cannon availed little when these waterborne enemies swooped in for the kill. Nevertheless, beginning about A.D. 800, Brunei developed a typical Malay adaptation of the Hinduized kingdom of the Javanese type, wherein the sultan exercised control over subsidiary fiefs held by hereditary nobles. Subsequently, the kingdom became Islamic.

The magnificent trading empire of Brunei, which monopolized most of the regional trade in Magellan's time and for 250 years afterwards, left in stone only the crumbling walls surrounding the then capital of Kota Batu (Stone Fort), and the stone tomb of Sultan Bolkiah. The splendid city, the multiwinged palace, the docks and ship berths, and the places of worship, all were built of wood and have vanished without a trace. Under British sponsorship as a protected state since 1888, Brunei became fully independent on January 1, 1984. The wealth accruing since the discovery of oil and gas in 1926 has made Brunei the richest per capita state in Southeast Asia. Brunei's present population of approximately 200,000 bustles with enterprises in import/export businesses, public schools, community hospitals, welfare programs, and well-trained police and army. The ancient kingdom lives on, now at home in the space age.

Last but not least in the Bornean rhythm of life represented by Brunei is the deeply felt desire of the overseas Malays to return to their sunny homeland, of the Ibans to return to the family security of their longhouses, and of the coastal peoples to hear the wavelets' slap-slap against the pilings that hold up their houses.

JAVA AND THE JAVANESE

Nearing the Center

We have been moving gradually from the periphery of forests and mountains towards the central plains, and from the outlying tribal and minority peoples towards the more densely populated areas of greater technological and national importance. It is the peoples of these densely populated plains who have felt the greatest impact of Islam, even though the measure of their acceptance and practice of its teachings has varied. And particularly as we approach the central island of Java we perceive more and more evidence of nearly four hundred years of Dutch influence and control, of four years of Japanese domination, and of the last thirty-odd years of independent progress and dignity. So we need to sketch briefly the era of the Dutch presence in the Indonesian archipelago.

The Dutch Presence

Four Dutch ships came to anchor in the port of Bantam in West Java in 1596, when sultanates at Acheh and in the Moluccas, and the kingdoms of Bantam and Mataram on Java, controlled trade in the whole region. In 1602 the Netherlands United East India Company agents bargained in the markets for pepper and cloves and paid taxes like all other merchants. Gradually, however, they gained control of the sea lanes and spice routes and secured an economic base. Economics often lead to politics, and politics to war. This was so in India under the British East India Company, and the Netherlands East India company was no different. Participating in local rivalries it gradually acquired control over the whole miscellany of islands and empires, sultanates and chiefdoms, and their scattered communities. As Dutch economic and political influence deepened the Javanese aristocracy continued to develop their refinement of culture in court etiquette and language, drama, textiles, and art well into the 1700s. The practical Dutch, however, using both free and forced labor reaped such profits from their coffee and other plantations that the sagging fortunes of the Netherlands were rescued, its debts reduced, and its merchant marine increased. Dutch brush-fire wars culminated in the suppression of Acheh because of its intolerable piracy in the Strait of Malacca. Beginning in 1873, the war dragged on for fully twenty-five years and cost a quarter of a million lives. By 1907 the Netherlands East Indies was organized much as it would be incorporated later into the Republic of Indonesia.

While independence (*merdeka*) may reveal more problems than it solves, it certainly transfers them to fresh shoulders. Merdeka brought into focus the two elitist groups on Java (the Javanese aristocracy and the Dutch-trained officials), and the provincial aspirants for advanced schooling and appointments to the new bureaucracy. The socioreligious *santri/abangan* divisions (as defined below) reappeared, but in the political arena. The *santri* bloc, of conservative Muslim groups, also included the merchants, and the Outer Island groups, who vied for power with the unorthodox (*abangan*) group of white-collar workers, Javanese laborers, and Communists. These and other fragmented factions in the country gave President Sukarno the opportunity to introduce his unifying concept of "Guided Democracy," a socialist program of government control adjusted to the traditional "Indonesian identity." This identity derives partly from past history and partly from present events.

Adat: Custom Based on Cooperation

A young man dressed in sarong, sandals, and the Muslim's black cap quoted an Indonesian saying in the national language, Bahasa Indonesia: "*Agama masuk dari laut, tetapi adat datang dari bukit.*" "Religion / comes in / from / the sea, but / custom / comes down / from / the mountain." That is, religion has been imported, but customs are our own. Much else came in besides religion, language for instance. (To begin with, there are two Sanskrit words in that sentence, *agama* and *tetapi*.) A constitution, representative government, statutory law, mercantilism and machinery, high-rise buildings, sliding windows, leather shoes, and much else came in from the outside. Very often such material, conceptual, and procedural items were accompanied by their foreign names for use in the description and handling of them. On the other hand, adat is local and embodies so ancient a pattern of behavioral standards or social mores that it has become both a set of customs and the local law. Outside the cities and their formal courts the local *lura* (headman or mayor) often acts as the justice of the peace. He may decide cases on the basis of his understanding of statutory law, or according to a Muslim Koranic precept, but usually on adat as known locally to everyone around him.

Throughout Indonesia (except New Guinea), village life is held together by certain basic principles. These include cooperation on community projects (road building, bridge repair, cleaning of irrigation ditches) and on neighborly assistance (house building, house moving); a family-like view of the community; open discussion at public meetings; and decision by consensus.

The Layered Beliefs

Another characteristic of Indonesia is the blending of time-related layerings of five strands of religious beliefs. (1) To the indigenous animism were added (2) the tenets of Buddhism in both Hinayana and Mahayana forms, (3) as well as various aspects of Hinduism. (4) Later the monotheistic beliefs and puritanical social conduct of Islam gradually became the main layer of religious synthesis. (5) With the Dutch and other Westerners came Christianity.

The first four strands have intermingled in common observance, and this blend constitutes the popular *abangan* (from Javanese *abang*, "red") tradition of peasant cultivators in the typical village. Purer forms of Islam characterize the market places and towns of northern Java, where the larger mosques and the more devout Muslims, the *santri*, may be found. Another philosophy of life has descended from the remnants of the old Javanese aristocracy, the *prijaji* (or *priyayi*). This philosophy, modified by the ideas and organization of the Dutch colonial rulers, has provided today's Westernized civil servants and government officials with a highly sophisticated, hierarchical, and faintly mystical outlook for life and the nation. They seem eons away from the humble villager. Yet there are no hard and fast demarcations between these various viewpoints, for the ideal Indonesian way allows to each his or her own preferred belief. So in the midst of Islam there are socially acceptable niches for Bali's Hinduism, Batak Christianity, Chinese Buddhism, and animism among the Papuans of New Guinea.

The Javanese

Were it not for the Javanese and the Javanese kingdoms there never would have been an Indonesia. Descendants of the Srivijaya, Madjapahit, and Mataram empires, the modern Javanese still preserve nine styles of language for speaking up to royalty and aristocracy and speaking down to commoners and juniors. It is this historic culture that inevitably sets apart Javanese officials and white-collar workers from their provincial counterparts, whose cultural and linguistic backgrounds lack these distinctions. To many Javanese the egalitarian national language, the Bahasa Indonesia, is almost an alien speech.

Markets serving four or five villages appear in all parts of Java. Hamlets and their tilled fields set among luxuriant vegetation alternate with settlements strung out along the dusty lowland roads or meandering rivers. The spartan furnishings of many homes—table and stools, bed, cupboard, kitchen utensils and dishes, and mats, sheets, and bolsters for children and visitors—do not indicate poverty but the simplicity of daily needs in a warm and salubrious climate. In many of these rectangular homes a married daughter dutifully nurtures her retired and aging parents in return for the inheritance of house and garden. Land, trees, and animals are shared equally by children of both sexes, whose marriages are designed to unite not only two individuals but, more importantly, two lineages.

Instruction and entertainment blend as soon as the radio is turned on, or the lights illuminate the sheet on which the puppet shadows are cast during the intensely popular narration of the *wayang kulit,* or shadow play. Amongst the throngs at these theatricals the black-capped Muslim merchants, and leaders of political parties or one of the endless number of action-oriented committees, are immediately discernible. Next to them are Chinese businessmen, officials in Western clothing, and matrons in colored blouses and brightly patterned *batik sarongs* (many-colored wrap-around skirts). Uniformed schoolchildren, messenger boys with their bicycles, bare-footed artisans and field laborers are there listening intently to the narrator against the background noises of passing horse carts and buses. The wit of the raconteur brings to life the royal intrigues and wars of a glorious yesteryear and brings uneasy shudders with folk stories of the rice goddess and malevolent spirits.

Just as the "Hindu-Javanese high culture" was the flowering of Indonesian society, so the subsequent overlays of the social and religious aspects of Islam, and commercial modernization, have produced the present standards of Indonesian conduct and enterprise. The diversity among the nation's peoples arises from the fact that each of the hundred or more distinguishable peoples preserves its own location, language, social organization, and sense of identity and pride, sometimes to the weakening of national loyalty.

THE FAR CORNERS OF INDONESIA

From the boulevards, universities, and airfields of Jakarta, the overseas shipping at Palembang, and the deadly volcanoes dominating Bali's templed hills, we look east to the fabled Spice Islands. Here in the Moluccas the sultan of Ternate once dominated the spice trade. Ambon, Ceram and Timor, all participate in the dual influences of trade and religion, both Islam and Christianity. Still further east the coastal areas of the Vogelkop (Bird's Head) of New Guinea (Irian Jaya) are Muslim areas. But inland the multitudes of peoples speaking Malayo-Polynesian and Papuan languages are mostly swidden farmers, technologically simple yet culturally complex.

Insular Southeast Asia resembles a gigantic triangle, and we can follow the base line from Acheh at the northwestern tip of Sumatra through Java, Bali, and Timor to half way through New Guinea. If then we could ride the destructive winds of a Pacific typhoon into the northern half of the triangle, we would see the islands of the Philippines, like a giant's fistful of 7,100 emeralds, scattered over 1,200 miles (1,920 km.) of the South China Sea.

THE PHILIPPINES

Weaving the Web of Identity

Before A.D. 1000 the Chinese, Borneans, and others took advantage of the northeast-southwest monsoon winds to trade or raid in the Philippines. Chinese traders came to the Manila area, to the island of Mindoro (then called Ma-i), and to the Calamian Islands nearby, and unloaded their goods on the beaches. Some months later they returned to pick up payments and new cargoes to sell in China. The huge glazed and ornamented jars which the traders brought in from South China from the A.D. 600s on became prized heirlooms in the Philippines. Somewhat later, in the 1200s the Sulu or Jolo Islands, located between the Philippines and Borneo, became "the trading crossroads of the Southern Seas," famous for their lustrous pearls and exotic merchandise.

Europe knew practically nothing about this island world and its peoples until Portuguese and Spanish reports came back in the early 1500s. In claiming the islands for Spain in 1521 Ferdinand Magellan prepared the way for Miguel Lopez de Legaspi, who arrived in 1564 with soldiers to conquer and friars to Christianize their peoples. Named for Philippe II of Spain, the islands were placed initially under the administration of the viceroy of Mexico. From this assignment came the era of trade with China, of the Spanish galleons, and of the millions of "Mexican dollars" flooding the cash drawers of East and Southeast Asia. Conquest, commerce, and kinship gradually united the country.

The Filipinos' pride in their locality of origin, language, and lineage finds further strength in bonds of a common ethnic group, religion, education, or occupation. Lowland Filipinos are commonly called Christians, meaning they belong to groups exposed to Christian teaching in Spanish times. Proportionate estimates for the major religious bodies show Roman Catholics to compose 80 percent, Protestants 9 percent, Muslims 6 percent, Animists 3 percent, and others 2 percent of the population. Sixty national minorities include the Moros, the Mangyans, and the highland-dwelling Igorots, Ifugaos, and Aeta (or Negritos), who in all number about five million persons. Specific names may be applied to lowlanders according to place of origin (Boholeño, from Bohol), or language (Tagalog, Ilonggo, Cuyonon), or by a word referring to both locality and language (Ilocano, Cebuano). Settlement programs for these lowlanders in the more sparsely settled areas have been so oppressive upon the tribal minorities (the traditional occupants), that PANAMIN (Presidential Arm for National Minorities) was set up to ensure the survival of these peoples on at least part of their ancestral lands.

Only one Philippine minority has been frustrated to the point of armed rebellion. When the Spaniards found Muslims in the southern Philippines, they called them Moros after the Muslim Moors of Morocco and Spain. Fiercely tenacious of their religious and linguistic distinction from the "Christian" lowlanders, the Moros steadily fought the Spanish, resented the Americans, and have maintained a smoldering war against the Manila government.

Sampling Public Transportation

In considering the Philippines as a textured whole, the geographic north-to-south alignment of these 7,100 islands resembles the longitudinal warp threads, and the nationwide system of interisland shipping and long distance bus lines constitute the horizontal weft threads, embroidered by airline routes. If one does not patronize the airplane for the trip from Moroland to Manila, a comfortable berth on a larger ship is available, or a deck cot chosen on a minesweeper-type steamer. There is nothing quite like the bright red intercity bus plying between port and city. Overloaded with chickens in baskets, fruit in crates, trussed pigs, clothes in hampers, assorted baggage, and many people, the bus careens at high

BOX 19-1 *INITIAL IMPRESSIONS*

Let us suppose our tour liner enters Manila Bay, past the historic island fortress of Corregidor, into waters that could harbor the fleets of all the world. We debark and taxi into this city of eight million people. We pass the gardens of the green Luneta Park and the Jose Rizal statue and on into the Intramuros, the old area of the Spanish walled city. Continuing past government buildings and across the steel Pasig bridge, we roll over the underground plaza, note the imposing cathedral on our left, and stop amid the gaily dressed throngs in downtown Manila. The name Manila, really May-nila', is compounded from the Tagalog words *may,* "to have," and *nila',* "a red water-borne flower." The southern islands, the Visayas, were named from the Indonesian empire of Sri-vijaya, of which they once were a part. The Spanish contributed many names, such as Mindoro, contracted from Min d'Oro, "mine of gold," and Corregidor, meaning "corrector" or "magistrate," for the island fortress at the entrance to Manila Bay.

Buses or jeepneys (minibuses on jeep chassis) take us to the outer-circle road and the prestigious University of the Philippines, the leader among several hundred colleges and universities in Greater Manila.

The skyline is filled with flour-milling towers and factories processing foods, tobacco products, textiles, and automobiles, an oil refinery, and large clusters of radio antennae. Further into the countryside lie extensive salt pans near the Bay, and at the Los Banyos research center some of the world's best miracle grains grow in neat paddies, as well as corn, tobacco, fruits, and vegetables. (Corn, cassava, tobacco, and sweet potato were Spanish contributions.) In the hills lumbering and livestock are big business. Coastal fishing utilizes everything from one-person *bancas* (hollowed-out canoes with double outriggers and perhaps mast and sail) to large "PT-boat" craft operating mechanical lift-nets. Turning north to the tribal areas near Baguio we find some of the richest gold mines in Asia, and elsewhere silver, copper, iron ore, and chromite. The farms of two thirds of the country's fifty million people carpet the plains and panel the hillsides of over seven hundred of its verdant islands.

speed around steep and hilly roads, protected only by the saint's picture on the dashboard.

Typical Lowlanders: The Tagalogs

Most prominent among the lowland populations, the Tagalogs occupy the broad, rich ricelands north and south of the commercial and administrative capital, Manila. Since they make up the relatively well-to-do population surrounding Manila, and most of the officials in this national center for education, art, communications, and government, and since their language is the basis for the national language, Filipino, the Tagalogs feel no need to conceal their well-earned self-satisfaction, or their wealth. In the suburbs, sandwiched between ornate mansions and shopping areas, one may find a typical country-style house. Set ten feet up on its stout posts, the base walls and flooring of stained and polished lumber are topped by upper walls of woven bamboo. Beneath the roof of galvanized iron or thatch, the sliding windows are set with tiny panes made of thin, semi-translucent seashells. At the foot of the broad wooden steps a visitor will call "Tao po!"— "Sir, (there's) someone (here)"—to be answered promptly by a cheery "Tuloy kayo!" —"Come on up, all of you." Ushered into the guest room and seated in a cool wicker chair the visitor will be offered tea, coffee, or a soft drink and, if late in the afternoon, expected to stay for supper. The visitor will already know, or the conversation will reveal, that the Tagalog family relates closely to both paternal and maternal lines, each with its mutual rights and duties. If the host is a teacher or professional man he will be wearing the *barong Tagalog* (Tagalog [formal] upper garment, which is both shirt and jacket). Everyone will be barefooted, of course, for shoes are always left at the foot of the steps outside or on the veranda. The hostess, if formal, might wear the lacy and starched blouse with high puffed sleeves at the shoulders, and a long skirt, a style patterned after Spanish originals. Should the visitor be passing through town, a mat, sheet, pillow and even a mosquito net, will be provided, and the night spent in comfort on the polished floor near the rest of the family and guests. The family is up at daylight, and the guest is provided with a substantial breakfast of rice, dried fish, vegetables, and chilis, or perhaps of rolls, margarine and coffee before leaving. Payment would be an embarrassment, but to bring on the next occasion a small gift or specialty not locally available is appreciated. This is the sincere "Philippine courtesy" for which the nation is famous.

Highlanders: The Bontoc Igorots

Houses of another kind can be seen from a mountain bus climbing steeply into Bontoc Igorot country 106 miles or so (170 km.) north of Manila. Twenty or more feet (6+ m.) high, like a very narrow A-frame hut, the thatch roof drops to within 18 inches (0.5 m.) of the ground, thus acting as both roof and walls. Stepping up, one crouches through a low doorway on to the main floor, which is perhaps 12 by 16 feet (4x5 m.) in area. The earth and stone fireplace near the door sends out heat enough for the one room and for the small upper platform where goods and smoked foods are kept. Some of the family also sleep on the upper platform. As with the Ifugao, so here among the Bontoc, a guest is expected to drink beer or wine with the host. If the guest drinks—fine; he is welcome. If not, he does not drink because he is at variance with the host. In time past the nondrinking guest could expect to be summarily speared. Even today it is a serious breach of customary etiquette. On the hillside below the house the pig occupies its stone pen, and near it an upright stick with a bundle of grass and twigs touched red with blood indicates the spirit shrine of the home. A chicken has been sacrificed to appease the spirits.

The Town as a Blending Mechanism

Northeast of Bontocland, in a country town in Isabella province, the bus will deposit the visitor opposite the inn in the short single street. If wise, the visitor heads for the mayor's house and requests lodging, which is always readily and courteously given. On this occasion it happens to be end-of-year graduation at the local academy. As special guest speaker the mayor delivers the appropriate "advices" in the dominant language, Ilocano, with its rather jerky glottal stops, then smoothly says the same thing in the liquid flow of the local language, Ibanag. Finally he gives a brief summary in English for the benefit of the guests and perhaps the Chinese storekeepers. Others present that evening are some tribal Gaddang people. A Chinese merchant also is there, together with several prominent persons representing stable and happy Spanish-Filipino and Chinese-Filipino marriages. The only ones not present are the members of the Negrito Aeta party, whose loincloth dress does not suit this lowland town. Jungle hunter and outside visitor, farmer and town-dweller mingle in the town, which serves as a blending mechanism. When it comes time for the visitor to leave, the farewell resounds, "When are you coming back? Come and visit us again!"

Part VII

Conclusion: The Mandala Completed

Chapter 20

The Whence
and Whither of Asia

Few people would venture definitive statements on the future of Asia. It is sensible, however, to examine some of the factors and conditions in Asia's past and present which might help us understand the directions in which the continent's peoples seem to be moving. For this purpose we may return to the mandala at the beginning of the book, and use it as a framework of inquiry and exploration.

THE MANDALA'S QUESTIONS

There are many ways to contemplate a mandala and the complex interrelationships it contains. The discussion here concentrates on the questions in the outer circle:

1. The "Who?" of Asia's Peoples
2. The "Whence?" of Asia's Uniqueness
3. The "What?" of Asia's Environments
4. The "Why?" of Asia's Dynamics
5. The "Whither?" of Asia's Destinies

THE "WHO?" OF ASIA'S PEOPLES

If all the world's peoples were paraded together today, about six of every ten persons would be an Asian. As intercommunication developed among them, princes and sheiks, soldiers and fellahin from Arab states could mingle cautiously with Cypriots, Turks, and Israelis. Palestinians and Kurds, Pathans and Afghans could exchange news of their various struggles for recognition and independence. The multicultural communities of Soviet Asia and Southeast Asia could accept the monocultural Chinese, Koreans, and Japanese.

All these peoples are conscious of their membership in a cultural community, with a fresh focus on and loyalty to the nation-state. While to the Muslim theologians and rulers the separation of religion and state is blatant heresy, in the Communist world the State is everything. Israel, India, South Korea, and the Philippines represent Asian nations whose political philosophies stress the secular stance of national policy, while preserving both religious integrity and religious freedom. Actually, each Asian nation is a state of mind as much as it is a political unit.

When fifty nations became charter members of the United Nations Assembly in 1945, few if any envisioned three times that number less than forty years later. Few foresaw that the roll-call of "Who's Who" in the world would soon list not only the major nations and the ex-colonial ones, but also such new countries as Israel, Pakistan, and Singapore, and such small communities as the Maldives, Qatar, and Bahrain.

The modern entity of the nation-state has overridden (or made itself coterminous with) older units such as kingdom, sultanate, and tribe. The modern state also has absorbed traditional solidarities such as the Bedouin and Ainu, or split them apart, as was the case with the Kurds and Mongols, Tajiks and Pathans. Communities large and small must adjust to new political and social patterns.

One of the benefits of the modern age to Asians has been longer life and a lower death rate. Yet this increased vitality brings with it the problem of burgeoning members. (Figure 20-1 illustrates the situation.) China already has one billion people. India probably will have that many by the year 2000. Each country adds about 15 million persons annually despite large-scale birth-control campaigns, so that, of the projected world population of six billion people by the year 2000, 4.66 billion will be in the less-developed nations. Asia also participates in the trend toward bigger cities. One third of the world's cities of 900,000 and over are located in Asia, including seven of the top twelve. Demographic statisticians project a stable world population of some fourteen billion people by about 2030, and many would hope such stability might foster world peace.

For all these peoples and nations the search for identity and the celebration of recognition are like twin bells ringing in the human spirit. Asia's progress and prosperity likewise have emanated considerably from the efforts of such men as Kemal Ataturk and Mahatma Gandhi who, seeing the problems realized that "Where there is no vision, the people perish" (Proverbs 29:18) and endeavored to guide their nations toward the realization of a vision.

Ultimately the "Who?" of Asia's peoples is each individual Asian, the Humanity at the center of the mandala. To each individual, life has its own purpose and hope, bafflement and wonder. An immense wealth of human *being* fills Asia, people being people, from the Arctic to the Equator, and from the remotest heart-

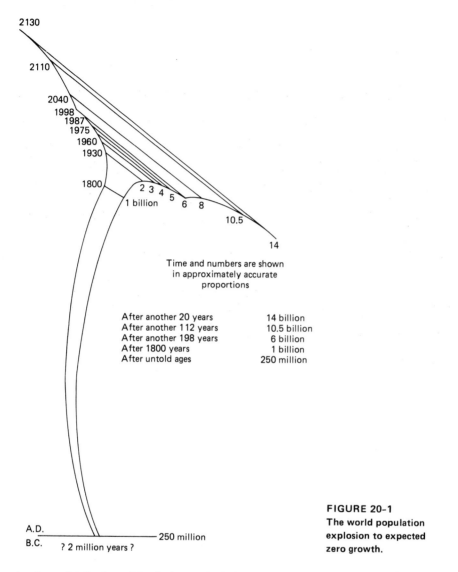

Time and numbers are shown
in approximately accurate
proportions

After another 20 years	14 billion
After another 112 years	10.5 billion
After another 198 years	6 billion
After 1800 years	1 billion
After untold ages	250 million

FIGURE 20-1
The world population
explosion to expected
zero growth.

land to the furthest island shore. And, just as no generality should obscure the Humanity who *are* Asia, so no statistic can separate them from their past.

THE "WHENCE?" OF ASIA'S UNIQUENESS

As tomorrow stems from today, so the present is the offspring of the past. The ultimate "Whence?" of Asia's peoples still remains hidden in the mists of that past. After perhaps 100,000 years of hunting-gathering came plant cultivation (15,000 B.C.), villages and towns, pottery (6800 B.C.), bronze age metallurgy

(3600 B.C.), and the basic shapes of things today. Civilization was nourished in several cradles, for just as the invention of writing added a new dimension to language, so the interchanges along the ancient trade routes cross-fertilized the civilizations of Egypt, Mesopotamia, the Indus Valley, and, a little later, China. Where the winds of change have blown lightly or never reached, in the fastnesses of forest and mountain, peoples from thousands of years ago would blend easily into villages of some sixty years ago in similar environments from Central India to the Philippines and Indonesia. But today is different.

Three major winds of change have blown over Asia during the past three millenia. The first wind of change was the founding and dissemination of the major expansionist religions: Zoroastrianism, Buddhism, Daoism (Taoism), Confucianism, Judaism, Christianity, and Islam. Second was the movement of nomadic peoples, from the Scythians to the Mongols and the Turkish confederations. The third wind was the coming of technologized industry. Cultures, residences, and political alignments were affected throughout the continent. The winds of change that developed scientists among the Mongols, and doctors among the Yakuts, also led to Indian-designed and built frigates and satellites, and to the colossal expertise that enabled Japan, in less than forty years after leaving a state of feudalism, to build battleships that destroyed the Russian fleet at the battle of Tsushima Strait in 1905. A fourth wind of change could be postulated, the wind of new ideas. Industrialism, individualism, nationalism, and communism have profoundly affected the patternings and problems of the nations internally, and externally have altered some of their territorial boundaries as well as their international alignments.

The maps of Asia show national identities and boundaries resulting from the pressures of international alignments (Figure 1-2). Note the present nations arising out of the break-up of the Turkish Empire after World War I (Figure 3-3) and the new nations of South Asia formed following the division of what was called British India (Figure 7-1). The establishment of Southeast Asia's entities is based on: international power plays (Vietnam, Laos, Kampuchea); geographic separation (Philippines, Indonesia); ethnic identity (Singapore); and the amalgamation of previously discrete sultanates (Malaysia) (Figure 17-1). Most of these Asian nations display intense concern to develop a sense of national identity, of "Indianness" in India, or of ethno-religious identity among the Arab peoples of Southwest Asia, for instance. Amid the bewildering diversity of "nationalities" in Soviet Asia, the U.S.S.R. likewise is endeavoring to foster the concept of a single Soviet citizenship.

THE "WHAT?" OF ASIA'S ENVIRONMENTS

The environments of Asia include such basic elements as the physical geography and climate of any given region; the outward factors of technology and industry; plus the cultural perception and social utilization of the prevailing political and religious surroundings. Daily contacts with the environment loom large to the participants: the removal of shoes before entering a mosque, a Hindu temple, or a Shinto shrine; the highly structured social space of a Mongol yurt or a reception hall in a Chinese home; or the caste discrimination that allows some to enter an Indian village store and determines who must remain outside.

The square inside the mandala suggests yet another approach to Asia's environments, consideration of the four elemental constituents of the universe: time, space, energy, and order.

Time

We have here considered "time" from three aspects: linear, cyclic, and relevant. The Western concept of time is basically *linear* and may be perceived from different angles for diverse purposes. The preceding chapters have illustrated the *maturational* view of time as societies grew into nations, accumulating their stores of knowledge, culture, and technology as events and processes followed each other through *chronological* or *calendrical* time. Nations grapple with the problem of *elapsed* time: the period between present stages of development and the fulfillment of their successive Five-Year Plans, and the culmination of current and seemingly inexorable trends. When will be the end of the arms race, of discrimination against minorities, of power squeezes against selected peoples and nations? When will malaria be eradicated, poverty remedied, famine averted, the desert sands halted, and water conserved? How long will it take for the desires of all humanity for peace and food, security and dignity, to be finally fulfilled?

The traditional historiography of China, and perhaps other Asian nations, stresses *cyclical* time, the historical rise, flourishing, decay, and fall of dynasties, as a repetitive process whose sequences of events have a fundamental sameness and differ only in their details. The cycles of years, seasons, days, and nights compounded together form the Chinese 60-year cycle. This cycle is the basis for the Chinese "Farmer's Almanac," for scheduling seasonal activities, and for the Chinese astrologer's calculations for fixing auspicious dates for weddings and the compatibility of prospective marriage partners.

In practice, the daily round for the millions of common people is a matter of *relevant* time, what is to be done now or in relation to a specific event. Any of the other aspects of time are of importance to most individuals only as they relate to fulfillment of assigned responsibilities. Time lost here may make impossible the prompt action necessary to avert war, to slow population growth, or to preserve political integrity. The nuclear arms race relates directly to relevant short-term and long-term considerations of time.

Space

General viewpoints. The significance of space is its *liveability*. A Tibetan yak herder would find crowded Hong Kong insufferably small, while a Calcutta businessman would be lost in the expanse of the Bornean jungle. What is the *carrying capacity* of a given region? One third of Asia's land mass is mountain and desert, one third steppeland and savannas, and perhaps less than one third will sustain any form of year-round agriculture. A third concept, that of *limited good*, comes into play when Israel diverts Jordan river water to irrigate the Negev, thus leaving less for Jordanian farmers to use, and when increasing thousands of Sri Lankans and millions of Chinese clamor for additional *lebensraum* (space to live in). Potentially devastating is the *empty land syndrome*, whereby each more advanced level of technology successively takes over land sites for more intensive exploitation. Asia's hundreds of expanding cities commonly take over good arable land that then disappears under asphalt and concrete. The reverse effort animates projects to reclaim parts of the Taklimakan desert for farming and to reforest mountains and hills in Israel and China.

Technologized Industry and Space

Technologized industry has been primarily responsible for some of the conditions mentioned above, for such industry perceives the environment as an inanimate entity whose only worth is its value in production. Even the *biosphere* is treated like a polluted dumpyard rather than as a complex living universe. Such industry also views people mainly as cogs in the machinery of procurement, production, and distribution of its products. Actually, the ethos of technologized industry perceives the entire world as empty land awaiting exploitation. Just as the agricultural transformation once drastically altered the earth, so the industrial revolution is changing it again. From Siberia to India and from Israel to Japan industries are variously preparing to drill for oil in the Arctic or the raging sea, manufacture rare and delicate crystals, produce compounds and medicines in space laboratories, or mine manganese nodules on the ocean floor. New strains of grain and fruit have been developed to replace taiga forest and pastoral steppeland and to reclaim the edges of the desert. Thousands of factories have been set up from the railroads and rivers of Central Asia to the seacoast export zones in Korea, Taiwan, and the Philippines, to produce everything from steel to textiles to chemicals. The price paid for material benefits and foreign currency in short-term values appears to be in the long-term effects of massive air and water pollution. There are no frontiers left to act as buffer zones, and the road ahead must be one of disciplined development.

Choke points and hot spots.   A crucial aspect of Asian space is the presence of "choke points" and "hot spots." Choke points are strategically located passageways through which traffic must pass. The ancient Silk Road was fraught with them, and today this region contains Chinese and Soviet space facilities that can lead to confrontation between their armies. Asia contains more than half of the major choke points in the world today: the Suez Canal, the Bab al-Mandab (el-Mandeb), the Strait of Hormuz, and the Strait of Malacca. Choke points on land could include the bridges at Istanbul, the Khyber Pass, and the Dzungarian Gate. The oil and gas pipelines across Jordan and Syria, and from Siberia to Europe, as well as the major shipping lanes, constitute elongated choke points. The Strait of Hormuz, for instance, passes tankers in and out of the Persian Gulf at the rate of one every two minutes, supplying half of Europe's oil and three quarters of Japan's oil needs. Terrorists are pointing to other choke points, the major air terminals, as part of the growing number of hot spots.

The hot spots of ongoing or potential international conflict include not only the Persian Gulf but also the Eastern Mediterranean region of Israel, Lebanon, and Syria, the Iraq-Iran war zone, the Russian-occupied areas of Afghanistan, and the eastern and southern sections of Mainland Southeast Asia. These hot spots may be heated through such doorways of threat as the eighteenth parallel in Korea, the American-built naval and air bases in Vietnam now utilized by the Russians, and the island of Diego Garcia in the Indian Ocean. The stakes are high in this deadly game of international chess, where the control of space—as circles of containment, strangulation points, and doorways of threat—constitutes the layout of dominance. The hostility or peace of Asian space confronts the future—and may determine it.

Energy

Human and animal labor, wind and water power, mineral, mechanical, solar, biomass, and nuclear energy, all find practical and scientific expression somewhere in Asia. Political structures affect where people live relative to energy sources, as when the U.S.S.R. and China combine the tapping of energy sources with the dispersal of expanding populations by building new cities close to those sources, and then linking the cities with transportation systems. The insufficiency of energy sources for rural populations has led to mass migrations of the unemployed to the cities, as seen in Karachi, Calcutta, and Manila. In Japan such energy is available, and Tokyo is a flourishing giant, one of the largest cities on earth.

India and China, with large and advanced industrial and scientific super-structures, are systematically grappling with the drastic problems of huge populations that must be provided with work opportunities. These two countries and Indonesia have extensive programs for employing otherwise idle hands in agriculture, cottage industries, fishing, and resource management. Many Third World nations, lacking a literate and trained industrial superstructure, face the problem of adjusting their agricultural economies to meet survival needs on the one hand, and of wanting to share in the affluence and progress of developed nations on the other.

One of the world's headaches is the possession, distribution, payment for, and use of oil as the present primary source of energy for industry and transportation. The oil-needy nations of the world were held to ransom by the oil-producing nations, whose billions of dollars of oil revenues threatened for a while to unbalance the structure of international finances. The gap between the "have" and the "have not" nations was dangerously widened as many developing countries were forced near to bankruptcy. Potential "hot spots" loom north of Japan, where Japanese and Soviet interests conflict over oil resources near Sakhalin Island, and in the South China Sea, where potential oil fields lie under the Sunda Shelf in areas claimed by China and Vietnam. Two other problems with wide implications face the world. One is the supply of water for personal and industrial use. Millions now facing thirst and famine, and the long-dead cities of Central Asia, Arabia, and Africa testify to the dread results of losing this key energy-supporting factor. The other problem involves hungry and frustrated sectors of humanity who do not have the capacity to mesh their bullock-and-hoe economy with machine-based technology. In an almost primeval sense, all cultures, societies, and patterns of economic activity are energy systems, and their breakdown means a chaos of energy. Only well-ordered energy can sustain human survival.

Order

When implemented in practical use, the concepts of ecology and harmony (stressed early in Chapter 1) can ensure the preservation of the environment and the prosperity of the human race.

Five elements are essential for human survival: food, shelter, water, warmth, and a spiritual dynamic. (It is true that "Man does not live by bread alone.") Communities must add another element: order, in the sense of community-wide cooperation. The various institutions of the United Nations and the provisions of regional pacts are generally designed to preserve order among the nations. The enemies of order include forces which cause divisions within the nation and instability on the international level. For Eurasian agricultural societies of the Middle Ages, the Mongols constituted just such a prime enemy of order.

Only a balanced patterning, wherein every constituent nation is conceded its intrinsic value, can provide international order. Humanity neither needs, nor should there be any place for, the unbalanced pattern wherein one nation or clique subjugates another. It is unnecessary to list such disorderly actions as the Soviet invasion of Afghanistan, the Vietnamese invasion of Kampuchea, and the Turkish invasion of Cyprus, where long-term domination occurred. But it may be helpful to ascertain why conflicts stymied the efforts of United Nations peacekeeping forces in Cyprus, the Sinai, and Lebanon. And it may be instructive that the nonregimented nations of Asia have the better record of peace and the higher standards of living, based on the dynamic initiatives of personal dignity and free choice.

THE "WHY?" OF ASIA'S PROBLEMS

Asia's many problems run deep. Few answers respond to the question "Why?" The problems arise mainly from within humanity itself, and the answers necessarily must come from readjustments in the attitudes and actions of individuals, multitudes of them, and the nations composed of them. Let us scan some of the problem areas.

Poverty.   The less-developed countries are characterized by poverty, whose roots and tendrils pervade society. Grants of money, tractors, and powdered milk are short-term palliatives. Only multiple major adjustments at both ends—"society" and "the poor"—will produce permanent society-wide solutions.

Warfare.   This century has been described as the bloodiest in human history. Tens of millions have died in at least sixty wars, many of them in Asia. Millions more have perished in some sixty-four civil wars. If "Love your enemies" is unrealistic, then at least "Live and let live" would change confrontation into toleration.

Wealth.   Money, power, privilege, prestige, and even health are very unevenly distributed in Asian countries. Money, as in the petroleum producing countries, has widened the economic gap between the affluent and the poor, even though billions have been spent on social improvements. Political power may be totalitarian (as in Soviet Asia, China, and North Korea), religious and then political (as in Iran), or secular. Privilege is commonly an acquired status, as in the case of party members in communist countries, who have access to perquisites not available to the general populace. Prestige may be class related in terms of lineage, education, occupation, or position, as in Japan and Indonesia; or, as in India, prestige may be based upon status dictated by religion.

Fortunately for most of Asia, with increased supplies and better distribution of food, there is a general lift in life expectancy. The increasing role of industry and education in Asian countries is giving rise to a middle class of professionals, business leaders, scientists, and teachers, who have better social amenities and national influence than their predecessors.

Wants and expectations. Credit the mass media and films for broadcasting visions of more food, better clothes, luxury housing, education, and idealistic lifestyles among the myriad Asians who lack these comforts. Expectations are presented where wants remain unfulfilled. Each want fulfilled prods a rise in expectations. The high school youth of China, disenchanted with unfulfillable expectations of party promises, pose a multidimensional social problem. Youth in Japan may join the growing cult of "tribal" (*zokir*) membership, don its regalia, practice its rituals, and be traditionally deviant. Or they may join a militant group and, armed with helmet, shield, steel chain, or pipe, give pitched battle to the police. The negative aspect of education is that it often discomfits people for the life which circumstances oblige them to live. Yet nations consider widespread basic education (indoctrination) as a first necessity for their people.

Ideologies. Soviet Communism and Western individualism vie with each other and with various types of Asian faith and fanaticism. Shi'ite fervor in Iran, the Muslim Brotherhood of younger Muslims, Israel's fundamentalist Gush Emunim or Bloc of the Faithful, and radical Buddhist sects in Japan such as the Soka Gakkai and the Rissho-koseikai, in part represent reactions against the disjunctive and secularizing influences of modernization. People hunger for wholeness.

Given the current medley of nationalities, languages, cultures, religions, and aspirations existing in Asia under widely different political and economic systems, it is easy to be pessimistic about achieving peace, security, and significant equality of comforts in the foreseeable future. Yet such is exactly the deliberate goal of socialist India, Communist China, autocratic Arabia, Islamic Iran, and bustling Singapore. The long-term well-being of Asia and Asians can be obtained only through adding a spirit of tolerance to the existing value systems and technologies, and harnessing all available resources to the chariot of progress to achieve freedom from want.

THE "WHITHER?" OF ASIA'S DESTINY

We have seen that in recent decades Asians have become better informed and respected than previously; they are better clothed and fed; and they participate more intimately in national politics and more directly in world affairs. We have seen the paradox that, while condemning the spirit and practice of colonialism worldwide, Asians war upon and colonize each other for the same age-old reasons: territory, religion, resources, national security, or economic and imperialistic control. As Asians have become more nationalistic (and therefore separatist), they also have become more conscious of their Asianness in a contracting world, bound by bands of instant communications into an ever-smaller compass. Communications have graduated from courier to cable, and the lonely lookout on the hilltop has been replaced by the satellite in the sky. Whither, then, is Asia going, and how fast?

The answer to the preceding question seems to be at cross-directions and in countercurrents with each other. The rush to have a place in the future may be simultaneous with a withdrawal into the past, as in the case of Iran. Highly conservative enclaves may argue on religious grounds to be exempted from the demands of the modern state, as in Israel. In a middle course there is an attempt to adapt the old and the new to make a harmonious present, as in Malaysia. New political and economic forces may alter a traditional culture, while the kinship and social interaction patterns of that culture are the only thing that enables the faulty and imposed economic system to work, as in the non-Russian communes in Soviet Central Asia (Humphrey 1983). Century-old invasion plans may become a reality, as in the Soviet occupation of Afghanistan, bringing one step nearer the goal of a southern port for the Soviet military empire (Luttwak 1983). Moreover, new nations enter the international arena, as did Brunei on January 1, 1984.

While some major hot spots fill the newspapers, some seemingly small incidents harbor great portent. For example, in the summer of 1983 Vietnam invaded and established a base on the Layang-layang Islands in Malaysian territorial waters about 150 miles off the west coast of Borneo. Malaysia promptly established a counter-base on nearby islands. Two factors appear to be in the background: first a Soviet desire for a base in this strategic sea route area (note the presence of British and/or United States bases on Diego Garcia Island in the Indian Ocean, Taiwan, and the Philippines). Second, the Layang-layang Islands are located on the Sunda Shelf, which is thought to contain some of the largest oil reserves in the world.

Other Asian crosscurrents surface in the abundance of automobiles and a dire shortage of cooking fuel in many areas; a desire both to be left alone and to receive substantial aid from outside; and the clash and interaction of modern ideas with traditional ideologies. Yet this interplay of cross- and countercurrents is neither new nor limited to Asia; *what is new* is the worldwide intensity.

Operational Dualisms

The trend toward secularism spurred by the achievements of science and industry is counterbalanced by the revival of supernaturalism in the religious activities of Islam, Christianity, Hinduism, and Buddhism, and also of spiritism. The authoritarianism of dictatorships, military juntas, and communism is paralleled by the rise of individualism in the political philosophies of the "free" countries and in the effects of wage labor upon the extended family system. The self-protective shield of nationalism runs alongside a growing recognition of the practical need for global cooperation. The value systems, education, capital, and equipment embodied in the concept of modernism (needed for economic survival) are challenging traditionalism as the bastion of ethnic and social stability. Pleas for peace and "ban the bomb" proceed alongside an accelerating race to sell armaments and to stockpile nuclear arsenals. Heavy industry has been the elusive glamor goal of many countries, while low-level industries in village (India), commune (China), and kibbutz (Israel) have provided practical solutions to underemployment and worker frustration. Industrial protectionism to nurse local industries and jobs is eroded by multinational firms which establish branches in competing countries or where labor is cheap.

Asia has been caught up in this maelstrom of conflicting ideologies and alternative national lifestyles and political alignments. China, India, Pakistan, and other nations continue to struggle with lagging rural economies and high-technology aspi-

FIGURE 20-2
Temple scene in Bali.

rations. Countries owning natural resources try to balance with exports their need to import energy, processed foods, goods, and machinery from the industrialized nations; if that fails they may try to force a balanced exchange by holding for ransom the natural resources the industrialized nations need.

Another Perspective

Thus far we have considered the mandala of Asia from a Western "rational" cause-and-effect standpoint. But other perspectives have equal validity.

Perhaps the best way to understand the effect of the technologized industrial wind of change on Asia is in terms of the Chinese concepts of yin and yang: *yin* the negative, the inward and downward, the night, cold; *yang* the positive, the outward and upward, the day, hot. Like the day and the night they interact, as one increases the other decreases; and neither exists without the other.

The larger the yang grows, so also the larger grows the yin it contains: the more certain aspects of technologized industry grow, the greater also the corresponding negative aspects. One yang aspect of technologized industry is that electronic communications and speedy transportation have linked people who otherwise would not have known one another and have made available goods which otherwise would not be obtainable in a region; the corresponding yin is that the pressures and patterns of modernity tend to break down extensive family ties and regional working and living patterns, often leaving loneliness and maladjustment in their place. The productive and scientific yang is the ready abundance of material goods and greater public health (gone are the days when within a month cholera swept tens of thousands from the earth); the yin is environmental depredation and pollution, and the problems of overpopulation. Further outworkings of this analysis are readily apparent. The impact of the technologized industrial transformation on Asia has become critical and will greatly alter the future.

Purposes, Rights, and Solutions

Amid the bewildering alternatives available to governments, groups, and individuals today, there seems to be an unwanted but unavoidable spirit of urgency, of being driven. Nations want more nationalism, world leaders want more internationalism; regional blocs want more internal cohesion and external confrontation; and the trend toward splinter-group terrorism is hardly balanced by organized protection. In the maelstrom of conflicting wants, and despite the continued technical missions sent by the advanced nations to the less endowed countries (and there are many such missions), two utterly divergent streams of purpose and endeavor appear to be emerging. The one stream is the outgrowth of frustration and desperation, leading to terrorism and revolution; the other is the search for certainty, however defined. For some certainty is the ultimate absolute, Deity; for some certainty is a world ruler; for others certainty (and stability) is international consensus.

Another critical area of Asian and worldwide concern relates to the definition of human rights. The Western-type democracies define human rights as (1) intrinsic rights or basic personal freedoms ("life, liberty, and the pursuit of happiness"), and (2) conferred rights granted by law. Such a definition restricts the powers of the state. The authoritarian governments recognize only conferred rights. By legislating what the citizen may do, they restrict the options of the people. Several nations attempt to steer a middle course between unrestricted freedom and iron-bound authoritarianism. Because one or another of these political philosophies affects every aspect of their social, legal, and personal lives the peoples and nations of Asia will be wrestling with the alternatives for a long time—as to whether their societies will provide them with a free choice, reasonable latitude, or with imposed decisions.

What humanity needs is not more education, inventions, or comforts. We already have all the knowledge necessary to use efficiently all the technology required for comfort and all the political expertise to fulfil freely all our aspirations. We need to act responsibly according to that knowledge. Representative of these desires are the calls by governments and peoples for a stable world order based on mutual respect and cooperation. For it is the hope of each individual on earth that there will be a worthwhile future both now and for coming generations. The earth itself and all that dwell on it form the mandala of life.

The Mandala's Answers

It is not in the nature of a mandala to answer questions, but rather to serve as a guide to understanding. The mandala used here for consideration of Asia applies equally well to the entire globe.

Both hope and desperation tinge the fate of the earth. Desperation stems from the global scope of many of the problems discussed with reference to Asia. These include: (1) destruction of the environment from the pressures of overpopulation, (2) the exploitative demands of technologized industry, as well as (3) politically enforced detrimental uses; (4) the real threat that modern transportation may cause the rapid spread of lethal diseases, and of fauna inimical to other biosystems; and (5) the threat of nuclear war. The four horsemen of the apocalypse—war, famine, disease, and natural calamity—may yet again cut a deadly swathe across the earth.

Hope arises from the growing global involvement in several patterns noted for Asia, including: (1) the increasing realization that our world is so interconnected that a major rupture anywhere must affect everyone; (2) a steady improvement in the use and application of already extant knowledge to better the quality of life and improve the environment; (3) the interaction and mutual enrichment of various spiritual and philosophical traditions; and (4) the international sharing and cooperation of many scientific and technical projects.

Perhaps the most profound hope lies in the incredibly beautiful mandala which is the earth itself—a precious living wonder amid the cold vast reaches of the universe—which raises thoughts beyond conscious understanding, and should help people to put aside their selfishness and squabbles to share in the grandeur of life in all its varieties throughout the world. It is difficult for an individual to lift his or her eyes from the incessant demands of daily life to see a greater being. But the basic message of Asia's major religions is an enormous hope for each individual. The profound vision of the cosmic island Earth, and the fertile crosscurrents of modern thought, might so influence many individuals that their combined actions could effect a deep change in the course of world events, and bring about a new hope for the future. From the mandala's questions we have come to the center.

At the center of the mandala, Humanity, the multipart entity, becomes a single whole. Asia, that vast human space, is at once the summation of its individuals' lives, and the embodiment of them. And each individual Asian stands at the center of the mandala, both forming it and being formed by it, yet in a certain sense also constituting the entirety of the mandala. The same applies to all peoples —everywhere on earth.

> Each brush-stroke in Chinese calligraphy must have
> a beginning, a middle, and an end.
> May this book be one brush-stroke in
> the calligraphy of understanding Asia and its peoples.

Bibliography

GENERAL

ARGÜLLES, JOSE and MIRIAM ARGÜLLES 1972 *Mandala*. Boulder, Colo.: Shambhala.

Asia 1984 yearbook 1983 Hong Kong: Far Eastern Economic Review.

Atlas of Man 1978 London: Cavendish Editions.

Atlas of the world 1981 Fifth edition. Washington, D.C.: National Geographic Society.

BELLAH, ROBERT N., ed. 1965 *Religion and progress in modern Asia*. New York: Free Press.

The Holy Bible

CALDER, NIGEL 1983 *Timescale: an atlas of the fourth dimension*. New York: Viking.

CLARK, GRAHAME 1977 *World prehistory in new perspective*. Third edition. London: Cambridge University Press.

CRESSEY, GEORGE B. 1963 *Asia's lands and peoples: a geography of one-third of the earth and two-thirds of its peoples*. Third edition. New York: McGraw-Hill.

DEAN, VERA MICHELES 1966 *The nature of the non-western world*. New York: NAL.

ELLENWOOD, DeWITT C. and CYNTHIA H. ENLOE, eds. 1981 *Ethnicity and the military in Asia*. New Brunswick, N.J.: Transaction Books.

FAIRSERVIS, WALTER A. Jr. 1981 *Asia, traditions and treasures*. New York: H. N. Abrams.

FREDERIC, LOUIS, compiler 1977–1984 *Encyclopedia of Asian civilizations.* Paris: Editions Jean-Michel Place.

FÜRER-HAIMENDORF, CHRISTOPH von 1981 *Asian highland societies in perspective.* New Delhi: Sterling Publications.

HAWKES, JACQUETTA, and SIR LEONARD WOOLLEY 1963 *History of mankind, Vol. 1: prehistory and the beginnings of civilization.* New York: Harper & Row.

——— 1979 *Atlas of world prehistory.*

LINCOLN, BRUCE 1981 *Priests, warriors, and cattle: a study in the ecology of religions.* Berkeley: University of California Press.

LUTTWAK, EDWARD N. 1983 *The grand strategy of the Soviet Union.* New York: Saint Martin's Press.

MANDER, LINDEN 1942 Lectures delivered at the University of Washington, Seattle.

METRAUX, GUY S. and FRANCOIS CROUZET 1965 *The new Asia: readings in the history of mankind.* New York: NAL.

MILLER, ELMER S. 1979 *Introduction to cultural anthropology.* Englewood Cliffs, N.J.: Prentice-Hall.

The New International Atlas 1982 Chicago: Rand McNally.

NOBE, KENNETH C. and RAJAN K. SAMPATH, eds. 1983 *Issues in Third World development.* Boulder, Colo.: Westview Press.

PARETI, LUIGI, PAOLO BREZZI and LUCIANO PETECH 1965 *History of mankind, Vol. 2: the ancient world, 1200 B.C. to A.D. 500.* New York: Harper and Row.

QUAYLE, G. ROBINA 1966 *Eastern civilizations.* New York: Appleton-Century-Crofts.

ROBINSON, HARRY 1967 *Monsoon Asia: a geographical survey.* New York: Praeger.

SCALAPINO, ROBERT A., ed. 1965 *The Communist revolution in Asia: tactics, goals, and achievements.* Englewood Cliffs, N.J.: Prentice-Hall.

SEVERN, TIMOTHY 1976 *The Oriental adventure: explorers of the East.* Boston: Little, Brown.

SMITH, HUSTON 1965 *The religions of man.* New York: Harper & Row.

The statesman's year-book: statistical and historical annual of states of the world for the year 1983–84. 1983 ed. John Paxton. New York: Saint Martin's Press.

Times atlas of world history, The revised 1979 Maplewood, N.J.: Hammond.

TURNEY-HIGH, HARRY H. 1968 *Man and system: foundations for the study of human relations.* New York: Appleton-Century-Crofts.

WELTY, PAUL T. 1976 *The Asians: their heritage and their destiny.* Fifth edition. Philadelphia: Lippincott.

WHYTE, ROBERT ORR and PAULINE WHYTE 1982 *The women of Asia.* Boulder, Colo.: Westview Press.

SOUTHWEST ASIA

Aramco handbook: oil and the Middle East 1968 Dharan, Saudi Arabia: Arabian American Oil Company.

ARBERRY, ARTHUR J. 1967 *Aspects of Islamic civilization: as depicted in the original texts.* Ann Arbor: University of Michigan Press.

——— 1976 *The Koran interpreted.* 7th printing. New York: Macmillan.

BARTH, FREDRIK 1961 *Nomads of South Persia.* Boston: Little, Brown.

BERGER, MORROE 1964   *The Arab world today.* New York: Doubleday.
BRASWELL, GEORGE W., Jr. 1977 *To ride a magic carpet.* Nashville: Broadman.
BRILLIANT, MOSHE 1970 *Portrait of Israel.* New York: American Heritage Press.
BURNEY, CHARLES 1977 *The ancient Near East.* Ithaca, N.Y.: Cornell University Press.
COLE, DONALD P. 1975 *Nomads of the nomads.* Chicago: Aldine.
COTTRELL, ALVIN J., ed. 1980 *The Persian Gulf States: a general survey.* Baltimore: Johns Hopkins University Press.
CRESSEY, GEORGE B. 1960 *Crossroads: land and life in Southwest Asia.* Chicago: Lippincott.
EICKELMAN, DALE F. 1981 *The Middle East: an anthropological approach.* Englewood Cliffs, N.J.: Prentice-Hall.
FERNEA, ELIZABETH WARNOCK 1969 *Guests of the Sheik: an ethnography of an Iraqi village.* New York: Doubleday.
FISHER, W. B. 1979 *The Middle East: a physical, social, and regional geography.* Seventh edition. New York: Methuen.
GARTHWAITE, GENE R. 1983 *Khans and Shahs: a documentary analysis of the Bakhtiyari in Iran.* Cambridge, Eng.: Cambridge University Press.
GULICK, JOHN 1976 *The Middle East: an anthropological perspective.* Pacific Palisades, Calif.: Goodyear.
HITTI, PHILIP K. 1949 *The Arabs: a short history.* Chicago: Regnery.
HODGE, CARELTON T. 1981 "Indo-Europeans in the Near East." *Anthropological Linguistics* 23(6):227–244.
HODGSON, M. G. S. 1974 *The venture of Islam.* Chicago: University of Chicago Press.
IRVING, CLIVE 1979 *Crossroads of civilization: three thousand years of Persian history.* Totowa, N.J.: Barnes & Noble.
ISMAEL, TAREQ Y. 1982 *Iraq and Iran: roots of conflict.* Syracuse: Syracuse University Press.
Jordan (Quarterly) 1979–83 Washington, D.C.: Jordanian Information Bureau.
KRAMER, SAMUEL NOAH 1981 *History begins at Sumer: thirty-nine firsts in man's recorded history.* Third revised edition. Philadelphia: University of Pennsylvania Press.
LEWIS, BERNARD 1966 *The Arabs in history.* London: Hutchinson.
MANSFIELD, PETER 1981 *The new Arabians.* Chicago: J. G. Ferguson Publishing Company.
MARTIN, RICHARD C. 1982 *Islam: a cultural perspective.* Englewood Cliffs, N.J.: Prentice-Hall.
NUTTING, ANTHONY 1964 *The Arabs.* New York: NAL.
PATAI, RAPHAEL 1971 *Society, culture, and change in the Middle East.* Third enlarged edition. Philadelphia: University of Pennsylvania Press.
RIVLIN, BENJAMIN and J. S. SZYLIOWICZ 1965 *The contemporary Middle East.* New York: Random House.
RZOSKA, JULIAN with contributions by J. F. TALLING and K. E. BANISTER 1980 *Euphrates and Tigris: Mesopotamian ecology and destiny.* Boston: W. Junk.
SAVORY, R. M., ed. 1976 *Introduction to Islamic civilization.* Cambridge, Eng.: Cambridge University Press.
SHILOH, AILON, ed. 1969 *Peoples and cultures of the Middle East.* New York: Random House.
SMITH, WILFRED C. 1963 *Islam in modern history.* New York: NAL.

STEWART, DESMOND 1964 *The Arab world.* New York: Time.
―――― 1967 *Early Islam.* New York: Time.
―――― 1982 *The Palestinians, victims of expediency.* New York: Quartet Books.
WEEKS, RICHARD V., ed. 1978 *Muslim peoples: a world ethnographic survey.* Westport, Conn.: Greenwood Press.
ZABARAH, MOHAMMAD AHMAD 1982 *Yemen, traditionalism vs. (sic.) modernity.* New York: Praeger.
ZIRING, LAWRENCE 1981 *Iran, Turkey, and Afghanistan: a political chronology.* New York: Praeger.

SOUTH ASIA

ABDULLAH, AHMAED 1973 *The historical background of Pakistan and its people.* Karachi: Tanzeem Publications.
ARIS, MICHAEL 1979 *Bhutan, the early history of a Himalayan kingdom.* Warminster, Eng.: Aris and Phillips.
BARTH, FREDRIK 1968 *Political leadership among Swat Pathans.* London: Athlone Press.
BEALS, ALAN R. 1964 *Gopalur: a south Indian village.* New York: Holt, Rinehart and Winston.
―――― 1974 *Village life in South India: cultural design and environmental variation.* Chicago: Aldine.
BISA, DOR BAHADUR 1967 *People of Nepal.* First edition. Katmandu: Department of Publicity, Ministry of Information and Broadcasting, His Majesty's Government of Nepal.
CARSTAIRS, G. MORRIS 1967 *The twice-born: a study of a community of high-caste Hindus.* Bloomington, Ind.: Indiana University Press.
COHN, BERNARD S. 1971 *India: the social anthropology of a civilization.* Englewood Cliffs, N.J.: Prentice-Hall.
CONZE, EDWARD 1980 *A short history of Buddhism.* Boston: Allen & Unwin.
DAS, VEENA 1977 *Structure and cognition: aspects of Hindu caste.* Delhi: Oxford University Press.
DOWNS, HUGH R. 1980 *Rhythms of a Himalayan village.* San Francisco: Harper & Row.
DUBE, S.C., ed. 1977 *Tribal heritage of India.* New Delhi: Vikas Publishing House.
FERNANDO, TISSA and ROBERT N. KEARNEY, eds. 1979 *Modern Sri Lanka: a society in transition.* Syracuse, New York: Maxwell School of Citizenship and Public Affairs.
FÜRER-HAIMENDORF, CHRISTOPH von 1969 *The Konyak Nagas: an Indian frontier tribe.* New York: Holt, Rinehart and Winston.
GHURZE, GOVIND SADASHUR 1961 *Caste, class, and occupation.* Fourth edition. Bombay: Popular Book Depot.
India News Washington, D.C.: Information Service, Embassy of India.
ISLAM, A. K. M. AMINUL 1974 *A Bangladesh village: conflict and cohesion, an anthropological study of politics.* Cambridge, Mass.: Schenkman.
KARAN, PRADYUMNA P. and WILLIAM M. JENKINS, Jr. 1963 *The Himalayan kingdoms: Bhutan, Sikkim and Nepal.* New York: Van Nostrand.
LUDOWYK, E. F. C. 1967 *A short history of Ceylon.* New York: Praeger.
MALONEY, CLARENCE, ed. 1974 *South Asia: seven community profiles.* New York: Holt, Rinehart and Winston.
―――― 1974 *Peoples of South Asia.* New York: Holt, Rinehart and Winston.

MINTURN, LEIGH and JOHN T. HITCHCOCK 1966 *The Rajputs of Khalapur, India.* New York: John Wiley.

NADARAJAH, DEVAPOOPATHY 1969 *Women in Tamil society: the classical period.* Kuala Lumpur: Faculty of Arts. University of Malaya.

NAIR, KUSUM 1965 *Blossoms in the dust: the human factor in Indian development.* New York: Praeger.

NOBLE, ALLEN G. and ASHOK K. DUFF 1982 *India: cultural patterns and processes.* Boulder, Colo.: Westview Press.

PATEL, SATYAVRATA RAMDAS 1980 *Hinduism: religion and way of life.* New Delhi: Associated Publishing House.

SLUSSER, MARY SHEPHERD 1982 *Nepal Mandala: a cultural study of the Kathmandu valley.* Princeton: Princeton University Press.

SPEAR, PERCIVAL 1967 *India, Pakistan, and the West.* Fourth edition. New York: Oxford University Press.

TYLER, STEPHEN A. 1973 *India: an anthropological perspective.* Pacific Palisades, Calif.: Goodyear.

VIDYARTHI, LALITA PRASAD 1976 *South Asian culture: an anthropological perspective.* Delhi: Oriental Publishers and Distributors.

WARD, BARBARA 1959 *Five ideas that change the world.* New York: Norton.

WARSHAW, STEVEN, C. DAVID BROMWELL and A. J. TUDISCO 1974 *India emerges: a concise history of India from its origin to the present.* San Francisco: Canfield.

ZAEHNER, R. C. 1966 *Hinduism.* Oxford: Oxford University Press.

NORTH ASIA

ANASTASIO, ANGELO 1952 *The Mongols: a study of pastoralism in its ecological and cultural contexts.* M.A. thesis, University of Chicago.

———— 1965 Lecture notes. Bellingham, WA: Western Washington University.

BLUNT, WILFRED 1973 *The golden road to Samarkand.* New York: Viking.

CZAPLICKA, MARIE ANTOINETTE 1969 *Aboriginal Siberia: a study in social anthropology.* Oxford: Clarendon Press.

DONNER, KAI, translated by Rinehart Kyler, Genevieve A. Highland, ed. 1954 *Among the Samoyed in Siberia.* New Haven: HRAF Press.

HEDIN, SVEN 1903 *Central Asia and Tibet: towards the holy city of Lassa.* Two volumes. New York: Scribner's.

HUMPHREY, CAROLINE 1983 *Karl Marx Collective: economy, society and religion in a Siberian collective farm.* Cambridge, Eng.: Cambridge University Press.

JAGCHID, SECHIN and PAUL HYER 1979 *Mongolia's culture and society.* Boulder, Colo.: Westview Press.

KOLARZ, WALTER 1954 *The peoples of the Soviet Far East.* New York: Praeger.

KRADER, LAWRENCE 1963 *Peoples of Central Asia.* Bloomington: Indiana University Press.

KWANTEN, LUC 1979 *Imperial nomads: a history of Central Asia.* Philadelphia: University of Pennsylvania Press.

LATTIMORE, OWEN 1930 *The desert road to Turkestan.* Boston: Little, Brown.

———— 1951 *Inner Asian frontiers of China.* Boston: Beacon Press.

LEGG, STUART 1971 *The heartland.* New York: Farrar, Strauss & Giroux.

LEVIN, MAKSIM GRIGOR'EVICH 1963 *Ethnic origins of the peoples of northeastern Asia.* Henry N. Michael, ed. Published for the Arctic Institute of North America by the University of Toronto Press.

——— 1964 and L. P. POTAPOV, translated by Scripta Technica, English transla-
tion edited by Stephen P. Dunn. *The peoples of Siberia.* Chicago: University
of Chicago Press.
LYDOLPH, PAUL 1977 *Geography of the U.S.S.R.* Third edition. New York:
John Wiley.
MICHAEL, HENRY N. 1962 *Studies in Siberian ethnogenesis.* Published for the
Arctic Institute of North America by the University of Toronto Press.
OSHANIN, L. V. 1962 *Anthropological composition of the population of Cen-
tral Asia, and the ethnogenesis of its peoples: I, II, III.* Cambridge, Mass.:
Peabody Museum.
PHILLIPS, EUSTACE D. 1969 *The Mongols.* London: Thames and Hudson.
POPOV, A. A. 1966 *The Nganasan: the material culture of the Tavgi Samoyeds.*
Bloomington: Indiana University Press.
POPPE, NIKOLAI NIKOLAEVICH 1978 *Tsongol folklore: translation of the
collective farm poetry of the Buriat Mongols of the Selenga region.* Wies-
baden: Harrassowitz.
RICE, TAMARA TALBOT 1965 *Ancient arts of Central Asia.* New York: Praeger.
RYWKIN, MICHAEL 1981 *Moscow's Muslim challenge: Soviet Central Asia.*
Armonk, New York: M. E. Sharp.
SCHWARZ, HENRY G., ed. 1979 *Studies on Mongolia: proceedings of the first
North American conference on Mongolian studies.* Bellingham, Wash.: Center
for East Asian Studies, Western Washington University.
SHIRAKOGAROV, SERGEI MIKHAILOVICH 1980 *Psychomental complex of
the Tungus.* New York: AMS Press.
STEIN, M. AUREL 1912 *Ruins of desert Cathay: personal narrative of explo-
rations in Central Asia and westernmost China.* Two volumes. London:
Macmillan.
SVERDRUP, translated by Molly Sverdrup. 1939 *Among the Tundra people.* La
Jolla. Distributed by Scripps Institution of Oceanography, University of
California, San Diego.
WHEELER, GEOFFREY 1966 *The modern history of Soviet Central Asia.* New
York: Praeger.
WINNER, THOMAS G. 1958 *The oral art and literature of the Kazakhs of Rus-
sian Central Asia.* Durham, N.C.: Duke University Press.

EAST ASIA

AHERN, EMILY MARTIN and HILL GATES, eds. 1981 *The anthropology of
Taiwanese society.* Stanford, Calif.: Stanford University Press.
BEFU, HARUMI 1971 *Japan: an anthropological introduction.* San Francisco:
Chandler Publishing Company.
BENEDICT, RUTH 1946 *The chrysanthemum and the sword: patterns of Japa-
nese culture.* New York: NAL.
BLUNDEN, CAROLINE and MARK ELVIN 1983 *Cultural atlas of China.* New
York: Facts on File, Inc.
BRANDT, VINCENT S. R. 1971 *A Korean village: between farm and sea.* Cam-
bridge, Mass.: Harvard University Press.
CHANG, KWANG-CHIH 1983 *Art, myth, and ritual: the path to political au-
thority in ancient China.* Cambridge, Mass.: Harvard University Press.
CHEN, CHI-LU 1968 *Material culture of Formosan aborigines.* Taipei: Taiwan
Museum.
China's Minority Nationalities: selected articles from Chinese sources. 1977 San
Francisco: Red Sun Publishers.

CLUBB, O. EDMUND 1978 *Twentieth-century China.* Third edition. New York: Columbia University Press.

COVELL, JON CARTER 1981 *Korea's cultural roots.* Salt Lake City: Moth House.

CRESSEY, GEORGE B. 1934 *China's geographic foundations: a survey of the land and its peoples.* New York: McGraw-Hill.

DAVIES, HENRY RODOLPH 1909 *Yun-nan, the link between India and the Yangtze.* Cambridge, Eng.: Cambridge University Press.

EBERHARD, WOLFRAM 1982 *China's minorities: yesterday and today.* Belmont, Calif.: Wadsworth.

EKVALL, ROBERT BRAINERD 1968 *Fields on the hoof: nexus of Tibetan nomadic pastoralism.* New York: Holt, Rinehart and Winston.

Facts about Korea 1977 Thirteenth revised edition. Seoul: Korean Overseas Information Service.

FAIRBANK, JOHN K., EDWIN O. REISCHAUER and ALBERT M. CRAIG 1973 *East Asia: tradition and transformation.* Atlanta: Houghton Mifflin.

FITZGERALD, C. P. 1972 *The southern expansion of the Chinese people.* New York: Praeger.

GOODRICH, L. CARRINGTON 1963 *A short history of the Chinese people.* Third edition. New York: Harper & Row.

HEDIN, SVEN 1909 *Trans-Himalaya: discoveries and adventures in Tibet.* Volumes one and two.

——— 1913 *Trans-Himalaya: discoveries and adventures in Tibet.* Volume three. London: Macmillan.

HENTHORN, WILLIAM E. 1971 *A history of Korea.* New York: Free Press.

Japan in Transition: One Hundred Years of Modernization. 1975 Tokyo: Ministry of Foreign Affairs.

JOHNSON, ERWIN 1976 *Nagura Mura: an ethnohistorical analysis.* Ithaca, New York: China-Japan Program, Cornell University.

KENNEDY, MALCOLM D. 1963 *A short history of Japan.* New York: NAL.

KIM, BYONG SIK 1970 *Modern Korea: the socialist North, revolutionary perspectives in the South, and unification.* New York: International Publishers.

LEI, KI-BAIK, W. Wagner, translator. 1983 *New history of Korea.* Cambridge, Mass.: Harvard University Press.

LI, DUN J. 1978 *The ageless Chinese: a history.* Third edition. New York: Scribner's.

LIU, WU-CHI 1972 *Confucius, his life and time.* Westport, Conn.: Greenwood Press.

LOWE, PETER 1981 *Britain in the Far East: a survey from 1819 to the present.* New York: Longman.

MARAINI, FOSCO 1952 *Secret Tibet.* New York: Viking.

Minorities of Southwest China 1978 (compiled by) Center for East Asian Studies, Western Washington University, Bellingham, Washington.

NAKANE, CHIE 1973 *Japanese society.* Berkeley: University of California Press.

NORBU, THUBTEN JIGME 1968 *Tibet.* New York: Simon & Schuster.

PENG, FRED C. C. and PETER GEISER 1977 *The Ainu: the past in the present.* Hiroshima: Bunka Hyoron.

REISCHAUER, EDWIN O. 1970 *Japan: the story of a nation.* New York: Knopf.

ROCK, JOSEPH F. 1947 *The ancient Na-khi kingdom of Southwest China.* Two volumes. Cambridge, Mass.: Harvard University Press.

Statistical Handbook of Japan. 1976 Tokyo: Bureau of Statistics.

STOVER, LEON E. and TAKEKO K. STOVER 1976 *China: an anthropological perspective.* Pacific Palisades, Calif.: Goodyear.

Studies on the I, Miao, and Pai tribes of Southwest China 1978 (compiled by) The Center for East Asian Studies, Western Washington University, Bellingham, Washington.

TAI, HUNG-HA 1962 *Korea—forty-three centuries.* Seoul: Yonsei University Press.

TERRILL, ROSS 1975 *Flowers on an iron tree.* Boston: Little, Brown.

TREWARTHA, GLENN T. 1965 *Japan: a geography.* Madison: University of Wisconsin Press.

TRUNGPA, CHOGYAM 1971 *Born in Tibet.* Baltimore: Penguin.

TUAN, YI-FU 1969 *China.* Chicago: Aldine.

TWEDDELL, COLIN ELLIDGE 1978 "The Tuli-Chinese Balk Line: Minimal Group Self-identity" in *Perspectives on Ethnicity,* eds. Holloman, Regina E. and Serghei A. Arutiunov. The Hague: Mouton.

WARSHAW, STEVEN, C. DAVID BROMWELL and A. J. TUDISCO 1974 *Japan emerges: a concise history of Japan from its origin to the present.* San Francisco: Canfield.

WOLF, MARGERY 1968 *The house of Lim: a study of a Chinese farm family.* New York: Appleton-Century-Crofts.

SOUTHEAST ASIA

ALI, ABDUL RAHMAN, N. RAJENDRA and V. NAJENDRA 1978 *World history for Sarawak secondary schools.* Book One. Kuala Lumpur: Longman.

ALLEN, SIR RICHARD 1970 *A short introduction to the history and politics of Southeast Asia.* London: Oxford University Press.

BANKS, DAVID J., ed. 1976 *Changing identities in modern Southeast Asia.* (papers from the ninth International Congress of Anthropological and Ethnological Sciences, Chicago, 1973). The Hague: Mouton.

BROWN, D. E. 1976 *Principles of social structure: Southeast Asia.* Boulder, Colo.: Westview Press.

BUCHANAN, KEITH 1968 *The Southeast Asian world: an introductory essay.* New York: Doubleday.

BURLING, ROBBINS 1965 *Hill farms and padi fields: life in mainland Southeast Asia.* Englewood Cliffs, N.J.: Prentice-Hall.

CADY, JOHN F. 1964 *Southeast Asia: its historical development.* New York: McGraw-Hill.

———— 1966 *Thailand, Burma, Laos, and Cambodia.* Englewood Cliffs, N.J.: Prentice-Hall.

CAREY, ISKANDAR 1976 *Orang asli: the aboriginal tribes of Peninsular Malaysia.* London: Oxford University Press.

COEDES, G. 1968 *The Indianized states of Southeast Asia.* Kuala Lumpur: University of Malaya Press.

CONKLIN, HAROLD C. 1980 *Ethnographic atlas of Ifugao: a study of environment, culture, and society in northern Luzon.* New Haven: Yale University Press.

DENTAN, ROBERT KNOX 1968 *The Semai: a nonviolent people of Malaya.* New York: Holt, Rinehart and Winston.

DUTT, ASHOK K., ed. 1984 *Southeast Asia: realm of contrasts.* Third revised edition. Boulder, Colo.: Westview Press.

FIRTH, RAYMOND 1975 *Malay fisherman: their peasant economy.* New York: Norton.

FOX, JAMES J. 1980 *The flow of life: essays on eastern Indonesia.* Cambridge, Mass.: Harvard University Press.

GEERTZ, CLIFFORD   1956   *The development of the Javanese economy: a socio-cultural approach.* Cambridge, Mass.: M.I.T. Press.
GEERTZ, HILDRED   1961   *The Javanese family: a study of kinship and socializa-tion.* New York: Free Press of Glencoe.
GIRLING, JOHN L. S.   1981   *Thailand, society and politics.* Ithaca, New York: Cornell University Press.
HAMILTON, JAMES W.   1976   *Pwo Karen: at the edge of mountain and plain.* St. Paul: Westview Press.
HANKS, LUCIEN M.   1972   *Rice and man: agricultural ecology in southeast Asia.* New York: Aldine.
HANNA, WILLARD A.   1976   *Bali profile: people, events, circumstances (1001-1976).* New York: American Universities Field Staff.
HASSAN, RIAZ, ed.   1976   *Singapore: society in transition.* Kuala Lumpur: Oxford University Press.
HICKEY, GERALD CANNON   1982   *Free in the forest: ethnohistory of the Viet-namese central highlands 1954-1976.* New Haven: Yale University Press.
HUDSON, A. B.   1972   *Padju Epat: the Ma'anyan of Indonesian Borneo.* New York: Holt, Rinehart and Winston.
JOCANO, F. LANDA   1969   *Growing up in a Philippine barrio.* New York: Holt, Rinehart and Winston.
KAHN, JOEL S.   1980   *Minangkabau social formations: Indonesian peasants and the world economy.* Cambridge, Eng.: Cambridge University Press.
KHAING, MI MI   1979   *Burmese family.* First AMS edition. New York: AMS Press.
KHAM, NGUYEN KHAC   1967   *An introduction to Vietnamese culture.* Tokyo: The Center for East Asian Cultural Studies.
KIMBALL, LINDA AMY   1979   *Borneo medicine: the healing art of indigenous Brunei Malay medicine.* Ann Arbor, Mich.: University Microfilms Inter-national for Loyola University of Chicago.
LEBAR, FRANK M., GERALD C. HICKEY and JOHN K. MUSGRAVE   1964   *Ethnic groups of mainland Southeast Asia.* New Haven: HRAF Press.
_____and ADRIENNE SUDDARD, eds.   1967   *Laos, its people, its society, its culture.* New Haven: HRAF Press.
LEBAR, FRANK M., ed.   1972-75   *Ethnic groups of insular Southeast Asia.* New Haven: HRAF Press.
von der MEHDEN, FRED R.   1968   *Religion and nationalism in Southeast Asia: Burma, Indonesia, the Philippines.* Madison: University of Wisconsin Press.
MOLE, ROBERT L.   1973   *Thai values and behavior patterns.* Rutland, Vt.: Tuttle.
MURDOCK, GEORGE PETER   1960   *Social structure in Southeast Asia.* Chicago: Quadrangle Books.
NASH, MANNING   1965   *The golden road to modernity.* New York: John Wiley.
NIMMO, H. ARLO   1972   *The sea-peoples of Sulu: a study of social change in the Philippines.* San Francisco: Chandler.
PROVENCHER, RONALD   1975   *Mainland Southeast Asia: an anthropological perspective.* Pacific Palisades, Calif.: Goodyear.
PYE, LUCIEN W.   1967   *Southeast Asia's political systems.* Englewood Cliffs, N.J.: Prentice-Hall.
STEINBERG, DAVID J., ed.   1971   *In search of Southeast Asia: a modern history.* New York: Praeger.
TILMAN, ROBERT O., ed.   1969   *Man, state, and society in contemporary South-east Asia.* New York: Praeger.
TWEDDELL, COLIN E.   1970   "The identity and distribution of the Mangyan

tribes of Mindoro, Philippines," in *Anthropological Linguistics* 12(6):189–207.

WARSHAW, STEVEN 1975 *Southeast Asia emerges: a concise history of Southeast Asia from its origin to the present.* San Francisco: Canfield.

YOE, SHWAY 1963 *The Burman: his life and notions.* New York: Norton.

Index

Note: This non-exhaustive index makes use of many categories to incorporate many single items under Geography, History, Language(s), Modernization, Dynasties, Treaties, Women, etc.